MALAYSIAN DEVELOPMENT

A RETROSPECTIVE

MALAYSIAN

DEVELOPMENT

A RETROSPECTIVE

Martin Rudner

CARLETON UNIVERSITY PRESS

OTTAWA

1994

Carleton General List #26

Printed and bound in Canada

Canadian Cataloguing in Publication Data

    Rudner, Martin
        Malaysian Development : a retropective

    ISBN 0-88629-220-4 (bound) –
    ISBN 0-88629-221-2 (pbk.)

    1. Malaysia—Economic Policy. 2. Malaysia—Economic conditions
    I. Title

HC445.5R825 1994   338.9595   C94-900185-6

Carleton University Press   Distributed in Canada by:
160 Paterson Hall
Carleton University   Oxford University Press Canada
1125 Colonel by Drive   70 Wynford Drive
Ottawa, Ontario   Don Mills, Ontario
K1S 5B6   M3J 1J9

Cover: Y Graphic Design

Typeset by: Phillip Bird, Bird Design and Service

Acknowledgments:
Carleton University Press gratefully acknowledges the support
extended to its publishing programme by the Canada Council and
the financial assistance of the Ontario Arts Council.

The Press would also like to thank the Department of Canadian
Heritage, Government of Canada, and the Government of Ontario
through the Ministry of Culture, Tourism, and Recreation, for their
assistance.

They who sow in tears,
Will reap with joy.

Psalm 126

For Judith...

*Who shared the journeys and
the experiences.*

TABLE OF CONTENTS

PREFACE

These collected papers on Malaysian development consist of articles written over nearly 25 years while working at academic institutions in different parts of the world. The various academic settings and experiences contributed, each in their distinctive way, to the ideas and approaches that are reflected here. The opportunity to work alongside scholars and policy-makers of varied backgrounds, expressing a wide range of perspectives on society and social processes, had a telling impact on the thinking about development that went into these studies. The work on these articles took place at a number of universities including the University of Oxford, the Hebrew University of Jerusalem, the Australian National University and, most recently, Carleton University, and in particular The Norman Paterson School of International Affairs. At various stages I was also able to benefit from the research facilities at the Harry S. Truman Research Institute (now the Harry S. Truman Institute for the Advancement of Peace) at the Hebrew University of Jerusalem, the Institute of Southeast Asian Studies in Singapore, and the Faculty of Economics and Administration at the University of Malaya. The Canada Council provided scholarship support for my initial work on Malaysian economic and political development at Linacre College, Oxford, and later the Harry S. Truman Research Institute awarded me a research grant for travel to Malaysia and Singapore.

I am grateful to the journals and books in which these articles originally appeared for their permission to reprint the material here. The original sources are cited fully in the Acknowledgements that follow.

The original publication of these articles in a wide number of journals and edited volumes published in different countries made access to them difficult with the passage of time, especially for students. The initiative taken by Carleton University Press in bringing these articles together as a collected volume accessible to a wider audience is commendable. I am thankful for the generous support of the Asian Pacific Research and Resource Centre at Carleton

University, and the Faculty of Social Sciences, for grants in aid of publication of this book.

Debts of gratitude are owing to many individuals for their support, good will, and intellectual exchanges during my years of involvement in the study of Malaysian development. A special word of appreciation is owed to Tun Datuk Dr. Awang bin Hassan, formerly Malaysian High Commissioner to Australia and afterwards Governor of Penang, now retired, for his friendship, encouragement and assistance; to Professor Shamsul A.B. of Universiti Kebangsaan Malaysia, who first suggested the need and urged me to publish these collected papers, while also arranging for their translation into Bahasa Melayu; and to the former Malaysian High Commissioner to Canada, Tan Sri Datuk Thomas Jayasuriya for extending his friendship and encouraging the production of this book also in a Bahasa Melayu edition.

Academic friends and colleagues, past and present, helped in many ways to shape and influence the ideas expressed in the articles in this volume. They include, in Malaysia, Dr. Halim Ismail, K.J. Ratnam, V. Selvaratnam (now at the World Bank), and M. Pathmanathan; in Singapore, Lim Chong Yah, Tham Seong Chee, the late Kernial Sandhu, and the late Wong Lin Ken; in Great Britain, D.A. Low, Len Watson, the late Maurice Freedman, and the late Mervin Jaspan; in Israel, Harold Schiffrin, Ellis Joffe, Avraham Altman, S.N. Eisenstadt, Reuven Kahane, Ben-Ami Shillony, Tuvia Blumenthal, Yitzhak Shichor, and Moshe Lissak; in Australia, Heinz Arndt, R.M. Sundrum, E.K. Fisk, Peter McCawley, John Drabble, Lenore Manderson, Philip Courtenay, Peter Drake, Colin Barlow, Audrey Donnithorne (now in Hong Kong), Christine Inglis, Rosemary Barnard, David Lim, Wang Gungwu (now in Hong Kong), the late James C. Jackson, and the late Lode Brakel; in the United States, Milton Esman, Charles Hirschman, and Dennis Rondinelli; and in Canada, Ozay Mehmet, John O'Manique, and Stephen Milne.

The Directors of The Norman Paterson School of International Affairs at Carleton University, Brian Tomlin, Christopher Maule and, currently, Maureen Molot, have given wholehearted support and encouragement for Southeast Asian studies as part of our postgraduate teaching and research programme. Brenda Sutherland, the School Administrator, has helped create a well-run institutional environment conducive to the pursuit of knowledge. It was my good fortune that Brenda also agreed to input the entire collection of typeset articles into computerized format. My Secretary, Janice

Fochuk, helped in many ways to ease the burdens of administration, always with good cheer. For all this I am most grateful.

My association with the Canadian International Development Agency (CIDA) provided me with many valuable insights into development policy, its formulation and implementation. The former President of CIDA, now President of the Queen's Privy Council for Canada and Minister of Intergovernmental Affairs and Minister responsible for Public Service Renewal, the Hon. Marcel Massé, introduced me to the world of development assistance. Jean-H. Guilmette educated me about strategic management. Jim Carruthers, Peter Morgan, David Spring and André Vinette shared some of their operational experiences with me, and gave instruction by example in the art of development programming and program delivery.

Members of my family were always highly supportive of the academic enterprise that resulted in this book. My father, Moe Rudner, and late mother, Esther, of blessed memory, maintained a faith and an affection that never wavered. My sister Bonnie, brother-in-law Alex, and nephews Brian, Avi, Danny and Shalom, and Margaret Moody, were always cheerfully tolerant of a long-distant relative. Their forbearance and good will merit acknowledgement.

I am deeply grateful to Susan McLellan for her devotion, her love of learning, enthusiasm for Malaysiana, and infectious cheerfulness. I also thank Susan for supplying photographs of Malaysia from her personal collection that enhance this volume.

My daughter Aliza Tamar spent her formative years growing up in those parts of the world where this research was accomplished. She is now pursuing her own university studies, and her progress remains a source of pride and anticipation to those who love her.

For Judith Levine, my former wife, this collected volume recalls the journeys and experiences shared. Judy is a woman of courage and values, wisdom and compassion, a friend and a dedicated professional whose calling has made a difference to the lives of many across the globe.

By three things is the world preserved: by truth, by judgment, and by peace.

Ethics of Our Fathers, I, 18

It is fitting that this book be dedicated to her.

It is also appropriate to acknowledge Judy's parents, Jack and Lena Levine, and sisters Dorothy and Trudi, for their friendship and good will over many years of association.

ACKNOWLEDGMENTS

The articles included in this collected volume made their original appearance in the following publications:

"Financial Policies in Post-War Malaya: The Fiscal and Monetary Measures of Liberation and Reconstruction," *Journal of Imperial and Commonwealth History,* Vol. 3, No. 3 (May, 1975), pp. 232-48.

"The Malayan Post-War Rice Crisis: An Episode in Colonial Agricultural Policy," *Kajian Ekonomi Malaysia*, Vol. 12, No. 1 (June, 1975), pp. 1-13.

"Agricultural Policy and Peasant Social Transformation in Late Colonial Malaya," in James C. Jackson and Martin Rudner, eds., *Issues in Malaysian Development*, Southeast Asian Publications Series No. 3, (published for the Asian Studies Association of Australia by Heinemann Educational Books (Asia) Ltd., Singapore, 1979), pp. 7-68.

"The Malayan Quandary: Rural Development Policy Under the First and Second Five-Year Plans," *Contributions to Asian Studies*, Vol. 1 (1971), pp. 190-204.

"Malayan Rubber Policy: Development and Anti-Development During the 1950s," *Journal of Southeast Asian Studies*, Vol. 8, No. 2 (September, 1976), pp. 235-59.

"The State and Peasant Innovation in Rural Development: The Case of Malaysian Rubber," *Asian and African Studies*, Vol. 6 (1970), pp. 75-96.

"Development Policies and Patterns of Agrarian Dominance in the Malaysian Rubber Export Economy," *Modern Asian Studies*, Vol. 15, Pt. 1 (February, 1981), pp. 83-105.

"Trends in Malaysian Development Planning: Goals, Policies and Role Expansion," *Review of Indonesian and Malayan Affairs*, Vol. 14, No. 2 (December, 1980), pp. 48-91.

"Changing Planning Perspectives of Agricultural Development in Malaysia," *Modern Asian Studies*, Vol. 17, Pt. 3 (July, 1983), pp. 413-35.

"Agricultural Planning and Development Performance in Malaysia," in Anita Beltran Chen, ed., *Contemporary and Historical Perspectives in Southeast Asia*, (Ottawa: Carleton University Printshop for the Canadian Asian Studies Association, 1985), pp. 196-218.

"Colonial Education Policy and Manpower Underdevelopment in British Malaya," in Barbara Ingham and Colin Simmons, eds., *Development Studies and Colonial Policy*, (London: Frank Cass & Co., 1987), pp. 193-209.

"Education, Development and Change in Malaysia," *South East Asian Studies*, Vol. 15, No. 1 (June, 1977), pp.23-62.

"Labour Policy and the Dilemmas of Trade Unionism in Post-War Malaya," *Review of Indonesian and Malayan Affairs*, Vol. 16, No. 1 (1982), pp. 101-11.

"Malayan Labour in Transition: Labour Policy and Trade Unionism, 1956-1963," *Modern Asian Studies*, Vol. 7, Pt. 1 (January, 1973), pp. 21-45.

MALAYSIAN CURRENCY VALUES

Period	M$ per £ sterling
•1890 to November 1967	8.57
• 20 November 1967 to 22 June 1972	7.36
• to end 1972	6.83
• to end June 1973	6.65
• to end December 1973	5.45
• end 1976	4.32
• end 1977	4.53
• end 1978	4.49
• end 1979	4.87
• end 1980	5.30
• end 1981	4.29
• end 1982	3.76
• end 1983	3.40
• end 1984	2.83
• end 1985	3.49
• end 1990	5.29
• end 1991	5.08
• end February 1992	4.54

Note: With the introduction of floating exchange rates after June, 1972, the rates indicated represent approximations of inter- bank exchange rates for given periods of time.

Sources: *Bank Negara Malaysia Report 1969-1971*(Kuala Lumpur, 1971); *Bank Negara Malaysia Annual Report 1972-73* (Kuala Lumpur, 1973); Malaysian Ministry of Finance, *Economic Report 1987/88* (Kuala Lumpur, 1988); United Malaysian Banking Corporation, *Business Conditions Malaysia*; adapted

INTRODUCTION

Malaysia has achieved a distinctive record of development. Over nearly four decades, the country has undergone a dynamic development process culminating in a substantial transformation of its economy, political system, social organization, and civic culture. Malaysia today ranks foremost among developing countries in its human development attainments, according to available indicators.

From the vantage point of the 1990s, some students of development may have difficulty recalling that Malaysia was once a relatively poor and deeply troubled country. At independence in 1957, the prognosis for Malaya (as it was then) was decidedly bleak. The country had an untested, fragile parliamentary government, under challenge from a Communist insurgency, with a depressed and dependent economy, which was ethnically stratified and afflicted by widespread poverty and social inequality. Nevertheless, in subsequent years the country made significant economic and social progress, largely out of its own resources. The path was neither smooth nor easy, nor has it been linear. Dynamic advances on the part of some was accompanied by lagging performance, or even relative deprivation, among others. As late as the 1970s, most studies of Malaysia's development prospects remained pessimistic, by and large.

Malaysia's development strategy is determined by the government of the day. Like the political process that governs it, development strategy is a matter of who gets what, when and how. Since Malayan independence, its economic and social development strategies have been formulated within the framework of a succession of national five-year development plans. Planning priorities underwent change as the role of development planning evolved and expanded. The ensuing implementation of plan policies and priorities determined the allocation of development resources. Planning and plan implementation thus determined, in good measure, the beneficiaries of the development effort, the leads and lags, and, I daresay, the residues of neglect and underdevelopment. For Malaysia, development planning has been the institutional centrepiece of its political-economic system.

Historically, Malaysia's planning institution has been distinctly positivist in its approach to development. Behind this positivist strategy there lies a complex political process. Political behaviour in Malaysia extends beyond the explanatory powers of any single analytical paradigm, whether political pluralism, class analysis, dependency theory, or patron-clientism, though elements of these may influence the political process at certain times and over pertinent issues. Malaysian politics express the interplay among modern and traditional authority structures, ethnicity and class, ideology and religion, region and sector, age and gender, bureaucracy and market. The process through which politics affects development planning and policy can perhaps best be treated by an analysis of the origins of political demands, and their structure and content in addressing the resource allocations at issue.

The collection of articles included in this volume examines some of the major policy issues in Malaysian development planning from the end of the colonial era down to the present. Most articles focus their analysis on the national political economic system, though for the historical case studies the emphasis is on the Peninsular Malaysian experience. Among the topics treated are development planning, as such, agricultural policy and development, evolution of the rubber export economy, education, labour relations, and the development of science in Malaysia and other Islamic countries. These articles appeared originally in various scholarly journals and books over many years. They are being brought together in this volume for the convenience of students of Malaysian economic and social development, especially in Malaysia itself.

Whereas these articles were individually written over a 20-year time span, they do reflect certain common approaches to political economic analysis. The focus throughout is on the policy-making and resource allocation process. In the context of Malaysian development the focal point is on the planning mechanism, its political inputs, management structure, and allocative outputs, and their impact on the politically stipulated goals of development.

By way of contrast with studies of Malaysia that postulate *a priori* either social class or ethnicity or institutional biases as their prime explanatory variable, the analytical framework applied in these articles is sensitive to an empirically determined matrix of interests, structures and goals addressing the policies at issue. The key components of this approach to political economic analysis include:

- Identification of the spectrum of interests arising in the political system and interacting over the policies at issue. These interests are analyzed according to their societal origins, whether ethnic, class, institutional, or cultural/ideological, and their demand content. Interests express the values of participants in the political process, translated into policy-directed action.

- Examination of the policy demands articulated by various interest groups acting or responding to the political process. Policy demands address the sought-after allocation of resources. Their composition may be analyzed in terms of mutually supporting versus conflicting interests. Not all demands on development policy are necessarily developmental in their implications. There are also demands on the part of vested interests, demands for policies leading to greater disparities in resource allocation, as well as demands for differential benefits arising from privileged status rather than from development effort. Analysis of the character of demands on a particular policy issue serves to elucidate the competing and conflicting interests at stake, and their role in the political process.

- Attention to the attitudinal perceptions and belief systems shared by policy-makers. The policy-making echelon includes the governing political party elite, as and where it intervenes in development planning and implementation, as well as bureaucratic managers. Their assumptions about the development situation, their definition of plausible alternatives, their perspectives about the means and ends of development, and their implicit paradigms and beliefs that underpin policy prescriptions are all embodied in the attitudinal prism through which policy-makers address their planning functions. Analysis of the perceptions reflected in this attitudinal prism permits an understanding of decision-making behaviour in response to the demands and constraints of the political process.

- Consideration of structure of decision-making within the political process and in planning institutions. Different policy-making institutions allow varying degrees of access to decision-making authority. Malaysia has a broadly representative parliamentary system of government, based on multi-party elections. As is often the case, however, certain other political and bureaucratic institutions are rather more skewed in their accessibility. Analysis of decision-making structures for their participatory biases reveals the relationship between ruler and ruled inherent in various political institutions and planning mechanisms.

• Assessment of the policy outcomes affecting the authoritative allocation of development resources among competing interests and objectives. Since development resources are innately scarce relative to competing demands on policy, the planning mechanism must give effect to resource allocations by way of prioritizing the preferred interests and objectives. Policy outcomes imply allocations of resources to some, while denying them to others. Among the policy instruments available for allocating development resources are extractive policies, like taxes, duties, tariffs, and other exactions which take resources from some; as well as distributive policies, such as subsidies, transfer payments and entitlements, which remit resources to others. Regulatory policies, which govern access to public goods and services, are another type of allocative instrument. There are also symbolic policies, policies that draw on generally respected social or cultural symbols but which embody implicit allocations of resources. Analysis of the allocative consequences of policy reveals the structure of rewards and penalties, and the beneficiaries and the activities so favoured, thus describing the prevailing policy regime.

• Evaluation of the development impact of the prevailing policy regime and its authoritative allocation of resources. Each policy-determined allocation of resources will tend to stimulate certain activities on the part of those who are favoured, while incurring opportunity costs in relation to those denied. The balance between resources gained as against opportunity costs may be assessed in the light of the goals of development. To be sure, a broad range of goals may be stipulated by the political system. Analysis of the goals being impacted upon by policy, as compared to the goals proclaimed in the original planning process, will reveal the effectiveness of the planning and policy mechanisms in achieving the politically-determined targets of development.

In reviewing the application of this conceptual framework in the articles contained in this collection, four analytical themes appear to have been salient in Malaysian development planning: (a) the evolution of strategic thinking about development in response to newly emergent social values and political priorities; (b) the changing pattern of interest articulation and conflicts of interest affecting policy alternatives; (c) the shifting attitudinal prism regarding prevailing perceptions of capabilities, constraints, and objectives; and (d) the changing goals of development as the political process interacts with development planning over time. These themes are essentially dynamic rather than static, highlighting the dynamism of the development process. It is this dynamism, its ebbs and flow, structure and direction, that the articles in this volume seek to capture and explain through the application of a policy-centred analytical framework and themes.

CHAPTER 1

FINANCIAL POLICIES IN POST-WAR MALAYA:
The Fiscal and Monetary Measures of Liberation and Reconstruction

In several significant respects, the restoration of British rule following the wartime Japanese inter-regnum made for alterations in the course of modern Malayan history. Politically, the reintroduction of British authority was designed to centralize and modernize government administration, hitherto divided among the Malay States and Straits Settlements, into a cohesive Malayan Union.[1] For society, the war experience generated a resurgent national feeling among the indigenous Malay community, while transforming the orientation of Chinese and Indians from transience to permanent stakes in Malaya. Yet if British policy had set its sights on certain political and social changes, considerations of economic policy were somewhat more complex and, accordingly, ambivalent. The Malayan legacy of colonial economic history was that of a "geographic region where capital and labour belonging to other economies found it convenient to carry on certain specialized operations, within the British monetary as well as political framework."[2] However, during the course of the Second World War, this essentially exploitative legacy was to be tempered by a new development goal that percolated into colonial economic policy and obtained institutional expression in the original Colonial Welfare and Development Act of 1941. Hence, the formulation of monetary and fiscal measures for post-war Malaya was confronted by the inertia cum momentum characteristic of economic policies in transition.

Financial policy for liberated Malaya originated in the "Malayan Planning Unit" established jointly by the British War Office and Colonial Office.[3] In the aftermath of conquest and liberation it fell upon public finance to re-establish the British colonial presence in Malaya and set in motion the process of reconstruction. Meanwhile

Journal of Imperial and Commonwealth History, Vol. 3, No. 3 (May, 1975).

the Colonial Office prepared a long-term financial directive for the British Military Administration (BMA) laying down fiscal and monetary guidelines towards future policy goals. Indeed BMA-Malayan Union finance policy was of much greater than purely Malayan relevance, since Malaya, the "Dollar Arsenal" of the Empire, was also expected to play an important part in sterling area post-war recovery.

Monetary Policy

Properly speaking, the currency board system that had been restored to liberated Malaya admitted to no "monetary policy" in the usual meaning of the term. The Malayan Currency Board (technically, Board of Commissioners of Currency for Malaya) undertook to administer an automatic currency board system for the monetary regulation of economic activity.[4] There was no provision within the currency board system for the monetary regulation of economic activity. [5] Where this system allowed some limited scope for discretion as regards exchange rates, extent of currency cover and investment reserves, policy was here subject to the direct control of the Colonial Office.[6] Under the Colonial Currency Board system, the Malayan authorities had virtually no jurisdiction over their monetary situation.

Among the first problems of monetary policy confronting the returning British was the value to be assigned to the Japanese currency circulated in Malaya during the occupation. This so-called 'banana' currency comprised unbacked military scrip denominated in dollars, and towards the end of the occupation it came forth in un-numbered reams from Japanese printing presses.[7] On their return the British decided to accord no value whatsoever to this currency. Demonetization of the "banana" currency was therefore embodied in the BMA Currency Proclamation published immediately upon Malaya's liberation.[8]

Demonetisation constituted a radical departure from the practice adopted for other liberated territories in Africa and Europe, and was motivated by a powerful combination of financial, military and political considerations.[9] Word of the Japanese authorities' resort to the printing press had escaped occupied Malaya, and British financial planners were understandably reluctant to expose their currency to heavy inflationary pressures from uncertain quantities of "banana" money. Furthermore, military strategists were unwilling to accord the Japanese a powerful economic weapon which could undermine the British liberation.[10] To the contrary, demonetization would help discredit Japanese authority behind their own lines, and therefore assist British operations. Demonetization accordingly became a valuable strategic instrument for Malaya's liberation.

Apart from financial and military considerations, political factors lent their weight to the decision to demonetize the Japanese scrip. Malayan planners envisaged the demonetization of the occupation currency as a definite and forceful reassertion of British authority in liberated Malaya. In addition, demonetization would cripple political opponents of the returning British. Collaborators and war profiteers in possession of quantities of "banana" currency would supposedly be hardest hit. Likewise the Malayan Communist Party, which, it had been learned, had accumulated large sums of occupation currency to underwrite its post-war political activities would now be (temporarily, at least) incapacitated.[11] Though it was admitted that "many reputable individuals" might be hurt by demonetization, the returning British proceeded to demolish utterly the Japanese occupation monetary system.

It is impossible, in the absence of statistical data, to determine the real impact of demonetization on resource allocation in liberated Malaya. In the official British view, then and now, the main effect was felt by "profiteers and collaborators" who were assumed to have amassed large cash balances in "banana" currency.[12] Whether this assumption was valid with regard to wartime Malaya, then in the throes of acute shortage and hyperinflation, is disputable. It is more than likely that, in the conditions prevailing in occupied Malaya, 'Gresham's Law' would have inspired wily profiteers to hoard scarce goods instead of cash, currency having ceased to be a common store of value. Conversely, consumers-at-large would be compelled to accumulate large cash balances in order to meet rapidly rising prices. In these conditions of an accelerated flight from currency, demonetization would not have hit profiteers hoarding goods, but would have impoverished others left by circumstances holding substantial (in money terms) cash balances. If this be true, then the incidence of demonetization was broader and more severe than officially admitted.[13] Of course, the largest transfer of real resources took place in favour of those issuing the new currency, the returning British.

To compensate for demonetization, the British felt impelled to put their new currency into circulation as speedily as possible. This was achieved through BMA's purchase of local supplies, hiring of labour, civil service salaries and payments to troops. By the end of the BMA period (March 1946), some M$179 million were put into circulation in these ways, amounting to an 80% increase over the pre-1942 currency issue.[14] Not only did this involve a massive transfer of real resources into BMA hands, but it also inspired a heavy inflationary spiral. The vast outpouring of currency notes by the BMA effectively subverted parallel measures aimed at restoring Malaya's post-liberation cost structure to pre-war levels as a means of bolstering commodity exports.

Inflationary pressures were further abetted by the inflation syndrome which had taken hold of Malayans since the occupation.[15] Shortly after the liberation, Malayan prices soared to 10 times their pre-war level, settling back to about eight times the pre-war level by the end of 1945. As supplies grew more abundant the downward trend continued, reaching four to five times the pre-war level in mid-1947, and three to four times the pre-war level by January 1948.[16] While real resources were being transferred to the note-issuing BMA, the real burden of inflation was borne by Malayan wage labour and government salaried personnel, whose money incomes were still geared by policy to their pre-war scales.[17]

Following demonetization the BMA introduced a new Malayan dollar valued at the pre-war rate of exchange, M$1=2s 4d. Although there was admittedly no economic rationale for resuming this historic rate of exchange, it was a taken-for-granted aspect of the return to normalcy. Yet the resumption of the pre-war exchange rate in the midst of spiraling post-war inflation implied a revaluation of the Malayan dollar in terms of sterling at a time when the Malayan dollar was rapidly depreciating in value. The result was an income deflation in Malaya, moderated only by the wartime depreciation of sterling.[18] After an initial round of inflation, Malayan money incomes, including wages and export earnings, accordingly continued under downward pressure through the late 1940s, at least until the devaluation of sterling itself in 1949.[19] By forcing Malaya's post-war money-cost structure to adjust to the pre-war sterling exchange rate, rather than the reverse, Malayan planners no doubt contributed to the political unrest culminating in the Communist Emergency that broke out in 1948, instigated in good measure by the post-war income deflation.[20]

Colonial currency boards were required to hold their reserve cover in London. A portion of this cover had to be held in liquid form while the remainder could be invested in approved interest-bearing U.K. or colonial (other than the country involved) securities. As a rule at least 70% of invested colonial currency reserves were retained in U.K. government debentures, with the colonies being required to maintain an overfull sterling backing to ensure that 100%

cover would always prevail. Pan-Malayan sterling currency reserves totalled M$272 million at the fall of Singapore, with over 70% invested in interest-bearing securities. Despite the doubling of the Malayan Currency Board note issue between then and the end of 1947, no additions were made in the investment portfolio so that the interest-bearing portion of Malaya's currency cover dropped to 41%, the difference being held in cash. Since dividends from Currency Fund investments yielded 4% on average,[21] this inability to invest these additional cash balances to the hitherto customary extent inflicted a substantial economic-welfare loss on Malaya and Singapore. Moreover, for 1946 the Malayan sterling cover was raised from 110% to over 115% of the currency issue.[22] It was certainly an anomaly of the colonial financial system that while idle Malayan sterling reserves accumulated to excess in London, Malaya itself was starved of capital for reconstruction and development.[23]

In the meantime access to London's capital market was blocked by the Capital Issues Committee, established by the Bank of England to ensure an "orderly" post-war money market but whose activities were "shrouded in darkness." As a matter of fact no colonial government loans were allowed to be floated in London until 1948.[24] The Malayan Union government did at one time contemplate approaching the London money market for a M$200 million loan to underwrite urgent reconstruction projects,[25] but was apparently dissuaded by the Capital Issues Committee. This violation of sterling area freedom of payments, hitherto one of its more valuable features, by the British monetary authorities implied the subordination of colonial financial requirements to the U.K. domestic economic policy. For Malaya it meant deferment of essential rehabilitation works.[26]

A second classic pillar of the sterling area, access to gold-dollar balances, was likewise seriously restricted in the post-war period. For purposes of foreign exchange, non-self-governing territories were treated as overseas adjuncts of the United Kingdom, and were expected to adhere to Bank of England exchange control policy.[27] The United States for its part had insisted that gold-dollar earning territories should be able to import American goods freely and not be bound by the payment problems of the less fortunate. The point was (reluctantly) conceded by the U.K.[28] Yet when Malayan businessmen demanded retention of a portion of Malaya's gold-dollar earnings for home use, this was categorically rejected by the expatriate Financial Secretary, presumably on instruction from the Colonial Office.[29] As the "dollar arsenal" of the Empire, Malaya contributed in 1946 and 1947 alone some 63.6 m pounds net to the sterling area gold dollar pool. Even during the six weeks of attempted sterling free convertibility from 15 July 1947, Malaya was unique among members of the sterling area in actually increasing its gold-dollar contributions. Nevertheless, in the aftermath of the convertibility debacle Malaya was required to further curb already restricted "hard currency" markets, so that as far as the U.K. was concerned its "dollar arsenal" constituted a "soft currency" buyer.[30] While Great Britain and the self-governing Dominions remained in gold-dollar deficit throughout this period, the real burden of sterling was borne by those sterling area members enjoying hard currency surpluses who had to forego essential imports to add to the gold-dollar pool. This post-war twist in gold-dollar pooling had the effect of forcing a transfer of current import measures from the less-developed dependent territories of the Empire, and pre-eminently among them Malaya, in favour of the more-developed Commonwealth, and especially Britain.

Although Malaya's monetary system had long been tied to sterling, fundamental changes had occurred in the monetary relationship between sterling's banker, the U.K., and the colonial empire after World War II. In the past sterling had served primarily as a lubricant of international trade, with monetary conditions in individual territories adjusting automatically to this flow. Colonies were included in the calculus of sterling policy on the same basis as the U.K. Following World War II, however, the chief aim of sterling monetary policy had become the creation of a new economic order in the U.K., and international payments were to adjust to the requirements of this objective. No longer were the colonies included on equal terms in calculations of economic policy, even though as overseas parts of its monetary system they were still automatically embraced by the sterling policy measures adopted by the U.K.[31] Because Malaya constituted the major gold-dollar earner among the colonial territories, it more than others had to subordinate its own interests in reconstruction and development to the imperatives of imperial economic strategy.

Fiscal Policy

Given the narrow latitude allowed for positive monetary policy within the currency board system, Malaya had to rely on fiscal techniques to define and realize public economic objectives.

Conditions in post-war Malaya placed heavy demands on fiscal policy. Conquest, occupation and liberation confronted government with the tasks of reconstruction at a time when war acted as a catalyst for new political claims on economic resources. Moreover, the bonds of empire, and the fundamental differences in economic structure between the former Straits Settlements and Federated and Unfederated Malay States, further complicated fiscal policy-making in an administrative entity that was hardly self-contained or homogeneous. These structural limitations on fiscal policy greatly impaired Malaya's financial capacities.

Public Expenditure

In the aftermath of World War II the new directions in British political economy precipitated changes in the perceived role of colonial government in economic affairs, from that of guardian over law and order to a more positive involvement in development. The cue for this fundamental transformation in the goals of governance originated in the new Labour government in London, which indicated its intentions by converting the wartime Colonial Development and Welfare Act into an instrument for planned colonial social and economic modernization.[32] According to the adopted view, the causes of colonial underdevelopment were seen in the "poverty of their environment and of their education," so that emphasis was placed on the development of education, public health and social reforms. As a concession to their socialist ethic, Labour also admitted that colonial poverty was due, to some extent, to the "maldistribution of profits," although here the suggested corrective was restricted to "improving the productivity of the colonial people themselves."[33]

In this "development" process colonial administration was to limit itself to advising local agriculture, co-operatives and labour and to creating infrastructure "which only government can provide and without which private initiative can do little."[34] Having instilled colonial administration with a development goal, Labour did not depart radically from past principles in confining public participation in goal attainment to providing the economic and social bases for privately inspired developmental activity.

Prompted by the new development inspiration, the Malayan Union government moved to focus its fiscal policy on assumed public needs. Yet the narrow representative character of Malayan Union Councils of State restricted societal participation in the determination of these needs, which had therefore to be postulated by the authorities *ex machina*.[35]

Underlining the ingrained conservatism of colonial government, budgetary economy in administration remained the "first principle" of policy, though this now meant "meeting . . . essential liabilities and providing essential services in the most economical way."[36] Economic reconstruction, covering both the public and private sectors, comprised a second objective of Malayan Union fiscal policy. To promote development, social services and especially education and health services were admittedly in need of improvement and attention. Yet by far the most radical aspect of Malayan Union fiscal strategy related to its declared intention of achieving equity in taxation, in the words of Governor Sir Edward Gent:

> My own thoughts lead me to the conclusion that compared with our own over-simple and possibly crude system of import and export duties which is the main basis of our present revenue system, there is a clear need to consider whether these cannot be replaced . . . with some form of tax on income which will reflect the ability of all members of the community, companies and so on, to make their due contributions according to the breadth of their shoulders and so carry their fair share of the burden.[37]

Income redistribution and growth, pursued by fiscal means, therefore became "a matter of public policy." This committed, the Malayan Union began underwriting reconstruction and cultivating development while overhauling its taxation system, all in the same short breath.

Under the Malayan Union constitution, policy-making authority on fiscal matters was vested in the government, with responsibility flowing upward to the Colonial Office. Although powers of initiative and veto rested with government, conventional practice had supply bills presented to the Advisory Council for discussion. Its essentially consultative constitutional role notwithstanding, the Advisory Council—and especially its British commercial members—regarded itself as intrinsically involved in public finance. Demands articulated in Advisory Council sessions were reinforced by the activities of its standing committees on budgetary problems. The Advisory Council's Standing Committee on Finance, consisting of British, Chinese and Indian commercial interests, undertook detailed investigation of proposed public spending. An Estimates Revision Committee, made up of representatives of British and Chinese commercial interests, sat continuously to consider possible savings on departmental expenditure. In addition, a Finance Review Committee of British, Chinese and Indian commercial professional and even labour interests was appointed to examine the overall state of Malayan Union finance in the light of post-war needs. None of these committees was actually engaged in fiscal policy-making, as their powers were limited to disclosure of expenditure. Nevertheless they regarded themselves as custodians of the public purse. This was especially true of the Finance Review Committee, which conceived its role as advising on "the necessary and proper economies" required to avoid "the eventual financial ruin" implicit in new taxation.[38]

There was strong support for the extension of social services among organized labour and teachers' associations. In Labour's view the purpose of government could best be served by reorganizing and reorienting administration towards the provision of social services: "It should be stressed that rehabilitation and restoration include not only replacement of machines and materials but rehabilitation and restoration in health, education and other social amenities."[39] Provision of social services ought not to be restrained by the budget, rather expenditure should be governed by the growing needs of Malaya's population.[40]

Business interests for their part demanded the strict curtailment of public expenditure in general and of social service spending in particular. To some, government operations were automatically too "lavish," "wasteful," "extravagant" and "costly."[41] Others conceded the social objectives of the government, but insisted with characteristic aplomb that these be deferred until such time as "financial stability" is "restored." Their favourite slogan, repeated at least a hundred times in budget debates, was: "We must cut our cost according to our cloth," and the government was reminded that "when a family runs into difficulties it begins by cutting domestic expenditure, in this case social service spending."[42] On the other hand commercial interests stressed that the "first duty" of the government was to "rehabilitate and restore" Malaya's war-shattered export sectors, regardless of cost. A central theme of British businessmen was the early restoration of a balanced budget, once their interests were satisfied, in order to forestall the introduction of additional taxation.

In its financial declarations the Malayan Union government came out in favour of increasing the supply of social services, extending public services into the less-developed areas of the former Federated and Unfederated Malay States, and effecting temporary transfer payments and subsidies designed to ease inflationary pressures, particularly in export sectors. However, actual public expenditures on the social services and rural areas did not represent a significant departure from pre-war policy.

Businessmen's complaints notwithstanding, the increase in total public spending between 1946 and 1948 did not keep pace

TABLE 1
Estimates and Actual Public Expenditures.
on Social and Agricultural Services, 1941-8 (M$ million).

	1941	1946*		1947		1948	
	estimated	estimated	revised	estimated	revised	estimated	actual
Total Expenditure	$138.7	$234.3	$214.0	$316.5	$308.7	$230.0	$209.9
Agricultural/Drainage & Irrigation	4.9	4.9	4.3	8.2	n/a	4.8	3.4
Social Services:	17.2	25.5	22.0	35.4	n/a	18.2	14.8
• of which Education	7.2	11.0	10.4	15.8	n/a	7.0	5.5
• of which Public Health	10.0	13.0	10.5	17.0	15.2	7.6	7.4
• of which Social Welfare	n/a	1.5	1.1	1.7	n/a	3.6	1.9

* April - December Only.
Source: *Finance Committee Report*, Table 9; *Malayan Union Estimates*.

with the inflation since the war. Hence government commanded a substantially smaller share of real resources in post-war Malaya than before the war. So far as the rural areas were concerned, government spending on agriculture and drainage and irrigation under the Malayan Union not only declined in money and real terms, but comprised a mere 1.5% of total actual expenditure in 1948 compared to nearly 5% budgeted in 1941. Social service expenditure likewise failed to catch up with inflation, and indeed actual spending between 1946 and 1948 was consistently less than even the already thin estimates. Interestingly enough, expenditure on public health exceeded that on education, reflecting the overriding concern of rubber estate and tin mining interests for the physical state of their labour force.[43] Although the demand for schooling expanded impressively following the liberation, especially among rural Malays, government spending on education remained severely restricted on budgetary grounds. By 1948 the colonial commitment to social and rural development was, for Malaya, more in the nature of a wish than a reality.

What amounted to an incomes policy for the rehabilitation period emerged as patchy and regressive, owing to the constraints of sterling coupled to the priorities of domestic reconstruction. In order to hold down local wage costs and counteract the pressure of an overvalued currency on Malaya's export sectors, the government embarked on an ad hoc programme of selective subsidization. Public servants received cost-of-living allowances rather than permanent upward revisions in salaries, mainly to avoid drawing up private sector wages. Still, public servants had valid complaints of falling real wages and salaries despite these allowances. Rice and other rationed staples were directly subsidized by a government "mindful" of the "desirability" of holding down food prices in order to maintain as best as feasible prevailing money wage rates in the export sectors. However in mid-1947 renewed pressure for budgetary restraint, emanating from sterling area difficulties, impelled government to reduce its subsidy on staple foodstuffs. Labour's reaction was predictably bitter:

> This action on the part of the Government to cut down the subsidies (on rationed foodstuffs) . . . contributed to a further deterioration of the living conditions of the working class. It is to be realized that due to inflated prices the real wages of the worker have shrunk to a fraction of his pre-war wages and one can easily picture the efforts of the Government to throw the main burden of the taxation on the shoulder of the wage earner, or the worker.[44]

When the crunch came, the government was indeed prepared to sacrifice real wages on the twin altars of sterling and reconstruction.

Rehabilitation of Malaya's war-shattered economy constituted the major domestic target of post-war fiscal policy. There were two types of calls on public monies for reconstruction, one to rebuild damaged public infrastructure and the other to assist private enterprise restore its productive capacity. Despite extensive planning by the Malayan Planning Unit for the early revival of public utilities, the stores and equipment that were ordered failed to arrive (they were installed only in 1948), so that considerable ingenuity and improvisation was necessary to put ports, railways, electricity and roads back in operation during the BMA period.[45] Following the resumption of civilian government, expenditure directed at rehabilitating public utilities and works absorbed the largest proportion of public funds, over a fifth in 1947. Even the Malayan Railways, normally operated on its own budget, required injections of some M$25 million from general revenues in 1946-7 to restore services, repair rolling stock, and re-lay track.

Their insistence on restraint in public spending notwithstanding, business interests joined in with their own demands for rehabilitation expenditure by government. The predominantly British F.M.S. Chamber of Commerce sought an "immediate" start on building new port facilities at Port Swettenham (now Klang), together with the speedy restoration of rail links, so as to corner the foreign trade of central Malaya. Penang merchants replied with demands for extensive modernization and improvement to Penang port. Such grandiose port developments had to await, however, the more urgent tasks of reconstruction.

Although resuscitation of commerce and industry in post-war Malaya was intended to fall to private enterprise, the magnitude of the task and the pressing need to resume gold-dollar exports prompted the government to assist with financial aid and help in securing priorities.[46] Shortly after its establishment the BMA advanced funds to British estate companies against promises of ultimate reimbursement.[47] Local producers, and especially proprietary rubber estates and smallholdings lacking the resources of London-based companies, also sought government assistance for rehabilitation.

In March 1947 the government responded with the Industrial Rehabilitation (Finance) Ordinance (No. 20 of 1947) extending its guarantee to commercial bank loans to enterprises engaged in the production of certain commodities. Only export industries were covered by the act, and since the guarantee related to bank loans its practical application was limited to larger British and Chinese concerns with access to the banking system. Smaller proprietary firms, customarily reliant upon traditional credit facilities, had therefore to forage for themselves for rehabilitation finance.[48] By introducing de facto differential access to low-cost rehabilitation finance, the government worked to increase effectively existing policy-induced inequalities between categories of producers, without regard to the relative operating efficiencies of different segments of the industry. The Industrial Rehabilitation Board established by the act guaranteed some M$27 million in low-cost loans through 1949, mainly to British rubber estates.[49]

Separate arrangements were made for rehabilitation assistance to the tin mines. Malaya's tin mining industry had suffered heavily in 1942 from the "denial" policy of the retreating British. To assist in the rehabilitation of the important export sector the Colonial Office offered disposal of a specifically created Chinese Tin Mines Rehabilitation Loans Board to extend low-interest loans to approved Chinese mines.[50] In addition, a large portion of the 1946 Malayan Union local loan was lent out to tin mines for rehabilitation purposes.[51] The allocation of loan funds distinctly favoured British producers who were normally responsible for 65% of total tin output but received over three-quarters of available loan funds. On the other hand, small Chinese mines were denied subsidized loans as a matter of policy.[52] Here again public policy served to increase unwarranted inequalities between producers, in favour of British interests.

Resource Mobilization

The greater part of rehabilitation finance for private industry was derived locally rather than from new capital from abroad. Although net inflows of private capital were relatively large in 1946, they declined considerably over the years 1947-49. Much of the finance required for industrial rehabilitation came from undistributed profits of overseas—mainly British—companies operating in Malaya, and commercial bank credit, aided and augmented of course by government-subsidized loans and grants.

Economic reconstruction therefore depended in good measure on the government's capacity to mobilize financial resources. For the Malayan Union government the revenue system was more than just a means of furnishing an "output" goal, i.e. its expenditure targets. Rather, taxation was also imbued with an "order" goal, in the form of a more egalitarian distribution of disposable income, through the imposition of a more progressive—or less regressive—tax structure. Malayan Union public revenue also aimed at a third goal, the curbing of inflationary pressures and their attendant economic and social ills.

Because of the limitations of the currency board system, there was no possibility of utilizing monetary policy as a means of realizing post-war Malaya's potential productive capacity. Indeed, this proved to be an especially severe shortcoming of the restored monetary system, since public investment in reconstruction had far greater efficiency as regards income creation than, say, more risk-bearing "development" expenditure. In the event, since short-term money could not be simply "created" by the monetary apparatus, the government had to rely instead on existing, hard-pressed fiscal resources, notably reserve funds, borrowing and taxation, in order to underwrite post-war rehabilitation.

Malayan government reserves constituted one important source of funds for post-war finance. Prior to the fall of Singapore substantial British Malayan reserve balances had accumulated in London in three accounts: the General Reserve Surplus, the Special Reserve Fund and the Opium Revenue Replacement Fund.[53] During the course of the war over M$60 million of Malaya's general reserves, in excess of its earnings, were expended by the authority of the secretary of state for the colonies, though no accounts of these transactions were ever published.[54] After the war successive Malayan Union budgetary deficits were financed largely out of reserve funds. Over the first nine months of civilian government deficit spending on rehabilitation consumed nearly three-quarters of the General Reserve Surplus plus a fifth of the Opium Revenue Replacement Fund, totalling M$72.9 million or a third of aggregate public expenditure. Although reserves were tapped less extensively during 1947, by the end of 1948 the General Reserve was exhausted.

TABLE 2
Malayan Government Reserves 1942-8 ($M million).

AT/Date	General Revenue Balance (1)	Special Reserve Fund (2)	Opium Revenue Replacement Fund (3)
15/02/42*	M$133.6	M$47.4	M$52.2
01/04/46	7.9	57.9	72.3
31/12/46	20.8	56.7	58.5
31/12/47	22.9	42.2	56.7
31/12/48†	—	39.9	50.0

* FMS and UMS only, later years include Malacca and Penang shares of SS fund
† Revised Estimates.
Source: *Malayan Union Estimates* (1946-8) adapted.

Government borrowing comprised a second means of mobilizing resources for public purposes. At first the Malayan Union authorities contemplated floating a $200 million London loan to finance rehabilitation, but balked in the face of U.K. restrictions on overseas lending. Britain insisted that the "financial burdens (of war) borne by the United Kingdom have been very much greater than those which have fallen on any other part of the Commonwealth" and therefore "expected" that the colonies would fully tap their own internal resources for reconstruction and development.[55] Nor were Colonial Development and Welfare Funds available for rehabilitation.[56] While the Malayan Union colonial authorities apparently accepted the logic of H.M. government's case with equanimity, local business interests decidedly did not. Demands for British aid for reconstruction pointed angrily to Imperial default in the defence of Malaya in 1942.

To enable the Malayan Union to commence internal borrowing the Colonial Office sanctioned the incurring of additional public debt from June 1946. Permission was given to float a local loan of M$50 million, "the maximum amount which it is likely to be possible to raise locally," and to issue treasury bills to a ceiling of M$20 million. A third savings instrument, Victory Savings Certificates, was later issued in low denominations to further mobilize the resources of small savers. By early 1947 the local loan was fully subscribed, and the government raised the issue amount to M$100 million. All told, M$66.5 million accrued to the government through the 1946 loan.

Although no legislative control was laid down for the 1946 loan, an undertaking had been given that the monies raised would be directed towards reconstruction.[57] In the first instance about a fifth of the monies borrowed went to the general expenditure and the remainder was advanced to municipalities and tin mines for rehabilitation, but without the required sanction of the secretary of state. Later reconstruction expenditure incurred on revenue account was transferred retroactively to loan account, with appropriate adjustments in the 1948 budget.

War damage compensation, promised by Britain in 1942 and subsequently accepted as a responsibility of the U.K. government, grossly undervalued the losses to Malaya and, in any case, did not materialize during the Malayan Union period. After lengthy procrastination a U.K. statement would only be considered on an "austerity" basis, with the main aim being to restore "productive enterprises," i.e. the export sectors. Not even the Malayan government could expect compensation for damage to its capital assets or those of its public enterprises, e.g. the railways, amounting to some £150 million. Of the £150 million in registered claims, the U.K. was prepared to entertain on this basis only £55 million, of which £11 million constituted legal liabilities arising out of war risks insurance. To meet these reduced claims the British government offered a £10 million free grant, £35 million by way of an interest-free loan and £10 million from expected Japanese reparations. Shocked by the paucity of this offer, a joint address of the Malayan Union and Singapore Legislative Councils pointed to the role of Malaya in the sterling area, to the default of the protecting power as the cause of the loss, and to the extent of the rehabilitation costs incurred, and asked for increased British participation in war damage compensation. Britain replied with a "final" offer raising the U.K. grant to £20 million pounds.

Since U.K. participation in war damage compensation was made conditional upon Malaya's maintaining a high level of sterling reserve balances, the real transfer of resources was substantially offset. Moreover the schedule of U.K. payments, extending well into the mid-1950s, assured that British war damage compensation arrived long after the actual reconstruction of Malaya's industries had been completed.

As expected, taxation comprised the major source of post-war government finance. Prior to World War II Malaya had acquired a highly fragmented and socially regressive tax system. The Federated Malay States (FMS), Unfederated Malay States (UMS) and Straits Settlements each imposed their own levies, with the duty on opium yielding the largest quantum of revenue for all the governments concerned.[58] It fell to the BMA to integrate and revise this tax system in line with the Colonial Office's financial directives and the War Office's own regard for H.M. Exchequer. This was achieved by extending the Federated Malay States' tariff system to encompass the entire BMA Mainland Division, including the FMS, UMS and Straits Settlements of Penang and Malacca (but excluding the separate Singapore Division), although special provision was later made for Penang's entrepot trade and tax rates were generally revised upward. Opium now being banned, its revenue ceased.

The taxation system introduced by the BMA effectively reasserted British rule in Malaya while harmonizing the country's several fiscal regimes. Incidentally, this integrated revenue system also served to shift a portion of the cost of military administration from the War Office to the people of Malaya. However, harmonization of taxation did not yet mean correction of its historically regressive incidence.

On taxation policy the Malayan Union government found itself squeezed between the upper and nether millstones of a pressing need for revenue and its express desire to reform the system. Indirect taxes, both import and export duties, generated the bulk of taxation collected under the Malayan Union, yielding over half the government's total revenues. Malayan Union authorities expressed concern about the socially regressive incidence of the tax system they inherited. Furthermore, they were aware that the prevailing system of indirect taxation exempted a considerable proportion of the national income from public levy. Reaction against the tax system was joined by labour interests as well as by the Malay-language press, which departed from their overriding concern with constitutional questions to condemn indirect taxation as inflationary. Commercial interests, on the other hand, rallied around indirect taxation as "always preferable" to any other form of government levy, being "less easy to evade" and "easier and less expensive to collect."[59]

Because of the economic and geographic proximity of the Malayan Union to Singapore, a Joint Advisory Board on Import and Export Policy was set up (August 1947) to achieve close co-ordination on fiscal matters between the two governments. Although this Board sought to achieve a unified application of policy, it had little real success. Failure was due primarily to "a big difference in the application of controls" between Malayan and Singaporean customs authorities such that laxity on the island implied competitive disadvantages for mainland traders as regards duty payments. Differences in enforcement of tax laws reflected the fundamental cleavage in fiscal policies between Kuala Lumpur and Singapore, the former being prepared to utilize taxation to advance national policy in a way that the latter was not. The fact that the two comprised a single economic market, especially with regard to capital flows, meant that Singapore "free trade" principles combined with its financial and commercial strength incidentally limited Malaya's own scope for fiscal initiatives. Furthermore, competition between Malayan ports and Singapore for foreign and entrepot trade made reciprocal action a virtual precondition for the political acceptability and economic effectiveness of taxation.

Import duties furnished about a third of Malayan Union general revenues. Most of these derived from three commodity groups, in descending order of yield: tobacco, liquor, and textiles. Petrol comprised another important source of import duty. The incidence of these duties was particularly regressive, prompting labour to ask that the government explore other sources of revenue to lift the burden of taxation from its shoulders.

The volume of dutiable imports into Malaya was subject to administration controls emanating from London, so that a substantial portion of government revenues lay at the discretion of sterling area policy-makers. Successive measures restricting hard currency imports into Malaya, despite the large Malayan contribution to the sterling area gold-dollar pool, effectively reduced the tax base of the Malayan Union. Although rates of duty were increased in mid-1948, this could not offset the enforced cutback in dutiable imports. Malayan business interests bitterly attacked this economic loss imposed on Malaya by Britain's action. Conceding the "considerable" losses incurred by colonial governments on behalf of sterling, the British government could only advise them to turn from dependence on import duties to "other forms of taxation."[60]

Export duties comprised Malaya's second most important source of tax revenue. The main items on which export duties were charged were rubber and tin, although other commodities, notably palm oil and coconut, also made minor contributions to the Treasury. Before World War II tin was by far the major source of export duty, yielding from two to eight times the revenue of rubber, but since then rubber had dominated export taxation. No less than four rates of duty were applied in succession to rubber exports up to the end of the Malayan Union period, in attempts to reconcile the revenue needs of government with rehabilitation of the rubber industry.[61] At the outset the FMS sliding scale, with a maximum duty of 3 1/4%, was levied on post-war rubber exports through the Rubber Buying Unit, though this was subsequently altered by the BMA (only a month before its disbandment) to a specific duty of 4 cents a pound. While the military authority might have facilitated introduction of this higher rate of duty, actually amounting to an eighth of producers' gross earnings at the fixed buying price for rubber, strenuous opposition to this "fourfold" increase in export tax was subsequently articulated in the Malayan Union Advisory Council:

> One recognizes the need for revenue at the present time but what with the low price at which this country is compelled to sell its rubber to America on the one hand, and the extraordinarily high rate of export tax on the other, this unfortunate industry, if I may put it crudely, seems to be "getting it" both coming and going, and this at a time when it is in need of every dollar it can muster to rehabilitate its dissipated resources.[62]

Although rubber estate demands for restoration of the pre-war sliding scale rate of duty went unattended,[63] following the U.K.-U.S. negotiated rubber price decline of November 1946 the British government permitted the Malayan authorities to reduce the export duty to 2 1/2 cents a pound, in order to maintain producers' returns. In February 1947 the rubber export duty was again changed to a 5% ad valorem tax, where it remained until 1950 when a new sliding scale was adopted. The incidence of rubber export duty, particularly at its specific rates, was particularly onerous on peasant smallholders, whose incomes were being taxed far in excess of what they would have been liable to in any other occupation.

Although chronic rehabilitation problems retarded the resumption of tin exports, the tin duty was reapplied at the pre-war rate.[64] At the official buying price fixed by the British government, the complicated tin export duty formula yielded about 14% of gross export value, or 16% of producers' gross earnings.[65] It had long been established that a portion of the tin export duty comprised a royalty to the State on a wasting asset—the royalty having been conventionally set at 5%, with the remainder representing a contribution to "the current administration and amenities of the country."[66] Chinese tin mining interests argued, however, that the prevailing rate of export duty constituted a one-third levy on their earnings, imposing on them an excessive share of the overall tax burden. They maintained, furthermore, that these duties inhibited exploitation of lower grade ores and therefore operated to the detriment of the Malayan tin industry.[67]

Mounting business opposition to further taxation inspired suggestions of other indirect means of filling the public purse. One of the more strenuously advocated of these was a public lottery, presumably designed to capitalize on the Chinese penchant for gambling. Though admittedly an "evil," lotteries were apparently less of an evil than new or higher taxation. The unofficial members of the Finance Review Committee, with the exception of trade union interests, supported the notion of a state lottery and also proposed a tax on rents, on the express assumption that landlords would be able to shift the tax forward; a tax on interest payments exceeding 8%, aimed explicitly at borrowers in the usurious traditional credit system; and a "windfall" tax on immovable property acquired during the occupation period. These proposals read more like a determined bid to inflict the burden of taxation on labour and peasantry than a serious effort at financial statecraft. These and other novel tax recommendations by business interests in the Finance Review Committee were in the end turned down as discriminatory and essentially regressive by the commissioner of income tax.

Movement towards a progressively graduated tax on incomes in post-war Malaya had been initiated by the Colonial Office's financial directive to the BMA, indicating that civilian government might well have to "consider" imposition of an income tax.[68] When the Labour government came to power income taxation was officially described as "the only practicable and fair method" by which sufficient revenues could be raised to meet Malaya's rehabilitation and development goals.[69] A one-man commission was dispatched to Malaya and Singapore ostensibly to "advise" on the suitability of income tax as a "basis for the taxation policy of either territory or both territories."[70] Although R. B. Heaseman's terms of reference were explicitly advisory, the secretary of state for the colonies duly informed the House of Commons that "the first task of the Commissioner of Income Tax will be to prepare the necessary plans for the introduction of the (income) tax."[71]

To the Malayan Union authorities, income taxation involved social as well as economic policy goals. That income tax was not viewed merely as a short-term revenue device was made abundantly clear. Indeed, the introduction of income taxation underlined a fundamental change in colonial Malayan fiscal objectives. Henceforth the government would pursue increased progressivity in revenue collection. This implied not only a notion of equity in taxation, but also meant a shift in its incidence away from labour, rubber and tin to other affluent but hitherto less taxed elements in the economy, notably the mercantile and professional groups.[72] The government's attraction to income taxation was indeed reinforced by its assumedly fixed incidence, placing the burden squarely on the broadest shoulders.

In addition to considerations of progressivity, the government also maintained that income taxation would secure for Malaya "a due share" of company profits especially of those remitted abroad. Such taxation would not, it was maintained, increase the levy on overseas shareholders since it would be deductible from their metropolitan (i.e. British) tax assessments.[73] Resident companies would of course bear the full burden of the new tax. In order to soften rubber and tin corporation resistance to income taxation, the government gave notice that export duties would be reduced once sufficient revenues were mobilized out of the new tax.

Pointing to the needs of development, the government further maintained that income tax would provide greater stability for public revenue as compared to the highly volatile rubber and tin duties. Broadening of the tax net, it was declared, should soften revenue fluctuations arising from changes in the fortunes of any one or two industries. Of course, in Malaya, where rubber and tin together accounted for more than a fifth of the national income in 1947,[74] it was unlikely that any tax could totally iron out cyclical fluctuations in revenue yields. The most that can be said for income tax in such circumstances is that a certain time lag is introduced, particularly regarding the self-employed, profits and rents, between income changes on one hand and assessment and collection of the tax on the other, thereby extending the time dimension of public finance beyond the immediacy of ordinary customs duties. This may serve to moderate cyclical fluctuations in government revenues and expenditures over time.[75]

Note was also made of the possible counter-inflationary attributes of income tax, though this was more a matter of future potentialities than current practicalities, given the needs of reconstruction. Far from aiming at deflationary finance, the immediate motivation behind the introduction of income taxation was the urgent need for additional expenditure on reconstruction and development.[76]

Progressive broadening of the tax base and the introduction of equity into taxation on the "ability to pay" principle were deemed by the Malayan Union government to be necessary fiscal reforms intended to "ensure the steadiest and most progressive development of the people and institutions of Malaya." Yet it was a curious commentary on the management of fiscal policy that the financial secretary could not even estimate the probable yield of the new tax for its first year, 1948.[77]

Vehement opposition to the introduction of income taxation was aroused among commercial and professional interests. Indeed, a Malayan Association was formed at the behest of British businessmen opponents of government fiscal initiative, as a counterpart of the Singapore Association to advocate the political interests of the business community, particularly in economic matters.[78] Arguments against the income tax ran along three main lines: the method of introducing the tax, supposed operational shortcomings of income taxation and alleged difficulties of enforcing income tax in Malayan society. Widespread resentment among commercial interests, even British, was expressed at the role of the Colonial Office in initiating the income tax: "If income tax is introduced it will not be introduced because in the Malayan Union it is a fair and desirable method of taxation, nor because it is necessary. It will be introduced because our masters in Whitehall have so decreed."[79]

Hostility towards the method of introducing income taxation also turned on the alleged inadequacies of Malayan Union policy-making organs. The "purely advisory" council was dismissed as an improper venue for "such a dramatic change" in fiscal policy, precisely by those who benefited most by imbalanced representation—the British companies. Not without irony, these same groups demanded "direct representation" as a "pre-requisite of direct taxation." In a bid for time, one Chinese councillor even asked that the tax legislation be deferred until the establishment of the successor of the Federation of Malaya, "when our Malay friends would also have the opportunity of expressing their views on the subject in a reconstituted council."

Opposition to the principle of income taxation focused on its alleged impropriety as an instrument of fiscal policy. A balanced budget was advocated as a preferable alternative. Demands for curtailment of public expenditure were calculated to forestall introduction of the new tax. Some of the arguments against the income tax bordered on the ridiculous, or the sublime: "The measure of a person's income is no criterion of his ability to pay." Others alluded to the difficulty of assessing incomes in the large and very affluent black market. In a poignant and colourful attack on income taxation and, implicitly, deteriorating norms of government integrity, one Chinese physician argued:

> To be really equitable, income tax should come down most heavily on those people who make the most money. Now, who make the most money in Malaya today? I would place murderers, robbers and extortioners right on top of the list. . . . Next I would put smugglers and blackmarketeers. Immediately below them—I must ask pardon for putting them so low—I would put officers of the Price Control Department and other Government Departments. If there was an Income Tax Department, I would place its officers above these of any other Government Department. I have searched in vain the Draft Bill for information on how the income of these people can be accurately assessed.[80]

Given the untappable wealth of the black market, the government was urged to devise a "pleasanter, more popular, and for the time being fairer" tax than income tax.

Probably, the most cogent argument against the new tax alleged that the war-rehabilitated Malayan industry was in no condition to shoulder an additional fiscal burden. The government was even warned that possible defaults on rehabilitation loans would more than offset the likely yield of the income tax.[81] Income taxation was further likened to "forcing people who are suffering from profound anemia to give blood transfusions." Shorn of its emotional appeal, this was but a classic plea for redistributing the burden of public revenue to other than commercial profits. The real effect of public finance on rehabilitation was determined not by the incidence of taxation alone, but by the comparative propensities of the government and private enterprise to actually engage in capital investment. The Malayan Union government's role in financing reconstruction, for the private as well as public sectors, was undoubted.

Fears were also expressed that income taxation would prove deflationary in practice. These fears were carried forward by some opponents *ad absurdum*:

> The heavier the tax, the more it restricts spending. . . . So if Income Tax is heavy enough it will stop spending and if there is no spending, there is no selling, which means no trade,

which means no income . . . to tax. I find it hard to believe that this incomeless stage is the objective towards which [the government] is striving.[82]

In fact, the inflationary or deflationary effect of any tax instrument, including income taxation, would be determined of course by the corresponding impact of government expenditure on aggregate demand. A development goal would here tend towards the inflationary.

Attention was also drawn by opponents to the alleged technical difficulties of administering income taxation in Malaya. The Chinese shopkeeper method of bookkeeping was said to be not amenable to income tax. Evasion, some maintained, would moreover be rife, with the main burden of the tax falling on the salaried and the honest. Others foresaw the mushrooming of a new and costly collection department and professed anxiety about "the baneful effect of tempting the government to be unnecessarily extravagant" by placing a new revenue source at its disposal.

In order to cement together the opposition to the income tax, twelve Unofficial Members of the Advisory Council, that is all except the two representing trade union interests, met in caucus to form a solid block against the measure. Support for their stand came from virtually all sectors of trade, industry, finance, commerce and professions in Malaya.[83] The government was urged to take cognizance of the strength and breadth of opposition to income taxation, claimed to represent the "majority opinion in this country." Interestingly, this opposition to income tax was typically accompanied by professions of altruism and social concern, and with strong denials of base motives of self-interest: "I may assure you with all the sincerity at my disposal that considerations of principle far outweigh any personal thought as to how much I may be called upon to foot in the way of my share of Income Tax, in the event of its becoming a *fait accompli.*"[84]

Support for the income tax came from labour representatives in the Advisory Council as well as from various quarters outside. Organized labour, including the Pan-Malayan Council of Government Workers, the Malayan Teachers Union and the large Communist-led Pan-Malayan Federation of Trade Unions declared strongly for the introduction of income taxation as the "most equitable" source of public finance.[85] Accompanying labour support for the measure were demands that the tax burden be shifted from indirect levies on mass consumption goods to broader, if less willing, shoulders and that the government's commitment to social development be fulfilled:

> What is the reply to the working classes of Malaya, when they ask for even the bare minimum of these essential [social] services? Are we to accept the reasons of the well-fed, racehorse-owning, cinema-building "representatives of the people" that the Malayan workers are to be content with a charitable dole? No Sir, I see in the introduction of this (income) tax some hope of carrying out the policy of social betterment of the people to which Government is committed and accordingly, Sir, it has my wholehearted support.[86]

Malaya's nascent nationalist parties, though more concerned with the great constitutional issues of the day, the transition from Malayan Union to a Federation of Malaya, nevertheless came out in favour of income taxation. The United Malays National Organization (UMNO), the leading Malay party; the radical Malay Nationalist Party; and the left-wing Malayan Democratic Union all supported the income tax.[87] Among the press, the Indian, Malay and left-wing newspapers generally expressed support for the new measure,[88] as did the influential English-language *Straits Times*.[89]

The debate on the Income Tax Bill found the Advisory Council sharply split. The official side and labour were in favour of the proposed legislation, commercial and professional interests were opposed. Upon division it was the latter who prevailed by force of numbers. In the meantime a similar debate took place in Singapore, with an identical outcome. Rejection of the income tax underlined the political gap inherent in these quasi-legislative organs between representation and responsibility. Thus, a major reform in fiscal policy, for which the government was responsible to the broad political community, was contradicted by its narrowly representative "legislative" institutions. Government was therefore placed in dilemma between its own responsibility and the need to override legislative opinion. In the end, the governors of Malaya and Singapore proceeded to enact the income tax by order, on 4 December 1947.

For its future promise, even more than for its current utility, the income tax constituted the most far-reaching economic policy reform undertaken by the post-war colonial government. Going beyond the point of the policy, the income tax principle opened the way to substantial changes in the ordering of national economic goals. The introduction of income taxation effectively challenged the colonial stratification of Malayan society with a new, albeit still potential, national and developmental leverage. Yet realization of the significance of this fiscal innovation had to await the transition to representative, responsible government upon independence, and its explicit acceptance of national development as its operative goal. For the time being, however, the colonial administration preferred reconciliation with the business community through a moderation of the actual tax proposals in their favour.[90] When introduced in 1949, the scale of income taxation was adapted to the needs of conservative public finance, with fiscal innovation, consistent with the larger colonial objective of maintaining intact Malaya's pre-war economic structure.

The Direction of Post-War Public Finance

Malaya emerged from World War II with her commercial structures shattered, her plantation economy ruined or obsolescent, food scarce and her labour force dislocated. In these circumstances of post-liberation prostration the restoration of the Imperial financial superstructure could only be an economic burden, with increasing political consequences. By way of contrast with some earlier stages of empire building, the post-war restoration of British rule did not entail a therapeutic inflow of sterling area capital for the economic development of Malaya. Rather, the main thrust of post-liberation monetary and fiscal policies was in a custodial direction: towards underwriting the re-establishment of a British colonial regime dominant over Malayan economic, as well as political, affairs.

The financial measures introduced into post-liberation Malaya were rooted in the cognitive scheme of a colonial economic order. Official attitudes typically envisaged the return to "normalcy" essentially in terms of the *status quo ante*, even if this went against the current of recent history. Monetary policies accordingly aimed at resurrecting the sterling area to its previous pre-eminence, notwithstanding the abandonment of fundamental rules of free intra-sterling bloc payments flows. This new unilateralism in post-war sterling placed Malaya, in particular, in the paradoxical situation of a massive contributor to the gold-dollar pool herself enduring an imposed liquidity shortage. Domestically, fiscal appropriations were clearly calculated to rehabilitate the international sector of the economy, that which was dominated by British-owned companies, ahead of competing local producers and the indigenous sectors. As before the war, the revenue base was still narrowly conceived and taxation remained regressive, while for the first time, reserves were drawn down. As a result of this web of financial measures designed to serve ultimate Imperial purposes, the formation of capital for post-war reconstruction imposed internal income deflation within Malaya, involving a terrific squeeze on Malayan resources—mainly labour but also capital enterprise and land.

The restored colonial financial structure was to prove, in later events, incapable of coping with the fiscal requisites of economic development. Even the income tax, a most significant fiscal innovation introduced at the initiative of the Labour government in London, had its progressive effects deferred in implementation at the behest of vested colonial administrative and business interests. When the golden opportunity did arise out of the Korean War rubber boom—one of the periodic great bonanzas of economic history—the considerable windfall was squandered for most intents and purposes, through the inadequacies of Malayan public finance.

Malayan economic reconstruction thus incurred a development cost, in terms of subsequent opportunities foregone owing to the deficiencies inherent in the pre-war financial system restored for Imperial purposes by post-war policy.

ENDNOTES

1. For studies of immediate post-war British policy in Malaya, see James de v. Allen, *The Malayan Union* (New Haven, Conn., 1956); Martin Rudner, "The Political Structure of the Malayan Union," *Journal of the Malaysian Branch, Royal Asiatic Society, Vol. 43 (1970)*; J. M. Gullick, *Malaya* (London, 1963) esp. chap. 9. For an official account see F.S.V. Donnison, *British Military Administration in the Far East* (London, 1956).

2. International Bank for Reconstruction and Development, *The Economic Development of Malaya* (Baltimore, 1955), p. 645 (Henceforth: *IBRD Report*).

3. On the structure and operations of the Malayan Planning Unit, see M. Rudner, "The Organization of the British Military Administration in Malaya," *Journal of Southeast Asian History*, Vol. 9, (1968), p. 96 *et passim*.

4. On the colonial currency board system, see Ida Greaves, *Colonial Monetary Conditions* (London, 1954). On the organisation and operations of the Malayan Currency Board, see Frank H. King, *Money in British East Asia* (London, 1957), and Sir Sydney Caine, "Malayan Monetary Problems," *Malayan Economic Review* (henceforward: *MER*), Vol. 3 (1958), pp. 25-32. See also Frank King's reply to critiques of his original study in "Notes on Malayan Monetary Problems," *MER* Vol. 3 (1958), pp. 30-41.

5. In fact the currency board system did allow for one form of indirect regulation of credit through fluctuations in the local currency issue achieved by shifting government reserves between London and Malaya. cf. P.A. Wilson, "Money in Malaya," *MER* Vol. 2 (1957), p. 62 on this point.

6. Cf. Greaves, Colonial Monetary Conditions, pp. 6-15, and King, *Money*, pp. 29-45. All legislation concerning currency or banking had to be referred to the secretary of state prior to obtaining the governor's assent. Under the BMA the controller of Finance and Accounts, responsible to the War Office, served as currency commissioner, and after the resumption of civil government the financial secretaries of the Malayan Union and Singapore jointly comprised the Board of Commissioners of Currency for Malaya.

7. Little has been written on Japanese monetary policy in occupied Far Eastern Territories. For a contemporary account from Malaya, see Chin Kee Onn, *Malaya Upside Down* (Singapore, 1946), pp. 212-13; see also King, *Money*, pp. 23.

8. Proclamation No. 4, B.M.A. *Gazette* Vol. 1, No. 1 (November 1945), p. 9.

9. On the fixing of exchange rates on other liberated territories in Africa and Europe between occupation and liberation currencies, see Frank M. Tamagna, 'The Fixing of Foreign Exchange Rates', *Journal of Political Economy* Vol. 53 (1945), esp. 62-6.

10. This would have been especially relevant had Malaya's liberation occurred gradually, through combat, as military planners had assumed. Then, any recognition according the Japanese scrip would enable them to virtually print sterling and therefore inflict serious economic damage on the liberation.

11. The role of demonetization as an anti-Communist weapon was first noted by T. H. Silcock and U. A. Aziz, *Nationalism in Malaya* (New York, 1951), p. 23, and this motive was subsequently accepted and reiterated by Gene Z. Hanrahan in his comprehensive study of the Malaya Communist Party, T*he Communist Struggle in Malaya* (New York, 1954), p, 55. Charles Gamba, *The Origins of Trade Unionism in Malaya* (Singapore, 1961), maintains the anti-Communist motive of demonetization, see p. 49. F. S. V. Donnison's official history of the British Military Administration nowhere mentions this point.

12. F. S. V. Donnison, *British Military Administration*, p. 223. Donnison's account provides an official history of British military policy and administration in Malaya.

13. It is interesting to note in this regard that the Malayan Communist Party and its General Labourers' Union, then the largest in the country, described the demonetization of "banana" currency as a cause of the impoverishment of labour: "Motions Brought Forward at the 1st Meeting of the Selangor General Labourers' Union," Document 2 in reprinted in Gamba, *The Origins*, p. 430.

14. Donnison, *British Military Administration,* pp. 226-7.

15. A long association with heavy inflation had created an inflationary outlook from which it was difficult to wean people. There was great uncertainty with regard to values and weak consumer resistance to upward price creep. Indeed the dollar and not the cent had come to be regarded as the lowest unit of currency. Cf. Donnison, *Brtitish Military Administration,* p. 227; Gamba, *The Origins*, p. 45, and *Singapore Annual Report* 1946 (Singapore, 1946), p. 13.

16. In the absence of proper cost-of-living indices of this period these figures represent crude estimates made by authoritative sources and are useful for orders of magnitude: cf. Malayan Union and Singapore Joint Wages Commission, *Interim Report on Wages*, (Kuala Lumpur, 1947) pp. 5, 19; *Economic Review of Malaya 1945-49*, Reference division, Central Office of Information (London, 1950), p. 14.

17. See Donnison, *British Military Administration*, pp. 212-3.

18. There is a striking resemblance between the resumption of the pre-war sterling exchange rate in Malaya and sterling's return to the pre-World War I gold standard in 1925. If the term "Malayan dollar" be substituted for "sterling", and "sterling" for "gold," and the orders of magnitude be multiplied, the following comment from John Meynard Keynes, A *Treatise on Money* (London, 1930), Vol. II, p. 181, becomes quite relevant:

> "It was necessary to raise the gold value of sterling by about 10 percent at a time when gold was not depreciating in value. This meant that the flow of money income per unit output, i.e. rates of earnings generally, had to diminish by 10 percent—except in so far as a depreciation in the value of gold came to the assistance of the transition. In other words there had to be an income deflation in the strict sense of the term."

Note that under the Currency Board system the Malayan dollar was even on a sterling standard "in the shadow of gold": F. H. H. King, *Money*, p. 29.

19. On the post-war fall in money incomes, see Donnison, *British Military Administration*, pp. 311-13; on wages, see Gamba, *The Origins*, pp. 44-9; and on export earnings, see Malek A. Merican, *Finance in Post War Malaya*, unpublished B. Litt. thesis (Oxford University, 1958), p. 37. Note that revaluation was not offset by lower Malayan dollar import prices owing to international controls and supply shortages.

20. Cf. Michael R. Stenson, *Industrial Conflict in Malaya* (London, 1970) on this point.

21. *Report of the Commissioners of Currency for Malaya*, (1941-6), (Kuala Lumpur, 1947).

22. Ibid. In 1934 Sir Basil Blacket in his *Report of the Commissioner Appointed by the Secretary of State for the Colonies to Enquire into the Question of Malayan Currency, Straits Settlements Paper No. 78*, recommended at 115% premium but this was rejected as excessive by the Straits Settlements financial secretary in favour of 110% cover.

23. See A. Hazelwood, "Colonial External Finance Since the War," *Review of Economic Studies* Vol. 21 (1953-4), where it is argued that colonial sterling reserves more than offset Colonial Development and Welfare Act aid and constituted a transfer of real resources from underdeveloped colonial territories to the U.K. Malaya did not qualify for CDW Act aid during reconstruction, but nevertheless maintained total sterling reserves of £125 million and £115 million in 1946 and 1947 respectively: *The Colonial Empire (1939-1947)* (London, 1947), Cmd. 7167, *p. 106.*

24. *The Colonial Territories (1948-9)* (London, 1950), Cmd. 7715, pp. 76-7. On the role of the Capital Issues Committee, see Greaves, *Colonial Monetary Conditions*, pp. 82, 88; and Hazelwood, "Colonial External Finance", p. 35.

25. Financial Secretary, Statement to the Malayan Union Finance Committee, *Report of the Finance Committee, 1947* (Kuala Lumpur, 1947), p. C438.

26. Financial secretary, *Malayan Union Advisory Council Proceedings* (henceforward: A.C. Proc.), 25 November 1947, p. B266.

27. For the pattern of post-war exchange controls in the sterling area, see Greaves, *Colonial Monetary Conditions*, p. 13, and Sir Gerald Clauson, *The Sterling Area* (London, 1948). Note that the self-government dominions were not bound so inflexibly to Bank of England policy. The mechanism for enforcing colonial

compliance was "informal" communications to their financial secretaries: Cmd. 7433, p. 87.

28. *U.S.-U.K. Loan Agreement Cmd.* 6968, Art. 7, and address by Assistant Secretary of the U.S. Treasury Harry D. White at luncheon of Civitan Club, Mayflower Hotel, Washington D.C., 9 April 1946 (Private Papers, Princeton University Library).

29. Financial secretary, *A.C. Proc.*, 25 Nov. 1947, B266: "Foreign exchange is not allowed on the basis of quotas for particular territories," p. 30. See, *Report of the Customs and Excise Department* (Kuala Lumpur, 1947), p. 8, and Cmd. 7433, p. 83, on this point.

30. See, *Report of the Customs and Excise Department* (1947), 8, and Cmd. 7433, 83, on this point.

31. Cf. Philip W. Bell, *The Sterling Area in Post War World; Internal Mechanism and Cohesion, 1946-1956*, (1956), pp.62-3.

32. See I. Greaves, *Colonial Monetary Conditions*, p. 87, on changed post-war sterling area relations between the U.K. and its colonies.

33. Cf. *General Statement on Colonial Development and Welfare*, London, 1940, Cmd. 7433, and Cmd. 7167, p. 11.

34. Colonial Secretary George Hall, *Hansard*, 9 July 1946. On the social responsibilities of colonial governments, see Cmd. 7167, pp. 53-71, and Cmd. 7433, pp. 41-58.

35. Colonial secretary George Hall, *House of Commons Debates*, 9 July 1946.

36. Martin Rudner, op. cit., 1970.

37. Governors' Address, *A.C. Proc.*, 19 Dec. 1947.

38. *A.C. Proc.*, 11 Dec. 1946.

39. *Report of the Finance Review Committee* (Kuala Lumpur, 1947), Para. 66.

40. V.N.N. Menon, *A.C. Proc.*, 4 Oct. 1947.

41. Rider to the Report of the Unofficial Member of the Finance Review Committee by Messrs. Chong Min Khee and P.P. Narayanan.

42. Kho Teik Ee, *A.C. Proc.*, 4 Oct. 1947. This criticism was not, unfortunately, without foundation, for gross inefficiencies and blatant budgetary malpractices were later discovered to have pervaded Malayan Union public finance; see *Report of the Audit of Accounts* (Kuala Lumpur, 1947), pp. 1-3. Be that as it may, business criticism was directed not at particular miscarriages, but rather at the principle of government spending.

43. Cf. *A.C. Proc.*, 24 Nov. 1947, addresses by Jules Martin and A. W. Wallich. Taking the case further, a "wholesome" return to the idea of the Post World War I "Retrenchment Commission" was envisaged in order to "call a halt" to all "non-essential" spending; see W.G.C Blunn, *A.C. Proc.*, 10 Dec. 1946, and Khoo Teik Ee, *A.C. Proc.*, 4 Oct. 1947. One Chinese merchant appointee from Malacca, Ee Yew Kim, was perhaps more consistent, though less practical perhaps, in demanding that reconstruction spending as well be curbed in order to balance the budget without additional taxation.

44. See the *Report of the Finance Review Committee*, op. cit., para. 22, on this point: ". . . Expenditure upon Medical and Health Department cannot be unduly stinted . . ." (p. 45); V.N. Menon, *A.C. Proc.*, 14 July 1947, p. B151.

45. For rehabilitation problems of the BMA, see *Report on British Dependencies in the Far East (1945-1949)* (London, 1949), Cmd. 7709, pp. 14-16.

46. Cmd. 7709, p. 8. Note that of all the British Far Eastern territories only in Malaya was private enterprise restored under government auspices; on this point, see Donnison, *British Military Administration*, pp. 257-8.

47. According to E.G. Holt, *Report on the Malayan Rubber Industry* (Washington, 1946), p. 8, about M$455 million was advanced by the BMA to estates. Only half of this amount was actually repaid by the estate companies under rules agreed to seven years later, and the sum due could be credited to war damage reparations; see *Report of the War Damage Commission* (Kuala Lumpur, 1953), p. 110.

48. On the structure of credit in Malaya, and its division between modern banking and traditional moneylender sectors, see, *IBRD Report*, pp. 126-7; and T.H. Silcock, "From Piracy to credit," in Lim Tay Boh (ed.), *Problems of Malayan Economics* (Singapore, 1959), p. 29.

49. For the working of the Industrial Rehabilitation Board see Merican, *op. cit.*, pp. 55-6, and C.C. Allen and A.G. Donnithorne, *Western Enterprise in Indonesia and Malaya* (London, 1957), p. 208.

50. For a history of tin rehabilitation, see the *Annual Report of the Administration of the Mines Department and Mining Industry (1947)* (Kuala Lumpur, 1948), Part 4.

51. *Report of the Audit of Accounts* (1947), pp. 6-7. Though no official figures have been published it is estimated that M$25 million were lent out to tin mines in this way.

52. Chinese Tin Mines Rehabilitation Loans Board advances were to be based on ore reserves, tin content or ores and mine operating costs. In fact the Board's practice in applying these criteria were characterised as "too" stringent by the *Mines Department Report* (Kuala Lumpur, 1947), p. 50. Fewer than half the Chinese mines actually received aid, compared to 90% of the British mines.

53. Other reserve funds included the Electricity and Postal Departments Renewals Funds and the Railways Renewals Funds, all of which were earmarked.

54. For a report on and a critique of this depletion of Malayan General Reserves by over a third, see *The Report of the Finance Review Committee*, pp. C414-15. A portion of the monies was spent on supplies ordered but not delivered before the fall of Singapore; on payments to internal Malayan Civil Service officers' families; and on deficiency payments to officers posted elsewhere for the duration. Note that increases accrued to reserves at 1 April 1946 included past interest on investments and Penang and Malacca's shares of Straits Settlements Reserve Funds.

55. Colonial Secretary's despatch to colonial governments cited in *The Colonial Review*, Vol. IV (March, 1946), pp. 134-5.

56. Governor's address, *A.C. Proc.*, 30 April 1946. Apparently C.D.W. funds were not available to Malaya at the time even for new port development.

57. *Report of the Audit of Accounts* (1947), para. 37. No schedule of loan expenditure was prepared as required by Section 4 of the 1946 Loan Ordinance, until 1949.

58. On taxation in pre-war Malaya, see Lim Chong Yah, *Economic Development of Modern Malaya* (Kuala Lumpur, 1946), chapter 9.

59. Report of the *Finance Review Committee*, p. C430. See also R.B. Heasman, *Report on Income Tax* (Kuala Lumpur, 1947), p. 5.

60. Cmd. 7433, p. 83.

61. For a study of post-war rubber taxes, see Lim Chong Yah, "Export Taxes on Rubber in Malaya," *MER* Vol. 5 (1960), pp. 46-50.

62. W.G.C. Blunn, *A.C. Proc.*, 29 June 1946, p. B57. See also reports by Sir John Hay to Kamuning (Perak) Rubber and Tin Co. Ltd. annual meeting, November 1945, and President T.B. Barlow's address to the Rubber Growers Association annual meeting, 25 April 1946.

63. On this basis the tax yield would have been merely 1 1/2 cents a pound, as against 4 cents a pound then exacted. An additional "cess" of 1/2 cent a pound was collected to finance the Rubber Research Institute of Malaya.

64. On the history of the tin duty see Lim Chong Yah, *Economic Development*, Chapter 9 (ii).

65. Cf. F. Benham, *National Income of Malaya 1947-49* (Singapore, 1950), pp. 39-40.

66. Sir Lewis Fermor, *Report on the Mining Industry of Malaya* (Kuala Lumpur, 1933), p. 109.

67. Col. H.S. Lee, *A.C. Proc.*, 4 Oct. 1947. Indeed, if the tin duty did include a royalty portion, there was no logical reason to charge an identical royalty irrespective of location and ore content. The existing form of royalty actually tended to discriminate against marginal Chinese producers.

68. See statement by Chief Secretary, *A.C. Proc.*, 24 Nov. 1947. Income tax had previously been imposed in Malaya as a temporary wartime measure in both wars.

69. Under-Secretary of State for the Colonies, D.R. Rees-Williams, *H.C. Deb.*, 10 Dec. 1947. First publication of HM government's intent to impose tax on Malaya was made in the House of Commons by the colonial secretary on 18 June 1945.

70. *Report on Income Tax*, p. 1.

71. Mr. Creech-Jones, *H.C. Deb.*, 22 January 1947.

72. Mercantile groups were a particular target of the new tax owing to the high—untaxed—profits earned during the period of post-war shortages: *Report on Income Tax*, p. 9.

73. It is interesting to note that a subsequent recommendation by the Joint Committee on the Income Tax that the proposed company tax rate be increased to 30% was turned down by the financial secretaries of both the Malayan Union and Singapore on the grounds that this higher rate of tax would add to effective corporate tax burdens and deprive HM Exchequer of revenue. Cf. "Note of the Action Taken By Government of the Malayan Union on Recommendations of the Committee, Malayan Union and Singapore," *Joint Committee on Income Tax Report*, Advisory Council Paper No. 34 of 1947.

74. Benham, *National Income*, pp. 23-4.

75. For elaboration of this point, see Lim Chong Yah, *Economic Development cit.*, pp. 513-4.

76. *Report on Income Tax*, p. 13.

77. Financial secretary comments on *Finance Review Committee Report*, p. C439.

78. *F.M.S. Chamber of Commerce Yearbook, 1947* (Kuala Lumpur, 1947). See also M.R. Stenson, *Industrial Conflict*, pp. 173-4.

79. Cf. S.B. Palmer, *A.C. Proc.*, 5 Aug. 1947, p. B163.

80. Dr. Ong Chong Keng, *A.C. Proc..*, 4 Oct. 1947, p. B223.

81. This was in fact a spurious argument, for such costs would be deductible from income tax as legitimate business expenses.

82. Dr Ong Chong Keng, *A.C. Proc.*, 4 Oct. 1947, B223.

83. For a listing of these groups, see the *Report on Income Tax*, pp. 23-5.

84. Ee Yew Kim, *A.C. Proc.*, 4 Oct. 1947.

85. *Rider to the Report of the Unofficial Members of the Finance Review Committee* by Messrs Chang Min Kee and P.P. Narayanan, pp. C436.

86. M.P. Rajagopal, *A.C. Proc.*, 25 July 1947, p. B165.

87. The list of the trades unions and parties supporting the Income Tax Bill was enunciated by trade unionist M.P. Rajagopal, *A.C. Proc.*, 25 Nov. 1947, p. B265, to counter opposition claims that they represented "majority opinion."

88. A list of press supporters of the tax is provided in the *Report on Income Tax*, pp. 4-5. The Report states, however, that left-wing Chinese newspapers opposed the tax (p. 4) but this is contradicted by a contemporary account in *British Malaya* ("Malayan Review", October, 1947, p. 271) indicating left-wing press support for the measure, which would be more consistent with socialist party aims and documents.

89. *Straits Times*, 21 August 1947.

90. Cf. M.R. Stenson, *Industrial Conflict*, pp. 173-6

CHAPTER 2

THE MALAYAN POST-WAR RICE CRISIS:
An Episode in Colonial Agricultural Policy

Malaya's conquest by the Japanese during the Second World War provided the British with the opportunity to reconsider past practices and plan a radical reorganization of the post-war Malayan colonial system. Working from London during the occupation, the colonial authorities produced a scheme involving the merger of the territories and populations of British Malaya into an integrated, unified Malayan Union, as a preliminary step towards eventual self-government.[1] Taken in the context of earlier developments, the Malayan Union proposal constituted a substantially new departure for the country's administrative constitutional and social growth. Yet, if political modernization comprised the avowed thrust of British planning for Malaya, it is significant that the treatment given the post-war economic system, and particularly agricultural policy, reflected a continuation of past ambiguities and, indeed, ambivalence.

In line with the ethnic-economic stratification of colonial Malaya, agricultural policy was historically bound up with Malay communal life and Britain's self-acknowledged role of trustee for the stability of traditional Malay society. The Malays, considered the native people of Malaya, constituted only a small plurality in terms of population, but enjoyed a special status particularly, but not exclusively, in the Malay States.[2] This, by virtue of the traditional authority of the Malay rulers buttressed by the principles of indirect colonial rule, was reinforced by a long standing British sympathy for the Malay aristocracy.

Politically, solicitude for the Malays was a centrepiece of pre-war British colonial ideology and, to a degree, practice. Traditional Malay social organization and cultural forms were maintained as a matter of policy, while members of the Malay "squirearchy" were enlisted into the colonial government service. Yet, most of the Malay population remained employed in subsistence agriculture, tied to a kampung (village) society that constituted the economic basis of their social and cultural order.

Padi cultivation was—and to a certain extent still is—closely identified with Malay tradition. Rice was long regarded as the occupational symbol of a stable kampung society.[3] Indeed, agricultural lands in Malaya, then as now, were mostly held on lease from the Malay States, conditional upon the cultivation of stipulated crops, generally padi. Over time, the Muslim laws of inheritance and population pressure on cultivated land resulted in the fragmentation of peasant padi land holdings. Consequently, the bulk of the Malay peasantry found itself occupationally locked in rice cultivation by the combined influence of colonial solicitude, customary sanction and administrative regulation. For this, Malay tradition incurred a high opportunity cost in terms of income foregone, during a period when the country's leading export and urban sectors were largely given over, by default, to other, non-Malay communities.[4]

It was symptomatic of this historical legacy that British post-war planners could conceive of their modernization goals for Malaya without involving the Malay peasantry directly in the process. Post-war agricultural policy remained devoid of a development thrust, to the ultimate cost of the Malayan Union experiment, and of the Malay community itself.

Attitudes, Interests and Post-War Planning

Colonial Office directives concerning post-war Malaya were translated into a Key Plan by the wartime Malayan Planning Unit, charged with preparing civil policies for the British return. The economic strategy underlying the Malayan Planning Unit and Key Plan operations emphasized Britain's determination to restore, as rapidly as possible, a semblance of pre-war "normalcy" in economic relationships within Malaya, and between Malaya and the world. Re-establishing the former economic system was also deemed critical for the procurement of strategic supplies for the anticipated ongoing war effort for business, for Malaya's own economic welfare and, not least, for the sterling area balance of payments. Post-war economic policy measures, therefore, aimed at restoring the pre-war level of wages and domestic costs as the bedrock of assumed "normalcy" oblivious of the inflation-wrought changes of the war years. With the return of the British, the wartime Japanese currency was entirely demonetized and replaced by a new British Malayan currency (a step which also led, incidentally, to a considerable transfer of Malayan resources to the British Military Administration); pre-war salary and wage rates were reimposed; and trade and prices regulated—though this last with rather less resolve.

The inevitable consequence was a massive income deflation within Malaya, an almost classic Keynesian instance of income contraction in reaction to monetary revaluation in an inflationary economy.[5]

As it was, the main burden of this income deflation had been borne by those groups whose incomes were primarily of domestic origin, notably labour and foodcrop agriculture. However, labour in post-war Malaya, freshly organized in militant communist-led trade unions, succeeded in redressing the disparity somewhat through industrial action between 1946 and 1948.[6] The organizationally—and economically—weaker rice-growing peasantry was left to cope with the deflationary incomes strategy, transmitted through and complicated by the conflict and confusion that characterized post-war agricultural policy.

Prior to the Second World War, Malaya, as a rice deficit country, was obliged to import some 60% of its requirements. Rice and other staples were expected to be in short supply, and therefore costly in the post-war period. The Malayan Planning Unit accordingly designed its agricultural policy to minimize foreign currency expenditures in line with imperial economic strategy. Food supplies for post-war Malaya were incorporated into the Key Plan on a minimal "disease and unrest" standard,[7] one usually applied to liberated enemy territory, and based on estimates of Malaya's likely needs. For its rice requirements, Malaya was to be tied once again to Burma, as before the war, thus keeping payments within the sterling area, but which meant an unfounded dependency on a war ravaged source of supply. Nonetheless, food policy planning for post-war Malaya was cast in the specific context of relief supplies, rather than agricultural policy proper, as a policy prologue for the resumption of "normalcy" on the pre-war pattern.

Of course, the post-war planners had hoped that Malayan rice cultivators would maximize their production for local markets, and thereby reduce the country's reliance on immediate imports. However, little attention and resources were devoted to the post-war expansion of Malayan agriculture. In fact, not much faith was placed on Malaya's potential as a rice producer:

> The production of rice was low in Malaya before the war . . . because it was a non-productive crop, and because it could

be produced as cheaply in other parts more favoured by climatic or other circumstances. I am not sure that we can count upon a large rice production being really profitable economically for Malaya in the future.[8]

Cost accounting, even more than comparative advantage criteria, and certainly more than developmental perspectives, dictated reversion to a policy geared to cheap imports and involving the stagnation of domestic agriculture. Agricultural pricing had prior consideration, inasmuch as rice was considered the major factor in restoring the pre-war wages-cost structure of Malaya's labour-intensive rubber and tin export industries.

During the course of the war, those interest groups still free and capable of making themselves heard in London attempted to exert their influence on the making of post-war agricultural policy, inter alia. Foremost among these, and the first to present its case, was the Association of British Malaya (ABM), composed of companies, civil servants, and other Britons with a stake in Malaya. An ABM Memorandum on the Reconstruction of Malaya, submitted to the Colonial Office in 1943, argued for post-war "encouragement of home produced food and (a) policy of small scale subsistence production."[9] Also, "land suitable for rice production and other food production" should be "reserved" for such purposes, notwithstanding the criteria of comparative economic advantage, and Malay Land Reservations should be "retained and possibly extended."[10] On the surface, the ABM proposals for agriculture exhibited the ingrained paternalism of "British Malayans," as they called themselves, towards Malay "children of the soil" whose traditional position was to be preserved as a matter of colonial trust.[11] But the Memorandum obviously aimed at more than just that. The ABM stand also reflected a widespread belief among British administrators and businessmen that Malaya's rubber trade cycle could best be "balanced" through diversification with food-crop, even subsistence, agriculture. This approach coincided with the underlying economic interests of British estate companies. Be that as it may, the ABM's emphasis on continued Malay involvement in a peasant subsistence economy offered scant scope for post-war rural development.

Not that the modernization of the rural Malayan economy and society was an accepted goal among British Malayans at the time. In a book published in anticipation of post-war deliberations, one prominent and influential British rubber company director argued strenuously that agricultural policy should leave the Malays "to their own traditions and way of life."[12] Waxing romantic, he urged that Malays (e.g., kampung society) be insulated from "the false values of Western materialism," so that "all" would be the "richer" for it.

According to this fundamentally anti-developmental conception of agricultural policy, government was to restrict itself to the alleviation of disease, ignorance, and the effects of natural calamity, while, of course, ensuring continuation of the existing patterns of production. In these, the rubber estate companies were vitally interested. Plantation companies were particularly concerned to have peasant smallholders deployed away from rubber, where they were keen competitors, to alternative crops. It is noteworthy that British rubber estate company spokesmen were among the strongest advocates of cultivation clauses for all land, so as to prevent peasant entry into rubber cultivation, ostensibly in order to promote a "balanced agriculture." Likewise they were vocal supporters of Malay Land Reservations, for the "protection of the indigenous people."

In fact, the Colonial Office had already decided to uphold the Malay Land Reservations in its planning for post-war Malaya.[13] These Land Reservations were a feature of the pre-war agricultural economies of most of the Malay States, and had been intended as a bulwark against the displacement of Malay peasant society. By the Second World War the area under Malay Land Reservations had grown to some 60% of British Malaya's rice-growing acreage. These acts of communal defence may have contributed to the preservation of the traditional Malay agrarian-based social system, but inevitably incurred an economic cost for the community. There is evidence that Malay Land Reservations led to an increasing concentration of wealth and income within Malay society, greater impoverishment among the peasantry, and a generally retarding effect on the Malay agricultural economy.[14] Yet, the British decision to preserve intact Land Reservations underscored the historical paradox of colonial trusteeship, the policy dilemma between tradition and development, while simultaneously cutting against the grain of the post-war egalitarian and modernization goals. However, this policy was probably dictated by a Colonial Office desire to reassure the Malays and cushion them from the shock of post-war change, at least by protecting their landed interests.

The Malay communal elite, social and religious, maintained its past conception of an agricultural policy linked to a stable rice-growing kampung society. To the extent that economic improvement was considered at all, this was conceived strictly in terms of the institutional, social and cultural status quo of the kampung.

Implicitly subsumed in the retention of the past patterns was the continuity of a peasant agricultural base rooted in padi cultivation. Even when confronted with the economic acuity of immigrant non-Malays, the Malay elite reacted by withdrawal, seeking communal salvation in a deeper, more total commitment to the traditional kampung society and its subsistence rice economy. That rice cultivation had become a Malay cultural fetish and shield for communal survival remained apparent in elite attitudes towards post-war agricultural policy proposals. Thus, a wartime statement issued by the Society of Malay Students in Great Britain clearly subordinated considerations of relative economic advantage to cultural maintenance and communal defence.[15] Their objective was put simply as:

> The preservation of an indigenous and stable landed peasantry which shall neither be forced into the state of landed proletariat labouring on huge alien estates nor be supplanted by other alien elements such as the Chinese.[16]

Alternative possibilities for the employment of Malay resources were explicitly rejected.

Yet the Malay peasantry had no way to make its own demands heard. The war and occupation expanded the distance, always great in itself, between peasantry and policy-maker. For all the emphasis placed by others on preserving the traditional rural agricultural system, there seems to have been no economic advantage in this for those actually involved: the peasant cultivators. Malayan padi yields were unsatisfactory by all accounts, and deteriorating tenure conditions resulted in subsistence incomes for the bulk of the Malay peasantry. Already during pre-war years individual peasants had begun to shift away from arduous and profitless padi cultivation to more lucrative rubber smallholdings but were restrained by custom and reinforced by law.[17]

Two groups, British mercantile interests and the Malayan Chinese, did actually dissent from the prevailing trend in post-war agricultural policy thinking. Within the ABM, an extraordinary controversy emerged over the agricultural policy demands in the ABM Memorandum. These, the merchants claimed, were included at the behest and in the interests of rubber planters, and drew an angry reply. In a reasoned rebuttal, one leading merchant argued for a comprehensive review of pre-war policy, "seeing that very little more than one third of the rice consumed in the peninsula is grown there."[18] In effect, the merchants were demanding the rational application of comparative ad-

vantage in post-war Malayan agricultural policy. Of course, increasing Malaya's dependency on international agricultural trade,
including the importation of lower-cost rice, would have been to
the benefit of commerce, directly through the business thereby
created and indirectly by benefiting the cost conscious entrepot
trade. Nothing was said, however, about alternative employment
for displaced peasants or about the broader problem of rural development. Indeed, the ABM demands tended to reflect more its
concern with company profit and loss accounts than any consideration for Malayan welfare and development. The Malayan Chinese,
like the Malays, were constrained in relating to future British policy by the Japanese occupation. However, one of the community's leading figures, Tan Cheng Lock, prepared a
"Memorandum on the Future of Malaya," on behalf of the Overseas Chinese Association.[19] This called for the immediate revision
of pre-war policy tenets concerning agriculture. The Memorandum argued for an end to Malay Land Reservations "in the interests and rights of other races," coupled with free entry for
Chinese into rice cultivation. The case for this was put in both ethnic and production terms:

> The Chinese, who are extraordinarily fine rice cultivators ca-
> pable of extracting from the soil two or more crops in a year,
> may be permitted and encouraged to work paddy fields . . .
> This would immensely increase the rice production of the
> country, which has had to import from abroad one half to two
> thirds of its rice consumption, which must be a highly unsatis-
> factory state of affairs.[20]

Age-old Chinese agricultural expertise, according to the Memorandum, could be used to promote agricultural self-sufficiency without sacrificing the cheap rice principle so dear to employers. While
granting that Malay farmers might require assistance to keep pace,
it was urged that this be done through the non-discriminatory
extension of social and advisory services and agricultural credit
to cultivators. If the Tan Memorandum embodied a highly optimistic evaluation of Chinese rice-growing capabilities, and therefore of Malaya's agricultural potential, it is significant to note that
its main policy criteria were not so much economic as communal. Not the promise of income advantage would be Chinese
padi cultivators, but the determination of the urbanized Chinese
leadership to root their community in the soil of Malaya, politically and socially, stood behind their proposals for post-war agricultural policy change. As with the Malays, the Chinese elite's

thinking on agricultural policy was coloured by communal, political and social factors outweighing any concern for rural development proper.

The Policy Dilemma of Famine

Japan's sudden surrender confronted the agricultural policy debate with the reality of rice famine. The returning British found Malaya in the throes of a rice shortage which, it was claimed, "no mere redistribution of internal stocks could cure."[21] This domestic shortage became acute when planned relief supplies from abroad did not materialize. Whether due to inefficiency, ineffectiveness, incompetence, or an unwillingness to spend hard currency for Malayan consumption, British post-war administrators failed to meet even the minimum ("disease and unrest") rice import requirements that had been set. Suddenly, domestic agriculture emerged as a major challenge for the British Military Administration, involving simultaneously economic recovery and civil pacification.

There was much to be done, since wartime damage and neglect had left Malaya's riceland irrigation and drainage network virtually unusable for the 1945-46 wet padi season. Yet, because wartime planning had relied upon imported supplies, it was only after it had become unmistakably clear that Malaya's food requirements would have to be met almost in toto from local production, that administrative attention reverted to domestic agriculture.[22] It was only in December 1945 that restoration work began on the country's irrigation and drainage facilities, with the hope of having them operable for the 1946-47 rice growing season. For immediate needs, however, it was already a matter of too little, too late.

In the meantime, administrative measures were introduced to efficiently distribute whatever Malayan padi there was. Strict controls were placed on the marketing of rice so that the first—and only—time in Malayan history, rice was subject to rationing.

However, the fixing of an official buying price for domestic padi, with which to facilitate rationing, placed the British administration on the horns of a policy dilemma. A relatively high price might have induced more supplies to the market and attracted additional resources to rice cultivation. However, the generally deflationary incomes policy of the British postulated a low price for rice. One possible solution, the short-term subsidization of Malayan rice production with British funds, so as to expand market supplies at low retail prices, was dismissed owing to an unwillingness in principle to tap the U.K. Treasury for colonial finance.[23] Instead, the British Military Administration resorted to an even more intensive effort at administrative regulation of the rice trade, from padi field to consumer. Bureaucratic control reinforced rationing as a substitute for the pricing mechanism for allocating domestic rice production, which implied, in effect, distributing the burden of the shortfall.

From December 1945, the official buying price for domestic padi was fixed at M$4.40 a picul, with the intention that the rice acquired would be channelled through licensed retail outlets by the newly established Food Control Department. In the event, almost no padi was forthcoming to government purchasers at the official price. Producers evidently regarded the fixed price as too low, so that their marketable surpluses went instead to the inevitable "free" market. There they fetched some six times the official price. Government licensed agencies themselves reportedly connived in the illegal sale and distribution of controlled foodstuffs. Official price and distribution policies produced the worst of all possible worlds, for while failing to induce increased agricultural output, available

TABLE 1

Malayan Padi Acreage and Production Pre-War and Post-War.

	Wet Padi			Dry Padi			TOTAL	
Season	Acreage ('000 acres)	Yield (million gantangs)	Average Yield	Acreage ('000 acres)	Yield (million gantangs)	Average Yield	Acreage ('000 acres)	Output ('000 tons)
1938/39	704.4	218.6	310	48.8	8.8	180	753.2	341.4
1939/40	727.5	212.0	240	65.8	11.1	169	793.3	335.1
1945/46	684.0	143.3	210	105.6	6.5	62	789.6	225.0
1946/47	732.6	171.3	234	80.9	8.9	109	813.5	257.1
1947/48	765.0	208.3	266	79.9	9.5	119	844.8	343.0

Source: *Federation of Malaya Annual Report (1948)*, adapted.

supplies were permitted to leak to the costly black market.[24]

As a result of the rice shortage, the British Military Administration adopted a more tolerant, if tacit, approach to land policy in order to expand rice production. Thus, Chinese squatters displaced from towns and the mines by the war, were not prevented from growing rice on government land.[25] Most of this was dry padi; therefore, although yields were low, they provided some relief from the food shortage.

Official figures show that although the padi acreage for the 1945-46 season was well above the pre-war planted area, particularly in the less productive dry padi sector, harvests were reduced considerably (Table 1). To some extent, this may represent an understatement of the padi harvest diverted to the black market. Even so, it would appear that the reduced production and failure to procure imported supplies left Malaya with only about a third of its consumption requirements by pre-war standards, without taking account of population growth.[26] The worsening shortage of rice generated mounting civil unrest, inspired by communist-led trade union agitation, which invoked in turn a tightening of the control and rationing mechanisms. However, administrative regulation had all but broken down with the flourishing black market, so that an uneasy British authority found itself impelled to review its overall agricultural policy for the 1946-47 season.

The Grail of Agricultural Autarky

Once the regulative measures had proven ineffective, if not actually harmful, the British administration shifted towards a more positive agricultural policy. The familiar call of the Agriculture Department for rice "self-sufficiency" was again taken up by expatriate departmental personnel in the military government. With civilian colonial rule in March of 1946, food production emerged as the declared "first object" of government policy.[27] Since imported rice was not available, revived belief in agricultural autarky offered the promise of a policy solution. Hence, further reliance on imports was officially eschewed, and the Malayan Union government avowed adherence to a "sound" agricultural policy "properly balanced" in favour of rice self-sufficiency.[28]

As often occurs in economic administration, short-run necessity crystallized into long-run virtue. And, in the absence of rational economic criteria, bureaucratic exhortation was to become the chief instrument of the new agricultural policy.

Unfortunately, the rice self-sufficiency goal was based on a double illusion, ecological and communal, originating in pre-war colonial thought. Advocates of rice self-sufficiency had predicated their view on the belief that Malaya was "eminently suited to rice cultivation."[29] This assumption was subsequently accepted and raised to an article of official post-war faith in the country's "considerable potentiality" as a rice producer.[30] In fact, this assumption was at best doubtful, at worst unfounded. Malaya did not possess any clear advantage, neither ecological nor economic, in the cultivation of rice.[31] Certainly she did not with the then available techniques and agricultural system. Whatever the attributes ascribed to autarky, this was not a pragmatic policy objective for Malaya, not even during the rice crisis of the 1940s.

It is noteworthy in this regard that the advocacy of agricultural autarky was in no way tied to a strategy for rural development. Rather the contrary. Beyond mere physical self-sufficiency, rice autarky was conceived as a means of consolidating the custodial British relationship with traditional Malay society. The spirit of trusteeship, troubled by guilt over wartime surrender and post-war political innovation, invoked a close communion between British officialdom and Malay aristocracy, which one scholar later described as "a genuine nostalgia for a leisured and ceremonial culture."[32]

Rice self-sufficiency was meant to ensure the continuity and stability of this Malay social and cultural order, by strengthening its agrarian underpinnings.[33] Herein lay the second of the post-war bureaucratic illusions, that economic growth could be promoted divorced from social and cultural adaptation and change. The policies implemented as part of the proclaimed self-sufficiency goal included various incentives for rice producers together with measures to expand Malaya's padi growing area. The apparent intention was to simultaneously intensify and extend rice cultivation, an ambitious undertaking at the best of times. But it was typical of colonial Malayan policy that government remained unwilling to make any real commitment to its goal. Thus, despite the nominal priority assigned to rice production, finances remained a more severe constraint on agricultural policy than for other government undertakings.

Financial inhibitions were to prove especially critical as regards the government buying price for padi. This was the key to increasing rice supplies through official channels, as opposed to the black market. With the introduction of the self-sufficiency goal, a higher purchase price of M$6 a picul was offered, but this was still inadequate. Due to widespread scarcities and inflation, producers tended to prefer payment in kind rather than cash. In the rice-surplus state of Perlis, the Resident Commissioner was able to purchase padi with cloth.[34] However, acute shortages of commodities, including cloth, precluded similar transactions on a broader scale. Otherwise, government rejected an alternative suggestion that it offer a more realistic price of M$30 a picul in order to secure padi, arguing that such a price would "knock the economic stability of the country completely sideways."[35] What was meant was that government might have to redirect public resources to foodcrop agriculture, which would necessarily require additional taxation or a re-appro-priation of expenditure. Neither appealed to the colonial fiscal regime then prevailing.[36] Inasmuch as consumers were already paying exorbitant prices for black market rice, the policy was made more regressive by financial stringencies.

By late 1946, Malaya's official rice ration had fallen to the star-vation level of 3/4 kati (i.e., approximately 1 lb. or 450 grams) per person per week.[37] Pressed, government raised its purchase price to M$10 a picul, and scarce cloth, kerosene and even tinned milk were offered in lieu of cash; on the black market, rice now fetched about M$60 a picul and retailed at double that.[38] In the face of mounting social unrest, government again doubled its buying price. Inducements in kind were routinely offered, and Perlis producers even received a premium payment of cloth for every picul delivered to the "Padi Purchase Scheme." In addition, cultivators were given subsidized and, sometimes, even free agricultural supplies.

Though still lagging, government had managed to slowly close the gap between the official and the black market price. Its propor-tion of domestic padi marketing also increased, from a mere 6% in 1946, to 20% in 1947, and to over 25% in 1948.[39] Large quantities of rice still escaped to the black market, however, owing to govern-ment's refusal to pay producers the economic price of its agricul-tural policy.

Meanwhile, government had also encouraged expansion of the area planted with padi as a means of increasing output. This ap-proach, rooted in the doctrine of "eminent suitability," was to cost the country dearly. A March 1946 "Foodcrop Production" directive required rubber plantations to cultivate at least 2% of their total acreage with padi. The rubber estates generally encountered diffi-culties in complying, and complained bitterly of having to expend resources for negligible returns.[40] By the end of 1947, government was compelled to concede failure.

At the same time, government had encouraged bringing new lands under rice cultivation. Chinese squatters continued to enjoy official tolerance. In addition, new padi lands were given to landless Malays and non-Malays, and even surrendered Japanese for padi cultivation. Though some doubt was expressed about their long-run viability, the "urgent and great need for food production" warranted the effort.[41] About 6,500 acres of new land were thus planted with padi. Further, a Short-term Food Production Organization was set up employing surrendered Japanese military personnel on "Govern-ment farms" located on newly-cleared lands.[42] This was the first and only occasion where the government involved itself in food-crop cultivation, even if through the employment of bonded labour. Over M$4 million was expended on the project up to June 1947, for a net yield of 196 tons of rice worth M$20,000—results which were termed "disappointing."[43]

Government farms were consequently abolished, and attention turned to the restoration of abandoned padi lands. A Food Production Board, established under the Agriculture Department, was given responsibility for food cultivation. Urgent steps were taken to put irrigation and drainage works back into operation, and to revive the pre-war colonization schemes, especially those in the main deficit areas of Perak and Selangor. Despite official blandishments, few Malay peasants were prepared to embark on new padi planting when rice earnings lagged behind alternative crops. Thus, the schemes were resumed more slowly than anticipated.

All told, with the opening of new areas and the gradual resettlement of the colonization schemes and the rehabilitation of existing areas, 89,400 acres of wet padi were planted during the 1947-48 season, over and above the 48,000 acre increase in the previous season. The acreage actually harvested, though a record at the time, nevertheless fell short of the 12% growth target.[44] Malayan rice production rose to a record 343,000 tons, amounting to a 52% increase over 1945-46. Yet, this was sufficient for only 43% of domestic consumption.[45]

By then, however, the increasing availability of imported rice had relieved the pressure of famine. Soon the self-sufficiency goal found itself consigned to the realm of rhetoric.

The Political Economy of Post-War Agriculture

The post-war economy of Malayan foodcrop agriculture was marked by a sudden income inflation subsequently reduced into stunted growth and, in the end, non-development. This turn of events reflected the dilemma of colonial agricultural policy following the British return. Colonial ambivalence was apparent in the disparity between official declarations of intent and actual allocations of governmental resources to the agricultural, particularly rice-growing sector. Hence at the nadir of the rice famine, in 1947-48, when officials were stressing the self-sufficiency goal, government investment in irrigation and drainage facilities amounted to some M$6 million altogether, or under 3% of total Malayan Union expenditure.[46] This was less than was expended on the Customs and Excise Department. Government's resource commitment to foodcrop agriculture compared poorly with efforts directed to rehabilitating and developing Malaya's main export sectors, rubber and tin, and their infrastructural and administrative facilities.

As a result of the rice shortage, the domestic terms of trade for foodcrop agriculture had turned extraordinarily favourable during this period. To be sure, the colonial authorities tried to subject rice supplies and prices to official control; however, the larger share of output was nevertheless channelled through a highly profitable black market. Even rice delivered to the government's Padi Purchase Scheme later obtained payment in scarce commodities. Within the agricultural economy itself, food consumption remained relatively high, averaging a reported 16 oz. a day,[47] when the consumer rice ration never exceeded 6 oz. per capita per diem. Early post-war agricultural incomes, expressed in terms of money, commodities or food intake, therefore showed significant and unprecedented gains.

This inflow of income to agriculture did not imply substantial improvement in the net returns to peasant cultivators, however. Regulatory controls, coupled with deteriorating land tenure conditions in the main rice growing areas, and particularly in the Malay Reservations, led to distortions in the distribution of gain. Inasmuch as tenancy had become increasingly widespread among padi cultivators, land rents and tenure conditions generally shifted in favour of landlords. The landlords, squeezed by the post-war money inflation cum income deflation, typically sought redress at the expense of the peasantry. There even occurred a displacement of tenants as landlords resumed use of their properties for their own food—or speculative—requirements.[48] Improved agricultural terms of trade were accordingly reallocated by policy and practice within the Malay community to the advantage of the rentier class. To aggravate the situation, the cultivators' own earnings tended to be affected by ineffectual controls and corruption, making for enlarged black market trading margins. Landlordism and profiteering together served to sap the peasant economy of its vitality.

Policy failures and structural shortcomings rendered Malayan foodcrop agriculture incapable of capitalizing on short-run postwar gains to promote its longer-run development. The rice growing kampung economy remained depressed, despite the ostensibly favourable terms of trade. Indeed, colonial agricultural policy remained distinctly non-developmental in purpose. Rice cultivation was still treated as a cultural symbol of communal stability on the part of the Malay elite and British authorities, rather than as a system of production to be modernized. Agricultural policy still related to a peasant, subsistence economy.[49]

Another element of policy ambivalence pertained to the post-war modernization. The wartime British architects of the Malayan Union had designed their scheme so as to overcome the obstructions symbolized by traditional authority systems. Yet, in their approach to agricultural policy, post-war planners and policy-makers still remained attached to the traditional agrarian social and cultural systems upon which this authority was based. Post-war agricultural policy defaulted, intentionally, over the mobilization of the Malay peasantry in the process of rural development. It is not without irony that peasant society was soon afterwards mobilized by the traditional Malay leadership in their political counter-attack against the Malayan Union.

ENDNOTES

1. On wartime planning for the Malayan Union see A.J. Stockwell, "Colonial Planning during World War II: The Case of Malaya," *Journal of Imperial and Commonwealth History* Vol.2 (1974); James de Verre Allen, *The Malayan Union,* (New Haven, 1967); Martin Rudner, "The Political Structure of the Malayan Union," *Journal of the Malaysian Branch, Royal Asiatic Society* Vol. 41 (1970).

2. The political and social structure of pre-war British Malaya is described, *inter alia,* in Rupert Emerson, *Malaysia. A Study in Direct and Indirect Rule* (New York, 1937); S.W. Jones, *Public Administration in Malaya* (London, 1953); and more recently in Gayl D. Ness, *Bureaucracy and Rural Development in Malaysia* (Berkeley, 1967); Gordon P. Means, *Malaysian Politics* (London, 1970); and William R. Roff, *The Origins of Malay Nationalism* (New Haven, 1967).

3. On the place of rice agriculture in Malay history and culture, see, e.g. James C. Jackson, "Rice Cultivation in West Malaysia," *Journal of the Malaysian Branch, Royal Asiatic Society* Vol. 43 (1972).

4. The structure of peasant agriculture is discussed in E.H.G. Dobby, *Agricultural Questions of Malaya* (London, 1944) and Ooi Jin Bee, *Land, People and Economy in Malaya* (London, 1963); on the economics of padi cultivation see T.B. Wilson, *The Economics of Padi Cultivation in Malaya* Pt. 1, (Kuala Lumpur, 1958) and Lim Chong Yah, *The Economic Development of Modern Malaya* (Kuala Lumpur, 1967), esp. Chap. 6. For a study of colonial attitudes and policies towards Malay peasant agriculture see also Lim Teck Ghee, *Peasant Agriculture in Colonial Malaya*, unpublished Australian National University Ph.D. thesis, 1971.

5. Vide. Martin Rudner, "Financial Policies for Post-War Malaya: The Fiscal and Monetary Measures of Liberation and Reconstruction," *Journal of Imperial and Commonwealth History* Vol. 3 (1975); M. Rudner, "Rubber Strategy for Post-War Malaya," *Journal of Southeast Asian Studies* Vol. 1 (1970).

6. Vide. Michael R. Stenson, *Industrial Conflict in Malaya* (London, 1970).

7. F.S.V. Donnison, *British Military Administration in the Far East* (London, 1956), provides an official account of wartime planning. See also A.W. Wallich, *Malayan Union, Advisory Council Proceedings* (henceforth: *A.C. Proc.*), 14 July 1947. Mr. Wallich was formerly a member of the Young Working Party responsible for food planning under the Malayan Planning Unit.

8. Secretary of State for the Colonies, *House of Commons Debates* (henceforth: *H.C. Deb*), 25 July 1946.

9. "ABM Memorandum on the Reconstruction of Malaya," *British Malaya* (August, 1943).

10. Ibid., p. 187 (emphasis mine).

11. See "The Reconstruction of Malaya," an explanatory statement on the original ABM Memorandum, *British Malaya* (July, 1944), pp. 28-9.

12. H.B. Egmond Hake, *The New Malaya and You* (London, 1945), pp. 47-8. Mr. Hake was at the time chairman of the committee of the ABM, and later President of the Rubber Growers' Association (U.K.).

13. Secretary of State for the Colonies, *H.C. Deb.*, 25 July 1946; see also *The Malayan Union and Singapore* (London, 1946) Cmd. 6724, p. 31.

14. On the economic consequences of Malay Land Reservations see the International Bank for Reconstruction and Development, *The Economic Development of Malaya* (Baltimore, 1955), p. 311-2; *Final Report of the Rice Committee* (Kuala Lumpur, 1956), and S. Gordon, "Contradictions in the Malay Economic Structure," *Intisari* Vol. 1, pp. 32-6.

15. Society of Malay Students in G.B., "Post War Malaya," *British Malaya* (January, 1945).

16. Ibid., p. 102.

17. Among the legal instruments designed to keep Malay peasants in padi and out of rubber were the Land Regulations compelling cropping with specified crops. Moreover, British officialdom and the Malay traditional elite conspired to deliberately hold back the extension of modern, especially English-language education among rural Malays lest this upset custom and wean peasants away from the kampung environment. For an account of the origins of this policy, see Thomas H. Silcock, "The Economy of Malaya: Relevance of the Competitive Laisser-faire Model", in C. Hoover, ed., *Economic Systems of the Commonwealth* (Durham, N.C., 1961), pp. 343-7.

18. Sir Arnold P. Robinson, "Going Back to Malaya," *British Malaya* (June, 1944), p. 15. Sir Arnold was together with H.B.E. Hake (see footnote 12, *supra*), delegated by the ABM to represent British private economic interests in the Malayan Planning Unit.

19. Tan Cheng Lock, "Memorandum on the Future of Malaya," *British Malaya* (February, 1945).

20. Ibid.

21. Donnison, *British Military Adminiustration*, p. 155.

22. Cf. *Report of the Drainage and Irrigation Department, 1946* (Kuala Lumpur, 1947), p. 4.

23. Donnison, *British Military Administration*, p. 227.

24. On the black market in rice, see Malayan Union, *Report of the Co-operative Societies Department, 1946* (Kuala Lumpur, 1947), p. 10: 55.

Awberry & F.W. Dalley, *Labour and Trade Union Organization in the Federation of Malaya and Singapore* (London, 1948), Colonial No. 234, p. 10; and Donnison, *British Military Administration*, p. 228. For a scathing critique of British mal-administration of food control, see Charles Gamba, *The Origin of Trade Unionism in Malaya* (Singapore, 1962), e.g. p. 46.

25. *Agriculture Department Report, 1946* (Kuala Lumpur, 1947), p. 12. On post-war Chinese squatters in agriculture, see Victor Purcell, *Malaya: Communist or Free?* (London, 1954), pp. 73-4.

26. Malayan rice consumption for 1939 was 1,000,108 tons, of which 34% was locally grown; in 1946, consumption had been depressed to merely 361,478 tons, of which domestic production constituted 62%. *Federation of Malaya Annual Report, 1948* (Kuala Lumpur, 1949), p. 52.

27. Secretary of State for the Colonies, *H.C. Deb.* 29 May, 1946.

28. *Agriculture Department Report, 1946*, p. 1.

29. D.H. Grist, *Malaya: Agriculture* (London 1936), p. 67.

30. Secretary of State for the Colonies, *H.C. Deb.*, 25 July 1946.

31. This has been shown in the 1930s by Sir Frank Stockdale, *Report on a Visit to Malaya, Java, Sumatra and Ceylon* (London, 1939) Colonial Office Paper CAC 454, esp. p. 9. E.H.G. Dobby, then Professor of Geography at Raffles College, Singapore, wrote:

> Rice does not in any case find Malaya its ideal setting. Soil deficiencies, the climatic rhythm, heavy cloud cover, and various difficulties arising from brackish water, not least of which are the insect carriers of diseases like Filariasis, all operate to make Malaya below optimum rice conditions. (Dobby, Agricultural Questions, p. 31).

Lim Chong Yah, *Economic Development*, pp. 287-94 points to the comparative economic disadvantages of rice cultivation in Malaya.

32. Silcock, "The Economy of Malaya," p. 344. See also Sir Frank Swettentham, former Governor of the Straits Settlements and High Commissioner of the Federated Malay States, *British Malaya* (London, 1948), esp. chaps. 10, 11, 15, on the manner of pre-war British-Malay elite relationships.

33. See Emerson, *Malaysia*, pp. 17-19, on colonial attitudes and policies towards the Malay peasantry. For a statement underlining the continuity of these in post-war Malaya, see the Secretary of State for the Colonies, *H.C. Deb.*, 25 July 1946.

34. *British Malaya* (October, 1946), p. 101.

35. Chief Secretary, *A.C. Proc.*, 9 October 1946.

36. On the attitudes, beliefs and values that composed post-war colonial public finance, see Martin Rudner, "The Draft Development Plan of the Federation of Malaya," *Journal of Southeast Asian Studies* Vol. 3 (1972), and "Financial Policies for Post-War Malaya."

37. *A.C.Proc.*, 5 September 1946, p. B108. The wartime Young Working Party had laid down, in its plans to supply Malaya food on the "disease and unrest" standard, that the minimum tolerable per diem rice ration was 12 oz. per capita.

38. *British Malaya* (January, 1947), p. 133.

39. *Federation of Malaya Annual Report, 1948*, p. 45.

40. S.B. Parmer, *A.C. Proc.*, 19 December 1947, Paradoxically, this was the form of agriculture that estate interests had demanded government impose on the peasantry.

41. Director of Agriculture, *A.C. Proc.* Paper No. 6, 30 April 1946, p. C8.

42. On the Short-term Food Production Organization see the *Agriculture Department Report, 1947*, p. 19.

43. Secretary of State for the Colonies, *H.C. Deb.*, 23 July 1947.

44. Governor's Address, *A.C. Proc.*, 14 July 1947; for targets and attainments of the 1946-47 padi season, see the *Agriculture Department Report, 1947*, pp. 6-7.

45. *Federation of Malaya Annual Report, 1948*, pp. 51-52.

46. *Ibid.*, p. 28.

47. F. Benham, *The National Income of Malaya, 1947-1950* (Singapore, 1951), p. 28.

48. Cf. Raymond Firth, *Report on Social Science in Malaya* (Singapore, 1948), p. 12. Tenant displacement was incidentally aggravated by the effects of the British Military Administration's Moratorium Proclamation which, by limiting rentals to one year at a time, contributed to the insecurity of agricultural land tenure.

49. On the continued poor state of Malay peasant agriculture in post-war years see, e.g., U.A. Aziz, "The Causes of Poverty in Malay Agriculture," in Lim Tay Boh, ed., *Problems of the Malayan Economy* (Singapore, 1959); and E.K. Fisk, "Features of the Rural Economy" and "Rural Development Policy," in T.H. Silcock and E.K. Fisk, eds. *The Political Economy of Independent Malaya* (Canberra, 1963). For studies of a later period see, e.g. R. Ho, "Land Ownership and Economic Prospects of Malayan Peasants," *Modern Asian Studies* Vol. 4 (1970); Martin Rudner, "Malayan Quandary: Rural Development Policy Under the First and Second Five-Year Plans," *Contributions to Asian Studies* Vol. 1 (1971); James C. Jackson, "Rice Cultivation in West Malaysia"; Manning Nash, *Peasant Citizens: Politics, Religion and Modernization in Kelantan, Malaysia* (Athens, O., 1974); M.G. Swift, *Malay Peasant Society in Jelebu* (London, 1965); and Marvin L. Rogers, *Sungai Raya: A Socio-Political Study of a Rural Malay Community* (Mimeo).

CHAPTER 3

AGRICULTURAL POLICY AND PEASANT SOCIAL TRANSFORMATION IN LATE COLONIAL MALAYA

The closing decade of colonial rule brought profound economic and social changes in Malayan rice agriculture.[1] In a process set in train by wartime dislocation and accelerated by the policies and practices of the early 1950s, the former pattern of subsistence agriculture had begun to give way before the encroaching commercialization of rice production. At the same time, integrative communal political mechanisms were evolving in response to a parallel movement towards representative, responsible government. Interaction between the agricultural and political processes of change crystallized in a transitional agrarian structure, mixing traditional and entrepreneurial forms. The ensuing allocation of resources in agriculture introduced certain disequilibria into the rural economy, heralding the goal conflicts and policy dilemmas of agricultural development planning after Independence.[2]

The significance of this agrarian transition was underscored by the scope and composition of the post-war padi sector. By the mid-20th century 15% of the Malayan cultivated area was planted with padi, the second most widespread crop after rubber.[3] Padi constituted the economic mainstay of the northern states of Perlis, Kedah, Kelantan, Trengganu, and Province Wellesley, and was a salient feature of agriculture elsewhere. The cultivation of rice was strongly identified with a single ethnic group for almost all padi farmers (97%) were Malay. Moreover, the employment of half the Malay labour force in rice farming testified to its centrality in that community's economic and social organization. Yet, the income generated by rice cultivation remained disproportionately low.[4]

Issues in Malaysian Development, eds. James C. Jackson and Martin Rudner, Southeast Asian Publications Series No. 3, (published for the Asian Studies Association of Australia by Heinemann Educational Books (Asia) Ltd., Singapore, 1979).

The historical pattern of economic development in British Malaya reflected the ambivalence of colonial purpose. The geographic extension of agriculture during the 19th and early 20th centuries, under the impetus of immigration from Sumatra, and its transformation to the higher yielding wet padi techniques, accompanied the expansion of international economic activities into the peninsula, but remained segregated in its particular institutional framework.[5] Colonial treaty and colonial trust led British colonizers to collude with the ruling Malay aristocracy in the custodial treatment of rural Malay society. To the limited extent that commercialization necessarily penetrated agricultural activity, it was strictly circumscribed at the margins by a combination of social sanctions, cultural norms, and policy regulations. The kampung (Malay village) was insulated from extraneous influences, with subsistence agriculture serving as the agrarian bulwark of a stable traditional social and cultural order. In a reversal of the dualistic pattern found elsewhere, in the developing economic environment of British Malaya subsistence agriculture was reduced to an enclave, a traditionalized kampung sanctuary amidst a modernizing, internationalized, and predominantly expatriate economy.

Post-war agricultural policy subsequently transformed the historical conception of the kampung economy. In examining the events of change, it is necessary to contemplate the situation as it was then, and to trace the attitudes, motives, interests and goals acting on agricultural policy and its structural consequences.

Agriculture in the Draft Development Plan

Once post-war reconstruction was completed, the colonial authorities introduced a Draft Development Plan (DDP) for the extension of public investment in the Malayan economy over the period 1950-55. Agriculture, however, unlike other economic issues, was not exclusively within the central, that is federal, government jurisdiction. For, consistent with past practice and continued again under the Federation of Malaya Agreement of 1948, land matters were among the particular Malay concerns still vested in the states. Governance of the Malay States was at the time emphatically oligarchic on the part of a traditional communal elite, a triarchy of Sultanate, court aristocracy, and officialdom. If the federal style of government was more secular and modernized, it was hardly less authoritarian. Colonial authority centered on an expatriate dominated civil service subject to overriding imperial control. Oligarchic influence was pluralized slightly by the deliberations of an officially nominated, narrowly representative Federal Legislative Council.[6] The impulse for economic planning, characteristically, emanated from the Colonial Office, as did its scale of priorities and policy guidelines.

The DDP was conceived accordingly in a limited vein as an outline programme for the expansion and upgrading of governmental services.[7] Subsequently expenditure targets were revised upward, in the wake of the Korean War inflation, but the policy essentials remained intact. For agriculture, planning related to public investment in irrigation and drainage schemes. This amounted to about 3.5% of the (revised) plan target, and entailed in addition a small share of general agricultural, infrastructural, and social development programmes.[8] The DDP was expected to generate a remarkable 70% increase in Malayan rice production, but the prescribed treatment of agriculture disclosed ambiguity and ambivalence of purpose.

The dominant agricultural policy objective imputed to the DDP was to lessen Malaya's dependence on imported rice through increased domestic production.[9] This output goal bridged the twin British colonial interests concerning Malayan agriculture. Sterling area balance of payments interests impelled the British to try to minimize imports of foodstuffs, among other consumption (and occasionally even capital) goods in its dependent territories. In consequence, import restraints were imposed on Malaya for much of the post-war period. This notwithstanding the country's consistent and substantial contributions to sterling area gold-dollar earnings, effectively subsidizing Britain and others' payments deficits.[10] However, it was felt that scope still existed to enlarge further Malaya's current account surplus by exploiting the hitherto untapped agricultural potential for large-scale import substitution.

The expansion of agriculture also related to the prevailing British ideology of colonial development. A linkage between increasing market-oriented agricultural production and the economic welfare of the peasantry figured prominently in colonial development doctrine. Conventional colonial beliefs assumed that a subsistence peasantry could be uplifted simply from its traditional agrarian environment and—without undue concern for the effects of customary and social ties—be placed on the path of entrepreneurial style progress.[11] Stimulation of peasant agriculture appeared to reconcile the colonial interest in greater rice self-sufficiency with the interest in orderly economic advancement. Malayan agriculture thus acquired an import substitution goal, one that was unrelated to the country's own comparative economic advantages or its favourable balance of payments record.

Official advocates of import substitution typically glossed over the question of its costs, implicitly assuming that these could or would be borne mostly by agriculture itself. Cost considerations were to come into their own, however, in the ensuing translation of DDP goals into policy priorities and actual resource allocations. Fears of rising rice import costs and delivery difficulties continued to colour official perceptions long after the easing of international supply conditions had relieved import substitution of any real policy urgency.[12] Hence the colonial authorities pledged to do "all that is economically possible" to expand Malayan padi acreage and yields.[13] Rather conveniently, the prevailing colonial doctrine of orderly agricultural development presumed, quite simplistically, that some technical assistance together with "a little" capital investment should suffice to increase peasant productivity, and therefore the marketing of domestic rice, within the existing agrarian framework.[14] However, reality inevitably percolated through the policy. Confronted by the costs of its agricultural programme, the government equivocally shifted its policy terms of reference to emphasize price and budgetary criteria. The resulting policy ambivalence and ambiguity of goals signified a fading commitment to the development of agriculture. Agricultural import substitution may have remained on the government agenda, but policy equivocation reduced its effective claim on colonial economic and fiscal priorities.

The established Malay elite generally supported the objective of import substitution. Indeed, some circles misconstrued the colonial government's intentions, in the enthusiasm of self-interest, as a quest for agricultural autarky. Following their wartime experiences and the subsequent resurgence of nationalism the traditional Malay elite had grown increasingly sensitive about the economic disparities between ethnic groups in Malaya.[15] Among the Malay aristocracy the poor condition of kampung agriculture was perceived, in typical ethnic-sectoral terms, as a product of indebtedness to and exploitation by the urban, non-Malay trading economy.[16] The self-sufficiency goal seemed to offer a policy panacea against ethnic deprivation among Malays, insofar as the government was to provide irrigation for improved land productivity together with assured domestic markets for increased output. Communal economic improvement could therefore follow without a need to adapt Malay rural society to the norms and patterns of urban, that is non-Malay, life.

Agricultural self-sufficiency was seen furthermore as strengthening the traditional institutional order of Malay society. For the rice economy constituted the occupational basis of the kampung community, and accordingly was closely associated with its cultural and status systems. Traditional values and social hierarchies would, it was believed, be buttressed by the linear expansion of rice production under governmental assurances of means and markets. Development, in the traditionalist Malay perspective, represented an essentially custodial economic mechanism serving

> . . . to maintain the peasants on the land, to check rural exodus and to prevent the displacement of the rural people from their traditional mode of life; and we owe it to their ultimate happiness and usefulness to achieve these objectives for they are the salt of the earth.[17]

Beyond this, the colonial authorities were warned against the developmental pursuit of "social progress," anathema to the traditional elite, which might disrupt stable kampung agrarian relations.[18]

This custodial elite concept of development forged an ideological doctrine out of the traditional fixation with rice. Rice and rice production alone assured traditionalists that development would remain harnessed to the established Malay cultural and social framework. A committee of inquiry (the Rice Production Committee) into the rice economy set up in the early 1950s and dominated by the Malay landed establishment, maintained that the social and cultural values embodied in the traditional kampung "way of life" were of greater policy significance than mere producer cost-benefit calculations.[19] To defend these values the Committee proposed to combat deviation from traditional economic forms, notwithstanding the opportunity costs for the rural Malay community. Such was the strength of its ideological concern for tradition that the Committee even recommended compelling Malay peasant innovators, who had embarked on other more remunerative occupations like rubber smallholding, to revert to customary padi cultivation.[20]

This emphatically retrogressive custodial stand highlighted the widening gulf between the conservative Malay squirearchy participating in colonial councils of state and the peasant occupational community. Elite representation at centres of colonial authority, introduced through indirect rule and continued, in essence, under the Federation, reinforced the traditional relationship of subsistence society. Patronage invoked an oligarchic style of communal political

leadership, rationalized by the patronizing, somewhat contemp-
tuous dismissal of the peasant mass as—in the words of one Malay
legislator—"simple" folk "apparently incapable of making the
smallest advance along the road to civilization."[21] Such attitudes
were not untypical of a traditionalist elite determined to keep
their charges bound to tried and true patterns of communal orthodoxy and authority. Yet post-war events and agricultural policies had led to new and evolving production relations in
agriculture. As a result of policies designed to cope with post-war
shortages of imported rice, Malayan agriculture shifted suddenly
and to an unprecedented degree to production for the market, as against subsistence.[22] Economic criteria accordingly became increasingly salient, in turn setting in motion a process of
differentiation among disparate levels and categories of agricultural interests. Economic motivations, coupled with a heightening
nationalism and the influence of inter-ethnic competitiveness,
weakened the traditional institutional ties of subsistence agricultural enclaves. Peasant interest no longer related to padi as a matter of custom or course.

The accelerated process of differentiation among agricultural
interests posed a dilemma for colonial economic policy-making.
Attitudinal and motivational changes among the peasantry were
manifest in the extent of their post-war occupational mobility. Agricultural resources were being re-deployed increasingly, and often
illicitly, towards more remunerative rubber or coconut cultivation.[23]
Also, for want of better rural opportunities, the urban drift of Malay
villagers reached major proportions. Even in the more tradition-
bound, subsistence rice growing east coast states, officials were
now prepared to entertain some movement towards cash-cropping
as a remedy for regional economic retardation. However, rural innovation came up against the traditionalist elite hold on state and
federal authority.

Elite defence of the established kampung institutional order
against perceived disintegrative economic influences engendered
policy measures designed to reinforce customary social sanctions
surrounding the rice economy. A two-pronged reaction was sought:
improved provision of government services, infrastructure, and
amenities to raise the effective social welfare level of kampung society, coupled with legal and administrative constraints on land
use, in particular, to consolidate the padi underpinnings of Malay
agriculture. However, the post-war entrepreneurial impulse was
manifest not only in outward bound innovations, but also inside

the rice economy. There, the deepening penetration of market linkages produced a structural metamorphosis in agrarian relations. Accelerated post-war agricultural commercialization, resulting from the policy stress on import substitution, invoked the formation of new classes of agrarian entrepreneurial and rentier landlord interests, cutting across customary patrimonial ties between aristocracy and subsistence peasantry.[24] This trend towards divergent entrepreneurial and traditional agricultural interests generated frictions over established institutional constraints, and led to new and competing claims on policy.

Non-Malay interests were divided over the DDP treatment of agricultural policy. The newly-established (1949) Malayan Chinese Association (MCA), as spokesman for the Chinese community, urged "genuine, bold and effective efforts" to bring Malayan rice output to self-sufficiency.[25] Behind this call lay the latent anxieties of a predominantly urbanized consumer community over possible recurrence of the traumatic early post-war rice shortages. Moreover, the better-off Chinese community had come to display an increasingly pronounced sensitivity to Malay consciousness of their economic plight. The realization that the economic advancement of the Malays had become the inter-communal quid pro quo for the participation of non-Malays in impending political developments promoted the MCA to advise the Chinese community: "Let us not grudge or envy the greater attention as well as the major financial assistance, given to the advancement of . . . our Malay brothers. Their needs are greater."[26]

Non-Malay concern for the economic advancement of Malays supported improvement in rural infrastructure and social services, albeit within the existing agrarian order. Improved rural amenities, it was hoped, would of themselves serve to keep Malay peasants in the kampungs, stemming the occupational mobility which was viewed as a threat to domestic rice production and a potential challenge to non-Malay preponderance in the cash-crop and urban sectors. Non-Malay enterprise exhibited a shared interest with the Malay establishment in retaining a stable peasant agriculture based on padi. Interestingly enough, the continued confinement of Malay peasants to padi was also accepted by the insurgent Malayan Communist Party, whose predominantly Chinese composition gave the party line a clear urban-proletarian outlook.[27]

British corporate interests in Malaya, for their part, professed their "utmost sympathy" for agricultural development of the type envisaged in the DDP. Nevertheless, British company spokesmen characteristically insisted that agricultural development be self-sustaining ("show the spirit of independence") without relying on subsidization by the so called "Welfare State."[28] Such strictures were quite oblivious to the relative paucity of government resources actually being committed to the rice economy. While British commercial business on the whole remained antipathetic, rubber estate interests gradually came round to a more positive predisposition towards the government's role in promoting peasant foodcrop agriculture. Indeed, by 1953 legislators representing the rubber estate companies were urging the government to go somewhat beyond DDP policy and introduce rice price policies calculated to stimulate domestic rice production.[29] It was manifestly in the self-interest of rubber estates to work towards reducing the comparative economic disadvantage of padi cultivation as a means of stemming the burgeoning (and illicit) tide of peasant entry into competitive rubber smallholding.[30] Thus the not inconsiderable political leverage of British rubber plantation and commercial interests was brought to bear to shore up the traditional institutional framework of Malay agriculture.

The prevalent attitudes among colonial administrators were strongly sympathetic to the aristocratic social order of the Malays.[31] If governmental declarations favouring rice import substitution and Malay advancement seemingly injected an economic growth objective into agricultural policy formulation, this was effectively circumscribed by the predisposition of colonial officialdom to contain the process of social change in rural Malay society. "Development" policy was therefore confined to the provision of such infrastructural facilities and social amenities as would comply with the time-honoured "agricultural bias" of kampungs.[32]

Post-war Malayan agricultural policy aimed at raising domestic padi production through a combination of measures designed to increase yield per acre, as well as by opening up several new regions for cultivation. The essence of the policy was land development. Under the original DDP, 59 irrigation schemes were to be constructed for improving some 300,000 acres of existing padi land, and for opening an additional 100,000 acres of new land for rice-growing.[33] Many of these schemes in fact were continuations of pre-war projects of the Drainage and Irrigation Department. Later, the 1952 revision of the DDP reduced the irrigation target to just 46 schemes costing M$30 million, for improving 283,000 existing acres and opening 84,000 new acres only. This reduction in irrigation targets reflected the shifting economic priorities of the colonial government as the 1950s progressed, away from the output goals previously assigned to foodcrop agriculture.

DDP agricultural project planning did not operate according to "economic" investment criteria. The mainsprings of agricultural policy were essentially social and cultural, to which economic factors were clearly subordinate. Quite remarkably, the DDP gave scant consideration to comparative costs and benefits in setting out its various irrigation projects.[34] Highly ambitious schemes to open up new areas for padi cultivation foundered on excessive costs, low yields, arduous toil, lack of amenities, and a market lack of response on the part of peasants, even at existing favourable terms of trade for rice.[35] Irrigation plans were revised downward again in 1954, in order to concentrate on areas already under cultivation, and to adjust for laggard implementation.

Actually, irrigation plan fulfillment under the DDP fell far short of the original targets, and even of the lowered revised targets. Only 36 schemes were completed by the end of 1955. Of these, some 219,500 acres of established padi settlement were improved through irrigation, and a further 55,600 acres of new lands were made available for wet padi cultivation. Government investment in irrigation amounted to M$21 million over the period. This much reduced financial commitment indicated the extent of underfillment of agricultural land development in existing and new irrigation schemes, by 28% and 45% under original targets, or 23% and 34% under revised targets, respectively.

Malay reactions to this shortfall illustrated the growing polarization among agrarian interests under the impact of commercialization. Landed interests pressed for greater attention to irrigation of existing settlement areas and against the extension of new areas. A class response in protecting and possibly augmenting the asset values of their holdings—as well as their more general concern for social stability. Meanwhile, the inarticulate peasantry manifested its own producer interests in practice. New padi planting was generally eschewed under current conditions, while many actually substituted (illicitly) more remunerative rubber or tobacco for rice on irrigation schemes in established settlement areas.[36]

The government also sought to promote the use of chemical fertilizers as a means of increasing padi yields, especially on the less developed east coast, where appreciable gains were believed possible. In 1952 a scheme was introduced to provide subsidized fertilizers in the states of Kelantan and Trengganu. Although the application of chemical fertilizer did double yields in Kelantan, the results of the popularization campaign proved disappointing. Despite the potential gains, only 210 tons of subsidized fertilizer were actually utilized for the 1952-53 padi season, 720 tons for 1953-54, and 296 tons for 1954-55, whereas local requirements were estimated at 40,000 tons per annum. Officially, lack of peasant response was blamed on low disposable incomes, as well as the ingrained conservatism of the east coast.[37] To these must be added surely the poor price incentives, difficulties of access to west coast markets, and institutional constraints built into the traditional kampung economic and social structure. Fertilizer subsidies did not apply, paradoxically, on the west coast, where padi cultivation had generally closer market linkages and entrepreneurial propensities were accordingly more pronounced.

Throughout the period, peasant agriculture was affected by official efforts at "diversifying" the Malayan economy away from what was termed its excessive dependency on highly cyclical primary exports. The Federal Department of Agriculture had long sought to "balance" agricultural export dependency by directing peasant resources away from rubber to the more "stable" padi.[38] This standpoint was translated into policy allocations by the combined working of two specialized agencies during the early 1950s, the Rice Production Committee, eager to enlarge the role of the padi sector, and the Rubber Industry (Replanting) Board, with its inclination towards diminishing the rubber smallholding sector as a means of maintaining higher export price levels. Under the rubber replanting programme then in force, smallholders were directed to replant with padi (or, infrequently, with other approved crops) whenever *soil conditions* were suitable, without regard to economic considerations.[39] Peasant rubber producers were in effect obliged to subsidize (through their replanting cess) their own removal from that industry where they possessed long-run competitive advantages, to other, lower income occupations as determined by soil circumstances.

It was ironical that the same official agencies ostensibly in charge of the well-being of the rural economy also took responsibility for transferring peasant producers out of rubber and into padi, despite the admittedly "limited" economic justification.[40] Consequently some 10% of rubber smallholding replanting, totalling 7,674 acres through 1955, was actually converted to other crops, mainly padi. In the meantime, a considerably larger area of land in traditional "rice bowl" regions, legally restricted to padi underwent illicit planting with rubber trees.[41] Occupational mobility towards rubber smallholding enhanced the structural differentiation of the kampung economy, notwithstanding the inherent weaknesses and difficulties of illicit enterprise. Yet this illicit form of agrarian commercialization influenced production relations and income distribution to the detriment of those peasants still attached to subsistence rice cultivation.

Meanwhile, the Malay establishment continued to adhere to its cultural fixation on padi. Although the web of regulations and sanctions was proving less and less effectual, the Malay official executive Member for Agriculture and Forestry, Tunku Ya'acob, nevertheless called to peasants who forsook padi for rubber to revert to rice cultivation out of their presumed "civic duty." Communalism had become the final appeal of economic traditionalism.

Although official rhetoric regularly attached great importance to increasing domestic rice production, in practice public investment in foodcrop agriculture tended to be systematically subordinated to other claims on public finance. Agricultural policy, as conceived, suffered a lack of funding and the absence of any real sense of urgency.[42] Chronic underspending diminished the pace of policy implementation to the point where overall federal and state expenditures on administration, research, and extension services for foodcrop agriculture aggregated less than was spent on general "public information" services—under 2% of current public expenditure. Invidious comparisons were made with the policy treatment of Chinese squatters being resettled as an "Emergency" measure in so called "New Villages," built on the economic foundations of cash-crop agriculture and comparatively well-provided with social services and amenities.[43] Even the more traditionalist Malays expressed resentment at the allegedly "highly discriminatory" treatment of "loyal" Malays as compared to resettled squatters. Malay complainants focused on the provision of social services, to be sure, typically ignoring the structural basis of economic betterment. This sense of ethnic deprivation served to galvanize the Malay communal elite into a major policy effort at imbuing traditional kampung agriculture with economic growth.[44]

The Rural and Industrial Development Authority

The Malay colonial power elite, the officially ensconced "Datocracy," looked to the post-war creation, the Rural and Industrial Development Authority (RIDA), as its catalyst for kampung economic improvement. RIDA represented a unique and specialized agency charged with reconciling the maintenance of tradtional Malay agrarian institutional arrangements with higher and rising levels of rural economic welfare.[45] The origins of RIDA lay in the emergent post-war pattern of inter-ethnic competition and accommodation. Thus, the elite-status Communities Liaison Committee set up shortly after the Federation came into being first mooted the reciprocal ethnic relations strategy of exchanging economic benefits for Malays in return for political enfranchisement of non-Malays. Subsequently, the counter-insurgency resettlement of Chinese squatters in New Villages fuelled Malay demands for compensatory policy provisions. In order to mollify communal grievances and to avert internecine conflict among the Malays, the colonial authorities agreed to the establishment of a governmental organ having specific responsibility for the economic advancement of kampung society.[46]

RIDA was formally constituted in August 1950, as an autonomous, quasi-departmental authority of the federal government. Chairmanship of the Authority was vested in Dato Onn bin Ja'afar, then the top ranking Malay political figure combining, as he did, nationalist leadership (as President of the United Malays National Organization (UMNO)) traditional legitimacy (as an aristocrat serving also as Mentri Besar, Chief Minister of the state of Johore), and colonial position (Executive Council membership, later with responsibility for Home Affairs). This form of organization enabled the traditional Malay elite to cope, through RIDA operations, with the exigencies of agricultural transition, then proceeding apace. Since RIDA was to channel certain developmental resources to the kampungs, in response to local initiatives, and also (vaguely) "co-ordinate" all other government department activities in rural Malay settlement areas, these mediatory functions induced the aristocratic elite to adapt to a new style of patrimonial role between the colonial centre and the traditional periphery. RIDA introduced and exemplified an emergent neo-patrimonial relationship among Malay agrarian interests, in which modern resources were allocated through the mediatory agency of established elites so as to sustain and improve the economic underpinnings of the traditional kampung institutional order.[47] For the colonial authorities, the notion of a separate RIDA combined the advantages of Malay elite responsibility with more strictly limited budgetary liabilities.

The establishment of RIDA gave policy expression to certain underlying economic assumptions espoused by the Malay establishment. Colonial officialdom conventionally condemned what they described as the ingrained conservatism of the Malay peasantry as the main obstacle to improved agricultural performance.[48] This view ignored the effects of institutional constraints on agricultural production, and conversely the gradual and increasing success of the new post-war class of entrepreneurial peasants in overcoming these. So far as the Malay communal elite was concerned, those institutional constraints were culturally and socially sacrosanct, whereas the entrepreneurial trend constituted part and parcel of the alleged motivational crisis confronting Malay agriculture. Hence Dato Onn himself attributed the assumed inadequacy of agricultural motivation to the "social deterioration" of the Malays' spirit and custom of group effort. This, in turn, was blamed on the patronizing effects of colonial tutelage in combination with alien capitalist exploitation (for example, the activities of non-Malay middlemen).[49]

In order to correct the causes of social breakdown and exploitation, and as an alternative either to secularizing commercialism or to submissive impoverishment, the Malay communal elite sought to mobilize public spirited social traits traditionally identified with the kampung institutional ideal. RIDA was to function, therefore, not so much as an instrument of public investment, though the provision of financial and administrative backing was of course not unimportant, but as a revivalist agency for the reactivation of pristine Malay values of self-help and, particularly, co-operative effort. By mobilizing latent forces of kampung tradition, RIDA could, it was believed, generate an indigenous process of economic betterment compatible with continuity of the customary Malay "agricultural bias" toward rice cultivation.[50]

This developmental mobilization of traditional values involved RIDA in intense organizational strains from competing tendencies towards bureaucratization of administration on the one hand and partisan federalist politics on the other. Whereas the original RIDA concept allowed that initiatives should come from below, as it were, from the kampungs, in practice RIDA programmes, as well as priorities, emanated from the top of the organizational hierarchy, its Executive and Planning Committees. Centralized decision-making emphasized bureaucratic control of the organization and its policy conduct, though at the cost of rendering local participation peripheral to RIDA's activities. Bureaucratic control furthermore accentuated the neo-patrimonial role assumed by the UMNO leadership. However, this produced a context of authority between the Malay elite at the administrative centre and the generally more conservative aristocracies of the Malay states. In a typically federalist response to centralizing tendencies several States objected to RIDA encroachment upon subjects within their constitutional jurisdiction, notably those relating to Malay custom, land and local administration. The issue was resolved, at least jurisdictionally, by incorporating State representation into the RIDA organization at all levels. In the course of events this federalist embodiment introduced incipient political party pressures into RIDA, while in turn adapting the Malay parties to a neo-patrimonial political role.

Shifting party divisions along federal lines coloured RIDA operations throughout the period. Dato Onn left UMNO eventually to form Party Negara of the established "Datocracy," which still retained a stake in the colonial authority structure. Meanwhile the oppositional UMNO-based Alliance was swept to power in each of the state elections in succession. The resulting federalist pattern of political party rivalry introduced an administrative dichotomy into RIDA, between electoral responsibility at the state government level and its central executive authority. The increasingly manifest political tension between authority and responsibility in RIDA administration contributed to the remolding of traditional agrarian patron-client relationships into a new, policy-directed neo-patrimonial style. This emergent neo-patrimonial order revolved around the political competition amongst Malay elites, between the "Datocracy" represented by Party Negara and the UMNO counter-elite, and was to condition agrarian responses to policy initiatives and change.

Organizational pressures and the hardening of bureaucratic forms wrought subtle but nonetheless significant goal changes in RIDA. As policies were being implemented, the original cultural emphasis on traditional kampung values for mobilization was transformed into a typically bureaucratic emphasis on orderly administration and output maximization. Aversion to possible local "mismanagement or muddle" promoted a tendency towards centralized direction of project undertakings, overshadowing RIDA's initial cardinal objective of fostering kampung initiative. Similarly, the operative meaning of "self-help" came to be diluted into kampung money payments for RIDA services rendered. Even the much avowed sponsorship of the kampung co-operative ethic was dispelled, in effect, by RIDA fiscal practices which, on the one hand invoked bureaucratic intervention that undermined any genuine co-operative effort and, on the other, tended to be more favourably disposed to individually managed, capitalist-type enterprise.[51] These goal changes underscored a functional shift in RIDA away from so-

cial mobilization and toward more narrowly specific and instrumental investment role in agriculture.

Ensuing allocations of administrative and financial resources
through RIDA reinforced the emergent neo-patrimonialism among
the Malay communal elite. At the outset RIDA obtained an annual
grant of M$5 million in order to fund its activities, and was ex-
pected to generate further income of its own through a revolving
loan account. Lending absorbed the bulk of RIDA's appropriations.[52]
According to regulations, eligibility for loans extended to projects
otherwise unable to qualify for normal banking credit, however
these were still expected to show "sound management" and reasonable commercial prospects. Schemes of a non-remunerative
type, but which advanced the RIDA concept of development, also
qualified for support under a separate and smaller provision for
non-reimbursable grants. Both categories were manipulated as

TABLE 1
Appropriation of RIDA Loans
Through Co-operatives, 1951-54 (M$ thousand).

Type of Loan	1951	1952	1953	1954
Seasonal credit	200	700	927	1,395
Rice milling	—	4	12	2
Coconut oil processing	20	4	—	—
Fish marketing	—	38	33	—
Rubber marketing	—	20	14	—
Retail shops	41	—	13	—
Farming	—	—	14	3
Transport	11	—	—	—
Total RIDA project loans	583	n/a	4,777	1,854

Note: Some project loans were appropriated for 1955
and 1956, but no figures are available.
Source: RIDA Annual Reports, Fredricks, 1974, p. 238.

part of the social and political dynamics of neo-patrimonial institution-building within RIDA.

RIDA lending activities were inaugurated with several relatively
large loans to newly formed rural co-operative credit organizations
(Table 1). The sponsorship of co-operative agricultural credit represented a major RIDA project combining the development of positive
traditional group traits with an attack on usury and exploitation. Yet
it soon became apparent that RIDA lacked resources to supply and
administer agricultural credit on a sufficient scale (see below). In-

stead RIDA began to redirect its lending more towards rural business enterprise now springing up with the commercialization of
agriculture. RIDA appropriation for commercial project finance
overrode the traditional insularity of Malay agriculture and ensured
that the emergent entrepreneurial class remained indebted—liter-
ally—to the new neo-patrimonial forms of communal patronage.
The utilization of RIDA project finance to underwrite a new patron-
client relationship with emergent rural entrepreneurs pointed to a
process of elite adaptation to economic transition. Yet, this adap-
tive process invariably diminished the efficacy of public investment through RIDA. By 1955 some three-quarters of the projects
sponsored had turned out "failures," while repayments of interest
and principal were reportedly "heavily" in arrears.[53] The effective
allocation of RIDA project finance tended to oversubsidize regressively formative Malay entrepreneurship, with little provision left for
the neediest agriculturalists.

The experience of RIDA sponsored schemes likewise reflected
the changes in organizational goals and communal patronage patterns.[54] Most of the schemes devised for the agricultural sector came
to naught. As its contribution to the agricultural self-sufficiency campaign RIDA had embarked on a much-vaunted scheme involving
the setting up of a network of tractor stations to spur the mechani-
zation of rice production. Despite much fanfare and heavy subsidization, the scheme eventually broke down as a result of high costs,
low utilization on the part of poor peasants, and technical and me-
chanical deficiencies. An experimental *daisha* hand-railway to facilitate padi transport (Tanjong Karang, Selangor) proved impractical
soon after its installation. A pilot rubber milling factory (Grisek, Johore) encountered such difficulties that RIDA thereafter abdicated
any further participation in the rubber sector. RIDA also established and managed a variety of non-agricultural schemes oriented
to the perceived needs of the rural economy, including ventures
in fishing-boat building, fruit canning, and kampung handicrafts.
Most of these suffered from ineptitude. In time far greater popularity
was attached to RIDA-instituted technical training schemes.
Nevertheless official ambivalence over the impact of such training on occupational mobility and urban migration provoked financial curbs on such activities. Consequently, RIDA's main
successes were concentrated in the non-controversial provision of
kampung social amenities, including roads, water supply, bridges,
community buildings, and the like. By the end of the colonial period such investment in rural infrastructure dominated the grants

schemes, absorbing a third of aggregate RIDA expenditure. In this RIDA served as an intermediary for the allocation of rural infrastructure between the colonial government and the rural population, a role that reinforced the neo-patrimonial function of the political party elites controlling the Authority.

Not surprisingly in the circumstances, RIDA activities were plagued by administrative malpractices and abuses. Government auditors' comments on RIDA annual reports regularly gave indication of unverifiable or improperly recorded assets, as well as other financial discrepancies.[55] RIDA schemes tended to ignore provision for upkeep or maintenance costs. In a practice tinged with corruption, RIDA procurements took place privately, without the usual public tender, and frequently at inflated prices. Moreover, inconsistencies and overlapping and duplicated effort frequently detracted from the efficiency of rural investment. Administrative co-ordination between RIDA and other government departments remained inadequate. Saddled with excessive administrative overheads, infected by miscalculations and failures, RIDA's role in late colonial rural development surely warranted the reported verdict, "insignificant."[56] For their part, RIDA officials preferred to blame mismanagement on inexperience, on federalist constraints, or on the alleged "experimental" character of their activities.[57] The colonial authorities undertook to remedy these deficiencies by the reorganization of RIDA in 1954 into a semi-autonomous public corporation. Apart from its formal implications, this move symbolized the transformation of RIDA from the initial notion of social catalyst to an institutionalized neo-patrimonial role.

Land Policy and Agricultural Credit

Whereas the Federation of Malaya Agreement provided for centralized authority over most important policy areas, the states retained jurisdiction over the communally sensitive subject of land. Constitutionally, the federal government had limited powers to ensure basic uniformity in land matters, to be sure, but the determination and application of land policy, especially with regard to alienation and use, was exclusively the prerogative of the individual states (and the then "settlements" of Penang and Malacca). Not only did land codes and tenure arrangements therefore differ according to state, but the reluctance of the federal authorities to exercise even those powers they possessed allowed considerable variation in standards of land administration throughout the Federation.[58]

State performance of the administrative function over land was commonly conceded to be "most unsatisfactory."[59] Persistent staff shortages prevented state land offices from coping with their duties. Administration was hamstrung by the failure of state governments to provide clear directives on land use policy. Consequently, throughout the 1950s land administration suffered from substantial backlogs of unregistered titles and transfers.

Problematic land administration masked deteriorating land tenure conditions. The DDP had already noted that what it termed "the growing evil" of landlordism had reached "serious proportions . . . without effective means having been found hitherto to check it."[60] Nevertheless, the concentration of land ownership subsequently continued on an ever-increasing scale. By the mid-1950s, tenancies reportedly encompassed the greater portion of rice growing lands in the Malay settlement areas of northwestern Malaya, and possibly elsewhere as well.[61] Similarly, disparities grew increasingly pronounced between the smallholding peasantry and large and medium landowners.[62]

The trend towards landlordism was accompanied by a parallel worsening of population pressures on available cultivable (officially "alienated") land. Together, the combined forces of monopolistic supply and intensified demand for scarce available land aggravated the plight of tenants and smallholders. Land rents rose substantially, in real terms, as did the general insecurity of tenancy.[63] The growing scarcity of agricultural land under population pressure compounded with the effects of policy constraints, administrative laxity, and commercial penetration, served to transform land from a communal preserve to an investment asset. In the process, agrarian interests were differentiated in relation to land as a basic form of agricultural capital.

This capitalization of land was to have a far more severe impact on land tenure conditions in the rice enclave than in the more open rubber sector. While pressure on cultivable land was felt everywhere, the combination with low income levels, insularity and restrictions on land use made the situation in the rice economy particularly acute.[64] Moreover, the Malay Land Reservation Enactment, covering most of the Malay settled rice growing areas, applied legal constraints on the movement of capital into agriculture. Malay reserved lands had access only to Malay sources for their capital requirements, effectively according the Malay gentry and salariat an investment monopoly.[65] With the peasant economy under pressure and forced to adjust its labour-land relationships, this investment monopoly led to large-scale agglomeration of land ownership by the Malay establishment. It was ironical that the Malay Reservations, introduced earlier in the century to prevent the displacement of Malay peasants from their land, by mid-century had come to serve in effect as an agency of encroaching Malay landlordism in the peasant economy.

Problems associated with land tenure were slow to emerge in national awareness. In part this was due to the decentralization of responsibility over land to the States. However, a conspiracy of silence—and consequent acts of omission—reflected the vested interests of the Malay landed establishment then predominant in government councils and administration. In fact, the Federal Executive Member portfolio with responsibility for land matters was throughout held by office bearers from the landed "Datocracy."[66] Until the Rice Production Committee had (incidentally) reported otherwise, and despite occasional warnings by rural representatives of widespread land hunger, official and conventional opinion maintained that tenancy was uncommon in Malay settlement areas. Where it existed its negative effects were said to be satisfactorily cushioned by customary patrimonial obligations operative in traditional Malay society.[67]

Whereas the established Malay classes were able to capitalize on the new asset value attached to agricultural land with the help of policy constraints, the peasantry were dispossessed of countervailing political means of protecting, or even articulating, their interests. A conspiracy of political silence surrounded the land issue. It was only in the fortuitous circumstances provided by the Rice Production Committee inquiry that peasant petitions were able to call public attention to the spread of landlordism, spiraling rents, insecurity of tenancy, and demand corrective measures from the government.[68]

Official treatment of the inquiry Report displayed tactful evasion on the part of the Malay landed establishment, in apparent collusion with sympathetic colonial officialdom. Conspiracy of silence became collusive conspiracy. Although the Committee had reported in March 1953, its Report was tabled in the Legislative Council only in June 1954 (No. 3 of 1954), without allowing for debate. Subsequently, a resolution moved by the representative of the minuscule Labour Party, calling for urgent implementation of the Committee's recommendations, was turned down by a conservative Legislative Council coalition built around landed interests and cautious administrators. Rejecting "immediate action," the executive Member for Natural Resources, Dato Ismail, resorted to the not unfamiliar delaying tactic of insisting on more time for the government ostensibly to gather additional facts on land tenure conditions, and to consult the states in whose jurisdiction the matter was stated to rest.[69]

Landlord politics of avoidance delayed further action. In time, however, this sidestepping the land tenure issue had to give way to the dictates of electioneering, in circumstances aggravated by agricultural recession. The collapse of rice prices at the end of 1954 brought severe hardship to tenant cultivators in particular, owing to high fixed cash rents previously contracted. Public criticism of governmental unresponsiveness acquired political leverage in anticipation of the first general elections scheduled for 1955. Making electoral capital out of the close association of the aristocratic Party Negara with the colonial regime, UMNO waged a campaign to mobilize Malay peasant support with populist demands for rent control and improved agricultural credit facilities.[70]

Prodded by partisan politics and pressed by the dictates of their own rice policy, the federal authorities finally moved in January 1955 to appoint a joint Federal-State Rice Committee of Inquiry to further investigate padi production and incomes. Moving quickly under pressure of events, this new Committee submitted its Interim Report in March 1955. This acknowledged the symptoms of land hunger, insecurity of tenure, and rising real rents flowing from current agricultural policy. Corrective legislation was introduced speedily by the federal government to fix statutory maximum rentals in kind for different grades of land, and provided for registration and security of tenancy. Though a federal enactment, implementation of the padi Cultivators' (Control of Rent and Security of Tenure) Ordinance, 1955, was delegated to the state administrations. Since local gentry still held political sway over the Malay State governments, vested landed interests were able to manipulate enforcement of the law so as to turn avoidance into virtually wholesale evasion. Tenure and tenancy conditions therefore remained for the most part unaffected by legal remedies.[71]

Deliberations on land policy did not go beyond the tenure question to deal with the more fundamental issue of the allocation of land resources in the colonial Malayan economy. Longstanding policies circumscribing the agricultural frontier, setting aside wide tracts as forest reserve, and stipulating utilization of "alienated" (i.e. assigned) lands, still remained sacrosanct. Restrictive land settlement and utilization served in effect to protect both the asset values of established landowners and the internal stability of the rural, social order and to preserve public finance from the costs of infrastructure.[72] Yet these private and public "savings" incurred considerable—and unquestioned—social costs in terms of potential income forgone and the retrogressive distribution of landed assets brought into being.

Overall land allocation policies directly affected the scale of agricultural activity in the Malay kampung economy, and indirectly its productivity. As a result of arbitrarily confined agrarian settlement on the one hand, and induced social immobility and rapid population growth on the other, the typical size of farming unit in rice-growing areas became, with time, inordinately small. It should be noted in this light that subdivision of inherited land into very small holdings had long been prohibited in the traditionalist state of Kelantan, with its particular social and religious fabric (as also in the more modernist Islamic societies of West Asia).[73]

Elsewhere among the Malay States a conservative interpretation of religious principle applied, giving moral justification for the terminal redistribution of land. In 1955, near the end of the era of colonial rule, the federal government finally proposed to break the impasse with a secular and universal prohibition on the parcelling of very small plots.[74] Interestingly, this move elicited the support of Party Negara, representing the Malay gentry. Nonetheless, religious opposition, joined by entrepreneurial interests in land, obliged the government to modify its proposed legislation, making the prohibition voluntary in effect. As a result, the efficacy of the prohibition was weakened in precisely that sector where subeconomic fragmentation of holdings was especially rife, that is in the kampung economy.

If excessive subdivision jeopardized the stability of the traditional agrarian community (hence the disquiet of the landed gentry) it conversely assured a continuing supply of agricultural land for investors. A shared, almost predatory interest in maintaining the supply of procurable land produced an alignment of expediency between the emergent classes of landlord capitalists and entrepreneurial peasants with religious orthodoxy. However, the post-war commercialization of agriculture had effectively altered the social context of the religious inheritance principle, in that land had come to be treated as a capital asset and concentrated in larger-scale ownership than hitherto. The successful challenge to the aristocratic position over the land inheritance reform testified to the growing power of the new classes of rentiers and entrepreneurial peasants in Malay society.

Closely related to problems of land tenure was the matter of agricultural credit. Historically, agricultural credit operated through informal moneylenders. The cost of agricultural credit of this type was comparatively high, denoting, in some part, the risk element attached. Agricultural credit costs were raised additionally as a result of institutional constraints on farmers' access to alternative sources of seasonal and investment finance. Such limitations derived from policies and practices both internal and external to the agricultural sector.

Constraints on investment capital in the agricultural economy arose out of the explicit restrictions attached to the Malay Land Reservation Enactments. These effectively cut off most padi cultivators from access to non-Malay sources of medium- to long-term finance. Instead, the widespread existence of Reservations conferred an exclusive ethnic monopoly in the provision of mortgage capital for land acquisition or improvement on a privileged set of Malay rentiers—mostly landlords or bureaucrats.

Seasonal credit requirements had to be met mainly through usurious traditional mechanisms, such as *padi kunca*. Because of the volume of short-term credit necessary and available only on such terms, peasant cultivators commonly became grossly indebted and dependent upon the omnipresent middlemen, usually non-Malays, operating in the rural economy.[75] Although commercial banking was relatively well developed in the urban and export sectors of British Malaya, it showed no inclination towards short-term agricultural lending, and was in any case disqualified from longer-term reserved mortgage finance. Even the central government, which had empowered District Officers to grant loans to padi cultivators, preferred to refrain on administrative grounds and for fear of mass default.[76]

Even at the peak of the post-war rice import substitution campaign, colonial officials, including the Directors of the Agriculture and Drainage and Irrigation Departments, objected to any use of public funds to underwrite agricultural credit facilities for padi cultivators, arguing Malay ineptitude in money matters. Indeed, post-war colonial policy on agricultural credit was largely conditioned by the contemporary bureaucratic stereotype of the Malay peasant, as someone "ill-prepared either in experience or in business capacity to handle problems arising out of the purchase of goods on credit and the borrowing of money on a business basis."[77]

Official disdain for peasant competence in money matters formed an attitudinal point of departure for the equivocal treatment of agricultural credit in post-war policy. The conventional stereotype supplied a rationalization for the 1948 report of a federal committee of inquiry into agricultural credits, recommending against government finance of loans to padi cultivators. Instead, the committee espoused the long familiar policy preference for building up rural co-operative credit organizations to mobilize and distribute indigenous agricultural financial capital. In the strenuously promoted view of colonial agricultural officials, the co-operative format suggested "the best" way to organize and manage agricultural credit in order to ensure that finance would be "widely available in the right amounts at the right time."[78] This viewpoint was subsequently incorporated into the DDP, which provided for the expansion of the rural co-operative credit society network under Federal Co-operative Department tutelage.[79] It was made explicitly clear at the outset that rural co-operative societies were not intended as a channel for government lines of credit to agriculturalists. Rather, co-operation was conceived as a practical device for mobilizing finance and dispensing credit within the agricultural economy itself, while at the same time serving as a school for instilling financial skills and responsibility among the peasantry.

This multiplication of concurrent RIDA goals, encompassing self-reliance, accessibility, and social training, exposed rural co-operative credit to inherent role conflict. In order to minimize such conflicts over the allocation of co-operative credit, ensuing organizational priorities stressed the principle of creditworthiness. Selectivity in terms of creditworthiness was applied through delegating local level responsibility for the apportionment of rural co-operative finance.

A considerable enlargement of the Co-operative Department was called for by the DDP to manage the envisaged expansion of rural co-operative credit. However, recruitment of departmental personnel lagged owing to persisting federal budgetary restraints on expenditure. Standards of co-operative administration declined decidedly, weakening this specifically designated federal contribution to the conduct of its agricultural credit policy.[80]

In practice, the working of the renovated post-war rural co-operative credit organization deviated in important respects from the precepts laid down earlier. For some time past, a strong body of Malay opinion tended to place high value on rural co-operative effort as a singularly appropriate bridging device linking traditional communal norms to current economic problem-solving. With colonial policy now emphasizing co-operative organization, the concept was taken up by the recently established RIDA and made into an operational centrepiece of its traditionalist development ideology. Co-operative agricultural credit was transformed accordingly into a remedial policy against perceived rural financial "exploitation." To combat usurious practices of customary moneylending, RIDA channeled most of its funds into rural co-operative credit societies through a concessional seasonal credit facility for agriculture. Very soon, RIDA emerged as the main source of agricultural credit at the disposal of co-operative societies.[81] RIDA's own financial resources proved too limited to enable co-operatives to meet more than a fraction of agricultural credit needs, however.

Social access to co-operative agricultural credit proved more restrictive than initially postulated.[82] Participation in co-operative credit was subject to financial and administrative constraints, leading to particular class and regional biases in membership. Contrary to the egalitarian assumptions of proponents of rural co-operation, prevailing incomes were so low and existing indebtedness so high as to depress the savings propensity of most of the agricultural population beneath the threshold for co-operative organization. Official attitudes disparaging peasant financial skills reinforced barriers from the administrative side. To ensure creditworthiness, co-operative rules and lending regulations emphasized banking principles over populist aims. The availability of co-operative agricultural credit was confined effectively therefore to better-off agricultural entrepreneurs and *rentiers*, predominantly in the more commercialized rice-growing areas on the west coast. Since the bulk of co-operative finance originated not in rural savings but in RIDA concessional lines of credit, the resulting transfer of resources amounted to a socially regressive subsidy for relatively advantaged producers and regions.

The limitations of rural co-operative credit policy were increasingly felt even by its beneficiaries. As the prolonged post-Korean War recession inflicted a deepening scissors crisis in agricultural incomes, worsening rural indebtedness gave rise to calls for a more liberal federal government approach to agricultural finance. Taking the political lead on this issue, UMNO appealed for enlarged government subsidies to rural credit institutions alongside direct seasonal loans to cultivators.[83] The peasants themselves solicited government support through the Rice Production Committee for the establishment of a specialized rural financial and marketing agency to replace private middlemen.[84] It is noteworthy that Malay officials of RIDA and the Co-operative Department reacted by opposing any policy change that might have assigned to other institutions a role in dispensing agricultural credit.[85] Already shaken by changes in the agricultural economy and at the state government level, the officially ensconced aristocracy was reluctant to forego its patronage of rural co-operative credit for partisan purposes, certainly not just before the impending general elections.

Despite debt crises and controversies, agricultural credit never became really one of colonial government's policy priorities. Certainly the budgetary commitment remained quite modest. In late 1954, acting on the advice of the IBRD Mission, the federal government set up the Rural Co-operative "Apex" Bank to replace RIDA as the central funding authority for the co-operative credit network, ostensibly to strengthen its financial underpinnings. When economic conditions in agriculture deteriorated further during the depressed 1954-55 padi season, the government's relief measures included a M$5 million grant to the Apex Bank for combatting worsening kampung indebtedness. Yet, agricultural co-operative credit was otherwise still kept on a short financial leash.[86] At the end of the colonial period only about 10 to 15% of Malaya's estimated short-term agricultural credit requirements could be satisfied through the agency of co-operative credit, even with Apex Bank support. Most agricultural credit needs still had to be met through customary, usurious financial arrangements.

Padi Price Policy

Emergency controls over the price and supply of rice, as well as other essentials, were instituted by the returning British in the unsettled conditions immediately following World War II. Price regulations on rice remained in force longer than on other commodities, despite their dubious achievements.[87] Domestic trading in rice was decontrolled only after October 1949. To safeguard padi cultivators against sudden falls in price or machinations of unscrupulous traders, the federal government decided to fix a guaranteed minimum purchase price for rice in future. This price was to be fixed annually, intentionally at a level below the estimated market price for the forthcoming season. This would constitute the government's standing offer as residual buyer. The minimum guaranteed purchase price was not construed in relation to an agricultural incomes goal. Rather, it aimed at providing so called "psychological" reassurance for rice cultivators on their re-exposure to a free domestic market.

The government certainly had no intention of intervening any longer in the ordinary market determination of domestic rice prices. Agricultural policy sought ways of expanding local marketable output, but without tampering with the price of rice, upon which the country's wages structure hinged. Because of the close rice price-wage cost nexus, Malayan rice price considerations extended beyond the realm of agricultural policy to involve also the main employer and labour concerns, including rubber estates, tin mines, mercantile groups, and the government itself. Given the structure of Malayan international trade and finance, rice prices furthermore impinged upon sterling area balance of payments sensitivities. In the hierarchy of colonial policy concerns, local staple food prices were invariably treated as subordinate and instrumental to the dominant strategy of a primary export, trade surplus economy.

Policies relating to domestic rice supply therefore emphasized competitive prices in an internal, free, but not wholly open market. Import competition in rice trading was unilaterally encouraged, as a means of holding down wage costs. However, the impact of rice imports on Malayan domestic agricultural terms of trade was cushioned by the post-war world shortage of foodgrains, at least until 1954. A discriminatory ban on the export of rice in the meantime prevented Malayan producers from obtaining upward leverage on the market value of domestic rice. The government rice price policy institutionalized deflationary pressure on Malayan producer prices, while upholding the guaranteed minimum as a cushion against sudden or severe adjustments.

Uncertainties in the international supply of rice complicated the adjustment of domestic prices, prompting the federal government to utilize its minimum price guarantee as a signal of short-run expectations for local producers. The manipulation of guaranteed prices served to mobilize Malayan agricultural resources in the face of fluctuating supply trends, without incurring the costs of longer-run agricultural income maintenance. As soon as the immediate post-war rice shortage had eased somewhat, the government cut its guaranteed price for the 1948-49 growing season by 25%, to M$15 a picul. Market prices held to a level somewhat above this floor, resulting in a lesser decline in producers' earnings though output had also fallen. The floor price remained unchanged during the Korean War Boom of 1950-51, when higher market prices and record yields brought "considerable prosperity" to Malayan rice cultivators.[88] However, rubber still attracted manpower resources even at peak prices for rice, so that the planted acreage and output of rice fell in 1951-52.[89]

Difficulties in securing adequate supplies of imported rice in 1952 led to a higher guaranteed price of M$17 a picul in a determined bid to stimulate local production.[90] Planted acreage and output responded upwards, and enjoyed even better market prices. The government itself acquired negligible quantities of rice under its policy; rather, periodic variations in the guaranteed price were used to juggle the level of domestic agricultural activity. By varying the guaranteed price according to exogenous circumstances, the government was able to capitalize on peasant psychological dependence in order to counterbalance fluctuations in international supply conditions at a minimum cost to the local market or to itself.

Rice cultivators were bitterly critical of the government's price policy, which they saw as the cause of instability in their product prices and incomes. In repeated submissions to the Rice Production Committee, cultivators argued for revising the guaranteed minimum price into a proper price support, or income maintenance measure. Such appeals fell on deaf ears. Reiterating official and conventional opinion, the Committee Report rejected as "clearly fallacious" the notion that higher rice prices might induce increased domestic production, despite the circumstantial evidence to the contrary provided by the manipulative guaranteed pricing practice.[91]

Underlying the Committee's patronizing approach to rice price policy lay a characteristically custodial conception of agriculture as a "way of life." This, it maintained, could not be and ought not to be subject to "ordinary commercial standards of assessment of its benefits to the padi planter."[92] By implication, price-related economic behaviour was perceived as a threat to the traditional Malay agrarian cultural and social order. Its defence of classical communal values impelled the Committee to eschew considerations of price and its behavioural implications. This ideological defence, incidentally, accorded well with the economic strategy of the colonial authorities.

The year 1954 provided the acid test for the government's rice price policy. Bountiful harvests in Burma and Thailand had brought about a significant decline in the world market price of rice.[93] Attracted by the prospect of cheaper rice during this time of recession in the country's export sectors and a forecast (though not realized) budgetary deficit, the federal government was quite unprepared to support domestic agriculture at the hitherto guaranteed price level.[94] The government therefore dropped its guaranteed purchase price late in the season from M$17 to M$12 a picul. Along with this sharp reduction in the floor price, official attitudes towards rice agriculture took on a curious ambiguity: on the one hand, the lowered price guarantee was justified as an indicator to marginal rice producers to shift into more gainful occupations, notably rubber tapping;[95] on the other, it was insisted that "the easing of tension in international rice affairs . . . give no grounds for complacency, and the intensification of local production . . . is still the policy of government."[96] The true policy function of the minimum price became apparent when, confronted with falling world rice prices, the government moved to exploit short-run cost advantages while retaining the guarantee as an adjustable safeguard against long-run uncertainties.

Meanwhile, the domestic terms of trade for agriculture deteriorated suddenly and sharply. The guaranteed minimum price was adjusted downwards, forcing the domestic rice production to adapt any future growth to a vulnerable and subordinate policy role. The economic distress caused by the ensuing deflation of agricultural earnings was magnified by the timing of the government's decision. Although the federal authorities were aware of impending large surpluses in Burma and Thailand, and of the prospect of falling prices, they were reluctant to commit the government to a guaranteed minimum until the market price could be accurately estimated. Delay afforded the government a way to avoid the risk of incurring price support expenditures in the event of an early overestimate, or of producing shortages in case of an under-estimate. Instead of fixing its guaranteed purchase price before the start of the 1954-55 planting season, as was the usual practice, the government therefore waited until December to announce the cut. By that time, of course, cultivators had already commenced planting and had contracted commitments based on previously assured price levels. By virtue of its exercise in statecraft, the government succeeded in shifting the costs of fiscal risk back onto peasant producers. Replying to charges of having forsaken the agricultural sector, the colonial authorities insisted that their price policy had remained consistent with avowed principles of market determination, at least when prices were falling.

The sudden and sharp drop in rice prices reduced already low agricultural incomes absolutely and relatively to other sectors of the economy.[97] While the area planted with padi reached a record acreage for the 1954-55 season, on the assumption of previously guaranteed price levels, harvested output increased only marginally due to subsequent price disincentives, compounded by poor weather. Immediate, and also prolonged, hardships were inflicted especially on tenant cultivators and, to a somewhat lesser degree, on the smallholding peasantry as well.[98] In a series of emergency gatherings in various rice growing areas, usually docile agriculturalists passed angry resolutions condemning the government's withdrawal of its previously guaranteed price.[99] Demands were made for a proper price support policy to maintain agricultural incomes above the subsistence level. Also making a political point, the meetings complained that colonial governmental institutions provided inadequate representation for agricultural interests, to their policy disadvantage. This was driven home by a not-very-tactful coincidence which further incensed agricultural sensibilities, when a general salary increase for the expatriate-run public service was brought into effect just as the price guarantee was cut.

Malaya's emergent political parties, warming up to the impending first general elections (1955), made political capital out of grievances over rice price policy. Party Negara, whose leadership had long been associated with colonial governance, now took considerable pains to dissociate itself from federal policy. Seeking to cast itself as the champion of kampung society, Party Negara argued for a large-scale, policy-induced redistribution of income in favour of the rice-growing sector. Ingredients of the policy package sought included rice price supports and protective tariffs for rural income maintenance, along with acreage payments calculated to maximize land utilization.[100] Yet, implicit in this policy advocacy was a characteristic Party Negara custodial predilection. Their apparent aim was to secure public financial support for sustaining intact the traditional relationships of subsistence agriculture between squirearchy as patrons and peasants—"Staple Men of the Kingdom"—as clients.

The leading Malay contender in federal politics, UMNO, presented an alternative policy approach. While supporting the popular opposition to the government's rice price policy, as a matter of course, UMNO went on to promote the economic welfare of peasant cultivators, as distinct from landlords. The UMNO leadership believed that the key to the problem of rural Malay poverty lay in intensified investment in agriculture infrastructure alongside institutional measures to eliminate so called exploitation, with price supports playing only a minor part, if any. UMNO was, without doubt, also under the influence of landed interests. At this stage in its election campaign, however, the party found it expedient to adopt a more populist stance against its rival's close association with the colonial establishment, and with striking political effect. Their MCA partner in the Alliance tactfully joined the denunciations of government price policy, and, as a gesture of inter-communal goodwill, went further to accept improved terms of trade for agriculture as a means of bolstering the rural Malay economy.[101] Though prepared to cater to the needs of rural Malay development as part of an Alliance political compromise formula, the MCA business constituency seemingly exhibited a policy preference for consumer cross-subsidization through agricultural terms of trade over fiscal subsidization through taxation.

British commercial interests, on the other hand, remained unalterably opposed to any manner of subsidization of domestic agriculture. Tax spending (on other sectors) was anathema, and legislators representing U.K.-owned rubber estates and tin mines strongly decried the dearer rice notion as a threat to the export orientation of the Malayan economy.[102] Nevertheless majority sentiment prevailed, without, however, reaching a consensus on precisely what ought to be done to help agriculture cope with the immediate scissors crisis. A Legislative Council resolution simply expressed "grave concern" at the sharp drop in domestic rice prices and incomes, and urged the government to review its policies in order to assure agriculturalists a "fair return." Responsibility for the future course of policy remained clearly with the federal authorities. Yet the Legislative Council had taken what was, for Malaya, an unprecedented initiative in impressing its sentiments on the colonial administration.

Responding to the political groundswell, the federal government appointed a Rice Production Committee under the (expatriate official) Member for Economic Affairs to investigate agricultural conditions following the fall in rice prices. However the scope of the Committee's recommendations was already limited from the outset by the government's categorical refusal to entertain price supports. This standpoint was justified officially by reference to past economic strategy, rationalized further by the allegedly regressive distributive effects of agricultural producer subsidies.[103] In a revealing disclaimer, the colonial authorities presumed that the benefits of any such measures would accrue mainly to landlords and middlemen, rather than to peasant cultivators themselves. The government's attachment to its agricultural price policy denoted a parting of the ways with erstwhile partners of the Party Negara "Da-tocracy." Policy differences were formalized subsequently by the recommendations of the Rice Production Committee's Interim Report, calling for legislation controlling rents and tenancies, together with immediate acreage payments directly to cultivators to maintain producer incomes.[104]

The federal government responded in March 1955, with land tenure legislation, discussed previously, and a special appropriation of M$15 million earmarked for the rice sector. Of this sum, M$5 million went to the Apex Bank for low-cost agricultural credit, with the remainder intended as acreage payments to cultivators producing for the market.[105] Neither of these financial measures was construed officially as redistribution or development. Rather, they were designed to provide fiscal relief, in a more restricted and immediate sense, to a minority of entrepreneurial peasants among the mass of poor subsistence cultivators.

As with the concurrent land tenure legislation, executive authority for the dispensation of relief funds devolved upon state governments. According to the agreed procedure, the latter were free to devise their own relief schemes provided they adhered to the general principles set out in the Interim Report.[106] By then it would seem that the 1955 rubber export boom had sufficiently repaired federal revenues so that the colonial authorities could afford a political gesture towards the electoral patronage of the UMNO-dominated State governments, in the name of administrative efficiency. Party Negara spokesmen protested vehemently, in view of the country's forthcoming first general election, but to no avail.

The M$10 million relief fund was allocated among the Malay States (and the then Settlements of Malacca and Penang) proportionally to their marketable output, with Kedah obtaining nearly half. Yet none of the state relief schemes became operative before the next padi season. In the event, only Kedah devoted its relief allocation wholly to direct acreage payments; other states adopted a variety of schemes including fertilizer subsidies, equipment loans, seed distribution, minor irrigation works, loans for land redemption (Perlis), and even rent subsidies (Malacca). As the urgency of the crisis faded over time, the belated application of fiscal relief became part agricultural subsidy, part agricultural investment, and part windfall gratuity to favoured classes of agricultural entrepreneurs.

Dilemmas of Change in Colonial Malayan Agriculture

Economic decision-making in Malayan agriculture in the late colonial period crystallized into a three-tier structure of subordination. At the production level, peasant cultivators retained scant scope for autonomous economic behaviour. Agricultural activity was constrained certainly by deficiencies and discontinuities of an enclave market, but was further subordinated also to traditional sanctions and resource-use restrictions. These last emanated from the overlying rural political order. The Malay aristocracy as representative of established cultural and social norms, composed a second tier. Elite influence was exercised through the medium of local hierarchies, administrative organs, and later, the political party apparatus, to condition communal attitudes, including economic propensities.[107] The top tier denoted an interventionist governmental authority, whose interventions regulated rural factors and incomes, but whose authority expressed the interests of colonial officialdom, expatriate commerce, and domestic oligarchies. Agricultural policy was thus squeezed between the upper and nether millstones of British economic priorities and Malay sociological illusion.

The policy decisions applied during the period were calculated to maximize short-run technical gains in domestic rice production. Emphasis on the short-run resulted in the concentration of policy resources in existing rice growing areas, where it was believed improved output could be achieved most readily. Exhortation and organization were to complement otherwise meager injections of public investment with the hope of realising more favourable incremental capital output ratios at even higher levels of marketed production. This style of policy treatment, emphasizing administration and persuasion, while de-emphasizing investment factors and price incentives, reflected prevailing attitudes towards peasant agriculture, and also underscored the priorities of colonial economic strategy. As molded by the interests of the Empire, colonial Malayan economic developments made a foremost object of building up related balances on revenue account and sterling area payments. This accumulation of externally held reserves, in effect forced savings, imposed a corresponding real income deflation on the domestic economy of Malaya. Certainly the deflationary impact was mitigated somewhat by the subsistence nature of a large part of agricultural income. Nevertheless, the welfare loss for the agricultural economy was compounded, in effect, by attendant regulatory obstacles blocking access to developmental resources and reinforced by traditional sanctions against social change.

The authoritative allocation of employment, assets, and incomes, more or less binding upon the agricultural economy, appealed to Malay communal elite sentiment. Yet, policy obsessions with increasing marketable rice output in the confines of a static rural social structure, incurred inescapable opportunity costs for Malaya's agricultural economy. Ruling economic and social priorities served to frustrate agrarian demands for expansion of Malaya's cultivable area.[108] Moreover, even within the existing agricultural frontier, agriculturalists continued to be penalized by constraints on land use and labour mobility. This confined and compulsory agrarian structure, blocking the two options of extending cultivation or redeploying resources towards more remunerative alternatives, effectively prevented the adjustment of agricultural factors to full economic potential. The ensuing distribution of income kept the returns to cultivators low, whereas land values and rents and consumer surpluses were upheld at deliberately high levels. Along with welfare losses, potential comparative advantages in Malayan agriculture were being sacrificed to policy tactics in support of an ulterior economic strategy.

Related governmental acts of omission and commission further depressed the state of Malayan agriculture. Federal neglect of land tenure and agriculture credit conditions allowed a large portion of the peasantry to subside into impoverishment by indebtedness, foreclosure of tenancy, and rent bondage. Agricultural incomes were negatively affected also by adverse marketing conditions, including poor communications, insufficient storage facilities, and a lack of recognized quality standards for domestic padi. The effects of market inefficiency were exacerbated by the federal road transport policy of providing licensed road haulers with local monopolies *inter alia* in the movement of rice.[109] Agriculturalists were therefore obliged to absorb the excessive (internal) marketing costs associated with deficient infrastructure, monopolistic practices, and multiple intermediaries.[110] It is no doubt revealing of the government's position that, despite official declarations on behalf of agriculture, no effort was made to produce proper statistical data for the rice economy, not even on such basic indicators as employment and market prices.

Insufficient investment in infrastructure and inadequate administrative treatment left agriculture vulnerable to the vagaries of climate. Capricious weather rendered the peninsula's main rice-growing areas prone to flooding or drought. In late colonial Malaya as in other traditional agrarian economies, climatic conditions remained a crucial determinant of stable crop yields.

Ecology and history had together structured the Malayan rice economy into two agronomically distinct subsectors, comprising wet and dry padi cultivation techniques, respectively.[111] The diffusion and spread of wet padi cultivation over the decades had systematically transformed the basis of lowland Malay agriculture. Meanwhile dry padi cultivation, as an economically inferior technology, invariably contracted, except for a brief resurgence owing to increased squatting and inter-cropping following the wartime

TABLE 2
Padi Acreage and Production 1938-1955.

	Wet Padi			Dry Padi			Total	
Season	Planted Acreage ('000)	Yield ('000 tons)	Average Yield (tons/acre)	Planted Acreage ('000)	Yield ('000 tons)	Average Yield (tons/acre)	Planted Acreage ('000)	Yield ('000 tons)
1938/39	704	n/a	n/a	49	n/a	n/a	753	341
1939/40	728	n/a	n/a	66	n/a	n/a	794	335
1945/46	684	n/a	n/a	81	n/a	n/a	765	225
1947/48	765	n/a	n/a	80	n/a	n/a	845	343
1950/51	829	685	.83	47	24	.51	876	709
1951/52	790	526	.66	41	13	.43	831	544
1952/53	790	684	.86	44	16	.36	834	700
1953/54	809	635	.78	37	13	.35	846	648
1954/55	843	633	.75	48	19	.39	891	652

Source: *Federation of Malaya Annual Reports*, 1948, 1954, 1955.

Japanese occupation. Thereafter dry padi cultivation retreated again to its remaining congenial environmental settings, the remote northeastern lowlands and the swidden (slash and burn) hill farming settlements of the interior. In the pattern that had emerged by the early 1950s, wet cultivation encompassed some 95% of planted padi acreage, and an even larger proportion of total yield (Table 2).

The area devoted to rice experienced spasmodic growth following the vicissitudes of wartime and post-war reconstruction. Planted padi acreage climbed steadily, reaching a post-war peak for the 1950-51 planting season. In this phase, expansion had been set in motion by the post-war policy determination to achieve greater self-reliance in rice supplies. Yet, the then high point in planting probably owed as much to the fortuitous import substitution effects generated by the preceding year's sterling devaluation and culminating in the Korean War commodity boom. This growth in the area under rice cultivation centred on the more price elastic wet padi, with dry padi retracting to its pre-war order of magnitude, though now smaller in proportion.

The ensuing international cyclical downturn led to reduced levels of economic activity also in Malaya. Planted padi acreage accordingly declined from Korean War heights, notwithstanding the policy accent then being placed on the self-sufficiency goal. However, since rice proved more resilient in the deepening international trade recession, domestic padi planting increased rapidly. Improving terms of trade for agriculture amidst general recession inspired a second phase of upward expansion in padi acreage, dry as well as wet. Because of restrictive land policies, this expansionary phase was mostly confined (in the wet padi subsector) to new government irrigation schemes. Elsewhere, institutional, policy, and market constraints eroded some of the gain. Planted acreage climbed above its previous peak by the 1954-55 season, marking the penultimate year of colonial governance, but just before the guaranteed price cutback had suddenly and drastically diminished agriculture's terms of trade.

The aggregate area sown with padi increased by 18% over the 15-year period to 1955. Most of this expansion occurred during the post-war reconstruction phase. In inter-war years deliberate policy restrictions kept acreage growth at 2% for the entire DDP-inspired quinquennium. The extension of Malaya's agricultural frontier had failed to keep pace with rural Malay population growth since the 1930s. This reversal of the earlier historical experience subjected the kampung economy to intensified population pressure on its agrarian resources. As a result, employment in the padi sector declined, for the first time, by over 15% during the decade 1947-57.[112] Ironically, custodial policy measures, imposed in a bid to preserve intact the traditional rural order, had contributed to an emergent peasant mobility through the forced movement of agricultural labour into alternative occupations.

Rice production tended to fluctuate markedly during the post-war period. Single cropping was then the rule and the proportions of planted acreage actually harvested remained contingent on a combination of market and natural forces. Since price data are lacking, supply elasticities for padi cannot be determined. Nevertheless, contemporary comment would seem to question the conventional colonial image of peasant imperviousness to price incentives. The level of output achieved per (planted) acre during the 1950s, though fluctuating, reached about double the pre-war average. Improvements in yields sprang from a substantial enlargement of the area of cultivation given to modern large-scale irrigation, which doubled under the DDP to about 450,000 acres, or half the total. Technical improvements facilitated producer responsiveness to the enhanced market orientation of the domestic rice economy.

With yields doubling overall, agriculture's share of national income rose from the subsistence levels of the past to a new post-war plateau.[113] Yet, despite apparent productivity gains, prevailing policy and institutional arrangements sustained and even exacerbated the maldistribution of income, assets and wealth in favour of privileged segments of the Malay community. The poverty associated with heightened inequality tended to aggravate the relative deprivation of the bulk of the peasantry, impelling the beginnings of an outward flow of manpower from the rice economy while fomenting internal unrest.

Indeed, the post-war increase in padi production under the impact of commercialization invoked far-reaching changes in the role of agriculture in Malayan economic and social development. Before World War II padi was cultivated by and primarily for the subsistence kampung economy. Production during the late 1930s satisfied only a third of the country's consumption requirements, leaving the export and urban sectors to rely on imported rice.[114] That enclave situation altered under the impact of the post-war greater self-sufficiency goal. By the early 1950s, local production had increased sufficiently to supply with regularity more than half of domestic rice requirements.[115] The incremental margin of production now going to market shattered the traditional insularity of the subsistence padi economy. Although commercialization came late to Malayan agriculture, the claims of economic policy on the kampung product imposed on agrarian relations an incipient class differentiation based on commercial marketing and landownership.[116]

The post-war thrust of commercial production injected a novel capitalist ethos into the patrimonial organization of subsistence agriculture. Market enterprise among agriculturalists was encouraged directly by the colonial authorities by way of public investment in large-scale irrigation works and concessional credit, and also indirectly through tax subsidies and forms of moral persuasion.[117] Changing conditions and incentives in agriculture tended to sharpen economic perceptions, and by differentiating among agrarian interests led also to the formation of a class of entrepreneurial peasants. While most, if not all, peasants engaged in some commercial sales, entrepreneurial peasants were distinguished by the significant share of their product going to market. Commodity market influences soon extended also to factor markets. Thus, the entrepreneurial peasantry took to augmenting marketable supplies through the hiring of labour, land acquisitions and rentals, usury, dealing, etc. The entrepreneurial peasant represented an agrarian capitalist outgrowth from subsistence agriculture in commercial transition. No statistical data are available to detail its role, but the emergence of an entrepreneurial peasantry clearly had the profound impact of a middle class between subsistence peasantry and landowning gentry.

The growth of entrepreneurial practice undermined traditional agrarian modes, weakening the symmetry of customary patrimonial relations within the subsistence economy.[118] Market forces tended to erode the status of local aristocracies as social and political patrons, but conversely served to strengthen landed economic power. Economic rents within the confined agricultural frontier increased in response to population pressures coupled with commercial demands. Since the government had itself taken over the role of agrarian improver, through its investment in irrigation works, other infrastructure, and extension services, landlords were being propped up as a privileged class of rentiers.[119] Cultivators holding land shared the benefits of increased economic rent, though their continued independence henceforward required their overcoming policy and institutional barriers to their development into an entrepreneurial peasantry. For most peasants dependent on tenancy and credit, the intrusion of fluctuating market conditions into patron-client obligations introduced new elements of insecurity into both their access to agricultural resources and levels of income. Market volatility and factor restrictions interacted with the spread of commercialism to rend the traditional kampung fabric, polarizing agrarian relations increasingly between the distinct economic interests of the landed and the dependent peasantry.

If peasants were becoming increasingly and manifestly more aware of their own interests, expressions of class tensions were moderated successfully by parallel political events. The strict ideological controls enforced under the anti-Communist Emergency inhibited radical political mobilization. At the same time, colonial tutelage towards self-government brought about the introduction of the Member System in 1951, followed by the holding of state-level elections after 1952, and the expanded participation of nascent political parties in the legislative process.[120] New avenues for the legitimate articulation of interests were opened, though predominant influences tended to accentuate ethnicity and ethnic competition in the emergent political process.[121]

Political representation tended to sensitize the authoritarian tenor of colonial administration, making it more responsive to social demands. It was this political sensitivity that led during the period to the adoption of some limited redistributive policies (e.g., RIDA credits, land tenure legislation, acreage relief payments) especially beneficial to entrepreneurial peasants, bolstering their position as an intermediary group between landlords and landless. A more general social brokerage function was performed by the nascent political parties. UMNO, in particular, established a network of village branches, enabling the party organization to serve as an integrative mediator—supplanting weakened old-style patron-client relations—between modern centres of authority and the more traditional agrarian periphery. This neo-patrimonial role was enhanced by the surrounding environment of ethnic competitiveness, in which Malays felt threatened by Chinese economic might. Communal defensiveness in the neo-patrimonial party manner lent Malay nationalism a particular cohesiveness of community, such that its other-directed goals overshadowed the antagonisms implicit in the political rivalry between the bureaucracy-rooted/kampung-branched UMNO and the Party Negara "Datocracy." The ascendance of a system of neo-patrimonial nationalist politics among the Malays dulled the cutting edge of conflicts of interest arising out of agrarian social changes.

This coincidence of agricultural commercialization with political democratization, albeit the result of separate and unrelated policy considerations, had a critical influence on the evolving structure of agrarian relations in Malayan agriculture. Policies introduced during the late colonial period both accelerated and telescoped the processes of agrarian class differentiation and electoral participation. The coincidence of timing and pace furthermore related these processes one to another in fostering the emergence of a modernist, nationalist, neo-patrimonial policy as a substitute for the weakening traditional forms of patrimonialism. Later, after Independence, this refurbished neo-patrimonial framework was to shape agricultural policy responses into a particular custodial-developmental configuration.[122] Because of this quite fortuitous neo-patrimonial linkage between social differentiation and political participation, Malay agrarian history was set apart from the radical experiences of Europe and elsewhere in Southeast Asia.[123]

ENDNOTES

1. The term agriculture as used in this chapter refers specifically to rice cultivation, unless otherwise noted.

2. Martin Rudner, "Malayan Quandary: Rural Development Policy under the First and Second Five Year Plans", *Contributions to Asian Studies* Vol. 1 (1971).

3. R. Ma & You Poh Seng, "The Economic Characteristics of the Population of the Federation of Malaya," *Malayan Economic Review* Vol. V (1957), pp. 10-45. Federation of Malaya, Ministry of Agriculture & Co-operatives, *Census of Agriculture 1960, Census Monograph 1, Kuala Lumpur, 1961).*

4. Detailed figures on the rice economy's contribution to national accounts are unavailable before 1955. However, V.V.B. Rao's study, extrapolating the composition of (peninsular) Malaysian real Gross Domestic Product, calculates "non-rubber agriculture" as comprising between 16 and 19% of GDP during the 1950s: V.V.B. Rao, *National Accounts of West Malaysia* (Singapore, 1976), pp. 57-60 and Table E. "Non-rubber agriculture" includes padi, fishing, forestry, tea, coconuts, livestock and oil palm; however, the item was heavily dominated by padi during the colonial period.

5. On the early development of the rice economy of Malaya, and the emergence of a social and cultural maintenance role for rural Malay society, see for example, Lim, 1967; Gayl D. Ness, *Bureaucracy and Rural Development in Malaysia* (Berkeley, 1967); William R. Roff, *The Origins of Malay Nationalism* (New Haven. 1967); Chai Hon-chai, 1964, *The Development of British Malaya 1896-1909* (Kuala Lumpur, 1964); Tan Soo Hai, Ding Eing, *The Rice Industry in Malaya, 1920-1940* (Singapore, 1963); Lim Teck Ghee, *Peasants and their Agricultural Economy in Colonial Malaya, 1874-1971* (Kuala Lumpur, 1977); R.D. Hill, *Rice in Malaya: A Study in Historical Geography* (Kuala Lumpur, 1977); James C. Jackson, "Rice Cultivation in West Malaysia," *Journal of the Malaysian Branch, Royal Asiatic Society* Vol. 45 (1972), pp. 76-96; E.K. Fisk, "Rural Development Problems in Malaya," *Australian Outlook* Vol. 16 (1962), pp. 246-259; D.H. Grist *An Outline of Malayan Agriculture* (Kuala Lumpur, 1936); G.E. Shaw, "Malay Industries, Part III, Rice Planting", in R.J. Wilkinson, (ed.), Papers on Malay Subjects (Kuala Lumpur, 1926).

6. Martin Rudner, "The Structure of Government in the Colonial Federation of Malaya," *South East Asian Studies* Vol. 13 (1976), pp. 495-512; Gordon P. Means, *Malaysia Politics* (New York, 1970).

7. Martin Rudner, "The Draft Development Plan of the Federation of Malaya, 1950-1955", *Journal of Southeast Asian Studies* Vol. 3 (1972).

8. *Federation of Malaya Draft Development Plan 1950-1955* (Kuala Lumpur, 1950).

9. In 1950, imported rice into Malaya and Singapore together totalled 436,000 tons, while Malayan gross production for the 1950-51 padi season reached 709,000 tons: *Federation of Malaya Annual Report, 1954,* (Kuala Lumpur, 1955), p. 137.

10. Rudner, "Draft Development Plan," pp. 71-75; A. Schoenfield, *British Economic Policy since the War (Harmondsworth, 1963); A.D. Hazelwood "Colonial External Balances since the War," Review of Economic Studies* Vol. 21 (1953), pp. 31-52 and "Sterling Balances and the Colonial Currency System," *Economic Journal Vol. 44 (1954), pp. 616-617; K.M. Wright, "Dollar Pooling in the Sterling Area," American Economic Review* Vol. 44 (1954), pp. 559-576; G.L.M. Clauson, "The British Colonial Currency System," *Economic Journal,* Vol. 54 (1944), pp. 1-25.

11. Secretary of State for the Colonies, *House of Commons Debates* (henceforward: *H.C. Deb.),* 17 July 1952.

12. *Federation of Malaya Annual Report 1949* (Kuala Lumpur, 1950) p. 149; *Federation of Malaya Annual Report 1952* (Kuala Lumpur, 1953), pp. 110-111; Federation of Malaya Annual Report 1955 (Kuala Lumpur, 1956), p. 145.

13. High Commissioner, *Federation of Malaya, Legislative Council Proceedings, 8 February 1950 (henceforth: L.C. Proc.);* Director of Agriculture, *Lc.C. Proc.,* 26 July 1950.

14. Secretary of State for the Colonies, *H.C. Deb.,* 17 July 1952.

15. *Leg. Co. Proc.,* speeches by the Mentri Besar of Negri Sembilan, 14 September 1951; Dato Haji Mohammed Eusoff, 20 September 1951.

16. *L.C. Proc.* speeches by, *inter alia,* the Mentri Besar of Selangor and Dato Haji Mohammed Eusoff.

17. Enche Mohammed Rashid, *L.C. Proc.,* 20 January 1955.

18. Dato Haji Mohammed Eusoff, *L.C. Proc.* 20 March 1953.

19. *Report of the Rice Production Committee* (Kuala Lumpur, 1953), para. 51.

20. Ibid., p. 152

21. Enche Nassaruddin bin Abdul Rais, *L.C. Proc.,* 8 May 1952.

22. Martin Rudner, "The Malayan Post-War Rice Crisis: An Episode in Colonial Agricultural Policy," *Kajian Ekonomi Malaysia* Vol. 12 (1975), pp. 1-13.

23. *Draft Development Plan,* para. 321; *Federation of Malaya Annual Report, 1952,, p. 110; Federation of Malaya Annual Report, 1953,* (Kuala Lumpur, 1954), p. 251-2; *Federation of Malaya Annual Report, 1959,* (Kuala Lumpur, 1960), p. 97.

24. James C. Scott and B. Kerkvliet, "The Politics of Survival: Peasant Responses to Progress in Southeast Asia," *Journal of Southeast Asian Studies* Vol. IV (1973), pp. 241-268.

25. *Interim Report of the Rice Production Committee* (Kuala Lumpur, 1955); Resolutions of the Congresses of Padi Planters at Kampung Sebrang and Simpang Tiga, Sungei Limau, Alor Star, cited in the *Straits Traits Times,* 1 January 1955.

26. Leong Yew Koh, *L.C. Proc.,* 26 November 1953.

27. G.Z. Hanrahan, *The Communist Struggle in Malaya* (New York, 1954).

28. C. Thornton, *L.C. Proc.,* 22 November 1950.

29. J.C. Mathison, *L.C. Proc.,* 20 March 1953.

30. Martin Rudner, "Malayan Rubber Policy: Development and Anti-Development during the 1950s," *Journal of Southeast Asian Studies* Vol. 7 (1976) pp. 235-239.

31. For a contemporary first-hand account of British officials' empathy for the leisured and temperate lifestyle of the Malay aristocracy by a critical British colonial servant (responsible for Malayan Chinese Affairs), see Victor Purcell, *Malaya, Communist or Free? (London, 1954).*

32. High Commissioner's address, *L.C. Proc.*, 19 November 1952.

33. *Draft Development Plan, 1950*, para. 239(i).

34. International Bank for Reconstruction and Development, *The Economic Development of Malaya* (Baltimore, 1955), p. 42 (henceforward: IBRD Report); *Final Report of the Rice Production Committee, 1956,* (Kuala Lumpur, 1956), para. 118.

35. Ooi Jin Bee, *Land, People and Economy in Malaya* (London, 1963), p. 230.

36. *Federation of Malaya Annual Report, 1954,*, p. 290.

37. *Federation of Malaya Annual Report, 1954*, p. 138; Ooi, *Land*, p. 244; *Final Report of the Rice Production Committee, 1956,*, Vol. 1, para. 73.

38. E.H.G. Dobby, *Agricultural Questions of Malaya* (Cambridge, 1949); Grist, *An Outline*; Rudner, "Malayan Quandary."

39. *Federation of Malaya Annual Report, 1954*, pp. 135-6.

40. *Final Report of the Rice Production Committee, 1956*; *IBRD Report*.

41. The illegal rubber planting area was estimated at a quarter million acres in 1955 (compared to a total legally recognised 3,665,000 acres, of which 1,650,000 was on smallholdings), mainly in Kedah, Perlis and Johore States: *Federation of Malaya Annual Report, 1955*.

42. Tunku Y'acob, *L.C. Proc.*, 20 March 1953.

43. Ness, *Bureaucracy*

44. *Report on Resettlement and Development of New Villages* (Kuala Lumpur, 1952; J.M. Gullick, *Malaya* (London, 1963); Purcell, *Malaya*; Ness, *Bureaucracy*

45. Ness, *Bureaucracy*

46. *RIDA: Progress Report up to 31 December 1951, Legislative Council Paper No. 24 of 1952*, paras. 1, 2; High Commissioner's Statement on RIDA, *Leg. Co. Proc.*, 19 November 1952.

47. Cf. S.N. Eisenstadt, *Traditional Patrimonialism and Neo-Patrimonialism* (Beverly Hills, Cal., 1973).

48. Ness, *Bureaucracy*, p. 125; D.C. Norton, Secretary of RIDA, quoted in the *Straits Times*, 5 August 1952.

49. Dato Onn, *L.C. Proc.*, 20 March 1953; *RIDA Progress Report,op. cit.*, paras. 1, 2, 3.

50. *RIDA Report, Legislative Council Paper No. 10 of 1951*; Ness, *Bureaucracy*, pp. 125-6.

51. *Vide.* Ness, *Bureaucracy*

52. L.J. Fredericks, "Free Enterprise and the Co-operative Movement in Malaysian Economic Development," *The Developing Economies* Vol. 12 (1974), pp. 229-244.

53. D.E.M. Fiennes, *Report on Rural and Industrial Development Authority 1950-5 (Kuala Lumpur, 1957), paras. 37,45* (henceforth: *Fiennes Report*).

54. Ooi, *Land*, pp. 245-6; *Report of the Rice Production Committee, 1953*, Vol. 1, para. 81.

55. RIDA *Annual Report, 1954* (Kuala Lumpur, 1954), Appendix A: Auditor's Report.

56. *Fiennes Report*, paras. 45, 53.

57. RIDA Chairman's Comments on the Fiennes Report, *Legislative Council Paper No. 15 of 1957*.

58. *IBRD Report*, pp. 57-60, 223; E.K. Meek, *Land Law and Customs in the Colonies (London, 1946); T.B. Wilson, T.B., 1954, "Some Economic Aspects of Padi Land*

Ownership," Malayan Agricultural Journal Vol. 37 (1954), pp. 125-135; R. Ho, *Farmers in Central Malaya* Department of Geography Publication G/4, Research School of Pacific Studies, Australian National University (Canberra. 1967); Zaharah Haji Mahmud, "The Period and Nature of 'Traditional' Settlement in the Malay Peninsula," *Journal of the Malaysian Branch, Royal Asiatic Society* Vol. 43 (1972), pp. 81-105.

59. High Commissioner's address, *L.C. Proc.*, 17 November 1954; *IBRD Report*, pp. 223-4.

60. *Draft Development Plan*, para. 316.

61. Properly speaking, Malay State lands were not "owned" but leased from the Rulers, though titles were permanent and transferable, within the limits set by land use regulations and Malay Reservations (Meeks, 1946). By 1954-55, tenancies comprised 75 percent of all padi land in Province Wellesley (Penang), 70 percent in Kedah, and 50 percent in Krian District, *IBRD Report*, p. 60; B.J. Surridge, *Report on Co-operation in the Federation of Malaya, Legislative Council Paper No. 41 of 1953*, p. 6; *Interim Report of the Rice Production Committee, (Kuala Lumpur, 1955), Appendix A, para. 8.*

62. Surridge, *Report on Co-operation*, para. 6, and J.J. Puthucheary, *Ownership and Control in the Malayan Economy* (Singapore, 1960), pp. 5-7, described the degree of concentration in north Malaya such that 2000 families owned some two-thirds the padi land.

63. Among these contract changes containing an implicit shift in costs and risks was the substitution of rental payment in advance in cash for previous payments post-harvest in kind, *IBRD Report*, p. 60; *Report of the Rice Production Committee, 1953*, Vol. 1, p. 46.

64. *Interim Report of the Rice Production Committee, 1955*, Appx. A, para. 12; *IBRD Report*, pp. 54-5.

65. *Report of the Working Party on Development of New Areas for Land Settlement, Legislative Council Paper No. 11 of 1956*, para. 61; Dobby, *Agricultural Questions*, p. 58; Puthucheary, *Ownership and Control*, pp. 10-12.

66. The portfolio for Natural Resources, which included land policy, was held by the following "Members" after the introduction of the "Member System" in 1951: Dato Mahud bin Mat, Dato N.K. Ahmad Kamil bin Haji Mohammed, and Dato Ismail bin Dato Abdul Rahman, the latter also a leading figure in the landed aristocracy's Party Negara.

67. *Federation of Malaya Annual Report, 1952*, p. 108.

68. *Interim Report of the Rice Production Committee, 1955*, Appx. A, paras. 8-9.

69. *Leg. Co. Proc.*, 18 August 1954.

70. Tunku Abdul Rahman, *L.C. Proc.*, 20 January 1955.

71. See the candid reply of the Minister of Transport on behalf of the (absent) Minister of Agriculture and Co-operatives, *Dewan Ra'ayat* (House of Representatives) Proceedings 26 April 1962. The only state where measures were undertaken consistently to enforce the law was Kedah.

72. T.H. Silcock, "The Economy of Malaya," in C. Hoover, ed., *Economic Systems of the Commonwealth (Durham, NC, 1961)*.

73. Kahar Bador, "Social Rank, Status Honor and Social Class Consciousness amongst the Malays," and Syed Hussein Alatas, "Religion and Modernization in Southeast Asia," both in Hans-Dieter Evers, ed., *Modernization in Southeast Asia* (Singapore, 1973); Syed Husin Ali, *Malay Peasant Society and Leadership* (Kuala Lumpur, 1975); W.R. Roff, *The Origins of Malay Nationalism* (New

Haven, 1973); R.L. Winzeler, "The Social Organization in Kelantan", in W.R. Roff, ed., *Kelantan: Religion, Society and Politics in a Malay State* (Kuala Lumpur, 1974).

74. Attorney-General, *L.C. Proc.*, 2 June 1955.

75. *Report of the Committee on Agricultural Credit, Legislative Council Paper No. 50 of 1948*, para. 48.

76. *Report of the Committee on Agricultural Credit, Legislative Council Paper No. 50 of 1948*, p. 240.

77. *Report of the Committee on Agricultural Credit, Legislative Council Paper No. 50 of 1948*, para. 56.

78. *Draft Development Plan*, pp. 59-60, 105.

79. Member for Home Affairs, *L.C. Proc.*, 18 November 1954.

80. *Federation of Malaya Annual Report, 1953*, pp. 165-5; *Fiennes Report*, para. 4.

81. *Report of the Rice Production Committee, 1955*, Vol. 1, para. 54.

82. "UMNO Memorandum on the Economic Position of the Malays," cited in the *Malayan Bulletin*, 25 March 1953; Tunku Adbul Rahman, *L.C. Proc.*, 20 January 1955.

83. *Interim Report of the Rice Production Committee, 1955*, Appendix A, para. 9.

84. *Fiennes Report*, para. 43.

85. Sheikh Ahmad b. Mohammed Hashim (President of Apex Bank), *Leg. Co. Proc.*, 5 May 1955, complained of Treasury refusal to grant requested funding for co-operative expansion.

86. Final Report of the Rice Production Committee, paras. 45-6.

87. *White Paper on Government Trading in Rice, Legislative Council Paper No. 27 of 1954*, paras. 1-2; Martin Rudner, "The Malayan Post-War Rice Crisis: An Episode in Colonial Agricultural Policy," pp. 1-13.

88. *Legislative Council Paper No. 63 of 1950*, p. B673; *Federation of Malaya Annual Report, 1951, p. 54.*

89. *Department of Agriculture Annual Report, 1952* (Kuala Lumpur, 1953), para. 34.

90. Ibid., paras. 3, 4.

91. *Report of the Rice Production Committee, 1953*, Vol. 1, paras. 52-61; *Federation of Malaya Annual Report, 1951*, p. 224.

92. *Report of the Rice Production Committee, 1953*, paras. 15, 51.

93. The effect of this decline on domestic Malayan market prices was accentuated by the resumption of commercial imports of rice around this time, *IBRD Report*, p. 48.

94. Member for Economic Affairs, *L.C. Proc.*, 20 January 1955.

95. Ibid.

96. *Federation of Malaya Annual Report, 1954*, pp. 137-8.

97. *IBRD Report*, p. 49.

98. *Interim Report of the Rice Production Committee, 1955*, Appendix A, paras. 7, 11.

99. Resolutions of Congresses of Padi Planters at Simpang Tiga, Alor Star, 1 January 1955; Sungei Limau, Alor Star, 1 January 1955; Kampung Sebrang, 1 January 1955; Langgar and Tajar, Alor Star, 5 January 1955; Sungei Prai, 6 January 1955. See also *Interim Report of the Rice Production Committee, 1955*, Appendix A, para. 9.

100. Dato Zainal Abidin, *L.C. Proc.*, 20 January 1955.

101. Heah Foo Seang and Leong Yew Koh, *L.C. Proc.*, 20 January 1955.

102. J.C. Mathison (rubber estates) and D.T. Waring (tin mines), *L.C. Proc.*, 20 January 1955.

103. Member for Economic Affairs, *L.C. Proc.*, 20 January 1955.

104. *Interim Report of the Rice Production Committee, 1955*, Appendix A.

105. Member for Economic Affairs, *L.C. Proc.*, 30 March 1955.

106. Financial Secretary, *L.C. Proc.*, 1 June 1955.

107. Husin Ali, *Malay Peasant Society*

108. *IBRD Report*, p. 41.

109. *Report of the Rice Production Committee, 1953*, Vol. 1, para. 55.

110. A.M. Thompson, *Report on the Marketing of Rice in the Federation of Malaya, U.N. Food and Agricultural Organization No. 278 (Rome, 1954)*.

111. On the regional, historical, and agronomic variations associated with the different sub-sectors, see Jackson, "Rice Cultivation," pp. 76-96.

112. Total employment in rice production given in the 1947 census was 470,692, and in the 1957 census 398,295. During the same period, employment in the rubber sector increased by 20 percent to 614,487: Ministry of Agriculture and Co-operatives, *Census of Agriculture 1960, Census Monograph 1* (Kuala Lumpur 1961) Extract No. 10.

113. Rao, *National Accounts*, gives the revenue product of non-rubber agriculture during the mid-1940s as 13-14 percent of GDP, rising to between 16 and 19% by the 1950s.

114. *Ooi, Land*, p. 131; Tan, *The Rice Industry in Malaya*.

115. Domestic production met 54% of total consumption in the hungry year of 1947, 60 percent in 1950, and 54% in 1955, *Malaysia, Official Year Book 1963* (Kuala Lumpur, 1963), Table 25, p. 519.

116. Clive Kessler, "Muslim Identity and Political Behaviour in Kelantan", in Roff, ed., *Kelantan*, suggests that colonial administrative interventions and the spread of cash cropping made agricultural class distinctions noticeable already in the 1930s.

117. On the element of tax subsidy for enterprising, better-off agriculturists, see C.T. Edwards, *Public Finances in Malaysia and Singapore* (Canberra, 1970), p. 369, Table 50.

118. Cf. Husin Ali, *Malay Peasant Society*; M.G. Swift, "Economic Concentration and Malay Peasant Society", in Maurice Freedman, ed., *Social Organisation: Essays Presented to Raymond Firth* (London, 1967) pp. 241-269; Eisenstadt, *Traditional Patrimonialism*; J.C. Scott, "Patron-Client Politics and Political Change in Southeast Asia," *American Political Science Review* Vol. 66 (1972); J.C. Scott and B. Kerkvliet, 'The Politics of Survival," pp. 241-268; J.D. Powell, "Peasant Society and Clientist Politics," *American Political Science Review Vol. 64 (1970), pp. 411-25*.

119. Wilson, "Economic Aspects of Land Ownership"; Swift, "Economic Concentration"; Fisk, "Rural Development Problems," pp. 246-259.

120. Rudner, "The Structure of Government in the Colonial Federation of Malaya."

121. K.J. Ratnam, *Communalism and the Political Process in Malaya* (Kuala Lumpur, 1965); Ness, *Bureaucracy*.

122. Rudner, "Malayan Quandary."

123. Scott and Kerkvliet, "Politics of Survival"; J. Barrington Moore, Jr. *The Social Basis of Dictatorship and Democracy (Boston, 1966)*.

CHAPTER 4

THE MALAYAN QUANDARY: Rural Development Policy Under The First and Second Five-Year Plans

The emergence of a competitive political system in independent Malaya, having its balance of electoral power located among the rural Malays, imparted new urgency to agricultural development. Clearly the conservative, uninspired treatment accorded foodcrop agriculture under the colonial regime could no longer be continued by a development-oriented Alliance government specifically committed to Malay economic advance. Indeed, for many in the Alliance, Chinese as well as Malays, the ultimate test of their inter-communal partnership was to be its capacity to cope successfully with rural Malay poverty as the quid pro quo for Chinese political rights. Yet if developmental aspirations abounded, their realization through policy had to overcome the deeply entrenched interests and profound cultural legacies of a traditional agrarian economy.

Political Conceptions of Rural Development

Behind the Alliance strategy for rural development lay an evaluation of the cause of Malay agricultural malaise. In the official view, widely shared though not without its critics, rural retardation stemmed from some "defect" in the Malay peasant "psychology and thinking" that rendered him impervious to economic advantage.[1] Having placed responsibility for their plight on the peasant's "inherent conservatism," the new Alliance Minister of Agriculture preferred to generate "enthusiasm and desire" for agricultural development by means of improved organization, co-operation and provision of infrastructure. However the innate conservatism of its leadership precluded radical institutional change from established policy. Malay Social Darwinism

Contributions to Asian Studies, Vol. 1 (1971).

and Alliance economic philosophy dovetailed to form the conventional wisdom underlying Malayan rural strategy.

Although agriculture carried a nominal first priority in the First Five-Year Plan (FYP) (1956-60), plan policy laid strong emphasis on the more advanced, urban sectors while trusting in backwash effects to convey development into the rural economy. To facilitate the operation of these linkages, the Plan provided for a "substantial" expansion of marketing mechanisms through improved rural transport, credit and co-operation. While government "primed the pump" the main effort at agricultural development devolved upon the peasants themselves. Indeed, the goal of Alliance rural strategy extended beyond merely raising agricultural output to the "cultural" objective of inculcating Malay peasants with a "spirit of independence" worthy of Merdeka.[2]

Malay rural interest welcomed the attention accorded agriculture but complained of the absence of a definite agricultural development programme in the First FYP. Regret was also expressed at the Alliance's failure to undertake even the modest reforms proposed by the Rice Committee Report (1956) to curb some of the more blatant evils of absentee landlordism in the rice-bowl of northwest Malay. However the landed gentry dominating the United Malays National Organization (UMNO), senior partner in the Alliance, preferred to look elsewhere than to institutional reform for a remedy for rural backwardness. Instead, the UMNO squirearchy indicated their faith in the classic formula of social amenities and economic infrastructure that came to denote Alliance strategy. Virtually, the only challenge to this conventional wisdom came from the University of Malaya, where economist Ungku Aziz strenuously attacked the persistent disregard for impoverished, land-hungry subsistence cultivators in policy calculations, insisting instead on comprehensive institutional reforms coupled to a massive programme of public investment aimed at raising rural productivity.[3]

By late 1958, it had become quite apparent that the First FYP approach had failed to prevent the continued decline of Malay fortunes. With the onset of the general election campaign, rural UMNO candidates pressed the government for positive measures to alleviate agricultural distress. Yet when the gesture did come, it was too little, too late, and the Alliance sustained important losses in the 1959 General Election, especially on the rural east coast.

The Alliance response to opposition electoral victories was to greatly expand its commitment to rural development in the Second Five-Year Plan (1961-65), incorporating a National Rural Development Plan.[4] Although the accent of policy remained unchanged, with emphasis still on the provision of economic and social infrastructure, the sum of public expenditure directed towards agriculture multiplied three-fold to M$150 million.[5] If there was innovation in agricultural policy under the Second FYP, it was not in the strategy of rural development but in the reorganization of administration aimed at mobilizing national effort towards the Alliance rural development goal.

The administrative structures, set up accompanying the National Rural Development Plan, were designed to render agricultural policy more responsive to rural needs, within the overall guidelines of official strategy.[6] A National Rural Development Council and Rural Development Executive Committee consisting of cabinet ministers and senior officials were established specifically to frame rural development policy and supervise its implementation. Political control over planning was reinforced by the creation of a Ministry of Rural Development, under the Deputy Prime Minister Tun Abdul Razak, whose tasks included co-ordinating the activities of all government departments and agencies engaged in rural areas. At the centre of this new administrative subsystem was the "Red Book" scheme, symbolizing the aggregation of peasant interests by District Rural Development Committees. Peasant demands reviewed by these Committees were then inscribed in Red Books located in Operations Rooms, thereby becoming at once the targets and indices of rural development attainment. While peasant participation in the political process thus increased, progress toward a genuinely responsive agricultural policy-making process was still impeded by the near-monopoly over the District Committees exercised by UMNO.

The National Rural Development Plan met with strong criticism from opposition parties for failing to cope with the real "causes" of rural poverty, notably class conflict and exploitation. Socialist Front spokesmen bitterly accused the Alliance of succumbing to vested interest in upholding the institutional status quo. True to its principle of inter-communal accommodation, the Alliance government vigorously denied that rural poverty stemmed from exploitation either by Malay landlords, Chinese middlemen or Indian moneylenders, and instead shrewdly redirected responsibility for agricultural backwardness on the legacy of "British Colonialism."[7]

In fact, the Alliance cabinet was itself seriously divided over rural development policy. Notwithstanding the National Rural Development Plan's adherence to the classic formula of amenities

and infrastructure, the maverick Minister of Agriculture and Co-
operatives, Abdul Aziz bin Ishak, expressed his intention to promote a more aggressive co-operative movement to combat rural
exploitation. Proclaiming himself "also a Socialist," Enche Aziz
sought to effect rural reform through co-operation if not through
legislation, as a vehicle for rural development along lines suggested by Professor Ungku Aziz (no relation) and supported by the
Socialist Front.[8]

Although the Minister of Rural Development, Tun Abdul Razak
likewise declared at the time in favour of a more "socialist" pattern
of agricultural development, albeit coupled to a "capitalist" urban
economy,[9] successive innovations in co-operative organization initiated by Abdul Aziz were still to be thwarted by a cautious
cabinet. Growing conflict between the Minister of Agriculture and
his cabinet colleagues led finally to his removal from that portfolio
and his leaving the government in 1962. Following the departure of
the popular Minister, the Alliance took great pains to renounce
"collective ownership" (read: producers' co-operatives) as "unacceptable" to the Malay peasantry. Instead the Alliance reverted to a
quest for "development" in context with the traditional agrarian
socio-economic structure.

The Padi Basis of Agricultural Policy

Alliance rural development strategy was firmly rooted in the
subsistence padi economy.[10] Continuing in the footsteps of its colonial predecessor, the newly elected government at the outset proclaimed its intention to aim at "eventual self-sufficiency in food"
(i.e., rice) and later even fixed the target date as 1963.[11] Despite rising world production and falling rice prices, the federal government
still insisted on maximizing domestic padi output. It was made quite
explicit, however, that the objective of agricultural policy under the
First FYP was less the augmentation of padi planters' income than
an increase in physical production.[12] Output rather than income
was the implied object of the self-sufficiency goal.

Most Malays originally applauded the Alliance self-sufficiency
goal. Indeed, some of the more fervent adherents to the Malay padi
culture demanded that land use policy be wholly redirected towards rice regardless of income considerations. Only a small minority of Malay "marginal men," among them university economists,
planters and entrepreneurs opposed this padi emphasis, which
"doomed" peasants to "perpetual poverty with not a ray of hope in
economic emancipation forever."[13] For the others only the intense

cultural shock of a massive Malay urban drift, an outcome of deteriorating conditions in the padi sector through the late 1950s, could induce change in traditional attitudes towards agriculture. Those still clinging to padi as an expression of the Malay ethos now asked the government to apply economic remedies, including the transfer of marginal lands to more remunerative crops, in order to bolster kampung life.

Among non-Malays, support for the self-sufficiency goal came from the trade unions, ever fearful of a recurrence of the early post-war rice famine. Indeed, it required a rural Malay to remind trade unionists that self-sufficiency might mean higher food prices, pointing to the contradiction in labour's interests. Chinese and Indian traders also approved movement toward self-sufficiency, in which they had a shared interest. On the other hand, rubber planters remained opposed to any policy that might raise rice prices and therefore labour costs, advocating instead steps to extend land settlement and raise rural productivity.

Neither was the Alliance cabinet united over padi policy. Whereas Malay ministers accepted the self-sufficiency goal, the Chinese Minister of Commerce and Industry argued that such a misallocation of national resources would bring about a decline in Malayan standards of living. The expatriate Economic Adviser found himself on a political tightrope between the demands of Malay communalism and the imperatives of rational development. In the end he came down for padi self-sufficiency "as well as" rubber-based development, but with priority for the latter.[14] This ambivalence was shortly to tell on policy.

When challenged by "theory peddling economists," the Minister of Agriculture originally justified his policy emphasis on padi, if not in terms of income, then on the grounds of the Malays' "inherited love of the land of their fathers." This allegedly protected them from vagaries of world markets:

> If the padi planter had lived by the tenets of the economist, scarcely a grain of rice would now be grown and we should be bound, hand and foot, body and soul, and at the mercy of the bulls and bears of the financial menageries of London and New York.[15]

Any illusion that padi would be immune from influences of the money economy were, however, rudely shattered by the 1958 recession. Under pressure from aggrieved rural interests, appeals to traditional ways gave way to economic realism. To be sure the verbal commitment to padi remained. Nevertheless, policy emphasis now began to shift towards crops yielding the highest marginal revenue product, notably rubber.

The Alliance response to the rural vote in the 1959 General Election, embodied in the National Rural Development Plan, resurrected self-sufficiency as an output goal but the substance of policy had now changed significantly. No longer was padi regarded simply as a Malay cultural predilection. Rather rice farmers were henceforward to be treated as economically rational, income-oriented producers. Producers incomes, and not merely sectoral output, now emerged as an object of rural policy. By 1965, Malayan padi output still satisfied only about 60% of domestic consumption. In the subsequent First Malaysia Plan (1966-70) the padi self-sufficiency goal was finally laid to rest.[16]

Agricultural Policy Instruments

In line with the Alliance approach to rural development, the direct involvement of government in agriculture under the First and Second FYPs was limited to the extension of economic infrastructure, especially roads and irrigation, and community development. Rural roads were regarded by the conventional wisdom as the veritable key to kampung development. Despite the fiscal stringencies of the late 1950s, the rural road programme exceeded its original First FYP target by over 35%, and this emphasis continued through the Second FYP.

Meanwhile, fulfillment of the irrigation plan, a vital component of the original padi policy, lagged seriously behind target. Following the failures of the previous Plan period, the Second FYP placed renewed emphasis on irrigation and drainage schemes as a vehicle for rural development. Cost-benefit considerations were henceforth to be applied to investment in irrigation works, while padi farmers came to be involved in the planning process through the Red Book scheme. By mid-1963, the Plan target of 300,000 additional padi acres drained or irrigated was substantially achieved, amounting to a 70% increase over the 1960 total. As a result, the acreage of padi given to double-cropping multiplied more than five-fold to 57,000 acres. Continuing this infrastructural approach, an expanded irrigation target of half of a million acres was incorporated in the subsequent First Malaysia Plan.

Accompanying the extension of infrastructure, strong emphasis was placed on social mobilization through community development efforts, as an instrument of kampung progress.[17] The conventional diagnosis of Malay agricultural retardation in cultural and psychological terms prompted a social rather than economic solution to the problem of rural underdevelopment. Whereas roads and irrigation were originally intended to serve the sectoral output goal of padi self-sufficiency, the creation of a progressive, development-minded Malay peasantry capable of mounting its own economic improvement was left to the social techniques of community development. Although community development was hardly new to Malaya, and indeed much was made of an alleged traditional co-operative orientation among Malays, it now assumed new vitality in the Alliance scheme of things. Community development was reintroduced with much fanfare as "a major force in the social, cultural and economic improvement of the people and the most important feature of national planning in this vital period of our history."[18] Yet after an initial flurry of activity, a shortage of funds and personnel brought the programme to a halt. By 1960 the kampungs involved had reverted virtually to their original state.

Following the failure of the community development programme, the Alliance government turned to charismatic leadership together with a military form of supervision to activate the peasantry towards its National Rural Development Plan. As part of this new mobilization scheme, the Minister of Rural Development took to extensive travelling throughout rural Malaya, exhorting peasants and impelling bureaucrats to act. Military symbols were used to lend a sense of urgency to rural development ("National Operations Room," "War against poverty," etc.), borrowing from techniques of the Malayan Emergency. At first efforts were directed towards overcoming bureaucratic lethargy by utilizing the Red Books as an index of their performance. Then, from late 1961, the "Second Phase" of the scheme was set in motion calling for the mobilization of peasant participation in rural developments. Kampungs were spurred on to "self-help" in organizing agricultural improvements and even small rural industries.

Together with this mobilization campaign, the Ministry of Rural Development launched an adult education programme against rural illiteracy, which later included Islamic teaching so as to cushion the "cultural shock" of development with faith. In spite of these efforts, the mobilization scheme still suffered the absence of independent, non-UMNO peasant associations capable of aggregating rural interests in agricultural planning. There existed no autonomous, rural-based mechanism for political communication between officialdom and agraria.

Malayan padi policy had also to contend with a price dilemma between cheap rice for urban consumers and dear padi for the advantage of padi producers. Padi planters constantly reminded the Alliance of electoral support given them and demanded in return incomes comparable to other sectors. Furthermore, padi farmers complained of middleman malpractices and sought appropriate redress. Although the Alliance government agreed to raise the guaranteed minimum price for padi, it otherwise declined to interfere with private trade in padi.[19] Even when a World Bank mission recommended a tariff on imported rice to stimulate domestic production, this was turned down by the Alliance. Although padi farmers were to be protected against sudden impoverishment, there was no intention to manipulate padi prices instrumentally towards either the self-sufficiency goal or raising rural incomes. Within limits of the politically acceptable, cheap padi was to remain a cornerstone of national policy, in the interest of export sectors and nascent industrialization.

Co-operative Marketing and Rural Credit Policy

Given the physical output goal of original padi policy, the task of raising producers' returns was assigned to an expanded rural co-operative movement, particularly co-operative marketing and credit. Over and above its economic attraction, co-operation also had important ideological appeal, especially for the then Minister of Agriculture and Co-operatives, Abdul Aziz bin Ishak. For him, co-operation constituted a defence against the emergence of a Malay exploiter class ("Malays eating Malays, Malay capitalists eating Malay non-capitalists") and would serve to redistribute the benefits of government policy among the rural populace.[20] Co-operation furthermore had strong affinity for Malay populism, both as an egalitarian principle and in terms of the traditional virtue of "self-help." To set their co-operative policy in motion, the Alliance promised important changes in its colonial organization and orientation. Their objective was the creation of a comprehensive co-operative marketing and credit system by 1960, so that rural producers would no longer be compelled to "unscrupulous middlemen."[21]

In practice, however, the middleman-producer nexus was closely bound up with inter-communal relations and therefore with the particularistic interests of the component parties of the Alliance. Thus the Alliance's formal commitment to the principle of co-operative marketing as a means of augmenting producers' returns touched upon tender communal nerves. To the then Minister of Agriculture and Co-operatives the issue was starkly clear: government action was necessary to "rid" peasant producers of "blood-sucking middlemen."[22] At the other end of the Alliance spectrum, the Malayan Chinese Association (MCA) staunchly defended Chinese traders in the name of "free enterprise" against "communistic" government monopolies.[23] Meanwhile, rural Malays complained bitterly of exploitation by middlemen, most of whom were Chinese. In its determination to reconcile its pluralism of interests and communities, the Alliance responded by acknowledging the need to "deal with the profiteers," but tactfully limited government activities to promoting competition through marketing co-operatives.

Although the introduction of co-operative marketing generally succeeded in raising producers' returns, it proved difficult to wean small padi farmers away from private dealers. By virtue of the seasonal credit they were able to offer, the latter, who were quite capable of intensive competition when motivated, frequently placed the young co-operative societies in difficulty. Not only did this diminish the lasting economic impact of co-operation, but further left its cultural goal unrealized. Following the promulgation of the National Rural Development Plan, tension between Abdul Aziz and the MCA sharpened over the more aggressive role envisaged by the Agriculture Minister for co-operative marketing.

In 1961, the Federal Ministry of Agriculture and Co-operatives adopted a radical course and convinced certain Malay State governments to accord co-operatives a monopoly over padi purchases in the major growing areas. The immediate success of this policy in strengthening the co-operatives and raising producers' returns inspired the Minister to contemplate establishing co-operative rice milling monopolies as well. At this point, the Prime Minister intervened at the behest of the MCA to ask the states to restore padi marketing licences to private, mainly Chinese traders. Though well aware of the significance of co-operative marketing to rural Malay welfare, Tunku Abdul Rahman was apparently even more concerned to uphold the delicate balance of communal interest within the Alliance. An astonished Abdul Aziz vigorously denied that the termination of rural exploitation by middlemen impinged upon inter-communal relations, but the stand of the Prime Minister prevailed. Following the resumption of Chinese business, widespread disillusionment among Malay peasants restored co-operative marketing to its previous, unsatisfactory state.[24]

On agricultural credit policy as well Abdul Aziz's Ministry embarked on a more positive role in the rural economy. By way of contrast with colonial practice, independent Malaya's rural credit co-operatives were no longer obliged to build up gilt-edged reserves in London. Instead, the newly created Rural Co-operative Apex Bank was to direct funds to local co-operative credit societies in order to provide members with financial capital. To assure liquidity, the Alliance government injected an annual line of credit into the Apex Bank. Yet the local credit co-operatives still retained their traditionally cautious approach to agricultural finance, not even fully using the resources placed at their disposal.[25]

As a result, the co-operative credit system was able to meet only a small portion of the estimated annual seasonal credit requirement of M$40 million for northwest Malaya alone.[26] While membership in rural credit societies grew slightly from 48,000 to 54,000 over the course of the First FYP, these consisted in the main of better-off peasants. The bulk of the peasantry had still to resort to usurious padi kunca for their seasonal credit requirements.[27]

Recurrent rural Malay demands favouring increased capitalization of credit co-operatives went unattended until after the 1959 General Election. Moved by electoral suasion, the Alliance government then decided to include a substantial expansion of co-operative credit facilities in the National Rural Development Plan. This brought to a head the conflict between the President of the Apex Bank and the Minister of Agriculture and Co-operatives over the place of co-operative credit in rural development. Abdul Aziz accused the Apex Bank of pursuing a negative, conservative policy in denying the use of co-operative credit as an instrument of rural social change. As far as the Ministry of Agriculture was concerned, the potential gains due to a more venturesome rural credit policy was well worth the possible added risks in co-operative lending. In the end an expert on cooperation banking from the International Labor Organization (ILO) was invited to Malaya to resolve the issue, but his recommended reorganization of the rural co-operative credit system came to be involved in the political intricacies of the Abdul Aziz "affair."

Following his attempts at innovation in the co-operative sector, pressure built up within the Alliance for the removal of Abdul Aziz bin Ishak from the Ministry of Agriculture and Co-operatives. In July 1962, his seven-year reign over this Ministry was brought to an abrupt end. Abdul Aziz quit the Alliance over issues of policy disguised as personality, and joined the Parliamentary opposition. In the last three years of his regime, membership in rural co-operative credit societies grew by 40%, even though available finance lagged behind. Subsequent to Abdul Aziz's departure, his successor, Minister of Agriculture and Co-operatives, obtained a substantially increased allocation of rural co-operative credit. However the co-operative movement now resumed its more traditional role as a rural banking institution, shorn of innovative initiative and redirected away from social reform.

Land Policy

Independent Malaya inherited widespread and severe land hunger as a colonial legacy.[28] Symptomatic of this endemic land hunger was the very small size of most padi holdings, almost 70% of which were uneconomic units of under five acres. Virtually all the holdings of one acre or less, nearly 10% of the total, were located in areas of long-standing Malay settlement.[29] Rapid population growth further accentuated the trend towards fragmentation into even smaller holdings. In such circumstances customary tenure relationships and rent control legislation were discarded in practice as landlords took increasing advantage of land hunger to expand their share of the agricultural product.

Malayan land hunger was less a result of inadequate cultivable land than the outcome of policy and administrative inertia. In fact less than one-fifth the potentially cultivable land area of the Federation was actually being farmed, with the remainder kept under

TABLE 1
Size of Peasant Farms in Malaya—1960.

Size Group (acres)	Number of Farms ('000)	Percent of Total
Below 1	45.9	10
1 - 1 ¾	79.6	18
2 - 2 ¾	78.0	17
3 - 3 ¾	57.4	13
4 - 4 ¾	41.7	9
5 - 7 ¼	72.1	16
7 - 14 ¾	56.9	14
15 - 99 ¾	17.7	3
Total	449.5	100

Source: *Census of Agriculture*. Ministry of Agriculture, 1960, adapted.

virgin jungle or forest reserve. In the poignant exclamation of one rural Malay MP, "There is land, land everywhere, but not an acre to possess." As the Federation's high standard of land administration precluded squatting, applications for new land had to proceed through regular channels. Yet land offices in the Malay States were typically given to interminable arrears in the processing of land applications, resulting in contrived land shortages. Efforts at overcoming this difficulty through formulation of a nationally co-ordinated land use policy floundered upon the jealousy of the states for their constitutional prerogatives over land. Deliberate restriction of Malay's land frontier apparently served the self-interest of the Malay landed gentry dominating the UMNO state governments.

The impact of population pressure on land fragmentation was further accentuated by the Islamic law of inheritance prevailing among Malays. According to Muslim custom followed extensively in Malay-settled areas, property holdings were divided among all heirs in fixed proportions. Since many of the inherited proportions were too small to be of economic viability, this practice when coupled to severe population pressure on alienated land effectively decreased Malay agricultural productivity.[30] Though well aware of the anti-developmental consequences of the trend towards fragmentation of padi-holdings, neither colonial administration nor their Malay officials were able to overcome religious-institutional resistance to change. Following the election of an Alliance federal government the UMNO leadership approached Malayan Muslim authorities with proposals to redefine Islamic practices regarding land inheritance, on the basis of precedents in the state of Kelantan and in the Middle East. Agreement was reached to restrict fragmentation of inherited land on new settlement schemes, but otherwise only when the heirs agree to forego their shares. In circumstances of acute land hunger, the policy sanction continued to be given Islamic land inheritance law resulted in an ongoing breakdown of Malay agricultural assets.

Within the cultivated areas large tracts of padi land lay under Malay Reservation. Created after 1913 in order to prevent the large-scale dispossession of Malay peasants, the Malay Reservations came to be regarded as a weapon of Malay communal defence against the economic achievements of the Chinese and Indians. However, instead of protecting the peasant, the Malay Reservations in practice served to facilitate concentration of landownership in the hands of the Malay rentier class, and this at a comparatively low cost to themselves.[31] Attempts on the part of the opposition Socialist Front to mobilize electoral support against the Malay Reservation system floundered upon the communal rock of rural Sinophobia, which alienated the Malay peasantry from other Socialist-sponsored proposals at reform as well.

Responding to political challenge, the Alliance put forward its own notion of a Jeffersonian-type "property-owning democracy" based on "decent . . . organized, sound farming communities."[32] Land hunger and resulting agrarian poverty were to be solved by the settlement of landless peasants on large-scale land development schemes. The Federal Land Development Authority, established in 1956, undertook the management of these schemes, which amounted to some 10,000 hitherto landless families cultivating 121,000 acres of new, high-yielding rubber by the end of its first decade.[33] As regards existing padi land, however, the Alliance still shied away from such "complex" matters as land tenure or concentration, preferring to leave these to the responsibility of the states. Despite strong pressure from rural Malays for a national land policy, the Alliance federal government would not or could not, encroach on state constitutional jurisdiction over land matters. Land policy remained decentralized and fixed.[34]

Rural Development 1956-65

Malayan rural development strategy over the decade covered by the First and Second FYPs did not succeed in generating substantial improvement in the rural subsistence economy. Despite the government's declared policy emphasis on padi, Malaya's total planted acreage expanded by less than 15% during the period 1956-65, considerably less than the estimated rate of kampung population growth. Moreover the differential between the acreage planted and actually harvested grew between the 1955-56 and 1965-66 seasons from 9 to 15%, indicating a worsening deterioration of agrarian assets. Still, output of padi did show gains of more than half in physical terms over the decade, due mainly to improved water control, increased double-cropping and the wider provision of economic and social services. Although federal authorities claimed to be satisfied with this performance, [35] a visiting Food and Agricultural Organization (FAO) consultant noted that the stress on physical output had resulted in a preponderance of low yield, often unmarketable domestic padi.[36]

Whereas physical padi output statistics indicated gains, the per capita income of Malayan rice producers continued its declining trend. Owing to declining labour productivity in the padi sector,

TABLE 2
Malayan Padi Acreage and Output 1955-1965.

Season	Planted Acreage ('000)	Harvested Acreage ('000)	Output ('000 long tons)	Percent of Home Consumption
1955/56	891	712	410.6	54
1960/61	941	798	560.2	61
1963/64	988	n/a	623.8	62
1965/66	980	840	860.0	60*

* Estimate.
Source: *Malaysia: Official Year Book, 1964; First Malaysian Plan.*

many Malay peasants, especially tenants, failed to receive even minimally adequate incomes.[37] Even the much-vaunted Chinese "New Villages" had deteriorated by the early 1960s into "a combination tropical slum and detention camp."[38] The annual growth rate of the padi sector during the Second FYP period averaged only 2.3% per annum, compared to an estimated annual increase in rural population of over 3%, and an overall growth rate of 4.8% for all agricultural produce (5.1% for export commodities). In spite of Alliance stress on stimulating the padi economy, the rate of growth and income levels in the rice producing sector still lagged far behind those of alternative agricultural sectors, to say nothing of the urban sector.[39]

The failure of development to take root in Malayan padi economy reflected a weakening in the Alliance government's real agricultural commitment. Despite the grand pronouncements accompanying introduction of the National Rural Development Plan, the actual allocation of governmental resources towards agricultural development fell considerably below target. The deficiency of over 14% in public capital investment in agriculture contrasted poorly with the over-fulfillment of the Second FYP overall by more than 23%. Although originally destined to receive a quarter of total public development expenditure over the period 1960-65, agriculture actually obtained only a fifth.[40] Yet this denial of capital to the agricultural sector cannot fully explain the failure of development. Just as important was the strict adherence of policy to traditional institutional forms, which both stifled peasant innovation in padi production and limited their redeployment towards other, more productive occupations.[41]

The Alliance government's conception of agricultural "development" assumed a persisting rural economic and social structure. There was little willingness, certainly not among the UMNO landed elite, to conceive of agricultural development as a socio-economic process involving basic modernizing changes in kampung structures and roles. If anything, Alliance policy sought to consolidate the traditional rural system while somehow making it prosper. In the event, vested institutional barriers arising out of established land tenure custom, the entrenchment of padi cultivation and exploitive marketing and credit relations continued to frustrate developmental innovation in subsistence agriculture. Declining agrarian fortunes and rural electoral pressures finally found expression in cautious institutional innovations introduced together with the First Malaysia Plan: from 1965, a Bank Bumiputra and Federal Agricultural Marketing Authority were set up with very limited capacity to correct distortions in rural credit and marketing arrangements, respectively.[42] And the goal of padi self-sufficiency was finally deferred to the indefinite future.[43]

To be sure, the balance of electoral power in the Malayan parliamentary system rested with the rural community and with Malay kampungs in particular.[44] Nevertheless rural interest articulation during the First and Second FYP period was still mediated by a conservative, landowning UMNO squirearchy. None of the opposition parties were capable of mobilizing mass rural support in the populous West Coast Malay settlement areas against the incumbent Alliance. Rather, the efficient UMNO machine proved quite able to garner sufficient kampung votes to ensure continued political predominance of the Alliance governing elite.[45] This was sufficient to ensure persistence of the past policy quandary of Malayan rural strategy: the dilemma of pursuing economic development without social-institutional adaptation.

ENDNOTES

1. Minister of Agriculture, *Federation of Malaya, Legislative Council Proceedings, 16* May 1956 (henceforth: *L.C. Proc.*).

2. *Report on Economic Planning in the Federation of Malaya in 1956* (Kuala Lumpur, 1956), p. 12.

3. Cf. Ungku Aziz, "The Causes of Poverty in Malaya" and "The Remedy for Rural Poverty," both in Lim Tay Boh, ed., *Problems of Malayan Economics* (Singapore, 1969).

4. On the National Rural Development Plan as a policy response to political demands expressed through the electoral system, see Gayl D. Ness, *Bureaucracy and Rural Development in Malaysia* (Berkeley, 1967), chap. 4.

5. *Federation of Malaya, Second Five-Year Plan* (Kuala Lumpur, 1961), p. 29. Actual public capital expenditure on agriculture under the First FYP totalled M$45 million, including the "subsistence" sectors only (padi, fishing etc.) and not the cash crops (rubber, oil, palm, pineapples, etc.) which attracted considerably larger sums of public investment.

6. On the operational machinery of the National Rural Development Plan, see Ness, *Bureaucracy*, Chap. 6; and C.G. Furgerson, "The Story of Development in Malaya," *Journal of Local Administration Overseas* (July 1965), p. 165.

7. Prime Minister Tunku Abdul Rahman, *L.C. Proc.* 28 April 1962.

8. Cf. *Federation of Malaya, Dewan Ra'ayat Proceedings* (House of Representatives), 9 December 1960 (henceforward: *D.R. Proc.*).

9. *D.R. Proc.*, 28 May 1963.

10. On Malayan agricultural policy and the padi economy, see E.K. Fisk, "Features of the Rural Economy" and "Rural Development Policy" in T.H. Silcock and E.K. Fisk, eds., *The Political Economy of Independent Malaya* (Canberra, 1963).

11. Minister of Agriculture, *L.C. Proc.*, 5 December 1955, and 10 December 1958.

12. Minister of Agriculture, *L.C. Proc.*, 30 April 1958. Neither did Malaya enjoy comparative advantages in rice production, since rubber growing was a more remunerative crop at virtually all ranges of realizable prices: cf. Lim Chong Yah, *The Economic Development of Modern Malaya* (Kuala Lumpur, 1967), pp. 30-3.

13. Cf. Dato Haji Yahya, a successful Malay businessman and M.P., *L.C. Proc.*, 11 December 1958.

14. *L.C. Proc.*, 9 December 1958.

15. Minister of Agriculture, *L.C. Proc.*, 7 December 1957, Among the so-called "theory peddling" criticizers of Alliance policy were Ungku Aziz and T.H. Silcock.

16. Cf. *Federation of Malaysia, First Malaysia Plan* (Kuala Lumpur, 1965), para. 25. According to the Plan, agricultural "self sufficiency" as an immediate objective was deemed beyond reach, and the aim of policy was limited to increasing the domestic component of rice consumption. However in the Ministry of Agriculture, at least, there remained those who aspired to padi self-sufficiency by the early 1970s, upon completion of the large Muda River irrigation scheme: cf. Minister of Agriculture, *Straits Budget* 17 February 1967 and G.M. Gullick, *Malaysia* (London, 1969), p. 249.

17. On Malayan efforts to promote Community Development during the 1950s, see Ness, *Bureaucracy*, pp. 133-5.

18. Yang di-Pertuan Agong's Address, *L.C. Proc.*, 3 December 1958.

19. Minister for Economic Affairs, *L.C. Proc.*, 9 December 1955.

20. *L.C. Proc.*, 13 December 1958.

21. Minister of Agriculture, *L.C. Proc.*, 10 December 1957.

22. *L.C. Proc.*, 11 December 1958.

23. Lim Joo Kong (MCA), *D.R. Proc.*, 7 December 1962.

24. According to Abdul Aziz himself, a "reactionary clique" within the Alliance, including by implication UMNO as well as MCA leaders, conspired against his radical

measures to rid the peasantry of exploitation, demanding his "head on a plate": *D.R. Proc.*, 27 May 1963.

25. *Federation of Malaya Annual Report, 1956* (Kuala Lumpur, 1957), p. 431.

26. *Final Report of the Rice Committee* (Kuala Lumpur, 1956), para. 45.

27. Cf. Gullick, *Malaysia*, p. 249 on the prevalence of padi kuncha as a means of rural credit in contemporary Malaysia.

28. *Report of the Working Party set up to Consider the Development of New Areas for Land Settlement* (Kuala Lumpur, 1956), section 5.

29. According to the Ministry of Agriculture and Co-operatives, *Census of Agriculture* (Kuala Lumpur 1960), 68 percent of Malay farms were of under five acres, 22% were of between five and ten acres and 10% were of over ten acres. Given an "economic size" for padi farms of eight acres, only 17% of all Malay farms equalled or exceeded this size. See Ooi Jin Bee, *Land People and Economy in Malaya* (London, 1963), pp. 193-4 and R. Ho, "Land Ownership and Economic Prospects of Malayan Peasants", *Modern Asian Studies* Vol. 4 (1970), pp. 83-92 on the structure of land-holding in Malaya.

30. On the anti-development effect of Islamic land inheritance practices amongst Malays, see Fisk, "Rural Development Policy," p. 171. Mr. Fisk noted that there are cases in Malayan Land Office records where as many as 32 separate individuals have registered as heirowners of a single holding of under two acres.

31. *Report of the Working Party . . . (on) . . . New Areas for Land Settlement*, Para. 61, and J.J. Puthucheary, *Ownership and Control in the Malayan Economy* (Singapore, 1961), pp. 10-2.

32. Minister of Agriculture, *L.C. Proc.*, 7 December 1957.

33. *Vide.* Martin Rudner, "The State and Peasant Innovation in Rural Development: The Case of Malaysian Rubber," in Martin Rudner, ed. *Society and Development in Asia, Asian and Agrican Studies* Vol. 6 (1970).

34. Ibid. p. 432 *et passim.*

35. Cf. Yang di-Pertuan Agong's Address, *D.R. Proc.*, 23 May 1963.

36. *Straits Times*, 7 September 1962. See also U. Narkswasdi, *A Report to the Government of Malaysia on the Rice Economy of West Malaysia* (Rome, 1968).

37. *First Malaysian Plan*, para. 16.

38. Tan Siew Sin (Minister of Finance, 1956-69), *L.C. Proc.*, 17 March 1956.

39. *First Malaysia Plan*, paras, 87, 250 and Table 7-1.

40. Ibid., table 2-6.

41. Cf. T.H. Silcock, "General Review of Economic Policy", in Silcock and Fisk, eds., *Political Economy*, p. 243 *et passim*, on the anti-developmental role of vested interests.

42. *First Malaysia Plan*, para. 342. Bank Bumiputra had an initial government capitalization of only M$5 million, barely a fraction of total rural seasonal credit requirements. The new Federal Agricultural Marketing Authority had no direct responsibility for the marketing of rural produce but was apparently intended to play a general supervisory role. The establishment of proper government Marketing Boards to supplant private traders, mainly Chinese, was envisaged only as a "last resort."

43. Ibid., para. 25.

44. See Martin Rudner, "The Malaysian General Election of 1969: A Political Analysis", *Modern Asian Studies* Vol. 4 (1970), pp. 10-12 on the urban-rural balance

of electoral power in Malaya. Until 1962 the weighting exponent of rural constituencies was constitutionally limited to 30%. That year article 116 of the Federation Constitution was amended to allow a 50% differential between (mainly Malay) rural and (mainly non-Malay) urban constituencies.

45. Cf. Marvin L. Rogers, "Politicization and Political Development in a Rural Malay Community", *Asian Survey* (1969).

| CHAPTER 5

MALAYAN RUBBER POLICY:
Development And
Anti-Development
During the 1950s [1]

The 1950s constituted a turning-point in the history of Malayan rubber. This was marked by a changed world rubber market, along with incipient changes in Malayan economic aspirations and policies. Internationally, the creation of a large synthetic rubber industry in the main consuming country, the United States, posed a challenge to the competitive position and long-run prospects of Malayan plantation rubber. While coping with this challenge, the rubber industry, as the mainstay of the Malayan economy, had to simultaneously satisfy emergent claims for domestic development. Indeed, Malayan rubber was itself confronted with two coterminous developmental issues: its own internal development towards more efficient forms of production; and the provision of a resource base for the development of other economic and social sectors. By way of response to these cumulative challenges, a transformation occurred with respect to the government's role in Malaya's rubber economy, with rubber emerging as the linchpin of an evolving development strategy. In the process, the Malayan rubber plantation industry was to undergo a fundamental and wide-ranging structural transfiguration.

Like all revolutions, the developmental transformation of the Malayan rubber industry during the 1950s was born in an *ancien regime*, political and economic. Here, as elsewhere, vested interests and historical preconceptions inhibited the processes of change until their grip on policy was finally released. It has been argued that the reversal in Malayan rubber industry fortunes took place during the early post-war period, between the British return and Malayan independence in 1957.[2] However, the history of post-war Malayan rubber development was rather more complex than

Journal of Southeast Asian Studies, Vol. 8, No. 2 (September 1976).

that view suggests. As will be seen, the manner in which policy coped with the multiple challenges confronting Malayan rubber was very largely conditioned by the prevailing constellation of interests, institutions and attitudes, and was in that way linked to development in the political system. Policies introduced with constructive intent during the late 1940s were of but little effect, and had manifestly failed to reverse the general deterioration of the Malayan rubber economy by the mid-1950s. Nevertheless, important groundwork had been laid, so that the transition to self-government in 1955 soon led to a chain of innovative measures aimed at the broad-based modernization of the Malayan rubber industry. This chapter portrays the predominant economic issues and policy dilemmas that beset Malayan rubber during the first half of the 1950s, and examines the later policy and institutional changes that set in motion a development revolution in Malayan rubber during the second half of that decade.

A Recourse to Price Diplomacy

Malayan rubber prices were of deep and abiding concern to producers: to the Malayan government, as an *ad valorem* source of export tax revenue; and to the United Kingdom as a key element in the post-war sterling area balance of payments. Yet the world market for rubber was painfully slow to find its post-war equilibrium. Supply conditions in particular remained in flux during the late 1940s and early 1950s. Political turmoil in Indonesia affected producers there, while in the main consuming markets the war-spawned synthetic rubber industries had not only emerged as forceful competitors, but were furthermore buttressed by protective measures. The Korean War (1950-53) led to a short spell of extraordinarily high prices for rubber, as for other strategic commodities, but once this passed, rubber entered a longer-run trend of secular price decline interrupted by periodic peaks. Although there was no question of returning to the output restrictions and price cartels of the past, Malayan rubber interests, official as well as private, nevertheless concentrated their policy efforts during this unsettled period first and foremost on prices and markets. Only after the new realities of the post-war rubber market were driven home in the wake of the post-Korean War recession did the lingering faith in price diplomacy finally give way to a changed policy emphasis on rubber industry development proper.

Although free rubber marketing was ostensibly restored following the termination of the early post-war bulk purchase agreements, rubber prices were nonetheless still subject to indirectly administered controls. In the United States, synthetic rubber benefitted from both subsidies and mandatory usage requirements, which together served as limiting factors on the marketing of natural rubber. Malayan rubber producers complained bitterly against the American government's trade restrictions, claiming that they held no fears for fair competition with synthetic ("we have a better product to sell").[3] Denying that genuine considerations of national security were involved in the American policy, Malayan producers charged that a "highly cohesive" group of user industries were using their political influence to force lower prices onto natural rubber.[4] Still, the Malayan rubber estate industry could scarcely appear as the advocates of freely competitive marketing, since only the shortest of American memories could forget the pre-war restriction schemes.[5]

The Malayan and British governments for their part sought to persuade the United States of the vital importance of rubber pricing to the counter-insurgency campaign then being waged in Malaya. The Communist "Emergency" which broke out in 1948 was a heavy drain on Malayan government resources, especially when rubber prices and, therefore, tax revenues declined during the post-Korean War trade cycle. The Malayan colonial authorities tried to convince the American government that the latter's policy of effectively subsidizing synthetic rubber was proving an "embarrassment" to the Federation's plans for economic and social development.[6] American rubber policy was said to weaken Malaya's capacity to wage its anti-Communist effort in the economic and social spheres, a clarion call that was quickly taken up by the Malayan estate industry. This quest for higher prices for natural rubber was joined by the British government, which pressed the United States to avoid discriminating "artificially" for synthetic and against natural rubber.[7] But the American government and user industries remained unmoved by the plight of Malayan rubber, partly through a determination to avoid a recurrence of past dependency on outside suppliers of strategic commodities. However, this determination took on a tinge of bitterness embodying the unfortunate memories of past restriction schemes, prompting an American desire to teach the "British monopolists" a lesson.[8]

An embargo on rubber deliveries to China, imposed during the Korean War as part of a United Nations ban on the shipment of strategic goods to the Communist states, continued to restrict Malayan rubber marketing even after the termination of hostilities.[9]

Continuation of the embargo against China brought strong criticism from Malayan rubber interests, including the otherwise strongly anti-Communist British-owned estate companies. The embargo was blamed for part of the post-Korean War price decline, and Malayan producers demanded that either sales to China be permitted again or else the United States be asked to make up the absorption of natural rubber by curbing its output of synthetic. That Malaya alone should have to bear a disproportionate share of the burden of Western strategic sanctions against China was felt to be distinctly unfair. The influential *Straits Times* went even further to suggest that Malaya be allowed to sell rubber to China in exchange for much-needed rice, arguing that in any case the Chinese had access to other Southeast Asian rubber producers.[10] As the responsible British authorities refused to relent, the unilateral embargo on Malayan rubber exports to China remained in force until rescinded by the newly elected government in 1956.

Gradually, Malayans became reconciled to the post-war market situation, and their inability to influence supply conditions in order to gain higher prices. As faith in price diplomacy faded, policy attention began to shift towards promoting efficiency in production in order to ensure the competitive advantage of Malayan natural rubber against the constantly improving American synthetic product. At first, government efforts concentrated mainly on rubber research to develop high-yielding clones and more productive techniques.[11] Government exhorted producers to replant their obsolete acreage with high-yielding stands, and even offered to provide smallholders with improved planting materials at nominal cost, without, however, designing policy supports to overcome the financial and technical problems involved. Rather, rubber development still remained subordinate to the ultimate policy aim of securing higher rubber prices. Thus, in early 1950, the Malayan government could still "hope" that the aging process would soon take sufficient acreage out of production so as to reduce output and thereby keep prices high.[12] Prices, profits and tax revenues rather than national income, employment and economic growth, remained the primary criteria for rubber policy then.

It was the post-Korean War slump that finally brought the development imperative home to Malayan economic policy-makers. Indeed, rubber industry development was made into a double imperative, to compete on price terms with synthetic, and to contribute to national economic growth. The policy solution was not new, but was given new urgency: intensified renewal of rubber plantations through replanting with high-yielding clones. So changed were official attitudes by the mid-1950s that even short-term rises in the price of rubber came to be feared, lest these stimulate further expansion of synthetic capacity to the detriment of longer-run natural rubber marketing.[13] Price diplomacy had given way to the quest for rubber modernization.

From Stabilization Fund to Replanting Scheme

In the past, relatively little effort had been devoted to the systematic renewal of aging rubber stands on Malayan plantations, with the consequence that a considerable portion had become obsolete already by the late 1940s. Whatever systematic replanting had been undertaken represented the private initiative of a few larger, more progressively minded, mainly British estates. For the majority of estate companies, replanting remained a costly, secondary activity, reserved for periods of prosperity.[14] High taxes and inadequate profit margins were typically blamed for failure to replant.[15] Not many estates conceived of replanting in the proper context of a necessary and regular procedure for maintaining, if not increasing, productive capacity. In the smallholding sector conditions were even worse, despite the government's offer of 1948 to supply replanting materials at nominal cost. Financial and technical factors inhibited smallholder replanting generally, with the colonial Government otherwise remaining unresponsive to their needs.[16] Indeed, government still regarded replanting as a private, plantation owners' affair, and was itself somewhat ambivalent about replanting in any case. Despite official declarations encouraging replanting, certain economic policy circles still looked to onsetting obsolescence as a means of reducing Malayan output and thereby achieving permanently higher prices for rubber.[17] Obsessions with price persisted in diverting thought towards output restriction, with deleterious effects on developmental imperatives.

Then, at the peak of the Korean War rubber boom, the Malayan government proposed the establishment of a "Stabilization Fund" designed to take the edge off mounting inflationary pressures. Compulsory savings accumulated in the Stabilization Fund could afterwards be utilized to protect the rubber industry against cyclical price declines and, government included, to finance replanting. Notwithstanding this essentially counter-inflationary initial approach, the proposal was to make a historic departure in government policy towards the rubber industry of Malaya. For, in putting forward the Stabilization Fund the government assumed implicit responsibility for ensuring the future of Malaya's rubber economy through replanting.[18] Particular stress was placed on government's intention to promote rubber modernization in those segments of the industry where little had as yet been done. The key was to be replanting, which thereafter emerged as the central theme of Malayan rubber policy.

First reactions to the Stabilization Fund proposal from among the rubber estates were predictably negative. The rubber estates, led as they were by British-owned estate companies, strongly opposed the creation of a counter-cyclical reserve fund, regarding this simply as new taxation in disguise.[19] Moreover, the larger plantations professed no need for compulsory measures which, they argued, would merely interfere with their own replanting programmes.[20] A joint statement of the influential Rubber Growers' Association and Rubber Traders' Association, both of London, denounced the proposed Stabilization Fund as "radically unsound," albeit "well intentioned."[21] After intensive negotiations with the estate companies, the colonial government accepted an industry counter-proposal that part of the anti-inflationary export duty already levied in 1950 revert back to producers as a replanting subsidy. The Stabilization Fund proposal accordingly came to be transformed into a proper replanting scheme, with government's commitment extending beyond the trade cycle to sponsoring the modernization of the industry.

The replanting levy (officially termed a "Schedule II Cess"), graduated according to rubber export prices, was collected from the beginning of 1951, although deliberations on the administration of the replanting fund took up most of the remainder of the year. Spokesmen for the rubber smallholders advocated a greatly enlarged replanting effort, coupled to an appropriately increased cess, and in this obtained support from smaller, locally domiciled, financially weaker estate companies. This was rejected by the larger, mainly British-owned estates, out of opposition to its implied redistributive effect on rubber industry resources. To reconcile these divergent interests, the Rubber Producers' Council, the industry's newly established representative body, decided in favour of separate replanting schemes for estates and smallholdings. Under this arrangement, the existing cess was segregated into two funds, A and B, for estates and smallholdings, respectively, on the basis of their relative production. Each scheme was to have its own levies, with the smallholders obliged to pay an extra cess

(Schedule IV) into Fund B, and their own methods of disbursal.[22] The evident intent was to sponsor accelerated replanting on both estates and smallholdings, though without invoking a redistribution of rubber industry resources between the sectors.

Another point at issue concerned the management of the replanting funds. From the outset, representatives of the rubber industry opposed government control over the funds, insisting that the industry manage its own resources. Estates and smallholdings both apparently shared a fear, not without foundation in the light of the comparatively high incidence of taxation imposed on their industry, lest the replanting cess be transformed by Treasury involvement into yet another impost on rubber producers. Agreement was finally reached for the formation of an autonomous executive authority to administer the replanting funds, the Rubber Industry (Replanting) Board, on which the rubber producers, and even the estate sector alone, enjoyed majority representation.[23] Government consented to only a minority voice on the Board, while retaining the usual reserve powers over Board decisions. The Board and the dual replanting funds it administered finally became operative in March 1952.

On the eve of the creation of the replanting funds, a tardy Rubber Smallholders' Enquiry Committee submitted, at long last, its Final Report to the Malayan Federal Legislative Council.[24] Three-and-half years in preparation, its recommendations served merely to confirm existing policy trends, and were in substance as well as timing quite anti-climatic.

If the larger, British-owned estates generally saw little use for the replanting fund so far as they themselves were concerned, other producers received the introduction of the replanting scheme with enthusiasm. The smaller, domiciled, mainly Chinese estates praised the scheme as "the first genuine effort at rationalizing the rubber industry . . . [so] as to put it on a sound competitive basis."[25] Smallholders' spokesmen also welcomed the replanting scheme as promising competitive continuity for their sector of the industry. This constellation of support took on an ethnic-communal style characteristic of the Malayan political economy. Malay communal leaders' sensitivity to the weak economic position of Malay smallholders, typically the smallest and poorest segment, and who composed about half the total number of smallholders, projected potentially powerful political aspirations onto the replanting scheme.[26] The Malay States, as federal partners and institutional expressions of traditional Malay society, also evinced a strong interest in replanting policy, especially as it affected smallholders.[27] This budding concern from among the Malay elite was to have a broad, long-run significance for rubber development in Malaya.

The Rubber Replanting Scheme, 1952-55

The Rubber Industry (Replanting) Ordinance, No. 8 of 1952, constituted the enabling legislation for the new rubber replanting scheme. Although signalling an innovation in policy intent, the new legislation still retained the long-standing administrative differentiation between estate and smallholding sectors of the industry. Replanting policy towards estates was to be limited to built-in automatic fiscal incentives, whereas policy towards smallholdings involved a comparatively high degree of administrative intervention and direction in replanting operations. This distinction in policy treatment reflected the legacy of colonial administrative bias, which considered the mainly foreign-owned, company estates to be the efficient, modern form of plantation enterprise, while smallholdings were typically dismissed as alien, peasant and in a way marginal to the industry.[28] Yet, the retention of this policy distinction, which was based on a structural illusion rather than on the empirical functioning of the two sectors, imposed in effect a bureaucratic constraint upon development capabilities. Continued adherence to *a priori* administrative differentiation restricted the possibility within the estate sector and between it and the smallholding sector, thus binding replanting policy to the structural continuity of the Malayan Rubber industry.

Underlying the economic policies of the colonial administration was a conception of development tied to the institutional status quo.[29] Thus, the rubber replanting scheme and its development bearings were implicitly envisaged in the context of the unchanging organization of the Malayan rubber plantation industry. Certainly there was no thought at the time of fomenting wide-ranging reforms in the ownership or holding patterns of the rubber industry. Still less was there any intention of introducing innovation on a scale that might jeopardize any vested interests. Rather, the framework of the replanting scheme was designed in essence to protect and preserve the existing structure of the rubber industry, in particular by ensuring the future competitive position and asset values of estate companies. Replanting accordingly came to be viewed primarily as a technical device, whose economic developmental significance was effectively circumscribed by the discriminatory designing of policy.

Bound as it was by established criteria, the original replanting scheme proved incapable of advancing the twin elements behind the modernization of Malayan rubber: large-scale asset renewal and the furtherance of comparative advantage. A substantial segment of Malaya's rubber acreage had reached obsolescence by the early 1950s, and stood in urgent need of renewal. The need was most acute on smallholdings, owing to the legacy of discrimination and neglect. At the same time, the long-run competitive capabilities of the Malayan industry required that modernization be directed towards the more efficient classes of producers. However, the structural rigidity built into the 1952 replanting scheme prevented the mobility of resources necessary to fulfil the "need" and "efficiency" criteria for rubber redevelopment. Instead, the scheme geared replanting to the established pattern of rubber industry privilege and protection.

Replanting policy towards the estate sector provided automatic fiscal inducements to replant. Apart from financial incentives, there was no other control or aim embodied in policy. Fund A rules allowed estates full and automatic rebates of their Schedule II cess upon proof of replanting, and made an unconditional refund of their additional (Schedule IV) cess. Furthermore, estate companies were entitled to deduct replanting expenses from their income tax liabilities.[30] This policy approach would seem to indicate the government had accepted the estate companies' line of argument that further intervention was unnecessary since replanting ostensibly was already a regular undertaking on estates. In fact, not all estates practiced systematic replanting. Many, especially the smaller firms, replanted only when they thought they could afford to. Because the replanting cess was directly proportional to the price of rubber, its yield would decline just when falling company revenues tended to reduce their inclination for replanting, so that the incentive element in the scheme tended to disappear during the long downward phase of the rubber trade cycle.[31]

As it emerged, the greater portion of repayments under the scheme went precisely to those more efficient, progressively managed estates having relatively higher productivity and regular replanting procedures.[32] Conversely, estates bordering on obsolescence, whose output was comparatively low and the need for replanting most urgent, received inadequate aid. Replanting policy thus tended to widen, rather than narrow, the modernization gap in the estate sector. Reactions to the Fund A scheme generally showed this disappointment. By 1954, disillusioned Chinese planters, generally the smaller, weaker estates, called publicly for a revision of the estate replanting scheme.[33] Meanwhile, the British companies' Rubber Growers' Association, was said to be unimpressed with the scheme as it stood.[34]

Smallholdings received separate and unequal treatment under the replanting scheme. Proceeds from smallholders' Schedule II and IV cesses were collected in Fund B for distribution to cover a portion of the cost only of *approved* replanting.[35] Reimbursement was not automatic as in the case of the estates' Fund, but was contingent upon bureaucratic authorization in each instance. Since federal government proposals for centrally directed, large-scale block replanting had not attracted support from the Rubber Smallholders' Enquiry Committee, it was decided instead to base the smallholding replanting scheme on individual smallholder enterprise.[36] The target for smallholding replanting was set at 500,000 acres over a six-year period, or about a third the total smallholding acreage.[37] According to Fund B rules, the smallholders were to initiate their own replanting and apply for approval and a conditional grant, which would cover two-thirds of the administratively determined "standard" cost, to the amount of M$400 per acre.[38] Hence the scheme neither completely assured nor fully covered the enterprising smallholder's replanting.

Smallholding replanting policy failed to take account of the structural, technical and socio-economic difficulties of asset renewal in a peasant plantation economy. No distinction was made between "medium" holdings of 25-100 acres, and the very small holdings of under 25 acres, which comprised over 80% of the smallholding area (1952), despite fundamental differences in capabilities and scale between them.[39] The Replanting Board argued correctly that replanting was technically feasible even on 3.5 acre holdings, the average size. However, what was technically feasible had proved to be overly onerous socially and economically, since replanting on such a small scale required sustained hard labour, exacting standards of maintenance, and deferment of income for six years until the new trees matured. It is hardly surprising in the circumstances that most applications for Fund B grants came from medium holdings, and even (illicitly) from subdivided estates.[40] Very small holders generally considered the replanting grant insufficient, even though it had been raised to M$500 an acre in mid-1955. Of those who did replant, a good number could not uphold the officially required standards of maintenance and consequently had their grants revoked.[41] Since few of the very small holdings were able to take advantage of the scheme, Fund B became in effect a regressive form of taxation on the whole smallholding sector to subsidize approved replanting on a few, mainly larger holdings.[42] The low rate of peasant participation caused the smallholding replanting scheme to lag behind, so that less than half the target of 150,000 acres was achieved up to the end of 1955.[43]

To some extent the lag in estate and perhaps even more so, smallholding, replanting during the early 1950s may have been due to the Emergency conditions. Yet, though it is impossible to determine the then effect of insurgency and counter-insurgency operations on producers' behaviour, the evidence suggests that rubber policy and institutional practices were rather more to blame for the poor state of Malaya's rubber economy at mid-decade.

Replanting policy during the period under review had a generally regressive distributive effect on the allocation of resources, and future income, in the Malayan rubber economy. Due to the segregation of replanting funds there was no redistribution of rubber industry resources between estates and smallholdings, the latter being the more needy overall. Indeed, the scheme ensured that high output producers among the estates, typically the best off, received the largest proportion of replanting grants. In the smallholding sector, though, a more distinctly retrogressive distributive mechanism applied, whereby replanting funds contributed by the sector as a whole went for the most part to better-off medium-sized holdings able to replant. This line of policy left the weaker estates and very small holdings in a relatively inferior position, whose inferiority was bound to deteriorate further as the regressive distributive impact of the replanting scheme accumulated over time.

Government policy also sought to utilize smallholder replanting to further other objectives, not necessarily consistent with peasant economic interests. Concerned over the excessive dependence of Malaya on rubber exports, the colonial authorities considered that smallholders should be transferred away from rubber cultivation, whose long-run prospects were felt to be "uncertain."[44] Fund B rules accordingly provided for replanting with approved crops other than rubber. The colonial Director of Agriculture, an official member of the Replanting Board and himself a leading advocate of diversification, had even declared his intention to encourage smallholders to replant with alternative crops.[45] Subsequently, the onus of diversification fell most heavily on peasant replanting. "Suitability of soil," rather than considerations of economic advantage, served as the main criterion for directing rubber smallholders to replant with other crops.[46] Support for this form of diversification came from the rubber estates (who themselves preferred to remain in that industry) and even from the Malay State governments.[47] In the event, "all possible encouragement" was given to redirecting smallholders away from rubber,[48] so that over 10% of the smallholding replanting that took place throughout 1955 involved other, officially approved crops.[49] Yet none of these alternatives promised smallholders similar returns to high-yielding rubber tress.[50] It was a curious twist of policy that the smallholders' own contributions to the replanting fund were used to induce their removal from that industry where they enjoyed a comparative economic advantage.

The introduction of the replanting scheme did not lead to a reconsideration of government's negative policy towards *new* planting in new areas as a means of expanding Malaya's high-yielding rubber acreage. While the previous ban on land alienation for rubber had been rescinded in mid-1947, hardly any additional land was released throughout 1955.[51] This impinged less on the larger estates, which usually possessed reserve lands for new planting. However, there existed among smallholders a widespread hunger for land for new rubber planting. In contrast with the difficulties of smallholding replanting, new rubber planting was especially attractive to peasants. Many were ready to undertake the necessary investment if land were obtainable.[52] A similar interest was shown by smaller, Chinese-owned estates. New planting thus had potentially significant social as well as economic advantages for Malayan development. Nevertheless, the authority over land remained conservative and restricting.

A powerful constellation of vested landed interests militated against any changes in the long-standing policy negation of new rubber planting. For one thing, agricultural diversification *away from* rubber was the economic slogan of the day. For another, land policy was in the constitutional jurisdiction of the Malay States and Settlements. The Malay States, in particular, retained a custodial interest in land, especially in the ethno-cultural quality of rural life. There existed a powerful predilection among the traditional Malay elite to preserve intact the Malay kampung society, rooted as it was in customary rice cultivation. This cultural fixation on the kampung tradition invoked restraints on Malay peasant initiative, especially against rubber planting with its implications for rural modernization and social change.[53] Nor were the Malay States eager to release their sovereign lands to non-Malays.

As for the federal government, whose policy leverage was not inconsiderable, there was reluctance to incur the infra-structural development costs of new settlement, and also a concern to uphold the capital values of existing rubber plantations.[54] Federal government opposition to new planting also derived from a Forestry Department determined to defend Malaya's timber reserves, though without having taken a proper economic accounting of this policy.[55] Demands for a more positive approach to new planting were turned down, with the excuse of avoiding "shifting cultivation."[56] New planting therefore remained outside the scope of the Rubber Replanting Fund, at least as far as smallholders were concerned, though estates could and did obtain Fund A rebates for planting their reserve lands.

Governmental strictures on their economic initiative impelled peasants towards illicit rubber planting, which increased over the years and was estimated to total a quarter-million acres by 1955.[57] Most of this consisted of inferior, unselected seedlings, which meant increased acreage but retarded modernization.

Rubber policy, by inadequately treating the needs of smallholder development, by encouraging redeployment towards other crops and discouraging new rubber planting, brought about a

TABLE 1
Summary Data on Rubber Replanting to 1955.

Total Rubber Planted Acreage, 1955 (thousand acres):

estates	2025
smallholdings	1650

Estates high yield acreage, 1955 (percent of total estate planted area):

immature	15.0%
mature	26.4%

Smallholdings Replanting Objectives, 1953-55 (thousand acres):

	Target	Actual
1953	40	29.5
1954	50	22.0
1955	60	25.3
Total	150	77.4

Smallholders actual replanting as proportion of total acreage = 4.7%
Illicit smallholding new planting: 250,00 acres (est.), or 15.1% of total smallhoding acreage.

Source: *Rubber Statistics Handbooks*, adapted.

grievous deterioration of the smallholding assets and with it declining productivity. By 1955 over half the smallholding acreage was over 30 years old, the point where diminishing returns set in, while less than 8% consisted of high-yielding stands.[58] What was worse in terms of Malaya's delicate communal balance was that the weakest, most vulnerable smallholdings were typically Malay-owned.[59] Prevailing rubber policy hence served to exacerbate Malay feelings of relative deprivation. Smallholders had also to endure the bias of other aspects of government policy which affected transportation and marketing in particular.[60] Ironically, government acts of omission and commission towards rubber smallholding had the effect of weakening that very sector which enjoyed a measure of freedom from the worst socio-economic afflictions of peasant agriculture.[61] Instead of pursuing the advantage, the structurally rigid colonial rubber policy in effect served to stifle a latent peasant potential for rural development.

The Political Turning-Point: The Mudie Mission and 1955 General Election

The worsening plight of the Malayan rubber industry during the first half of the 1950s, when prices fell drastically from their Korean War boom peak, gave rise to calls for a public inquiry. Concern was prompted by reduced wage rates on plantations, falling smallholder income, a weakening government revenue base and a deteriorating competitive position for Malayan rubber internationally. Yet, the influential British estate sector stood adamantly opposed to any new departure in government policy towards rubber, and framed its opposition in characteristically scathing and self-righteous terms:

> Great pressure is being brought to bear by some antagonistic journalists and educational leaders in Singapore for a fact-finding mission into the rubber industry. The only apparent reason for this campaign is ignorance on the part of its instigators and jealousy that the industry does not conform to their (socialist) political ideals but has been brilliantly successful.[62]

> . . .

> The estate sector has nothing to fear from such an inquiry and it is difficult to understand the necessity for it.[63]

By mid-1954, however, the pressures for an inquiry had become overwhelming as the fortunes of rubber sank to a trough. Moving shrewdly, the estate companies manoeuvred the Rubber Producers' Council alongside the Federal Government jointly to appoint a Mission of Enquiry under Sir Francis Mudie, with explicit and narrow terms of reference. The Mudie Mission reported in October 1954, making urgent recommendations on taxation and planting policy: "This is probably the last chance that a large part of the natural rubber industry will have of setting its house in order before the storm breaks. . . . It is no exaggeration to say that if the rubber industry were to be allowed to fall into irretrievable senility Malaya's present type of developing economy would collapse."[64]

Initial reactions to the Mudie Mission recommendations were mixed. Government recognized the vital need for an expanded replanting effort, but demurred over accepting reduced rubber taxation.[65] British estate representatives dismissed the recommendations as "far fetched."[66] Yet not even the fortuitous rubber boom of 1955 could disguise for long the seriousness of the long-term challenge confronting the aging Malayan rubber economy from the now denationalized, increasingly efficient American synthetic industry, and from the growing West African natural rubber stake. It remained for imminent political developments to attune Malayan rubber policy to the imperatives of economic modernization and structural change.

In the event, the transition from colonial to elected self-government proved to be the hammer of policy change, with the Mudie Mission Report serving as the anvil for forging new policy directions. Indeed, the advent of constitutional change had itself, in advance of the elections and the attendant political reorganization, infused the outgoing colonial authority with renewed energies. Even in the last remaining months of their *ancien regime*, colonial officialdom took up the challenge of rubber with a White Paper giving directives for future policy development.[67] The Mudie Mission had emphasized the need to achieve a maximum rate of rubber production at lowest per-unit cost by no later than 1964, when synthetic rubber prices were expected to fall. The solution was seen in urgent, accelerated replanting measures: "There is no time to lose and . . . everything must be done to replant as large an area as possible as quickly as possible."[68] The urgency of the rubber situation was multiplied by the urgency of political change. Working against time, and with the zeal of those whose mission has been revealed, the twilight colonial administration moved to stabilize the rubber industry and determine its future directions, before handing over to a novice, nationalist elected authority.

This residuary British interest in Malayan rubber development undoubtedly reflected not merely an abiding concern for fixed corporate assets, but also for longer-run hard currency earnings of the Sterling area (to which soon-independent Malaya remained committed). The Colonial Office kept abreast of policy deliberations and concurred in the invigorated replanting programme, provided always that the federal Malayan government ensured itself against revenue losses.[69] Consequently, the federal Government rejected on revenue grounds the Mudie Mission recommendation that rubber export duties be reduced and even abolished at lower price levels, as a means of revitalizing the industry. Instead, the sliding rates of export duty were decreased slightly at lower price ranges, and raised correspondingly at higher prices, together with the levy of an anti-inflationary cess.[70]

Rubber still remained Malaya's fiscal milch cow. Without denying accusations of tax discrimination, the federal Government sought to justify its policy position by insisting on the importance of rubber revenues to the Treasury, "which cannot be replaced."[71] Moreover, it was argued that the smallholding sector was too "inefficient" to be able to capitalize on tax benefits. Apparently the colonial authorities' interest in modernizing the rubber industry paled before the vested interest in maintaining Malaya's old revenue system substantially unaltered. It was characteristic of colonial Malaya's political economy that fiscal preservation should have precedence over development of national income.

Ironically, the modernizing inspiration of the late colonial officialdom was met by attitudinal ambivalence from the Alliance Party heirs to power, and particularly its United Malays National Organization (UMNO) senior partner. To be sure, expatriate officers serving the elected government, among them the Economic Adviser, had reached the conclusion that only a rejuvenated rubber industry could ensure acceptable levels of income and employment for the future.[72] However, the UMNO leadership, for its part, clung to the view that Malaya must be freed from the vagaries of the world commodity market through agricultural diversification leading to food (i.e., rice) self-sufficiency.[73] The Malay bias against rubber persisted down to the Second FYP period (1961-65), when the then Minister of Rural Development (later Prime Minister), Abdul Razak, could still insist that the problem of rural development was essentially one of relieving peasants of their "dependency" on rubber.[74] The Malay elite tended to regard rubber planting as an alien, "capitalist" venture, and indicated a strong cultural preference for rice cultivation in the traditional kampung way. Interestingly, it was Malay spokesmen from the more backward, mainly rice-growing east coast states who argued for rubber planting as the key to regional economic progress. By way of reconciling divergent opinions, the Alliance government opted to pursue both sides against the middle, to strive towards agricultural diversification and rice self-sufficiency, while proceeding to deal with the more pressing problems confronting rubber development. It is hardly surprising, in the circumstances, that policy initiatives apropos the rubber economy took shape slowly, and then cautiously.

The Gradual Revolution: The Revised Replanting Scheme

Estate company objections to certain of the Mudie Mission recommendations led the Rubber Producers' Council to offer its own replanting scheme as a counter-proposal. This was rejected in turn by government as being quite inadequate to the task envisaged. (Nevertheless, the government agreed not to extend the four and one-half cents per lb. smallholding cess to estates as well, as had been recommended by the Mudie Mission Report.) Instead, the colonial authorities proceeded to draft an expanded replanting scheme with the underlying intention of providing assistance where most needed. The declared objective was to enable the weaker segments of Malaya's rubber industry to redevelop into efficient, high-output producers.

The revised replanting scheme, calling for a M$280 million investment over a seven-year period, was introduced in June 1955, following a lengthy Federal Legislative Council debate during which the parties competing for the coming general election contributed surprisingly little. Like its predecessor, the revised scheme comprised two distinct programmes, for estates and for smallholdings. Estates were to benefit from a M$400 per acre grant, to be paid automatically for all replanting done up to a maximum of 21% of their planted acreage. By basing the estate sector's replanting grants on *actual* replanting instead of on past production rates as hitherto, and by imposing an acreage ceiling, the scheme redirected a greater share of Fund A resources towards the more needy plantations. In the estate sector, at least, a "need" standard for replanting policy had begun to apply.

This "need" standard did not at the time pertain equally to smallholding replanting policy. Replanting funds under the revised scheme were still allocated between estate and smallholdings sectors according to their relative production, with 60% going to the former. This allocative formula in effect penalized smallholders for the discriminatory policies they suffered in the past, and for their consequently greater present needs. Although smallholders were to be given a higher replanting grant, set initially at M$600 an acre, this was not automatic upon evidence of replanting (as with estates) but still required prior application and follow-up inspection. Furthermore, in line with the Alliance diversification goal, smallholders were still being "encouraged" to replant wherever feasible with crops other than rubber, the criteria being soil quality rather than income potential.[75]

The revised replanting scheme was subsequently integrated into self-governing Malaya's First FYP (1956-61).[76] In fact replanting became the largest single development item in the Plan, amounting to almost 15% of its target expenditure for the quinquennium. Although in policy terms, the revised scheme was not a substantive departure from the original scheme, the amounts spent achieved a new significance during the course of Plan implementation. Quantitative increase reached the point of, and resulted in, qualitative innovation. The very momentum of the replanting scheme yielded a substantial modernizing thrust, impelling a broad-based development of the Malayan rubber industry.

As in other fields of economic policy, the attitudes and responses of the various enterprises engaged in rubber cultivation conditioned the acceptance, and eventually the performance, of the revised scheme. The leading British estate companies generally received with disfavour this act of government involvement in the affairs of their traditionally individualistic industry. Those estates that were already substantially modernized condemned the measure as redundant.[77] What was more, the more predatory planters among them dismissed the scheme as downright "inequitable," since by assisting the weak to replant, it would serve to preserve the existing industrial structure against further "consolidation" by the strong.[78] Some also reiterated the long-standing fear of "overproduction," causing industrial recession, if a large proportion of Malaya's rubber acreage should be replanted with high-yielding trees. To such as these, government would have done best to concentrate instead on "law and order and on an equitable system of taxation," and leave the rubber industry alone.[79]

There were those British estates which went further to oppose entirely what they condemned as the "soon ripe, soon rotten" principle of replanting.[80] Their managerial style had been bred during the Great Depression, when the art of survival rested on minimizing labour costs per unit output. Bound by this legacy of insecurity and defensiveness, these estates rejected the more comprehensive input-output calculations inherent in the replanting scheme and adapted to the changing real world rubber marketing situation. Even among those British-owned estates that supported replanting, there existed a fear, sometime articulated, usually latent, that the advent of representative, responsible government to Malaya might bring about, sooner or later, a change in official attitudes towards private overseas investment.[81] In the event, the economic realities of rubber industry modernization were soon to overtake those lacking in courage or conviction.

As a result of the revised replanting scheme, the average annual rate of replanting in the estate sector doubled during the five years after 1956, compared to the previous quinquennium.[82] In part, this improvement reflected the progressive amelioration of Emergency conditions in the rural areas. Yet the main impulse of industrial modernization, and the explanation for its variations, seem to come from rubber policy. As before, the best replanting performance was generally turned out by the larger, more progressively managed estates. Indeed, by the end of the decade those same British planters who had earlier dismissed the replanting scheme now praised the "active and far-sighted" government policy, even expressing their "debt of gratitude."[83] In addition, many estates which had previously defaulted on replanting and incapable financially of modernizing on their own, were now able to use the opportunity of the scheme to begin redevelopment, many, but not all.

A number of estates still did not replant, preferring to disinvest through enlarged dividend payments instead of reinvesting in asset renewal.[84] Some of these estates were so aged that they had become economically unviable—except for asset capitalization —even if replanted up to the 21% ceiling. By 1960 there were some 530 estates, including 11 British-owned, and totalling 103,000 acres, with no high-yielding acreage at all.[85]

For smallholders, the revised replanting scheme brought about virtually the redemption of that sector's competitive economic advantages. Once the low-cost rubber producers, smallholders' comparative advantages were reversed by pre-war regulations and post-war restrictions on planting.[86] By mid-1955 the smallholding sector had consequently come to be regarded as the "comparatively inefficient" sector,[87] though the potential was still there. So grave was the situation that some Malayan political leaders foresaw a "danger of a big social and political upheaval" in the countryside.[88] Smallholding replanting emerged as a critical policy key designed to revitalize that sector while ensuring rural stability. For the Malayan Chinese Association (MCA) partners in government, the revised smallholding replanting scheme had the additional attribute of serving Malay socio-economic advancement without necessarily encroaching on the economic position of non-Malays.

In order to stimulate smallholding replanting, the revised Fund B sought to cope with the structural and technical difficulties inherent in that sector. Generally, smallholders whose applications were authorized received a M$600 per acre grant for up to a third of their acreage. Smallholders working less than 30 acres were entitled to replant a third plus an additional five acres. Smallholdings of under five acres were to be permitted to new plant an equivalent area of up to five acres, so that they would be assured subsistence, provided they undertook to cut down their old trees once the new, high-yielding rubber matured. Replanting policy thus allowed the thin edge of the new planting wedge, except that new planting was tied as a "special case" substitute to replanting, limited in scope, purpose and material effect on the peasant rubber economy.[89]

In another move, the elected government helped set up a Malayan Council of Smallholders Associations, as a sectoral industrial association designed to mobilize the smallholding constituency for replanting, and to service communications with the authorities.[90]

Smallholding replanting under the revised scheme during the First FYP showed a three-fold increase over the 1950-55 period. Smallholdings owned by Chinese and Indians replanted "reasonably well" by virtue of the revised scheme. Nevertheless, replanting still failed to attract many of the poorest Malay smallholders.[91] About three-quarters of the Malay smallhold acreage remained untouched even by the revised scheme. For the very small and poorer peasants, inadequate finance and onerous regulatory procedures still loomed as imposing obstacles to replanting. As smallholding replanting lagged behind schedule and the 1959 General Election approached, the government made an electoral gesture of accelerating the payment of grants under Fund B. But this merely expedited things for those better-off smallholders already participating in the scheme, without solving the difficulties of those worse off who still could not replant. For them government preferred to rely on conventional blandishments and increased replanting propaganda, with doubtful effect. By 1960 only 310,000 acres of the original six-year smallholding target of 480,000 acres were replanted; of this, less than a third was undertaken by Malays.[92]

The revised smallholding replanting scheme, like its predecessor, served as a redistributive mechanism for transferring the compulsory savings of poor smallholders to further replanting on better-off medium holdings. As a result, inequalities within the smallholding sector increased, with the weakest smallholdings left in a deteriorating position. However, while the problem of the unrelieved poor was still pressing, the smallholding sector as a whole had indeed succeeded in turning the corner towards rubber redevelopment. The overall sectoral decline had been halted, and even reversed. Indeed, the very resilience exhibited by their propensity for modernization had thrust the smallholding sector into the fore-

TABLE 2
Rubber Estate Smallhold
Planted Acreage, 1945-1966 (thousand acres).

Year	Total	Estates	Smallholdings	Percent Smallholding
1947	3325	1945	1580	47.5
1950	3551	1964	1587	44.7
1955	3675	2025	1650	44.9
1960	3848	1942	1960	50.9
1966	4342	1813	2529	58.2

Source: *Rubber Statistics Handbooks*, adapted.

front of the independent Malayan development effort. Rubber smallholding had emerged by the 1960s as a leading growth sector, and this in turn heralded the structural revolution which was to transform the smallholding sector into the mainstay of the Malayan rubber economy during the subsequent decade.

Malaya's acreage under high-yielding rubber, mature and immature, grew during the First FYP from 30 to 46% of the total rubber area.[93] This was chiefly a result of replanting. Rubber replanting was subsequently described as the "outstanding economic achievement" of the First FYP. Later, economic planners noted that the revised replanting scheme had made Malaya into "the most progressive and efficient producer of natural rubber in the world—able to compete effectively and profitably in world markets against the mounting rivalry of synthetic rubber."[94] Replanting had clearly revealed the potentials of modern plantation and peasant initiative for rural economic development. Admittedly, the revised scheme did not depart radically from the policy lines of the original, less-successful colonial replanting scheme; nonetheless it constituted a quantitative leap forward in rates of investment and participation, which induced a qualitative change in the organization and performance of the Malayan rubber economy. Taking its cue, the Second FYP (1961-65) invoked a more intensified replanting programme aimed at furthering the redevelopment of the rubber industry, especially among very small holdings.

By-Products of the Revolution: New Planting and Subdivision

The revised replanting scheme and rubber objectives of the First FYP related primarily to replanting, yet the prevailing conception of large-scale asset renewal opened the door, however slightly at first, to fresh policy initiatives in the direction of new rubber planting. What began as a hesitant and conditional concession to economic reality led, by virtue of the legitimization resulting from policy acceptance, to inevitable economic, social and political pressures for expanding Malaya's rubber acreage. The long-standing colonial government opposition to new planting began to bend following the Mudie Mission's recommendation that new planting be permitted in order to attract investment to the rubber industry.[95] Accelerated capital formation in rubber was deemed essential to maintain per capita incomes at a time of rapid population growth. While the colonial authorities still refused to allow unfettered new planting, lest it pare down the capital values of private and public investment in already established areas, but they grudgingly conceded new planting in "special circumstances," provided this would not be "detrimental to the replanting scheme taken as a whole."[96] The newly elected Alliance government subsequently accepted this "principle" of new planting. Yet acceptance of the principle did not yet produce new policy initiatives, for rubber policy was still officially perceived in terms of replanting and redevelopment rather than development anew.

Alliance government policy regarding new rubber planting began on this cautious and conservative footing. New planting, to the extent permitted, was tied for the most part to the revised replanting scheme. Estates were allowed to plant on their reserve lands, and then only up to 21% of their existing planted acreage. Smallholding new planting was restricted to those units of less than five acres, subject to the conditions of the replanting scheme for very small holdings. Meanwhile, the Malay States' governments justified their unwillingness to make land grants for rubber planting by insisting that they were merely adhering to federal government policy directives urging that new planting be denied in favour of replanting.[97] One Malay State, Negri Sembilan, did announce its preparedness to grant land for estate new planting, but not for smallholdings.[98] The State's leadership based this discriminatory policy on the professed desire to protect traditional Malay *kampung* life from dependency on a cyclical cash crop, claiming always that their custodial outlook was consistent "with the wishes of the people."

Even so, estate planters and peasant smallholders alike indicated their strong desire for new lands for rubber planting.[99] They were joined by peasants eager to gain entry into the rubber economy, and by the National Union of Plantation Workers concerned to broaden their employment base. Yet, if many estates still had reserve lands on which to plant, smallholders (and would-be smallholders) complained of the inability to acquire land for rubber.[100] Indeed one angry rural Malay parliamentarian went so far as to accuse Federal Agriculture officials of sinister "ulterior motives" in redirecting Malay peasants away from rubber to other, less remunerative crops.[101] On the economically backward east coast, Malay spokesmen called for the accelerated extension of new rubber planting as their vehicle for regional development, arguing justifiably that existing replanting schemes benefitted mainly the more developed west coast areas already under rubber.[102] With pressure mounting, the state governments tried to link their custodial land policies to national rubber policy, thereby shifting political accountability over to the federal government. This served in effect to bolster the authority of the centre just at a time when economic policy conceptions were in the throes of post-independence change towards a more resolute development goal orientation.[103]

Following the Report of a Working Party on Land Settlement and the Development of New Areas, which had been set up by the newly elected Alliance government, a Federal Land Development Authority (FLDA) was established in 1956.[104] Though designed to promote land settlement first and foremost, FLDA was committed to ensuring settlers' economic viability through planting with remunerative crops, particularly rubber.[105] FLDA settlement schemes were carried out by clearing large tracts of virgin land and preparing it for subdivision into 10-acre family holdings, of which eight acres were planted with high-yielding rubber and the remainder with fruit trees, padi, etc. All economic and social services for the settlement areas were supplied or coordinated by FLDA, which also provided settlers with maintenance loans until maturation of their rubber, when repayment was to begin by installments. FLDA schemes were intended to combine the efficiency of rubber smallholding with the economies of estate-type scale. Although difficulties over land and finance kept FLDA from realizing its original target, 22 settlement schemes involving 30,000 acres and 3,500 families, mostly poor Malays, were under development by the end of the First FYP period.[106] If the gilt was perhaps tarnished by the settler indebtedness incurred during the course of settlement, nevertheless the development prospects were believed to warrant a substantial expansion in the scope and magnitude of FLDA operations under the Second FYP.[107]

Of even greater development significance, however, was the separation of new planting from the replanting scheme, and its incorporation into a strategy of expanding the rubber frontier.

The separation was achieved in fact by FLDA, but the re-integration of new rubber planting as part of an expansionary land policy had to await the further evolution of independent Malaya's nascent political leadership and their economic philosophies. One of the early advocates of a national development strategy based on new rubber planting was the influential estate planter and MCA back-bencher in the newly elected Federal Legislative Council, Tan Siew Sin. In parliamentary deliberations, Tan advocated accelerated new rubber planting, "as fast and as much as possible," as the most suitable means of solving Malaya's two most pressing problems: domestic economic stagnation and Malay peasant poverty.[108] Appointed Minister of Commerce and Industry in mid-1957, he set about devising an expansionary new rubber planting policy designed to induce capital formation at a high aggregate rate, but of broad social and ethnic composition, on an expanding agricultural frontier. This policy envisaged the planting of one million acres of high-yielding rubber over the decade, and called upon the states to make available the necessary land.[109] The very immensity of the new planting target emphasized the moment of policy change.

While FLDA settlements comprised the cornerstone of federal new planting programmes, other measures were also introduced for new rubber planting in the neighbourhood of already settled areas. A Smallholder New Planting Scheme inaugurated in January 1958, provided federal financial support for block new planting undertaken under state auspices on the fringes of existing settlements of up to 75,000 acres. Block planting constituted a reversal of long-standing colonial policy opposition to this form of combined smallholding undertaking, and was intended to ensure the quality of smallholding plantations developed under the scheme. The states were of course expected to make lands available. Some 186,000 acres of fringe land was actually planted with rubber over the first five years.[110]

In April 1961, a modified fringe scheme was introduced to cater to the needs of very small holdings. In a separate development, the state government of Kelantan, controlled by the opposition Pan-Malayan Islamic Party, adopted an alternative policy of allowing lands for new rubber planting by pioneer settlers.[111] Agricultural diversification still remained an article of faith, to be sure, but the pattern of rural development that had crystallized during the later 1950s stressed the growing momentum of peasant involvement specifically in the rubber economy, through intensified asset renewal and expansionary new planting.

TABLE 3
Rubber New Planting, 1958-1963 (thousand acres).

Year	Estates	Smallholdings	Total
1958	13.9	10.8	24.7
1959	14.1	20.9	35.0
1960	21.7	25.1	46.8
1961	17.7	67.4	85.1
1962	10.0	82.5	92.5
1963	8.7	100.3	109.0
	86.1	307.0	393.1
of which FLDA:		197.0	

Source: *Rubber Statistical Handbook*, 1964

Clearly, with the advent of self-government the political power of the British estate companies and colonial retainers had dwindled, and with it the capacity of vested interests to forestall the expansion of the smallholding stake in Malaya's rubber industry.

Progress towards the renewed development of Malaya's rubber industry, even during the later 1950s, was by no means linear. Even as policy innovations were being introduced in the areas of replanting and new planting, an increasingly widespread phenomenon of estate subdivision was retarding, and to some extent even reversing, the development process. Estate subdivision reached critical proportions after 1957, so that by 1960 numerous plantations had been fragmented through resale to rentiers and speculators. The reasons for the foreign, mainly British, estate companies' disposal of their holdings in the manner were to be found in the deepening doubts over their ability to compete in future in world rubber markets, compounded by anxieties over Malayan nationalism on the coming of independence.[112]

When the effects of estate subdivision were first felt, in late 1957, the Ministry of Natural Resources set up a departmental Working Party, consisting of expatriate British senior officials, to examine its economic implications. In a remarkable exercise, reflecting relaxed commercial interests, the Working Party reported that estate subdivision was neither serious nor widespread, and anyway constituted a valuable device for creating a large class of rubber smallholders.[113] British officials serving the newly independent government, including the Economic Advisor, thereafter insisted that the authorities refrain from "intervening or interfering" with the "legitimate and lawful" disposal of property, whatever its domestic social and economic consequences, lest this ward off future overseas investment.[114] The British expatriate view was firm in its belief that no domestic economic or social objective should prejudice the freedom of capital, particularly foreign capital.

On the basis of the Working Party report and the exhortations of its senior expatriate advisors, the Alliance government accepted estate subdivision as inevitable and even desirable. Indeed, it was argued that subdivided plantations were more productive and more efficient, so that subdivision actually led to economic benefits.[115] This marked something of a reversal of the long-standing official bias regarding estates as the efficient, productive sector. The interests of estates, rather than the state of its interests, still apparently coloured governmental perceptions of its policy obligations. Concern about the displacement of labour was allayed by ministerial assurances that there appeared to be no large-scale increase in unemployment, and that most of those displaced were not "federal citizens" anyway, a curious turn of rationale.[116] At the heart of the independent government's acceptance of subdivision was a belief, cultivated by the Working Party, that the fragmentation of estates had "social advantages" by way of "increasing the number of small *landowners* who would thereby possess a stake in this country."[117] Estate subdivision accordingly dovetailed with the Alliance ideological goal of "property-owning democracy."

The main criticism of estate subdivision came from rubber trade unions, later joined by the opposition Socialist Front. Labour interests were greatly concerned over the effects of subdivision on employment, since only about 23% of the original work force remained after estates were subdivided, on terms far inferior to previous collective agreements.[118] While concurring that labour displacement was grievous, the Socialist Front also laid stress on the alleged social disabilities of unrestrained estate subdivision. Socialist politicians argued cogently that estate subdivision did not in fact satisfy land hunger, nor did it produce a real redistribution of assets or income, as government maintained, but constituted a "backward economic movement" impeding rubber industry development.[119] However, the flurry of business activity around estate subdivision dulled the edge of criticism for the time being: plantations were bought, sold and leased, so that the demand for rubber land was met, at a price, and yielded high returns to the investments of rentiers, middlemen and speculators. Unfettered enterprise in land created in its way, a welcome aura of profits for rubber.

Yet as the negative consequences of estate subdivision became increasingly evident, they gained political expression through the electoral process and competitive party system. Following the 1959 General Election, the first after independence, when the Socialist Front attracted strong support from estate labour, an Opposition motion was tabled calling for a Parliamentary Commission to investigate the subdivision of estates. The re-elected Alliance government's reaction was to set up its own committee of officials, state, Rubber Producers' Council and trade union representatives, charged with inquiring into the "social advantages" as well as disadvantages of subdivision. In its Interim Report the Committee expressed some concern over the plight of displaced labour, but was otherwise inconclusive as to the impact of estate subdivision on the rubber economy.

Nevertheless, the Interim Report did recommend that the federal government undertake to uphold standards of social services on subdivided estates, including housing, sanitation, public health and water supplies hitherto provided by estate companies.[120] This the government refused to do, claiming that it could not formulate policy without having "all the details necessary."[121] In the meantime the Economics Department of the University of Malaya was commissioned to prepare a comprehensive study of estate subdivision. When the Final Report of the Subdivision of Estates Committee appeared at last in August 1963, it found that the economic consequences of estate subdivision amounted to "anti-development."[122]

For all the controversy accompanying this report, which generated rather more heat than light,[123] it had little policy relevance by now as the high tide of subdivision had since passed, leaving behind a substantially reorganized rubber economy embodied in fact.

The period of heavy subdivision, when most of the activity took place, covered the years 1955-1960. During this period some 290 estates totalling about 232,000 acres were subdivided, amounting to 12% of total estate acreage. Of the subdivided plantations only about 8% were owner-cultivated, the remainder having become tenancies.[124] The prevalence of tenancy and widespread displacement of labour left the subdivided holdings far removed from the ideal of a property-owning democracy. Moreover, the impact of unrestricted estate subdivision on the rubber economy offset much of the modernizing trends then occurring in the sector. The subdivided acreage was equivalent to nearly 65% of the area replanted by (other) estates during the same period, yet little, if any, replanting had taken place on subdivided estates before or after. Worse still was the asset deterioration that had set in. Subdivided estates, and especially the tenancies, generally suffered declining standards of maintenance resulting eventually in an inferior quality and quantity of rubber production.[125] By refusing to cope forthrightly with estate subdivision, a policy line inspired by economic ideology and sustained by commercial interests, the federal government had in effect undercut its own rubber modernization objective.

Perspectives on the Rubber Revolution

In historical perspective, the 1950s witnessed the start of an industrial revolution in Malaya's rubber economy. This revolution occurred along two dimensions: in the asset structure and social structure of the industry. On the asset dimension, the resources of the Malayan rubber industry underwent a dramatic modernization during the 1950s decade. Spotty and uneven at first, the pace of modernization picked up and spread out with the policy innovations in replanting and new planting that followed self-government. Though still retarded somewhat by shortcomings in replanting and new planting policy, and particularly by the negative consequences of estate subdivision, this modernization process led to large-scale renewal and expansion in the Malayan natural rubber economy. As a result, the Malayan industry was placed in a comparatively advantageous long-run competitive position in the international rubber trade.

The process of modernization also produced a transformation of the social structure of the Malayan rubber industry. Policy initiatives towards accelerated replanting and new planting had the effect of releasing the growth potential of the hitherto confined smallholding sector. Consequently, the smallholding sector overtook the estates in terms of planted rubber acreage and, significantly, new rubber planting, by the end of the decade (Tables 2 and 3). Estate companies no longer predominated over the rubber industry, and the future trend was against them. To be sure, smallholding production remained less than estates, owing to past discrimination, but their relative position would improve as their late-planted, high-yielding acreage reached maturity during the 1960s.[126] This social transformation of the Malayan rubber industry was to have far-reaching economic and political implications. Suffice it to say here in this context that the transformed economic position of the smallholders, coupled to their electoral power, effectively altered the terms of reference of future Malaysian rubber policy.

ENDNOTES

1. The author expresses his gratitude to the Harry S. Truman Research Institute of the Hebrew University of Jerusalem for its support for the study of modern Malaysian economic history and development, upon which this paper is based; and to the Institute of Southeast Asian Studies, Singapore, for a Visiting Fellowship which facilitated its preparation for publication.

2. See P.T. Bauer, "Post War Malayan Rubber Policy: A Comment," *Journal of Southeast Asian Studies* Vol. 4 (1973)(henceforward *JSEAS*). For a rejoinder, see Martin Rudner, "A Reply to P.T. Bauer's Comment on Post-War Malayan Rubber Policy", *JSEAS* Vol. 4 (1973).

3. Chairman's addresses to the Rubber Growers Association, London, annual general meeting, 31 March 1948 and 12 April 1949.

4. Sir Eric MacFadyen, address to Lanadron Rubber Estates Ltd. 20 July 1949; Sir John Hay, address to United Sua Betong Rubber Estates Ltd., 25 May 1949.

5. On the rubber restriction schemes set up between the First and Second World Wars, see John H. Drabble, *Rubber in Malaya 1876-1922* (Kuala Lumpur 1973); and P.T. Bauer, *The Rubber Industry, A Study in Competition and Monopoly* (London, 1948).

6. High Commissioner Sir Gerald Templer, address to the Malayan Planting Industry Employers Association, Kuala Lumpur, June 1952.

7. Secretary of State for the Colonies O. Lyttleton, *House of Commons Debates, 17 July 1952* (henceforth: *H.C. Deb.*)

8. *Vide.* Thomas H. Silcock, *The Economy of Malaya* (Singapore, 1957), p. 19.

9. Peter Thorneycroft, President of the Board of Trade, *H.C. Deb.*, 20 March 1952; 3 April 1952; and Written Reply, *Federation of Malaya, Legislative Council*

Proceedings, 2 April 1951 (henceforth: *L.C. Proc.*). At the same time destination controls were applied to Malayan rubber shipments to assure the U.K. and "friendly countries" a "full and regular" supply and deny the Communist bloc more than its pre-Korean War "normal civilian consumption."

10. *Straits Times*, 21 Oct. 1952.

11. Federation of Malaya, *Legislative Council Paper No. 10 of 1949*.

12. Member for Agricultural and Forestry, *L.C. Proc.* 20 March 1950.

13. See R.F. Mudie, *Report of a Mission of Enquiry in the Rubber Industry of Malaya* (Kuala Lumpur, 1954), pp. 2-3, (henceforth: *Mudie Mission Report*).

14. Ibid., para. 30.

15. Sir Sydney Palmer, "Rubber in the Post War Period," *British Malaya* (April 1953), 201-4; see also Sir John Hay, address to United Sua Betong Rubber Estates Ltd, annual meeting, 25 May 1949.

16. *Final Report of the Rubber Smallholders Enquiry Committee*, Legislative Council Paper No. 8 of 1952.

17. Cf. Member for Agriculture and Forestry, *L.C. Proc.*, 20 March 1950.

18. Member for Economic Affairs, *L.C. Proc.*, 11 July 1951.

19. Cf. Major A.C. Smith (rubber estates appointee), *L.C. Proc.*, 11 July 1951.

20. *L.C. Proc.*, 11 July 1951; addresses by H.H. Facer and Khoo Teik Ee, Rubber estates appointees; see also Sir John Hay, address to United Sua Betong Rubber Estates Ltd., general meeting, 30 May 1951.

21. Cited in *British Malaya* (December, 1950), p. 141. This statement emphasized alleged administrative difficulties.

22. On the operating principles of Replanting Funds A and B, see Lim Chong Yah, "The Malayan Rubber Replanting Taxes," *Malayan Economic Review* (*MER*) (1961), pp. 47-8.

23. The Rubber Industry (Replanting) Board had 18 members, of whom 15 were representatives of the industry's Rubber Producers Council. Of the 15 producer representatives, 10 went to estate organizations, 4 to the Rubber Growers Association of London, 3 to the Malayan Estate Owners Association, and 3 to the United Planting Association of Malaya, amounting to a clear majority overall for the estate subsector; 5 went to smallholders, divided between 4 Malays and 1 Chinese, despite the fact that at least half the smallholdings were non-Malay owned and cultivated (*Rubber Statistics Handbook* (Kuala Lumpur, 1952), Table 28ii). Since there were no smallholder associations in existence yet, the smallholding representation on the Board was held in trust by officials of the Rural and Industrial Development Authority. Government sent 3 representatives of its own to the Board, one of which was given over to the Malay States (together with the-then Settlements).

24. The Rubber Smallholders Enquiry Committee was established by Federal Legislative Council resolution in October, 1948. The Committee produced a three-page *Interim Report* (*Legislative Council Paper No 48 of 1950*) in 1950 and submitted an eight-page *Final Report* (*Legislative Council Paper No. 8 of 1952*) two years later.

25. Khoo Teik Ee, *L.C. Proc.*, 20 March 1952.

26. *L.C. Proc.*, 20 March 1952, addresses by Enuche Nasaruddin bin Abdul Rais and Y.M. Musa bin Raja Mahadi.

27. Mentri Besar (Chief Minister) of Selangor, *L.C. Proc.*, 20 March 1952.

28. On the earlier effects of colonial administrative prejudice on the discriminatory treatment of rubber estates and smallholdings, see Martin Rudner, "Rubber Strategy for Post-War Malaya, 1945-48," *JSEAS* Vol.1 (1970), p. 28 *et passim*.

29. On this point see Martin Rudner, "The State and Peasant Innovation in Rural Development: The Case of Malaysian Rubber", *Asian and African Studies* Vol. 6 (1970), esp. pp. 75-85; and T.H. Silcock, "The Economy of Malaya", in C. Hoover, ed. *Economic Systems of the Commonwealth* (Durham, N.C., 1961).

30. Although allowed as a tax deduction for estate companies, it can be argued in economic terms that the cost of replanting should actually be treated as new investment. Replanting is, to be sure, essential to the survival of the plantation, however it represents the investment of current earnings to retrieve historic costs (the normal attrition of rubber trees), rather than a cost of current output. Plantations that replant without new borrowing therefore replace assets of little worth with assets of greater value, out of current earnings. See T.H. Silcock, chairman, "Rubber Industry Arbitration Board Report," *Legislative Council Paper No. 59 of 1949*, col. 15-16.

31. *Mudie Mission Report*, paras. 30, 31. At the relatively high price of M$1 a pound the replanting cess yielded only 1.8 cents; at under 60 cents a pound it vanished altogether.

32. Ibid.

33. Heah Joo Seng, *L.C. Proc.*, 7 Oct. 1954.

34. Sydney Palmer, Chairman's address to Rubber Grower Association general meeting, 1 May 1953.

35. *Rubber Industry Replanting Ordinance*, No. 8 of 1952, Art. 4 Smallholders' Fund B was to be managed by its own board composed of the five smallholders representatives from the Replanting Fund Board, which held overall responsibility; together with the Member for Economic Affairs and Director of Agriculture, both colonial expatriate officials; and a representative of the State and Settlement governments, the Keeper of the Rulers Seal, a Malay aristocrat.

36. Federal Government suggestions that it undertake block replanting for smallholdings were rejected by the Malay States and Settlements, while another proposal for cooperative smallholder block replanting failed to attract sufficient support from the various authorities. Vid. *Final Report of the Rubber Smallholders Enquiry Committee, paras. 43-5.*

37. *Annual Report of the Rubber Industry (Replanting) Board, Legislative Council Paper 53 of 1954.*

38. The actual adjudication of Fund B applications was delegated by the Board to Replanting Officers in each State and Settlement.

39. *Final Report of the Rubber Smallholders Enquiry Committee*, para. 19; on the size distribution of Malayan smallholdings at the time see the *Rubber Statistics Handbook 1952*, Table 28ii.

40. *Mudie Mission Report*, para. 69; See also Lim Chong Yah, "The Malayan Rubber Replanting Taxes", 49-52 and A.H.H. Tan, "The Incidence of Export Taxes on Small Producers", *MER* (1967), p. 97, on the matter of pseudo-subdivided estates' exploitation of the higher Fund B replanting grants.

41. *Mudie Mission Report*, para. 68. On the standards of maintenance required by the replanting authorities for continuation of the grant, which was paid by installments over time, see the *Federation of Malaya Annual Report, 1954* p. 136.

42. A.H.H. Tan, "The Incidence of Export Taxes," p 97; and Rudner, "The State and Peasant Innovation," p. 93. The extent to which the replanting scheme represented a form of regressive taxation on smallholders may be seen in the cumulative excess of Fund B revenues over disbursements, which totalled over M$76 million at the end of 1956 (when new policies were about to be introduced); vid. *Annual Report of the Rubber Industry (Replanting) Board for 1956, Legislative Council Paper 58 of 1957*, p. 5. The four and one-half cents a pound additional cess proved an especially heavy burden imposed only on smallholders, and not estates, even when rubber prices were low and the ordinary Schedule II cess declined or was removed.

43. The Replanting Scheme for Smallholdings envisaged the replanting of 40,000, 50,000 and 60,000 acres in 1953, 1954, 1955, respectively; actual smallholding replanting for these years was only 29,500, 22,600 and 25,300 acres, totalling 77,400 acres out of the 150,000 acre target: *Rubber Statistics Handbook 1957*, Table 12 (amended figures).

44. *Interim Report of the Rubber Smallholders Enquiry Committee*, para. 10.

45. Member for Agriculture and Forestry, *L.C. Proc.*, 20 March 1952.

46. Ibid.

47. Cf. Mentri Besar, Selangor, *L.C. Proc.*, 20 March 1952; J.C. Mathison, *L.C. Proc.*, 20 March 1952 and 26 November 1953. Mathison, an appointed representative of rubber estate interests, called for government to promote smallholder replanting with crops having "greater stability and more *security* of income than natural rubber" (emphasis added), though no such alternative crop offered a potential income level even equal to rubber, as the estates themselves were aware.

48. Member for Economic Affairs, *L.C. Proc.*, 25 November 1953.

49. *Federation of Malaya Annual Report, 1955*, p. 142. By 1955, 7,674 acres had been replanted with other crops, and 78,891 with rubber, under Fund B.

50. International Bank for Reconstruction and Development, *The Economic Development of Malaya* (Baltimore, 1955), p. 34 (Henceforth: *IBRD Report*).

51. *IBRD Report*, p. 40; *Mudie Mission Report*, para. 87; see also M. Rudner, "A Reply", p. 302.

52. *Mudie Mission Report*, para. 84.

53. On this point and its impact on agricultural and rubber policies, respectively, see Martin Rudner, "Malayan Quandary: Rural Development Policy Under the First and Second Five-Year Plans," *Contributions to Asian Studies* Vol. 1(1971), esp. pp. 193-197; and "A Reply," p. 302.

54. See T.H. Silcock, "The Economy of Malaya," p. 338.

55. *Federation of Malaya Annual Report, 1955*, p. 168.

56. Member for Economic Affairs, *L.C. Proc.* 20 March 1953. It is difficult to imagine natural rubber cultivation, as a cash crop with a lengthy (35 years) productive life and liable to subsequent replanting, being prone to "shifting cultivation."

57. *Federation of Malaya Annual Report, 1955*, p. 143. The main areas of illicit rubber planting were Kedah, Perlis and Johore.

58. Federation of Malaya, *Taxation and Replanting in the Rubber Industry* (Kuala Lumpur, 1955), p. 17.

59. *Rubber Statistics Handbook 1952*, Table 28ii. Chinese smallholders tended to predominate on medium size holdings.

60. Cf. *Mudie Mission Report*, para. 124.

61. *IBRD Report*, pp. 54-6; and P.T. Bauer, "Malayan Rubber Policy" in T.H. Silcock, ed. *Readings in Malayan Economics* (Singapore, 1961), pp. 306-7, on this point.

62. T.B. Barlow, chairman's address to Highlands and Lowlands Para Rubber Co. Ltd. general meeting, 27 May 1953.

63. Sir Sydney Palmer, Rubber Growers Association general meeting, 1 May 1953.

64. *Mudie Mission Report*, paras. 7, 15.

65. *Taxation and Replanting in the Rubber Industry*, pp. 6-7.

66. G.M. Knocker, rubber estates appointee, *L.C. Proc.* 10 November 1954.

67. *Taxation and Replanting in the Rubber Industry*, published in April, 1955, with the general elections scheduled for August.

68. *Mudie Mission Report*, para. 28.

69. Member for Economic Affairs, *L.C. Proc.*, 4 May 1955.

70. *Taxation and Replanting in the Rubber Industry*, pp. 6-7.

71. Member for Economic Affairs, *L.C. Proc.*, 4 May 1955.

72. *L.C. Proc.*, 10 December 1958.

73. Minister of Agriculture and Cooperatives, *L.C. Proc.*, 7 Dec. 1957.

74. *D.R. Proc.*, 28 May 1963.

75. See the Minister of Commerce and Industry's review of replanting policy, *Malaya* (April 1963), pp. 9-10.

76. For a study of the Five Year-Plan and its place in modern Malaysian economic history, see Martin Rudner, *Nationalism, Planning and Economic Modernization in Malaysia: The Politics of Beginning Development* (Beverly Hills, Calif., 1975), and Ness, *Bureaucracy*, esp. chap. 3.

77. H.B. Husey, *L.C. Proc.*, 5 May 1955.

78. Sir John Hay, chairman's address to United Sua Betong Rubber Estates Co. Ltd., annual general meeting, 8 June 1955.

79. Ibid.

80. See, for example, J.K. Swaine, chairman's address to Padang Senang Rubber Ltd., annual meeting, 21 March 1956, and to the Perak Rubber Plantations Ltd. annual meeting, 27 October 1955, where he denounced the "false assumption that rubber trees are economically finished by their 30th year, a fallacy which is amply exposed by yields on this Company's fine old property. . . . This Company will certainly cling to its 36 and 42 year old trees" so long as they continue to give fair yields per tapper. "Modern planting methods rely on yield per acre rather than on yield per tapper, but all who have piloted estates through the two great slumps of 1921 and the early thirties know that it is the latter that counted during the lean years."

81. See G.M. Knocker, *L.C. Proc.*, 5 May 1955.

82. The annual average rate of estate replanting reached 72.7 thousand acres between 1956 and 1960, compared to only 45.1 thousand acres between 1950 and 1955: *Rubber Statistics Handbook 1960*, Table 13.

83. See C.D. Shearn, address to Rubber Growers Association annual meeting, 9 May 1958; Sir Eric MacFadyen, chairman's report to London Asiatic Rubber and Produce Co. Ltd., annual general meeting, 20 June 1960.

84. On this point, see also W.M. Corden, "Prospects for Malayan Exports", in Silcock & Fisk, eds., *Political Economy*, p. 95.

85. *Rubber Statistics Handbook 1960*, Table 6. The *Straits Budget* of 12 October 1960 gives the figures of 600 estates totalling 160,000 that defaulted on replanting.

86. On smallholders'.comparative advantages in natural rubber production, see P.T. Bauer, *Malayan Rubber Policy*, pp. 306-7.

87. Minister for Economic Affairs, *L.C. Proc.*, 3 December 1955.

88. See Dato Sir Clough Thuraisingham, *L.C. Proc.*, 6 December 1955.

89. Minister of Commerce and Industry, Tan Siew Sin, *L.C. Proc.*, 7 December 1957.

90. The MCSA, set up in February, 1956, was assured of Federal Government financial support for the first five years, as the Association was regarded by the newly-elected Government as an integral part of its rubber development policy. Previous attempts to form a national association of smallholders out of their representatives on the Rubber Producers Council were all stillborne, mainly for reasons of finance. Cf. Minister of Commerce and Industry, *L.C. Proc.*, 14 November 1956.

91. Minister of Commerce and Industry, *L.C. Proc.*, 7 December 1957; *Federation of Malaya, Report of the Subdivision of Estates Committee*, Cmd. 29 of 1963, pp. 96-7.

92. Minister of Commerce and Industry, *L.C. Proc.*, 22 April 1959; Chief Replanting Officer, quioted in the *Strait Times*, 28 September 1961.

93. *Federation of Malaya, Second Five-Year Plan, 1961-65* (Kuala Lumpur, 1961), para. 25.

94. Ibid., para. 5.

95. *Mudie Mission Report*, para. 115.

96. Member for Economic Affairs, *L.C. Proc.*, 4 May 1955; see also *Taxation and Replanting in the Rubber Industry*.

97. Mentri Besar, Selangor, *L.C. Proc.*, 6 March 1957.

98. Mentri Besar, Negri Sembilan, *L.C. Proc.*, 13 December 1957.

99. *L.C. Proc.*, addresses by Yap Kim Hock, (Smallholders Association of Malaya), 3 December 1955; and S.N. King (rubber estates), 13 November 1956.

100. Enche Abdul Jalil, *L.C. Proc.*, 13 December 1957.

101. Enche Abdul Ghafar, *L.C. Proc.*, 6 March 1957.

102. Enche Ibrahim Fikri, *L.C. Proc.*, 3 December 1955.

103. For a study on the emergence of a development goal in Malaya following the transfer of power to the elected government, see Gayl D. Ness, *Bureaucracy*, chaps. 1-4; and Martin Rudner, *Nationalism*.

104. On FLDA and its attendant social and economic policies, goals and performances, see Ness, *Bureaucracy*, chaps. 5-8; Syed Hussain Wafa, "Land

Development Strategies in Malaysia: An Empirical Study," *Kajian Ekonomi Malaysia (1972)*, 1-28; and Martin Rudner, *"The State and Peasant Innovation,"* pp. 88-96.

105. *Report of the Working Party Set up to Consider the Development of New Areas for Land Settlement in the Federation of Malaya, Legislative Council Paper No. 11 of 1956*, para. 91. (Henceforth: *Report of the Land Settlement Working Party*).

106. *Second Five-Year Plan*, para. 29.

107. Average settler debt to FLDA was approximately M$7,228, or more than three years' net income, by the time the land reached full production; see Minister of Natural Resources, *D.R. Proc.*, 26 April 1962. However, the FLDA schemes tapped for the first time in 1963 yielded an average gross monthly family income of M$317, or M$197 net after deduction of production costs, including taxes, and loan repayments: *Colombo Plan Annual Report, 1963* (London, 1964), Cmd. 2529, p. 157. This compared well with the average rural Malay monthly income for 1957 was only M$128, and which, if anything, would have declined with the continued adversity affecting Malaya's rice economy by 1963; see *Household Budget Survey of the Federation of Malaya, 1957-8* (Kuala Lumpur, 1958).

108. Tan Siew Sin, *L.C. Proc.*, 6 March 1957.

109. Tan Siew Sin, Minister of Commerce and Industry, address to the Annual Installation of the Seremban Rotary Club, 5 July 1958 (*Straits Times*).

110. Minister of Rural Development, *D.R. Proc.*, 28 May 1963.

111. On the Kelantan scheme, see D. Ali, "Kelantan's unique go-it-alone Plan," *Straits Budget*, 14 Dec. 1960; Rudner, "The State and Peasant Innovation," p. 91 *et passim*; Wafa, "Land Development Strategies."

112. A total of 290 estates, of 231,800 acres, were subdivided during this period. As independence approached British investors became "somewhat anxious" of their holdings in Malaya: see P.B.L. Coughlin, report to Anglo-Malayan Rubber Plantations Ltd. annual meeting, 4 December 1956. Some leading estate groups began to disinvest through capital redistributions and dividend increases which were admittedly unjustified by current earnings; Sir John Hay, reports to the general meetings of United Sua Betong Rubber Estates Co. Ltd., 12 June 1957; Kamuning (Perak) Rubber and Tin Co. Ltd., 28 November 1957; Linggi Plantations Ltd., 27 March 1958; P.T. Barlow, report to Highlands and Lowlands Para Rubber Co. Ltd. annual meeting, 5 June 1957. This disinvestment to reduced these companies' investment exposure in independent Malaya "lest the possession of ample funds . . . be made the pretext for further exactions": Sir John Hay, report to Linggi Plantations Ltd. general meeting, 30 March 1955. On the other side of the coin there were British planters who deprecated suggestions of economic withdrawal from Malaya, arguing that the Malayan nationalists were committed to "a firm and just Government determined to maintain law and order . . . (and) . . . sound economic conditions . . . (as an) . . . antidote to agents of disruption": Sir Eric Miller, report to Petaling Rubber Estates Ltd. annual meeting, 4 April 1956. See also the *Interim Report of the Subdivision of Estates Committee*, Cmd. 15 of 1961, pp. 4-6.

113. Report No. CFLM 65/57 (N.D., 1957?), reproduced in the *Report of the Subdivisional Estates Committee*, General Appendix 1. The Committee commented in its Report: "Either the Committee (i.e. the Working Party) was incompetent in relation to its tasks, or it deliberately overlooked certain facts for motives that need not be the concern of this report". See also Ungku Aziz, "Land Disintegration and Land Policy in Malaya", *MER* (1958).

114. Economic Advisor, *L.C. Proc.*, 12 December 1958.

115. *D.R. Proc.*, 23 February 1960, addresses by the Minister of Finance (Tan Siew Sin) and Minister of External Affairs.

116. Minister of Labour, *D.R. Proc.*, 23 February 1960.

117. Assistant Minister of Rural Development, *D.R. Proc.*, 23 February 1960. Emphasis added.

118. See the *Report of the Subdivision of Estates Committee*, pp. 99-106, for the effect of subdivision on labour.

119. *D.R. Proc.*, 23 February 1960, addresses by V. David, V. Veerappen, K. Karam Singh.

120. *Interim Report of the Subdivision of Estates Committee*, para. 32.

121. Minister of Rural Development, *D.R. Proc.*, 9 August 1960.

122. *Final Report of the Subdivision of Estates Committee*, p. 124.

123. See for example, the Minority Report attached to the Final Report; the *Straits Times* editorial, 15 August 1963, and the Rubber Producers Council statement (*Straits Times*, 16 August 1963), all taking exceptions to the findings and conclusions of the Final Report.

124. *Final Report of the Subdivision of Estates Committee*, p. 14 and Chapter V.

125. Ibid., p. 92-95.

126. Thus by 1970, smallholding production reached 48.6 of total peninsular Malaysian output, as their high-yielding trees on the replanting and new planting schemes of the late 1950s, early 1960s, came under full tapping: *Federation of Malaysia, Second Malaysia Plan 1971-1975* (Kuala Lumpur, 1971), para. 335.

CHAPTER 6

THE STATE AND PEASANT INNOVATION IN RURAL DEVELOPMENT: The Case Of Malaysian Rubber

Contemporary inquiry into the development process has drawn attention to the role of creative innovation as an engine of economic progress. Innovation in underdeveloped economies has generally been characterized as originating in the activities of "marginal men" or "leading" enterprises.[1] By virtue of certain ascribed characteristics, these marginal or leading producers are typically seen as innovators in the mobilization of capital, the application of new techniques or the searching out of new markets. Underlying this notion of innovation is an assumption that economic creativity is the restricted province of a specified minority, with the central problem of development therefore being that of transmitting leaders' gains to the laggard majority. Yet it may properly be asked whether economic innovation must necessarily be tied to a marginal or leading few. Have there occurred instances where the propensity to innovate was demonstrably present in a broad-based social group, only to be frustrated by legal-institutional barriers imposed by vested interests? It is the contention of this chapter that contemporary Malaysian rural development has been rooted in a smallholding peasantry able and willing to innovate, so that the progressive removal of legal-institutional obstacles, coupled to the provision of critical supports by government, resulted in real gains in rubber productivity.

Since the First World War natural rubber obtained from the latex of the tree hevea brasiliensis has been virtually synonymous with the prosperity of the Malayan peninsula.[2]

As the economic mainstay of Malaya, natural rubber generates about a quarter of the country's national income and has been largely responsible for its relatively impressive growth performance.

Asian and African Studies, Vol. 6 (1970).

During the turbulent years between the World Wars Malayan natural rubber sales to the United States earned as much gold-dollar exchange as all domestic British exports combined, earning for the then colony the appellation, "Dollar Arsenal of the Sterling Area." Malayan rubber was of global significance as well, with more than half the world's supply of this vital commodity over the inter-war period coming from the peninsula's plantations.

The Malaysian rubber industry has been from its inception divided structurally into two sectors: the estate and smallholding. Whereas British-owned companies dominated the estate sector, nearly 40 percent of Malaya's pre-World War Two acreage consisted of peasant smallholdings. Precise statistics are unavailable, but it may be estimated that about half the inter-war smallholding acreage was Malay-owned, 40% Malayan Chinese and the remainder Malayan Indian, Eurasian or other Asian.[3]

Significantly, the average size of the Chinese or Indian smallholding was almost twice the Malay average of 3.2 acres. Over 98% of all Malay smallholdings were less than 25 acres, while more than a quarter the Chinese and a third the Indians held between 25 and 100 acres. All told, smallholdings produced some 40% of total Malayan rubber output through the 1930s, even though this was hardly indicative of their true comparative efficiency. For most of the inter-war period, Malayan rubber was beset by restrictive regulations heavily weighted in favour of the large estates, notwithstanding the fact that smallholdings were the lower-cost sector.[4]

Despite discriminatory policies, rubber remained an eminently suitable peasant crop, capable of yielding satisfactory economies of scale on smallholdings.[5] Its non-seasonal character rendered rubber smallholding relatively free from the social evils traditionally associated with peasant agriculture, viz., indebtedness, foreclosure and absentee landlordism. Rubber smallholding in Malaya, therefore combined comparative efficiency with the creation of a relatively stable, prosperous and independent peasantry. Rubber smallholding offered Malaya a promising formula for rural development.

Despite the social and economic prospects for rubber smallholding development, official attitudes and policies in colonial Malaya strongly favoured the estate sector at the expense of peasant producers. To British expatriate officers of the colonial administration, rubber was virtually identified with the British estate companies. Evidence to the contrary aside, British estates were officially deemed the more efficient sector, so that colonial policy-makers aimed at achieving the "economic benefits" of estate rubber production albeit "without its admitted social ills."[6] This predilection for estate agriculture on the part of British colonial administrators reflected an ingrained bias in favour of neat, well-ordered Western-style plantations, exemplified by large British estates, as against the alien character of peasant smallholdings.

TABLE 1
Malaysian* Planted Rubber
Acreage, estate and smallholding ('000 acres).

Years	Estates	Smallholding	Percent Smallholding of Total	Total Malaysian*
1925	1480	975	40	2455
1932	1939	1276	40	3215
1940	2113	1351	39	3464
1947	1945	1580	45	3525
1955	2025	1650	45	3675
1960	1942	1960	50	3848
1962	1933	2061	52	3994
1966	1813	2529	58	4342

* Malaysia-Malaya only.
Source: *Rubber Statistical Bulletins*, adapted.

So far as British planting circles were concerned, the smallholders' capacity to produce rubber at prices below the profitability threshold of estates instilled in them the fear that the Malayan rubber industry would eventually "go native." This fear inspired leading British planters to utilize their access to centres of colonial political authority to obtain policies aimed at protecting the capital values of the estate sector.[7] The international rubber restriction schemes, originally intended to maintain export prices, accordingly came to be applied in colonial Malaya as a calculated device for undermining the long-run competitive position of peasant smallholdings. Well after the expiration of the international rubber agreement, spokesmen for British estate interests still advocated the removal of peasants from rubber to other, non-competitive, less-remunerative crops.[8]

The Malay aristocratic elite, linked to Britain through the nexus of indirect colonial rule, exhibited little enthusiasm for rubber smallholding. For them, padi, closely associated with traditional kampung society and culture, remained the ascribed crop for Malay peasant cultivation. Not only was padi farming identified with maintenance of the Malay social order and culture, but total and exclusive Malay involvement in padi was further seen by the traditional communal elite as a defence against the perceived threat of Chinese economic domination. This affinity for padi impelled the Malay aristocracy to join the British officialdom in measures designed to keep the Malay peasantry in rice and out of rubber.[9] In their enthusiasm for padi, the Malay communal leadership went so far as to urge the peasantry to forego incremental income in order to adhere to the traditional Malay "way of life." Declarations favouring kampung economic betterment notwithstanding, some were even prepared to compel those Malays who had already responded to the attractions of rubber smallholding to return to arduous, impoverished padi.[10]

As a result of this predisposition against rubber smallholding on the part of those with access to colonial political authority, Malayan rubber strategy aimed primarily at supporting the estate pattern of plantation agriculture on the one hand, and upholding the traditional pattern of kampung life on the other. Rather than capitalize on the potentials of rubber smallholding for rural development, colonial policy deliberately stifled peasant innovation in pursuit of its custodial goals.[11] New entry into rubber growing was restricted by a ban on new planting, which was unilaterally maintained in Malaya even after the expiration of the International Rubber Regulation Agreement. When the ban was finally lifted in 1947, government's continuing refusal to alienate additional lands for smallholding rubber effectively restricted peasant entry into new rubber, whereas most larger estates already possessed adequate reserve lands to plant. Discriminatory practices of government agencies, such as the Rubber Research Institute of Malaya, directed the greatest part of their activities towards the estate sector, to virtual exclusion of the smallholdings who were thus made to finance the improvement of their immediate competitors.[12] Moreover, rubber smallholders bore an extraordinarily heavy share of the public purse through the rubber export duty, in effect a severely regressive tax on peasant income.[13] Such restrictive regulations and discriminatory measures effectively served to undermine the efficiency and independence of colonial Malaya's rubber smallholdings. By the late 1940s the bulk of the smallholding acreage had already been forced into obsolescence.[14]

Be that as it may, rubber still remained the most attractive crop for peasant producers. Those already engaged in rubber smallholding enjoyed rewards far greater than for any alternative crop, despite the heavy incidence of direct and indirect taxation. So great was the appeal of rubber planting that a large unsatisfied demand for land for new rubber planting persisted among the peasantry.[15] Rural Malays in particular demanded entry into rubber smallholding as a means of social and economic betterment. When land was not forthcoming, many of the more venturesome peasants took to illicit planting, though with low-yielding, unselected seedlings. By the end of the colonial period an estimated 15% of smallholding acreage consisted of inferior stands of this type, planted in evasion of government restrictions. Some peasants even turned to the insurgent Malayan Communist Party in response to its promise to eliminate colonial barriers to rubber smallholding-based rural development.[16]

Colonial rubber policy not only threatened to extinguish peasant economic development, but further jeopardized the competitive position of Malayan rubber in world markets. Whereas Malayan rubber acreage remained virtually stagnant owing to restrictions on new planting, the Netherlands East Indies (which had not participated in the Stevenson Scheme) expanded its rubber acreage and output until it exceeded Malaya's production in 1941. Since most of Indonesia's rubber acreage consisted of smallholdings, they loomed as a major low-cost competitor for Malaya.

This competitive threat was especially troubling since the rubber restrictions had effectively hampered progressing Malayan rubber technology, limiting the development of high-yielding natural rubber and its extension to local producers. Comparative stagnation in Malayan natural rubber technology contrasted poorly with the advances in synthetic production following the Second World War. Indeed, some Americans even viewed the newly established synthetic rubber industry as a convenient stick with which to beat the "few very powerful individuals who are the owners of rubber plantations" for their past efforts at cartelization,[17] punishing Malaya for the deeds of Mincing Lane.

In the event, the availability of synthetic rubber served to stabilize the post-Second World War international rubber market at relatively lower prices. Malayan rubber accordingly had to endure a competitive squeeze precisely when the demands on the industry were greatest, owing to the needs of post-war reconstruction, Sterling area weakness and rising economic expectations accompanying emergent Malayan nationalism.

The unreality surrounding post-war Malayan rubber policy was prolonged by the transient prosperity wrought by Sterling devaluation in 1949 followed by the Korean War "Boom." Thus in early

1950 the colonial authorities could still "hope" that onsetting obsolescence would curtail Malayan rubber output and thereby maintain
high prices.[18] Colonial rubber strategy implicitly favoured high unit
prices over efficient production, estate company profits over Malayan national income. It required the post-Korea recession to impel
government at long last to adopt developmental policies aimed at
raising the productivity of Malaya's rubber industry. As prices declined, the colonial authorities became acutely aware of the need
to compete with Indonesian natural and American synthetic, and
began looking to replanting with high-yielding clones to achieve the
desired improvements in productivity. However new planting by
smallholders remained, as before, effectively proscribed.

Malaya's first Rubber Replanting Scheme was originally suggested during the Korean Boom as a counter-inflationary device,
but met with strenuous opposition from British estate interests. Following lengthy deliberations with estate representatives on the
newly created Rubber Producers Council, a mutually acceptable
arrangement was worked out involving the establishment of separate replanting schemes, Funds A and B, for estates and smallholdings respectively, to be administered by an autonomous Rubber
Industry (Replanting) Board. Finance for these schemes was to be
derived from a cess on rubber exports, divided between the two
funds in proportion to the output of the respective sectors. The resource distribution for replanting the estate and smallholding sectors therefore reinforced existing inequalities among producers
instead of meeting their relative needs.

Under the split scheme, estates received an automatic rebate of
their cess payments upon proof of replanting, whereas smallholdings had first to apply and then qualify for a Fund B grant. Since
federal proposals for large-scale block replanting of smallholdings were rejected by state governments jealous of their constitutional prerogatives over land matters, smallholders were left to
replant on an individual basis. Smallholders wanting to do so had
to initiate their own replanting and then apply to the Rubber Industry (Replanting) Board for a grant to cover two-thirds the standard cost (i.e., M$400 per acre) of approved replanting. The target
for smallholding replanting under the scheme was set at an ambitious 500,000 acres, or two-thirds of the total smallholding area, over
a six-year period from January 1953.

Actual implementation of the Smallholder Replanting Scheme encountered basic structural, technical and financial impediments.[19] In
the official definition of smallholding, i.e., rubber plantations aggre-

gating less than 100 acres, no account was taken of the very real differences in structure and scale of operations between so-called "medium" holdings of 25 to 100 acres and very small peasant holdings of under 25 acres. Whereas the medium holdings could replant without much difficulty, replanting on peasant holdings of an average size of 3.5 acres entailed sustained physical labour, exacting standards of maintenance as well as the forgoing of income for six years until the new rubber trees were tappable. In this context the Fund B replanting grant was wholly inadequate to cover both costs and sustenance,[20] while failure to uphold standards of maintenance meant, for many, the discontinuation of their grant. Though ostensibly free to modernize their holdings through replanting, peasants in fact found themselves effectively denied the necessary technical and financial supports for carrying through the task. Inasmuch as participation in the scheme came mainly from medium holdings, the operations of Fund B served to regressively redistribute real resources away from smaller to larger producers, thereby worsening the relative position of peasant proprietors.[21]

To the extent that smallholdings did take advantage of Fund B, "all possible encouragement" was given to their replanting with crops other than rubber.[22] This approach to replanting satisfied government's concern over Malaya's "excessive" dependency on rubber, as well as catering to traditional Malay emphasis on padi and estate desires to reduce competition. This policy of promoting replanting with alternative crops stressed as its criterion "suitability of soil" rather than income, implicitly admitting that no other crop offered smallholders equivalent returns to high-yielding rubber. As a result of this diversification policy, over 10% of smallholders' replanted acreage through 1955 was given over to alternative crops having a lower revenue yield than rubber. Here smallholders' contributions to Fund B had actually financed their removal from that industry, where they were potentially the most efficient producers, to lower income occupations.

Meanwhile new rubber planting by smallholders remained virtually frozen as a matter of policy. Fund B was specifically precluded from extending assistance to new rubber planting. Although larger estates could and did plant new rubber on their reserve lands, persistent demands by peasants for additional land for rubber planting were firmly turned down. The official excuse for denying smallholder new planting was to avoid a return to "shifting agriculture."[23]

In reality this indicated government's commitment to uphold vested economic and institutional interests. Nor were Malaya's colonial authorities prepared to underwrite the social overhead capital costs of new settlements, despite prevailing conditions of oppressive land hunger. Instead, overriding governmental concern for vested interests and treasury revenue balances obstructed potentially large-scale peasant investment in new rubber development.

These legal-institutional barriers to peasant innovation seriously limited the effectiveness of the Rubber Replanting Scheme. In its early years rather less than half the target acreage was actually attained. Yet by 1955 over half the smallholding acreage consisted of trees more than thirty years old, at which time declining output begins, while less than 8 percent comprised high-yielding rubber. Hardest hit by obsolescence were the Malay peasant holdings, typically the smallest, poorest, most in need of renewal. It is a sad commentary on colonial policy in Malaya that weakened precisely that sector of an industry capable of liberating the rural population from many of the traditional socio-economic evils afflicting underdeveloped peasant agriculture.

Malaya's peasantry did not meekly succumb to the restrictions inherent in colonial rubber policy. Some joined the Communist-led insurgency campaign against British rule. Many persisted in applying for land, despite continuing refusals, while others took to illicit new rubber planting. Numerous official commissions were presented with petitions of their grievances, but smallholders lacked the means to apply political leverage onto their demands. Their nominal representative in the Federal Legislative Council, a Malay civil servant appointed by the colonial authorities, not only failed to press smallholders' demands but frequently lent support to government measures detrimental to smallholding interests.

Worsening conditions among producers finally resulted in the appointment of a special commission under Sir Francis Mudie to inquire into the deterioration of Malaya's rubber industry, over the objections of the larger British estates. The Mudie Report, published in October 1954, placed great emphasis on the urgency of policy changes for the modernization of Malayan rubber:

> This is probably the last chance that a large part of the natural rubber industry will have of setting its house in order before the storm breaks. . . . It is no exaggeration to say that if the rubber industry were to be allowed to fall into irretrievable senility Malaya's present type of developing economy would collapse.[24]

Yet the Mudie Mission proposals for revitalizing the Malayan rubber industry, based on a vastly expanded government commitment to replanting and even new planting, still failed to arouse the colonial authorities to action.[25] Before major policy changes designed to stimulate innovation could be adopted, custodial interests would have to be deprived of their clamp on policy. But first they would have to be separated from political power.

Malaya's first General Election of July 1955 marked the political watershed giving rise to fundamental changes in rubber strategy. To be sure, the United Malays National Organization (UMNO), senior partner in the elected Alliance Party government, retained a traditional Malay ambivalence towards rubber. Some UMNO leaders saw rubber smallholding as the key to rural Malay socio-economic advancement. Others, however, reiterated fears of the vagaries of world rubber markets, while still others of a more traditionalist bent insisted on continued emphasis on padi. The Malayan Chinese Association (MCA), UMNO's partner in the Alliance, for its part, strongly favoured measures aimed at resuscitating Malaya's rubber industry, especially since the greater part of its support stemmed from Chinese rubber plantation owners. Rubber, furthermore, suited the communal criteria of the UMNO-MCA Alliance, since it offered an avenue for bringing economic development to the Malay kampungs without undue encroachment upon the Chinese. In 1957 the MCA apostle of positive economics, Tan Siew Sin, assumed the portfolio of Minister of Commerce and Industry and immediately declared for the planting of 1,000,000 acres of high-yielding rubber over the coming decade in order to assure the country's economic growth and rural development. Despite initial hesitancy within the predominantly Malay, padi-oriented Ministry of Agriculture, the emergence of a responsive, elected government assured the ascendancy of a development goal in Malayan rubber policy.

Significantly, the elected Alliance government, shortly after coming to power undertook the organization of a Malayan Council of Smallholders Associations to aggregate smallholding interests and ventilate their demands on policy-making. This reflected the Alliance belief that the successful modernization of Malaya's rubber industry required better integration of peasant producers within the political process. This departure from normal governmental practice in organizing and financing a particular interest group indicated the depth of Alliance commitment to rubber development.

On the eve of the 1955 General Election the Colonial authorities responded to the Mudie Mission Report by expanding somewhat the original Rubber Replanting Scheme. This revised scheme was subsequently adopted by the elected Alliance government. Rubber replanting thereafter became the largest single item in Malaya's First Five-Year Plan (FYP) (1956-1960), involving M$280 million or 15% of planned public capital expenditure for the quinquennium. Although basic replanting strategy remained unchanged, the Alliance looked to extensive replanting of smallholdings to improve rubber productivity and raise peasant incomes.

A further change designed to facilitate replanting on very small holdings, termed the Rubber Industry (Replanting) (Smallholders) Scheme, was introduced in April 1956. By virtue of this new Scheme, the smallholders' replanting grant was raised by a fifth to M$600 per acre, with holders of less than 30 acres being entitled to replant a third of their acreage plus 5 acres. To cater to the financial difficulties confronting smaller holdings, special provision was made for peasants with less than 5 acres to new plant an equivalent area up to 5 acres under the auspices of Fund B, on condition that the old stands were cut down once the new rubber matured and subsistence was assured.

Although the Smallholders Replanting Scheme was a move in the direction of supporting peasant replanting, it did not go far enough with regard to the needs of very small holdings. By the end of the First FYP some three-quarters of the original smallholding replanting target had already been realized, mostly on Chinese and Indian medium-holdings. Less than 30% of the replanting had been undertaken by Malays, as these smallest holdings still came up against severe financial difficulties and administrative deficiencies obstructing their attempts to modernize themselves.[26] Strenuous demands by rural UMNO Members of Parliament on their behalf, manifested at the onset of the 1959 General Election campaign, moved the Alliance government to respond to the plight of Malay peasant smallholders by accelerating the rate of payment of Fund B grants. However, this proved to be too little, too late, at least in terms of the First FYP replanting target. Once again the operations of the replanting scheme had served to artificially widen the productivity gap between very small and larger producers of natural rubber.

Malaya's second General Election of 1959 and the local council elections of 1960-62 impelled the Alliance to further extend its policy commitment towards rubber smallholdings in order to maintain its political position among the rural electorate. The Second FYP, introduced in 1961, accordingly provided some M$165 million for rubber replanting, of which 42% was to be directed at the small-holding sector on the basis of their proportion of total output. In order to stimulate replanting among peasant producers, the re-planting grant was raised to M$750 an acre, with an additional M$50 an acre paid holders of less than 5 acres upon successful completion of replanting. Furthermore, contractors were now to be employed to clear and prepare smallholdings for replanting, thereby easing the physical burden as well.

This revised replanting programme, termed Scheme 3 of Fund B, succeeded in arousing active Malay interest in replanting at last. By the end of 1965, about half the smallholding acreage, some 800,000 acres, had been replanted with high-yielding material, and the new policy was continued in Scheme 4 introduced in December 1966.

So great was the growth in demand for replanting assistance on the part of smallholders that in 1967 the Malaysian government had to restrict annual replanting for budgetary reasons to 45,000 acres a year, until 1970. Once enabled to do so, peasant determination to replant with high-yielding rubber rapidly outstripped the resources available to Fund B for their finance. Henceforth, the continued arbitrary division of replanting funds according to estate-smallholding past production ratios, as against present needs or future capabilities, comprised a major institutional barrier to further peasant innovation through rubber renewal.

Alongside its replanting scheme, the elected Malayan government also embarked on a large-scale new planting programme subsequently described as "the most ambitious . . . ever undertaken in tropical agriculture."[27] Shortly after coming to power, the Alliance appointed a Working Party to consider the opening up of new areas for land settlement as a means of overcoming the near-desperate land hunger in the Federation. Despite traditionalist Malay preferences for "diversification" through padi, the government accepted the Working Party recommendation that new land settlement be based on rubber, in order to ensure settlers' prosperity.[28] In 1956, the Federal Land Development Authority (FELDA) was established to administer land settlement in conjunction with the state governments. By way of contrast with previous, not-very successful padi settlement projects, FELDA schemes were to be devoted primarily to rubber smallholding with its prospect of high settler income.

Under FELDA, large tracts of suitable virgin jungle were to be prepared by contractors for subdivision into 10-acre family holdings, of which 8 were planted with high-yielding rubber and the remainder with fruit trees and foodcrops. As part of the undertaking, FELDA granted financial assistance to settlers, including a maintenance stipend until the rubber matured, and co-ordinated the provision of all necessary economic and social services on its schemes. Selection of settlers was by interview, on a point system, with priority going to landless young married Malays having agricultural experience. Only when their new-planted rubber actually matured were settlers expected to repay their FELDA loans, by instalments. Through careful preparation of all factors and diligent aftercare, FELDA aimed at establishing productive and remunerative land settlement schemes based primarily on rubber smallholding.[29]

FELDA's original accent on profitability underlined its transitional state between a custodial and truly developmental role. Owing to the large sums of public monies committed to it, FELDA was originally expected to yield an accounting "profit" in the finest tradition of colonial enterprise. At the same time, however, the Alliance leadership made it clear that land settlement under FELDA was to proceed without undue concern for capital repayment and interest, reflecting an awareness of the urgency of the rural development problem. To reconcile these two considerations, it was resolved in the end that FELDA schemes would be "sound economic propositions able, eventually, to pay their own way and based initially on sound financial provisions;" yet for the sake of immediate development, actual profitability could be relegated to the future.[30] Development, rather than near-term accounting "profits" thus gained ascendancy among FELDA objectives.

The introduction of FELDA was greeted with widespread enthusiasm on the part of the peasantry, and especially the landless Malays. FELDA offered Malayan peasants an outlet for innovation through the redeployment of resources from subsistence agriculture to comparatively high income-generating rubber smallholding. Still, several of the Malay States governed by a more traditional elite and enjoying constitutional jurisdiction over land matters, declined co-operation with FELDA in favour of continued emphasis on padi. It required sustained political pressure on the part of rural Malay interests to impel state participation in FELDA-sponsored land development schemes.

Continuing, growing peasant interest in rubber settlement schemes manifested over successive general elections further induced increasingly larger provisions for FELDA in the post-election Second FYP (1961-65) and First Malaysia Plan (1966-70) periods. Expanded rural involvement in the Malaysian political process, through elections and interest articulation, brought about a substantial mobilization of social and economic resources for rubber smallholding-based land settlement. By 1967, some 67 FELDA schemes had come into operation, involving 121,000 acres of new, high-yielding rubber stands.

On these FELDA schemes about 10,600 families were settled in 48 new villages serviced by more than 2,000 miles of road and 44 schools with 14,000 pupils. A further 450,000 acres of FELDA land settlement schemes for 65,000 families were in various stages of planning by the late 1960s. While high-yielding rubber retained its primacy, the First Malaysian Plan also expressed the intention to broaden FELDA's scope to include other satisfactorily remunerative crops. Henceforth, crops hitherto restricted to estate-type cultivation, notably oil palm, citrus, bananas and coffee, were to be available to smallholders on FELDA schemes. In pursuing diversification, it is significant that considerations of income were now utilized as criteria to justify resource allocations on FELDA schemes, in the interest of rural development.

Policy requisites for successful peasant innovation can perhaps best be illustrated by contrasting the operations of FELDA with other Malayan land settlement schemes. As a supplement to FELDA the federal government initiated in 1956 a Smallholder New Planting Scheme, later revigorated as the so-called "Fringe Alienation Scheme." These schemes applied to the fringes of existing kampungs, where adjacent tracts were to be block-replanted with high-yielding rubber in order to augment villagers' income potential.[31] Under this scheme, the original plots were to ensure peasant earnings until the fringe block matured, when they too could be replanted. Although some 190,000 acres of new rubber were planted under Fringe Alienation Schemes through 1963, most of the responsible state governments failed to provide adequate aftercare to maintain the standards required for continuation of Fund B grants.

Another land settlement pattern was promulgated in the east coast states of Kelantan and Trengannu following the election there of Pan-Malayan Islamic Party (PMIP) state governments in 1959. Refusing co-operation with the Alliance-run FELDA, the PMIP state governments proceeded to introduce their own "land settlement" schemes based on the designation of uncleared blocks of jungle for settlers to plant without further aid or support.[32] Despite pressing land hunger and poverty in east coast Malaya, conditions on these schemes proved too arduous for successful peasant innovation. When PMIP rule in Trengganu collapsed in 1961, the federal government joined with the restored Alliance state government in an accelerated programme of FELDA-managed schemes, located strategically near the border with PMIP-governed Kelantan.

Party manoeuvring aside, the PMIP State and Fringe Alienation schemes both pointed to the immense difficulty of peasant innovation in a plantation industry demanding the highest technical standards unless adequate financial support, preparation and aftercare were assured.

Simply increasing the acreage of rubber under smallholdings did not, of itself, generate rural development. Between 1957 and 1960 some 300 rubber estates totalling about 230,000 acres were sold by despairing foreign owners for subdivision into smallholdings. Most of the subdivided acreage was disposed to small businessmen searching for investment opportunities, who in turn let out their subdivided holdings to tenants.

The Alliance government, even after being confronted with the social and economic evils accompanying estate subdivision, staunchly refused to interfere with the disposal of private property. Rather, the federal authorities preferred to believe that estate subdivision had "social advantages" by way of "increasing the number of small landowners who . . . possess a stake in this country."[33] In fact, fewer than 8% of subdivided holdings were owner-occupied. On tenancies, standards of management and maintenance deteriorated considerably so that few were capable of regular renewal of their assets through replanting. There can be little doubt that the unrestricted subdivision of estates introduced "anti-development" into peasant smallholding, effectively subverting much of the progress being made in revitalizing the Malayan rubber industry.[34] Resulting increases in nominal smallholding area notwithstanding, the absence of safeguards for improved peasant productivity on subdivided estates inhibited the innovation necessary for rural development.

Much of FELDA's success stemmed from its combining the organizational methods of large-scale plantation agriculture with the economic and social advantages inherent in smallholder rubber cultivation. While the operational basis of FELDA schemes remained the smallholding peasant, FELDA management offered settlers certain benefits of scale usually accruing only to larger estates, such as quality control, working capital, and the provision of adequate infrastructure. Later replanting schemes were similarly organized to make available to smallholders the benefits of scale at specific stages of the production process. The evolution of Malaysian rubber policy thus resulted in new forms of organization of production in which economies of scale were wed to the economics of smallholding, thereby releasing peasant innovation for rural development.

Malaysia's experience in rubber smallholding provides an interesting illustration of the relationship between state and peasantry in promoting rural development. At the core of this relationship lay a web of authoritative rules and institutions expressive of official policy. This legal-institutional framework regulated productive activity and allocated resources within the economy, according to which innovation was either barred or stimulated. The shift in rubber policy in favour of innovators denoted changes in the character of the peasant-state relationship that followed upon Merdeka:

1. Changed attitudes towards the rubber industry: A central feature of this new relationship was the changed conventional attitude towards rubber smallholding. Underlying official actions there generally rests a theory of economic life that serves as guidelines for subsequent policy. To the colonial mind, Western-style, large-scale, estate-type rubber plantations were inherently preferable to alien, native smallholdings. This preference reflected itself in resulting policy, despite the comparative economic advantages that rested with the peasant producers. Considerable harm was therefore caused to the rural economy and society, as well as to the competitive position of Malaya's leading industry. Only when the attitudal underpinnings of rubber policy were modified to accord with economic reality could remedial action be taken to restore the productive potentiality of the smallholding sector.

2. Political changes and policy revision: This revision of official attitudes mirrored changes in the constellation of political interests. Under the colonial regime, British estate interests enjoyed close access to the sources of political power, while rubber smallholders remained unorganized, inarticulate, and without direct representation in the councils of state. In such circumstances, pressure for policy changes could come mainly through the sobering effects of declining rubber prices on government revenues. It was the introduction of representative, responsible government in 1955 that inaugurated the transfer of ultimate political power to Malaya's peasantry. Since that time the need to maintain electoral support impelled governments, even at state and district levels, to respond through policy to rural demands. Elections and the party mechanism effectively included peasants within the Malayan political process, providing ventilation for rubber smallholding interests in policy formulation.

3. Legal-institutional patterns and innovation: Realization of their economic potential required, first, that rubber smallholders be liberated from legal-institutional barriers to their optimal performance. Smallholder innovation, directed at large-scale new investment in natural rubber, had been stifled by restrictions on new planting as well as by structural, technical and financial obstacles to replanting. With the onset of responsible and representative government in Malaya, policy changes were undertaken to expand rubber acreage and facilitate smallholding replanting. Over the decade 1955-66, Malayan rubber acreage grew by 18%, with the most significant expansion occurring in the smallholding sector, which increased in size by more than half. In 1960 smallholdings overtook estates to become the larger sector in terms of planted acreage. Even though a large portion of this acreage gain consisted in fact of less-efficient subdivided estates, smallholding production still increased by 49% over the decade. Even greater gains in smallholding productivity were promised once newly planted, high-yielding acreage reached maturity.

4. The role of government in fostering technological progress: Peasant investment in a high technology industry such as natural rubber required governmental supervision over maintenance and improvement of technical standards. Rubber research, financed by an export cess, produced high-yielding clones which then had to be made available to smallholders for replanting and new planting. Field supervision was further necessary to ensure adequate standards of maintenance on high-yielding smallholdings. Successive modifications to the smallholding replanting scheme rendered high-yielding rubber accessible even to peasant producers. New forms of smallholder organization, such as FELDA schemes and "block" planting, made for optimal deployment of the new technology. Capital expenditure on rubber replanting and land development undertaken by the Federal Government increased from M$170.1 million under the First FYP to M$250.7 million during the Second FYP period.[35] In 1967 applications for assistance exceeded the resources available to Fund B for replanting. By then some 56% of smallholding acreage (compared to 86% of estate, and 68% of total peninsular Malaysian acreage) consisted of high-yielding material. Average yield per acre reflected this process of modernization, having increased from 460 lbs. per acre in 1951 to 900 lbs. per acre in 1966. However, where legal-institutional restrictions continued to bar smallholder innovation, as on subdivided estates, improvement failed to take root and was overtaken by "anti-development."

5. Resource allocations for rubber development: Whereas removal of legal-institutional barriers and application of research might release peasant innovation, the Malaysian experience further indicates that large-scale, urgent progress in rural development requires a major commitment of national resources towards rubber smallholding. Under Malaya's colonial regime, the smallholding sector served virtually as the milch cow of the federal Treasury, owing to the excessive, regressive duties on rubber, and gained little in return by way of public services. With the advent of self-government the tax burden remained, but the government's growing commitment to rural development at least directed an increasing portion of public expenditure toward improving the rubber smallholding sector. Capital expenditure on land development accordingly grew from M\$16.7 million under the First FYP to M\$129.8 million under the Second FYP, reaching a target of M\$375.9 million in the First Malaysia Plan. Most of these funds went for the provision of economic and social infrastructure on FELDA schemes. Where such essential infrastructure was not provided, on Fringe Alienation schemes and on the Kelantan land scheme, smallholder innovation floundered upon environmental obstacles. Significantly, the enlarged appropriations towards rubber smallholding were no longer conditional upon annual variations in federal revenue, as was typical under colonial fiscal practice; instead, "sound" finance and strictly balanced budgeting had given way to long-term planning for expanding rural productivity. This underlined the ascendancy of a development goal in Malaysian economic policy.[36]

Malaysia's commitment to rural development also extended to ensuring peasant producers a more favourable distribution of rubber income. For the Alliance to toy with income redistribution through intervention in the free market would indicate a significant departure from its basically conservative outlook. Yet in response to electoral pressure, the federal government in 1962 charged its *Majlis Amanah Ra'ayat* (Rural Development Authority) with financing group processing facilities for rubber smallholders, 70% of whose production had hitherto been sold unprocessed at a 20%

discount. Up to 1967 some 260 such group centres were set up, processing about 8% of smallholding rubber. That year the heveacrumb process for "Standard Malaysian Rubber" (SMR), recently developed by the Rubber Research Institute of Malaya, was introduced into the smallholding sector.

Henceforth, smallholding rubber would obtain SMR prices based on stated technical specifications, rather than endure visual appearance discounts as in the past. Though apparently willing to adopt measures for enlarging peasant producers' shares of rubber earnings, the Alliance government remained firm in its refusal to apportion replanting funds other than according to proportional output. In so doing, Malaysian replanting strategy effectively sacrificed smallholders' greater needs to the canons of conservative finance. Alliance commitment to smallholder development was evidently limited to the point where redistribution became unpalatably radical.

Peasant innovation achieved more than merely the revitalization of the smallholding sector and with it Malaysia's rubber industry. Significant advances followed in peasant smallholders' standard of living. A 1966 survey showed that an average-sized holding of 7.4 acres planted with high-yielding rubber provided a net annual return of M$4000 (equivalent to US$1,300 or £540), described as "a reasonable income for a rural family."[37] If much remained to be done by way of assisting "marginal men" into rubber development, according to FELDA's slogan, there was "No Need to be Poor."

ENDNOTES

1. Among the major works in this line of enquiry are Everett E. Hagan, *On the Theory of Social Change* (Homewood, IL, 1962) Albert O. Hirschman, *The Strategy of Economic Development* (New Haven, 1960); and W.W. Rostow, *The Stages of Economic Growth* (Cambridge, 1958).

2. For an historical survey of the Malaysian rubber industry and its role in economic development see Lim Chong Yah, *The Economic Development of Modern Malaya* (Kuala Lumpur, 1967), chap. 3; and J.H. Drabble, "The plantation industry in Malaya up to 1922," *Journal of the Malaysian Branch, Royal Asiatic Society* (1967).

3. Lim, *Economic Development*, p. 114.

4. The Stevenson Scheme (1922-28) and International Rubber Regulation Scheme (1934-43) were intended to control the production of natural rubber, and therefore prices, but actually operated the expense of Malayan smallholdings. P.T. Bauer, *The Rubber Industry: A Study in Competition and Monopoly* (London, 1948) argued that this discrimination was deliberate; T.H. Silcock, "A note on the working of the rubber regulation," *Economic Journal* (1948). pp. 335-68, maintains that

discrimination was based on ignorance in evaluating the output of the smallholding sector.

5. On the comparative efficiency of smallholdings in natural rubber production in Malaya see P.T. Bauer's classic study, *Report on a Visit to the Rubber Growing Smallholdings of Malaya, July-September 1946* (London, 1948). (Henceforth: Bauer. Report).

6. Secretary of State for the Colonies, G. Hall, *House of Commons Debates*, 25 July 1946, col. 242.

7. See K.E. Knorr, *World Rubber and its Regulation* (London, 1945), pp. 108-12 on this point.

8. J.C. Mathison, rubber estate representative, *Federation of Malaya, Legislative Council Proceedings*, 20 March 1952, pp. 98-100. (Henceforth: *L.C. Proc.*).

9. Among the legal measures restricting mobility of Malays and Malay lands from rice to rubber were the Malay Reservations and Land Regulations which fixed tenure and obliged cropping with padi. In addition, the planting restrictions embodied in the International Rubber Agreement limited new entry into rubber. British officialdom and Malay aristocrats further conspired to deliberately hold back English-language education from the kampungs, lest its introduction upset traditional custom and entice Malay peasants away from padi: Cf. *Proceedings of the Federal Council of the Federated Malay States, 1930*, addresses by Raja Sir Chulan ibni Almarhum Sultan Abdullah, Raja di-Hilir of Perak, and the British expatriate Director of Education, pp. B65-105.

10. Federation of Malaya, *Report of the Rice Production Committee* (Kuala Lumpur, 1953), paras. 51, 152. For a comparison of the marginal revenue products of rice and rubber at various price levels for rubber see Lim, *Economic Development*, pp. 29-33.

11. For an evaluation of colonial rubber policy see T.H. Silcock, "The economy of Malaya," in C. Hoover (ed.). *Economic Systems of the Commonwealth* (Durham, N.C., 1961).

12. See Bauer, *Report*; and Federation of Malaya, *Final Report of the Rubber Smallholders Enquiry Committee* (Kuala Lumpur, 1952), Para. 11 on this point.

13. A.A.H. Tan, "The incidence of export taxes on small producers," *Malayan Economic Review* (1967).

14. Bauer, *Report*, esp. p. 25.

15. Evidence of strong smallholders demand for new investment opportunities in rubber was provided by the *Final Report of the Rubber Smallholders Enquiry Committee*, Para. 27, and by the International Bank for Reconstruction and Development, *The Economic Development of Malaya* (Baltimore, 1955), p. 40.

16. Bauer, *Report*, p. 38.

17. See the remarks by Mr. Stuart Symington, then head of the U.S. Reconstruction Finance Corporation testifying before the Preparedness Subcommittee of the Senate Armed Services Committee, 1951, quoted in Charles Gamba, *Synthetic Rubber and Malaya* (1959), p. 28. Like their British counterparts, the American authorities ignored the very large peasant stake in Malayan rubber in treating the industry as though it comprised solely British estate companies.

18. Member for Agriculture and Forestry, *L.C. Proc.*, 20 March 1950, p. 101.

19. On smallholding replanting difficulties see Sir Francis Mudie, *Report of a Mission of Enquiry into the Rubber Industry of Malaya* (Kuala Lumpur, 1954), Paras. 68-9. (Henceforth: *Mudie Mission Report*).

20. In October 1954 the grant was retroactively raised to M$500 an acre, and while this covered most of the direct costs of replanting the smallholders had no compensation for 6 years' waiting for the trees to mature. Outside work possibilities during this period were limited by the need to tend to the replanted holding to exacting standards of maintenance.

21. Pseudo-subdivided estates, contrived to take advantage of higher Fund B grants, gained an especially large portion of smallholding replanting funds at the expense of very small producers. See A.A.H. Tan, "The incidence of taxation," p. 97 on this matter.

22. *Federation of Malaya Annual Report 1955* (Kuala Lumpur, 1956), p. 142.

23. Member for Economic Affairs, *L.C. Proc.*, 20 March 1953, col. 263-4. It is difficult to imagine rubber, a cash crop with a very lengthy productive life (35 years) being prone to "shifting agriculture."

24. *Mudie Mission Report*, paras. 7, 15.

25. Among the proposals put forward by the Mudie Report were enlargement of the replanting scheme, promotion of new planting and reduced taxation of rubber producers. Of these only the first was implemented by the colonial government.

26. Chief Replanting Officer, *Straits Times*, 28 Sept. 1961.

27. *Federation of Malaya Yearbook 1962* (Kuala Lumpur, 1962), p. 299.

28. Federation of Malaya, *Report of the Land Settlement Working Party* (Kuala Lumpur, 1956), Para. 91.

29. For a study of FELDA activities see Gayl D. Ness, *Bureaucracy and Rural Development in Malaysia* (Berkeley, 1967), p. 136 *et passim*.

30. Minister of Commerce and Industry, *L.C. Proc.*, 7 March 1957, col. 252.

31. On Fringe Alienation Schemes see J.C. Jackson, "Smallholding cultivation of cash crops," in Wang Gungwu, ed., *Malaysia* (London, 1963), pp. 261-2.

32. D. Ali, "Kelantan's unique go-it-alone Plan," *Straits Budget*, 14 Dec. 1960, p. 11.

33. Assistant Minister of Rural Development, *Federation of Malaya, Dewan Ra'ayat Proceedings*, 23 Feb. 1960, col. 1846.

34. For a scathing critique of estate subdivision and its impact on Malaya's economy, including a detailed analysis of the subdivision process, see Ungku Aziz, *Subdivision of Estates in Malaya 1951-60*, Vol. 1, Appendix A to the *Final Report of the Subdivision of Estates Committee* (Kuala Lumpur, 1963), esp. pp. 135-6.

35. Federation of Malaysia, *First Malaysia Plan* (Kuala Lumpur, 1965), Table 2-6, pp. 28-9.

36. Gayl D. Ness, "Economic development and the goals of government," in Wang Gungwu, ed., *Malaysia*, pp. 307-17.

37. Quoted in *National Rubber News*, July 1967.

CHAPTER 7

DEVELOPMENT POLICIES AND PATTERNS OF AGRARIAN DOMINANCE IN THE MALAYSIAN RUBBER EXPORT ECONOMY

Since Malaysian independence over two decades ago, rubber production there has undergone a significant and far-reaching structural transformation, in social as well as economic dimensions. This transformation represented the outcome of policy responses to changing world market conditions for the export of natural rubber, which coincided with a political transition to independence and parliamentary government. In its response, government policy since the mid-1950s released many of the earlier administrative constraints on the spread of new rubber planting.[1] The ensuing entrepreneurial reawakening led to large-scale replanting and new planting with high-yielding rubber. This increasingly widespread wave of technological innovation was accompanied by the dissolution of marginal estate enterprises, which was more than offset by a parallel expansion of peasant participation in rubber cultivation. Productivity and therefore producer incomes generally tended to improve, notwithstanding cyclical fluctuations in world rubber prices. Yet, by the middle 1970s this policy trend favouring technological cum entrepreneurial innovation appears to have altered direction. Indeed, recent Malaysian rubber policy indicates that structural transformation has run its course, at least for present intents and purposes. As will be seen, the current policy goal has reverted to protecting the newly established economic and social order in the Malaysian rubber planting against further pressures for developmental change.

This policy reversion has critical implications for long-run Malaysian development. Rubber and, to a somewhat lesser extent, tin have constituted the main sources of Malaysian economic growth over recent decades.[2] Although the contribution of rubber planting

Modern Asian Studies, Vol. 15, Pt. 1 (February, 1981).

to Malaysian Gross Domestic Product has in fact declined, from around a quarter during the 1950s to about 10% in the mid-1970s, rubber exports still yield between a fifth (in 1975, a year of poor prices) and a quarter (in 1976, a better year) of total export earnings.[3]

Nor has rubber constituted a narrow enclave-type export sector. Malaysian rubber planting succeeded in generating a network of supply and demand linkages with other sectors of the economy. A substantial portion of rubber export earnings has consequently been retained through domestic accelerator and multiplier effects.[4] Furthermore, rubber export duties and associated company taxes continue to finance a significant proportion of government expenditure, including the increasingly comprehensive scale of development planning. Annual average real rates of growth of Malaysian Gross Domestic Product accelerated from the 3 to 4% level of the 1950s to over 5.5% during the 1960s, and reached 7.5% over the first half of the 1970s. Meanwhile, a reducing rate of population increase during this period resulted in a credible improvement to average real income per capita.[5] Whereas the rubber economy made a prime contribution to Malaysia's past growth performance, recent policy shifts invoke a three-tier situation of dependency: Malaysian development has been and still is heavily dependent on rubber export earnings; rubber export earnings are in turn dependent on continuing policy support for technological and entrepreneurial innovation for improved productivity; yet the conduct of policy has come to reflect a style of governance dependent politically on conservative, entrenched interests in the rubber economy itself.

Economic historians of Malaysia have recounted the deleterious impact of past administrative intervention in the allocation of resources between rubber estates and smallholdings on productive efficiency and ensuing economic developments.[6] In a somewhat different vein, and referring to agriculture generally, recent writings in the social history of Malaysia and elsewhere have underscored the effects of constraints deriving from landlord-peasant conflict upon agrarian modernization.[7] Be that as it may, the earlier structural distortions in the Malaysian rubber economy had virtually disappeared once the termination of colonial rule deprived the largest, mainly British-owned, estates of their former administrative patrons.[8] Nor does there appear to exist any great landlord-peasant dichotomy, at least not in the rubber planting sector of Malaysian agriculture.[9] The fact of the matter is that in contemporary Malaysia neither large estates nor landlordism can be said to constitute, as such, a vested interest against rubber development.

In a recent and seminal essay, D. A. Low has called attention to the newly emergent phenomenon in Asia of, what he has termed, "dominant peasantism."[10] This dominant peasantry is distinguished as a class by its comparatively large (for peasants) holdings of land, its relatively high degree of capital utilization in production, its market-oriented productive activity, its employment—usually informally—of outside labour, and by its close tie with political authority. The dominant peasantry is characteristically involved in commercialized agriculture, as a peasant entrepreneurial class. While in most instances elsewhere in Asia, this dominant peasant phenomenon apparently centred on food cultivation for local markets, where it typically benefitted from policy intervention and support from governments.

In Malaysia, by way of contrast, a dominant peasantry has emerged as a salient feature in a specifically export-oriented commodity sector, natural rubber.[11] Here the role of government in influencing market conditions is necessarily more subtle, but certainly no less significant. Arguably, the dominant peasant class of Malaysian rubber producers has been the prime beneficiary of policy developments since independence. The recent goal reversion in rubber policy may be explained precisely by reference to this role expansion of dominant peasantry, which induced policy responses designed to protect the stability of their newly acquired asset values and income shares against forces of competition and change. To discern the developmental implications of this policy transformation, it is instructive to look back at the history of the Malaysian rubber economy, from which the lesson may best be learned.

The pattern of production that emerged in the Malaysian rubber economy reflected the interaction between international trade and finance on the one hand, and government policy on the other, upon domestic and overseas investment activity in rubber planting. From the formative stage, two distinct types of planting enterprise evolved in peninsular Malaysia, differing in organizational form and factor mix.[12] One such type was represented by rubber estates, a corporate-style enterprise built around the relatively intensive utilization of both capital and (mostly immigrant) wage labour on large-scale plantations; the other comprised peasant smallholdings, characterized by family enterprise and labour. A legal provision fixed the dividing line between estates and smallholdings, for official purposes, at 100 acres (40.5 hectares). Throughout the period up to the late 1940s, government policy served to mediate the influence of the world rubber market, itself highly cyclical and prone to regular price fluctuations, on the local plantation economy. Authoritative allocations of public resources, such as land, new technologies, permissions and subsidies, effectively determined patterns of production and, accordingly, the direction of Malaysian rubber development. The rubber export market constituted, to be sure, the anvil upon which policy forged domestic production into its historical pattern. Yet the allocative process remained, at root, political rather than just economic in design and intent.

British colonial administration displayed a fundamental policy bias in making available public resources to the nascent rubber planting economy. Already from the formative, expansionary phase of rubber planting in British Malaya, allocations of policy resources tended to treat estates as the quintessential institution of the plantation industry. Conversely, peasant smallholders were conventionally perceived to be inefficient and peripheral producers.[13] Hence, the policy provision of land, infrastructure and economic services accorded real locational and concessional advantages to the estate subsector, bolstering their competitive position in relation to the smallholdings. What began as incidental preference soon translated into deliberate policy discrimination.

During the 1920s and again during the 1930s world demand for rubber experienced sudden and sharp downward cyclical trends. As prices and quantities demand fell, British Malayan rubber policy adapted its export strategy and internal resource allocations to cope with declining incomes. International commodity agreements were concluded through British initiative, the Stevenson Scheme (1922-28) and the International Rubber Regulation Agreement (1935-43), as a means of restricting the output of natural rubber and therefore raising its price.[14] Two policy instruments were applied. Export quotas were determined so as to restrict current production, while regulatory controls were introduced to limit the longer-run growth of rubber acreage and supply potential.

As the world's largest single producing country, Malaya was obliged to undertake a relatively greater cutback in order to have the restriction schemes accepted by others. Within Malaya, however, administrative discrimination tended to shift the burden of restriction onto smallholder producers disproportionately. In the administration of export quotas, relatively favourable treatment was given to the estate subsector, so that excessive curbs had to be imposed on smallholding output. Worse yet, the prohibition on the release of additional lands for rubber planting, and on new planting, had particularly grievous consequences for the long-run cost-competitiveness of the smallholding subsector. If the economic rents arising out of the restriction schemes at least made for higher current earnings, however unequally distributed, for established rubber growers, the ultimate penalty befell would-be smallholders who were denied entry into rubber planting and who had been kept back in alternative, comparatively disadvantageous occupations.

The Second World War altered drastically the conditions for international rubber trade and finance. In the main consuming country, the United States, synthetic rubber had emerged as a substitute for the natural product over a range of purposes and prices. Mandatory content requirements enforced by the American government in early post-war years bolstered the production of synthetic at the expense of incremental demand for natural rubber. Meanwhile, Britain came to depend heavily on Malayan rubber (and tin) exports to the United States to relieve the chronic post-war sterling payments deficit.[15] And although Indonesian production was temporarily curtailed owing to revolutionary turmoil, Sumatra loomed large as a prospective rival in the natural rubber export trade. Since these post-war challenges were perceived by the colonial authorities merely in relation to marketing, rather than allocative efficiency, the initial adjustment was therefore limited to Malayan export strategy.[16] Previous restrictions on output were removed, and producers freed to maximize current export earnings. However, the internal policy bias within the Malayan rubber economy, between estates and smallholdings, still persisted. A more comprehensive reform of Malayan rubber policy had to await future political developments.

By that time, a considerable portion of Malayan rubber acreage was threatened with approaching obsolescence, especially, but not only, on smallholdings. Substantial investment in asset renewal and growth was required to avert impending economic decay.[17] Nevertheless, post-war rehabilitation measures had directed their benefits first and foremost to the estate subsector.[18] Meanwhile, the continuing colonial administrative ban on the allocation of additional lands for rubber planting invariably bolstered asset values and economic rents accruing to owners of existing holdings, and to estates most of all. Yet, apart from serving vested interests, Malayan land policy also gave expression to deep underlying anxieties about the rubber export economy.[19] These anxieties were shared by both British officialdom and traditional Malay elite. The colonial administration often voiced its concern about Malaya's alleged excessive dependency on rubber exports, and the resulting dangers of possible "oversupply" in an unstable world market.

Such fears, vigorously exploited by interested parties, prompted an attitudinal predisposition favouring the constriction of Malaya's rubber area along with diversification (particularly of peasant producers) towards other foodcrops, especially rice. At the same time, the Malay aristocracy regarded rice cultivation as the traditional agrarian bulwark of Malay values and identity. Deliberate efforts were made to keep Malay peasants in subsistence agriculture and out of rubber, so as to preserve the inherited social order even at the expense of economic welfare and development.[20]

The main thrust of the post-war Malayan rubber modernization drive centred on replanting obsolete acreage. Already by the 1950s, a large segment of Malaya's planted area stood in urgent need of renewal. The inauguration of the rubber replanting scheme in 1952 heralded a shift in the goals of government intervention, away from protection to development. As originally conceived, the replanting scheme comprised simply an instrument of taxation and cross-subsidization.[21] Yet this was to pave the way—in the wake of subsequent political changes—to more decisive policy innovations.

Official concern for agricultural diversification was given expression in replanting policy for the smallholding subsector. Administrators of the smallholding replanting scheme laid down suitability of soil as their main criterion for redirecting smallholder asset renewal towards crops other than rubber.[22] Over 10% of smallholding replanting during this period therefore involved shifting to alternative, officially approved crops. Yet none of these alternatives promised smallholders equivalent returns to high-yielding rubber cultivation. Pursuit of smallholding diversification through the replanting scheme in effect coupled retrogressive redistribution with resource misallocation. Colonial agricultural policy took on a curious twist in that the special replanting taxes exacted from the rubber smallholding community were being utilized to induce their removal from that occupation where they enjoyed comparative economic and social advantages.

Post-war colonial Malayan economic policies reflected a notion of development contained within the institutional status quo. Thus, rubber replanting policy was conceived on the assumption of structural continuity in the Malayan rubber economy. Certainly there was no intention of fomenting such structural reforms as might tend to undermine established, vested interests. Rather, the rubber replanting scheme was designed to protect and preserve the existing pattern of production and privilege through asset modernization. Bound by institutional rigidities sanctioned by policy, the modernizing impulse of this original replanting scheme proved incapable of generating a broad developmental momentum. Instead, administrative discrimination continued to serve mainly the interests of estates, in which the British component loomed large. Conversely, ongoing policy constraints on the economic activities of peasant producers inhibited any technological or entrepreneurial innovation on their part.

In these circumstances, rapidly deteriorating terms of trade for rubber in the aftermath of the Korean War boom carried the decaying Malayan rubber economy to the brink of crisis by the mid-1950s.[23] Coming at a time of impending transition to self-rule, the effects of this rubber crisis were acutely felt particularly among peasant smallholders and estate wage labourers, and in government revenues. Through it all, the influential British estate companies, then engaged in heavy disinvestment, maintained their adamant opposition to any corrective intervention by government. However, mounting concern for the future induced the colonial administration to appoint a mission of enquiry (the Mudie Mission) into the rubber economy. In its report (1954), a watershed in the development of the Malaysian rubber economy, the Mudie Mission called for new directions in replanting policy.[24] The subsequent train of political events prompted urgent adoption of the recommended course.

Malaya was about to advance to representative, responsible government, a move which would accord peasants—including rubber smallholders—the electoral means of furthering their economic interests. The altered political setting presaged a release from many of the most discriminatory earlier policy constraints on rubber smallholding.[25]

Following the advent of self-government, Malaysian rubber policy expressed an overriding economic development goal, supplanting the custodial inclination of the past.[26] To cope with worsening world market conditions for natural rubber over most of this period, Malaysian policy responded by adapting its export strategy and internal allocation of rubber resources to the requirements of income maintenance and growth, even at the expense of structural

TABLE 1
Area and Production of Rubber
in Peninsular Malaysia, 1925-77 (selected years).

Year	Estates Planted ('000 ha)	Estates Production ('000 tonnes)	Smallholdings Planted ('000 ha)	Smallholdings Production ('000 tonnes)	Total Planted ('000 ha)	Total Producion ('000 tonnes)	Percent Smallholding Planted Area	Percent Smallholding Production
1925	598.9	n/a	394.6	n/a	993.5	213.4	39.7	n/a
1930	763.3	237.8	482.8	218.4	1,246.1	456.2	38.7	47.9
1935	815.9	243.9	470.6	135.1	1,286.5	379.0	36.6	35.6
1939	849.9	246.9	536.6	116.8	1,386.5	363.7	38.7	32.1
1948	790.4	409.5	640.2	298.9	1,430.6	708.2	44.7	42.2
1952	808.1	346.7	647.5	245.4	1,455.6	591.9	44.5	41.5
1955	815.5	357.5	667.7	290.0	1,483.2	647.3	45.0	44.8
1957	814.0	373.9	692.0	272.4	1,506.0	646.1	45.9	42.2
1960	782.9	419.9	765.7	297.6	1,548.6	717.5	49.4	41.5
1965	752.3	498.9	1,021.9	353.3	1,774.2	852.2	57.6	41.7
1970	646.6	621.2	1,077.2	594.8	1,723.8	1,216.0	62.5	48.9
1973	589.4	673.8	1,104.6	791.7	1,465.5	1,465.5	65.2	54.0
1974	574.2*	659.5†	1,117.7*	800.9†	1,691.9	1,460.4	66.1	54.8
1975	563.3*	599.0†	1,131.5*	817.5†	1,694.8	1,416.5†	66.8	57.7
1976	556.4*	679.1†	1,147.7*	884.5†	1,704.1	1,563.6†	67.3	56.5
1977	545.7‡	652.8†	1,164.7‡	883.9†	1,710.4‡	1,536.7†	68.1‡	57.5

* Malaysian *Monthly Statistical Bulletin*, December 1977.
† *Rubber Statistical Bulletin*, Vol. 32, No. 8.
‡ Malaysian *Annual Statistical Bulletin*, 1977.
Sources: C. Barlow, *The Natural Rubber Industry*, Kuala Lumpur, 1978, Table 3:2
(years 1925-73), adapted.

maintenance. The lifting of many of the obstacles to peasant innovation, coupled with the wider and more progressive provision of critical administrative supports, served to accelerate the modernization of estate and, especially smallholding, assets. Indeed, this process of adaptation occurred even in face of the unfavourable terms of trade for natural rubber prevailing during the 1960s. As these policy adjustments unfolded, the propensity towards entrepreneurial and technological innovation that were fostered engendered substantial developments in the rubber economy. Along with increased acreage, output and productivity, the thrust of reform also wrought organic changes in the structure of rubber production in peninsular Malaysia (Table 1).

Yet, however substantial its impact, the scope of reform still remained incomplete. The effects of policy-induced innovation failed to filter on down to the very smallest and weakest elements, for the most part.[27] Resulting discontinuities in degrees of development set apart this peasant underclass, consisting mostly of Malays, from the emergent pattern of dynamic and high-yielding smallholdings.[28] That pattern, to be sure, had appreciably upgraded the efficiency of larger-scale, modernized smallholdings, heightening their role to virtual dominance over rubber policy. Once the world rubber market situation altered after 1973, incipient tensions arising out of differential patterns of modernization threatened the privileged economic position of the now-dominant smallholders, and foreshadowed a reversion to a more custodial policy perspective.

Between the Korean War boom of 1950-51 and the oil-inspired commodity boom of the early 1970s, the structure and terms of trade for natural rubber endured prolonged and pronounced market difficulties.[29] Much of the problem revolved around the sharpening competition between natural rubber and an increasingly sophisticated synthetic rubber industry in the major consuming countries. Not for the first time in international commodity trade, a natural product encountered increasingly sharp price competition from a close synthetic substitute, which happened to enjoy technical advancements along with declining costs. Already during the 1950s, a relatively unsophisticated synthetic rubber had managed to expand its market penetration from a quarter to about half of total world rubber consumption. The introduction of so called "stereo-regular" synthetics in 1961 gave the synthetic product certain definite price, supply and technical advantages.

Ensuing inroads made by the various synthetic rubbers narrowed the market for natural rubber to only around a third of global demand by the end of the decade. This market displacement aggravated the deterioration in natural rubber's terms of trade. Natural rubber prices experienced a protracted declining trend over the period, despite the periodic, short-lived cyclical "boomlets" of 1955, 1961, 1966 and 1970. Had it not been for the policy responses that led to a doubling of output despite a price decline of half over the 1960s, the Malaysian rubber economy would have endured a grievous income inflation, with disinvestment leading to inevitable stagnation.

The reduced advantages of rubber planting invoked some pol-
icy-supported diversification of plantation resources, at the margin,
towards alternative, more apparently remunerative export crops,
notably oil palm.[30] Oil palm cultivation has expanded rapidly in recent years, though rubber still remains far and away Malaysia's
largest agricultural export sector in terms of land use, employment and domestic value added.

The direction and priorities of rubber policy were determined
within a framework of exogenous constraints imposed by export
conditions and endogenous constraints arising out of the domestic
political process. Malaysia's transition to parliamentary government
broadened the sphere of political influence on decision-making
through the general elections held at regular intervals of every five
years or so.[31] Even though government has been dominated from
the first by a single coalition party, the Alliance, their conduct of
policy demonstrated a pronounced sensitivity to the ebb and flow
of electoral sensibilities. The practice of weighting parliamentary
constituencies somewhat in favour of rural areas tended to accentuate the political strength of agrarian electorates. Hence the coalition alignments molded in the contours of this electoral setting
came to serve as a political bulwark, in effect, ensuring the dominance of established smallholding interests over the formulation of
rubber policy.

One early by-product of Alliance government rubber policy reform was a sudden rash of dissolutions of company estates. Dissolutions reached a crest between 1957 and 1960. During these years
some 300 rubber estates, encompassing about 230,000 acres, or
over 11% of total estate acreage, were disposed of for subdivision
into smallholdings.[32] Such estates were, typically, economically marginal enterprises with low-grade or obsolete stands, despairing the
removal of bygone policy protection. Many, if not most of these,
were hitherto British-owned. The Alliance government tolerated
estate disinvestment with equanimity, believing that the subdivision of properties proffered "social advantages" by way of "increasing the number of small landowners who . . . possess a stake in
this country."[33]

In point of fact, fewer than 8% of subdivided estate properties
were let out to tenant smallholders through intermediary land
speculators. Subdivided in this way, tenancies undoubtedly retarded the modernization of the smallholding subsector as a
whole.

However, the accelerated divestment of marginal, protection-dependent estates had the effect of ending the long-standing policy antagonism between estate and smallholding subsectors of the Malaysian rubber economy. The former political obstacle to policy reform was finally dismantled. Henceforward, the political leverage now accruing to peasant smallholders would channel this convergence of established planter interests towards asserting their own dominance over rubber policy.

The policy reforms introduced on the initiative of the independent Alliance government displayed a four-pronged approach to the development of the Malaysian rubber economy. This approach combined specific policy provisions relating to accelerated asset renewal, controlled acreage expansion, and improved marketing capabilities, with a wider-ranging expansion of public investment in general economic and social overhead facilities for the rural populace. Underpinning this policy approach lay a conception of development predicated on a dual formula for structural change. One, involving producer behaviour, invoked policy measures calculated to inspire and spread innovative responses in the rubber economy so as to overcome the market crisis situation. The other, involving resource reallocations, called for policy measures to reconcile the restructuring of rubber production with the requirements of allocative efficiency engendered by the open export strategy.

Successive adjustments to these policy terms, in response to domestic political sensibilities, served to broaden their effective scope. Although producer participation in policy-generated developments was thereby enhanced, the progressive extensions of policy carried the benefits boundaries forward, but still did not eliminate structural barriers to development. For their implicit allocative criteria, rendering policy benefits available to some, while denying them to others, tended to discriminate against certain structural disabilities. By way of conception and application, the prevailing policy approach patently favoured the behavioural role of established entrepreneurial classes of producers, specifically dominant peasants and estates. Inadequate policy resources were committed to coping with the residual, hard-core structural deficiencies constraining the modernization of poorer peasants on very small, inferior holdings.

The structural changes promoted by these policy reforms altered the dimensions and functions of production in the Malaysian rubber economy. Between 1957 and 1960, as has been noted, most economically marginal, protection-dependent estates were subdivided into smaller holdings. As estate subsector acreage declined, this was offset by the expansion of the area under smallholdings. Moreover, government-sponsored FELDA land settlement schemes and other new planting provisions accelerated significantly as a result of political and social pressures.[34] Owing to new planting schemes and the subdivision of estates, aggregate

TABLE 2
Proportions of High Yielding Rubber and
Average Yields, Peninsular Malaysia, 1950-75 (selected years).

| Year | Percentage High Yielding (replanted & new planting) | | Yield (kg/ha/year) | |
	Estates	Small-holdings	Estates	Small-holdings
1959	10	1	570	465
1965	24	8	550	432
1960	48	29	758	437
1965	68	54	953	590
1970	89	63	1,189	752
1975	95*	67†	1,520*	970*

* Estimates.
† *Economic Report, 1978/79.*
Sources: B.C. Sekhar, *Malaysian Rubber Review*, Vol. 1, No. 1, p. 27;
Malaysia, Ministry of Finance, *Economic Report, 1978/79.*

smallholding acreage overtook the planted area of estates after 1960. The proportion of smallholding rubber in total planted acreage grew rapidly following independence, from the 40% level of the 1930s and 1940s to in excess of 65% by the 1970s.

Along with this resource redistribution, an accelerated process of resource modernization took place within the rubber planting frontier. Progressive improvements to the rubber technology and the expansion of replanting schemes led to increasingly widespread asset renewal with high-yielding rubber (though some estates chose to diversify to alternative export crops, notably oil palm.)[35] By the 1970s, therefore, estate acreage was almost entirely replanted with high-yielding rubber (Table 2). New smallholding schemes likewise consisted of high-yielding material. By contrast, replanting with high-yielding rubber had occurred only on 65% of traditional smallholding acreage, which formed three-quarters of total smallholding area. The remaining inferior, low-grade smallholding acreage characteristically comprised very small properties, and was mainly Malay-owned (Table 3).

TABLE 3
Rubber Smallholdings by Ethnic Distribution
And Average Size, Peninsular Malaysia, 1977*.

	Number of Small-holders ('000)	%	Total Registered acreage ('000)	%	Average Size of Holding (Acres)
Malays	280.1	67%	1,168.6	50%	4.17
Chinese	132.8	32%	1,098.6	47%	8.27
Others	5.9	1%	54.5	3%	9.27
Total	418.9	100%	2,321.7	100%	5.54

* Smallholdings registered under RISDA but individually owned and managed only. Excludes FELDA, FELCRA, estate fragmentations, state land schemes and other individually owned rubber smallholdings not registered with RISDA. RISDA–registered acreage represents approximately 80% of total Rubber acreage.
Source: RISDA, cited in *Economic Report, 1978/79*.

The great expansion of public investment in rural economic and social infrastructure in recent years, and the introduction of group processing and block rubber facilities, may have been of general benefit. However, here too, the major advantage went to precisely those planters who already acquired high-yielding rubber.

Although the trend in world prices for natural rubber fell by half during the 1960s, Malaysian output had doubled. This output effect reflected the productivity gains due to replanting and new planting with high-yielding material.[36] Whereas improved productivity maintained producer incomes, more or less, despite deteriorating terms of trade, remaining structural constraints had an income redistribution effect of severely regressive proportions. To the extent that dominant peasants and estates had capitalized on policy provisions for planting with high-yielding material, their income levels were cushioned by ensuing productivity increases compounded by the benefits of government provided services and facilities. The worst incidence of income deflation affected differentially the smallest holdings unable structurally or under prevailing policy to replant.

The relative deprivation of very small holdings was further aggravated by the rubber export duty component of Malaysian fiscal policy. Rubber export duty constituted, in effect, an income tax levied on the gross export incomes of rubber producers. The effective rate of the tax has been well in excess of the ordinary income tax applicable to all occupations (including, of course, rubber planters as well). Its incidence was notoriously regressive on smallholders, particularly in relation to the incomes of the smallest peasant producers.[37] This fiscal burden had an undoubtedly deleterious impact on these smallholders' capacity to generate internal savings for capital improvements. Inasmuch as the poorest peasants generally lacked access to government development benefits, the regressive impact of the rubber export duty on their incomes was doubly onerous.

Resulting policy tensions came to the fore, ironically, just when the world market conditions for rubber had been shifted in favour of the natural product by the oil and commodity boom of the early 1970s. Action taken on the part of the Organization of Petroleum Exporting Countries (OPEC) in raising petroleum prices increased the costs of oil-based synthetics accordingly. This had a substantial positive substitution effect on the market for natural rubber. Having gained long-run comparative cost advantages, the market for natural rubber restored itself at sharply and dramatically improved terms of trade. While enabling natural rubber to overcome the competitive disadvantages of the recent past, ironically this same OPEC price action had an immediate downward, cyclical impact on the rate of rubber absorption in world markets. Because of the economic recession in the industrial countries during the mid-1970s, derived demand for rubber weakened. Rubber prices dipped along with declining absorption, though remaining at levels well above their historical trend.

Consequently, towards late 1974, the Malaysian rubber economy experienced a new and different crisis.[38] Export viability was no longer an issue. Rather, the crisis was internal, arising out of latent structural dichotomies between classes of rubber producers (Table 4). Existing differentials in productivity, particularly among smallholdings, were greatly exacerbated by the tribulations of the rubber market. An unprecedented domestic inflation had undercut the effects of improved terms of trade on output, while aggravating the effects of falling (derived) demand on export earnings.[39] Those already modernized, high-yielding plantations—smallholdings as well as estates—soon realized the advantages of their greater productivity. However, these same exogenous pressures had a scissors-like effect on the incomes of lower-grade smallholdings. Many of these relatively deprived and anyway marginal peasant holdings were now rendered patently sub-economic. Looming destitution drove impoverished, mostly Malay peasant smallholders to mass protests against the policy system that was crushing them. Though

TABLE 4
Malaysian Rubber Output and Average Prices, 1965-78.

	Production ('000 tonnes)	Precentage Change	Prices*	Percentage Change
1965	917	+6.1	154	-6.7
1966	928	+1.9	144	-17.3
1967	991	+13.8	119	-1.8
1968	1,100	+15.2	117	+31.4
1969	1,268	+0.1	154	-19.2
1970	1,269	+4.3	124	-18.3
1971	1,325	-1.5	102	-8.0
1972	1,304	+18.3	94	+76.8
1973	1,542	+0.4	165	+9.2
1974	1,549	-4.6	181	-24.9
1975	1,477	+11.0	136	+46.3
1976	1,639	-1.6	199	+0.5
1977	1,613	+1.5	203	+6.9
1978	1,637†		217†	

* RSSI, F.O.B. Kuala Lumpur, M. cents/kg average.
† Estimates.
Sources: Malaysia, The Treasury, *Economic Report, 1974-75*;
        Malaysia, Ministry of Finance, *Economic Report, 1977/78*;
        Rubber Statistical Bulletin, Vol. 32, No. 8;
        Malaysia, Ministry of Finance, *Economic Report, 1978/77*.

localized and easily suppressed by the authorities, the unrest succeeded in shaking the dominant order to its policy foundations.

The differential social impact of this market crisis posed a challenge to the existing political order. Government responded in late 1974 by introducing its so called National Crash Programme designed to restore producer income levels and sectoral shares. This Crash Programme, as implemented, entailed an immediate modification to the rubber export strategy and internal policy allocations.[40] In order to boost rubber prices in the short-run, deliberate policy measures were adopted curtailing current output and regulating the availability of supplies for export. For political reasons, it was important that the prospective benefits be distributed more or less progressively, so therefore the curbs on output were applied most stringently to estate production. In the event, the smallholding share of total output grew only marginally. However, with export prices rising above the previous trough, smallholdings secured a more favourable share of incremental income. Given the disparity in smallholding productivity between high-yielding and low-grade properties, the major benefit would have again accrued to the former, larger, dominant peasant producers.

The Crash Programme remained in force for just over a year. During this time, it paved the way for a far-reaching reassessment of policy norms affecting rubber export strategy and the structure of production.

At the same time as the Crash Programme was being implemented, Malaysia figured prominently in multilateral negotiations over a broader international rubber supply regulation agreement under the aegis of the Association of Natural Rubber Producing Countries (ANPRC). As a result, an International Natural Rubber Agreement on Price Stabilization was concluded in November 1976 between Malaysia, Indonesia, Singapore, Sri Lanka and Thailand.[41] This Agreement pertained to more than just price stabilization, to be sure, for it also incorporated a price increasing component. By design, the price stabilization mechanism has been integrated into the price increasing scheme. Price stabilization is to be served by the creation, under the Agreement, of a buffer stock contributed and managed by the participating producer countries.[42] However, the price range around which the buffer stock operates is to be maintained through a related scheme for supply rationalization.

The object of supply rationalization according to the Agreement is to uphold the equilibrium of its target stabilization price by adjusting exportable supplies of natural rubber to anticipated levels of world demand. This rationalization scheme would include determination of an aggregate export quota, which in turn would be allocated through export entitlements among participating countries, broadly in proportion to their production capabilities. For the initial period of the Stabilization Agreement, Malaysia's entitlement was to be set at 52.45% of the overall supply quota, through 1978. Domestic output would in turn have to be adjusted accordingly by means of internal policy constraints, to the level warranted by current export entitlements. The return to output restriction marked a reversion to an intrinsically custodial policy approach.

The Rubber Stabilization Agreement testified to the wholesale conversion of Malaysian official thinking to the hypotheses on international commodity trading postulated by the United Nations Conference of Trade and Development (UNCTAD), and symbolized in the so called "New International Economic Order."[43] If the assumed economic benefits of commodity agreements ostensibly validated the reversion to a restrictive export strategy and internal policy constraints, by promising improvement to the international terms of trade, domestically the implications seem somewhat more problematic. Among producers, the promise of price stabilization cum supply rationalization measures would clearly appeal most of all to the dominant vested interests in the Malaysian rubber economy. For the impact of interlocking constraints on price and output is likely to fortify existing structural differentials among rubber planters. Moreover, any economic rents that arise would tend to be distributed differentially in accordance with relative productivity. Invariably, the major benefits would accrue to the comparatively larger, higher-yielding holdings belonging mostly to dominant peasant planters and estate companies. Indeed, their privileged economic position would acquire protection through the prospective regulation of output.

Any such supply restrictions must perforce affect the prospects for new entry into rubber planting on the one hand, and the spread of advanced rubber technology to additional smaller peasant planters on the other. The effects of policy constraints on entrepreneurial and technological innovation may well protect the economic returns of a particular class of dominant peasants and estates against further new competition; meanwhile, the Malaysian rubber economy would itself incur a high opportunity cost on account of the prospective development potential forgone.

Until now, Malaysia has been in the vanguard of natural rubber production and innovation. Yet, adherence to the Rubber Stabilization Agreement implies a double threat to the future of Malaysia's rubber growing economy. Precisely because of its leading role, Malaysia will undoubtedly be called upon to play the Saudi counterpart and sacrifice its own potential in order to uphold the supply rationalization component of the Agreement. But unlike Saudi Arabia, Malaysia is still a comparatively poor developing country; and unlike petroleum, rubber is not an inimitable geophysical endowment, but merely a plantation industry that could be replicated elsewhere. Output restriction is bound to erode Malaysian comparative advantages in natural rubber production. The reassertion of administrative constraints on output would inhibit the propensity for further producer innovation, while the accrual of economic rents would tend to diminish the efficiency of those beneficiaries of the policy, the dominant peasants and estates. Consequently, Malaysia's long-term role as a low-cost rubber producing country would be placed in jeopardy.

TABLE 5
ANPRC* and World Production of Natural
Rubber, 1967-77 ('000 tonnes, selected years).

		1967	1970	1975	1976	1977
ANPRC	Malaysia	990.4	1,269.2	1,477.6	1,639.7	1,613.2
	Indonesia	700.8	815.1	822.5	847.5†	835.0
	Thailand‡	216.1	287.1	348.7	392.4	424.5
	Sri Lanka	143.2	159.1	148.7	152.1	146.2
	TOTAL	2,050.5	2,530.5	2,797.5	3,018.9	3,018.9
Non-ANPRC	India	62.3	83.4	82.7	82.4	(83.0)†
	Philippines	10.4	20.1	52.2	60.0†	65.0†
	Vietnam	40.6	28.4	20.0†	32.5†	37.0
	Liberia	62.3	83.4	82.7	82.4	(83.0)†
	Nigeria†	52.0	65.0	67.7	52.5	59.2
	Zaire	30.1	40.0†	30.0†	29.2†	(30.0)†
	Latin America†	28.4	31.9	31.3	37.3	40.6
	Others	185.9	213.3	97.6	64.7	107.2†
	GRAND TOTAL†	2,522.5	3,102.5	3,315.0	3,365.0	3,392.5
Proportions of	ANPRC (%)	81.3	81.6	84.4	85.8	84.0
World Production	Malaysia (%)	39.3	40.9	44.6	46.0	44.9

* Association of Natural Rubber Producing Countries.
† Estimates.
‡ Domestic consumption plus exports.
Source: *Rubber Statistical Bulletin*, Vol. 32, No.8.

In the meantime, those other producer countries remaining outside the Agreement (notably India, Liberia, Nigeria, the Philippines and Papua New Guinea), which altogether now produce about 15% of the world's natural rubber, are likely to expand their respective production roles so as to capitalize on the price incentives and supply restrictions subscribed by the ANPRC International Natural Rubber Agreement signatories (Table 5). By ignoring the Agreement, these outsiders could in future alter the rules of the international rubber market.

Like its predecessors of the 1920s and 1930s, the workings of the current International Natural Rubber Agreement threaten the

Malaysian rubber economy with structural stagnation and eventual competitive decay. As in the past, the stabilization effort might confer short-run gains on sectional beneficiaries: economic rents for established planters, along with continued dominance for privileged classes of producers, while relieving government of the attendant costs of structural change. Yet, the revenue product generated by natural rubber continues to represent a major source of employment, export earnings and national income. Its curtailment through the effects of output restriction could undermine the longer-run potential contribution of rubber agronomy to the overall economic development of Malaysia.

The recurring quest for administrative solutions to problems of rubber supply reveals a persisting distrust, among vested producer interests as among officialdom, of the market mechanism. Quite unreasonably, custodial policies seem to be preferred, however discredited by past experience. The impulse towards production controls reflects the predilections of a counter-developmental compact in which bureaucratic tendencies are jointed in the defence of economic privilege. The resulting custodial outlook implicitly would deny the spread effects of technological and policy advances to lower classes of peasant producers—all in the name of stability. This would appear to be an object example of Santayana's dictum about those who ignore the lessons of history being doomed to repeat it. Only, the possible future damage may not be so readily remediable.

ENDNOTES

1. Martin Rudner, "Malayan Rubber Policy: Development and Anti-Development During the 1950s," *Journal of Southeast Asian Studies (JSEAS)*, Vol. 8 (1976), pp. 235-59. For a detailed analysis of the economics and technologies of Malaysian rubber production and their development over recent decades, see the encyclopedic work by Colin Barlow, *The Natural Rubber Industry* (Kuala Lumpur, 1978). Whereas rubber policy decisions introduced since 1963 were generally all-Malaysian in their scope, the following discussions of policy and structural changes relate more specifically to the main rubber growing areas of peninsular Malaysia, the former Federation of Malaya. The application of policy in the East Malaysian States of Sabah and Sarawak is generally similar; however, historical and environmental factors have resulted in somewhat different conditions.

2. Lim Chong Yah, *The Economic Development of Modern Malaya* (Kuala Lumpur, 1967), describes rubber as the engine of Malayan post-war economic growth. On the contribution of rubber to Malaya/Malaysia's subsequent growth performance, see David Lim, *Economic Growth and Development in West Malaysia, 1947-1970* (Kuala Lumpur, 1973), esp. pp. 6 *et passim*. Writing in 1972, David Lim was fundamentally pessimistic about the future of Malaysian

rubber, but one year later, the OPEC oil price rise improved dramatically the long-run competitive position of natural versus synthetic rubbers in world markets.

3. Economic data cited in this paragraph are derived from the following sources: The Treasury, Malaysia, *Economic Report 1975-76* (Kuala Lumpur, 1976); Ministry of Finance, Malaysia, *Economic Report, 1976/77* (Kuala Lumpur, 1977); Federation of Malaya, *First Five-Year Plan 1961-1965* (Kuala Lumpur, 1961); Federation of Malaysia, *First Malaysia Plan 1966-70* (Kuala Lumpur, 1966); - , *Second Malaysia Plan 1971-75* (Kuala Lumpur, 1971); - , *Third Malaysia Plan, 1976-80* (Kuala Lumpur, 1976; V.V. Bhanoji Rao, *National Accounts of West Malaysia, 1947-1971* (Singapore, 1976), esp. Ch. 4 and Table E.

4. J.T. Thoburn, "Exports and Economic Growth in West Malaysia,", *Oxford Economic Papers* Vol. 2 (1973), p. 89 *et passim*.

5. David Lim, *Economic Growth*, p. 127.

6. P.T. Bauer, *The Rubber Industry: A Study in Competition and Monopoly* (London, 1948). Bauer's arguments were also set out in several journal articles, including: "The Working of Rubber Regulation," *The Economic Journal* Vol. 56 (1946), pp. 391-414, and "Malayan Rubber Policies," *Economica* Vol. 14 (1947) pp. 81-107. On policy regulation in the early post-war period, see Martin Rudner, "Rubber Strategy for Post War Malaya," *JSEAS* Vol. 1 (1970), pp. 23-36. In Malaysian practice, estates and smallholdings are classified by the size of the aggregate plantation, with the dividing line being legally defined at 100 acres, or 40.5 hectares.

7. Cf. J. Barrington Moore, Jr., *The Social Origins of Dictatorship and Democracy Landlord and Peasant in the Making of the Modern World* (Boston, 1969); James C. Scott, *The Moral Economy of the Peasant* (New Haven, 1976); Lim Teck Ghee, *Peasants and their Agricultural Economy in Colonial Malaya 1874-1941* (Kuala Lumpur, 1977); Martin Rudner, "Agricultural Policy and Peasant Social Transformation in Late Colonial Malaya," in James C. Jackson & Martin Rudner, eds., *Issues in Malaysian Development* (Singapore, 1979).

8. Martin Rudner, "The State and Peasant Innovation in Rural Development: The Case of Malaysian Rubber," *Asian and African Studies* Vol. 6 (1970), pp. 75-96.

9. *Vide*. D.W. Fryer & James C. Jackson, "Peasant Producers or Urban Planters?" *Pacific Viewpoint* Vol. 7 (1966), esp. pp. 203-9.

10. D.A. Low, *The Asian Revolution of the Mid-twentieth Century* (Canberra, Asian Studies Association of Australia, 1976, mimeo). Low's "dominant peasantry" resembles the Russian kulak, though its structural and behavioural attributes include factors other than just size of holding.

11. Cf. Fryer & Jackson, "Peasant Producers." Their notion of "Urban Planter" closely resembles, and indeed is analytically coterminous with, D.A. Low's "dominant peasantry" in the context of non-food, export-oriented agricultural production. See also Voon Phin Keong, "Size Aspects of Rubber Smallholdings in West Malaysia," *Journal of Tropical Geography* Vol. 34 (1972), pp. 65-76.

12. On the origins and historical organization of the Malayan rubber economy, see: John Drabble's writings on *Rubber in Malaya, 1876-1922* (Kuala Lumpur, 1973); "The Plantation Rubber Industry in Malaya up to 1922," *Journal of the Malaysian Branch, Royal Asiatic Society* Vol. 40 (1967), pp. 52-77, and "Investment in the Rubber Industry in Malaya," *JSEAS* Vol. 3 (1972), pp. 247-61. Other valuable studies of the formative period of Malaysia's rubber industry include James C. Jackson, *Planters and Speculators, Chinese and European Agricultural Enterprise in Malaya, 1786-1921* (Singapore, 1968);

T.R.McHale,"Changing Technology and Shifts in the Supply and Demand for Rubber: An Analytical History," *Malayan Economic Review* (*MER*) Vol. 9 (1964); Lim Teck Ghee, *Peasants*, esp. chaps. 3, 5 and 6; Barlow, *Natural Rubbber Industry*, esp. chaps. 2 and 3.

13. P.T. Bauer, *Report on a Visit to Rubber Growing Smallholdings in Malaya* (London, 1948); Drabble, *Rubber in Malaya*.

14. John Drabble, "Peasant Smallholders in the Malayan Economy," in James C. Jackson & Martin Rudner (eds), *Issues in Development*; P.T. Bauer, "The Working of Rubber Regulation."

15. Andrew Schoenfield, *British Economic Policy Since the War* (Harmondsworth, 1963); Martin Rudner, "The Draft Development Plan of the Federation of Malaya," *JSEAS* Vol. 3 (1972), esp. pp. 71-5.

16. Rudner, "Rubber Strategy for Post-War Malaya."

17. Bauer, *Report on a Visit to Rubber Growing Smallholdings in Malaya, op. cit.*

18. Rudner, "Rubber Strategy for Post War Malaya." Note that internal Malayan restrictions on rubber land utilization were cancelled only from 1947, though the original International Rubber Regulation Agreement itself terminated already in 1943.

19. Federation of Malay, *Legislative Council Proceedings, Report of the Rice Production Committee* (Kuala Lumpur, 1953).

20. Rudner, "Agricultural Policy and Peasant Social Transformation in Late Colonial Malaya," and "Malayan Rubber Policy."

21. Rudner, "Malayan Rubber Policy," esp. pp. 240-6; Lim Chong Yah, "The Malayan Rubber Replanting Taxes," *MER* Vol. 6 (1961), pp. 47-8.

22. *Federation of Malaya Annual Report 1955* (Kuala Lumpur, 1956), p. 142 Indications of official colonial concern to redirect smallholders away from rubber to alternative crops, on essentially non-economic grounds, may be seen in the *Interim Report of the Rubber Smallholders Enquiry Committee*, Federation of Malaya, *Legislative Proceedings Paper No. 48 of 1950*, para 10, and in statements by the colonial executive Member for Agriculture and Forestry, *Legislative Council Proceedings*, 20 March 1952, and Member for Economic Affairs, 25 November 1953. See also Rudner, "Malayan Rubber Policy," p. 244.

23. By 1955, over half Malaya's smallholding acreage was over 30 years old, the point where diminishing returns set in; less than eight percent of the smallholding acreage, and only around a quarter of estate acreage, consisted of high-yielding stands: Federation of Malaya, *Taxation and Replanting in the Rubber Industry* (Kuala Lumpur, 1955), p. 17.

24. R.F. Mudie, *Report of a Mission of Enquiry into the Rubber Industry of Malaya* (Kuala Lumpur, 1954) (*Mudie Mission Report*).

25. On the role of political development in releasing policy constraints on the development of the Malayan rubber economy, especially its smallholding sector, see Rudner, "The State and Peasant Innovation in Rural Development"; and Gayl D. Ness, *Bureaucracy and Rural Development in Malaysia* (Berkeley: University of California Press, 1967), esp. chap. 3.

26. Federation of Malaya, *Report on Economic Planning in the Federation of Malaya in 1956* (Kuala Lumpur, 1957). See also Martin Rudner, *Nationalism, Planning and Economic Modernization in Malaysia: The Politics of Beginning*

Development (Beverly Hills, 1975), esp. chap. 4, and "Malayan Rubber Policy," p. 248 *et passim*.

27. See the Chief Replanting Officer quoted in the *Straits Times*, 28 September 1961; Minister of Commerce and Industry, *Legislative Council Proceedings, 7 December 1957.*

28. Differential incomes and earnings to high yielding as against low yielding rubber smallholders have been estimated by the Rubber Research Institute of Malaysia, and can range as high as a factor of 10: Pee Teck Yew and Ani bin Arope, *Rubber Owners Manual 1976* (Kuala Lumpur, 1976), pp. 197-201, esp. Table 15.3.

29. For an account of the deteriorating competitive position of natural rubber in face of improving synthetic rubber technologies, bringing worsening real terms of trade for Malaysian production during the 1960s, see Lim, *Economic Growth*, esp. chap. 3. P.W. Allen, P.O. Thomas & B.C. Sekhar, *The Techno-Economic Potential of NR in Major End Uses* (Kuala Lumpur, 1975), provides a study of the comparative costs and benefits of natural rubber as against various types of synthetic for specified purposes.

30. Lim, *Economic Growth*, esp. chaps. 6 and 11; Harcharan Singh Khera, "The State and Peasant Innovative in Rural Development: The Case of FELDA Oil Palm Schemes," in Stephen Chee & Khoo Siew Mun, eds., *Malaysian Economic Development and Policies* (Kuala Lumpur, 1975), pp. 194-204.

31. On the operations of the Malaysian political process, see, *e.g.*, R.S. Milne, *Government and Politics in Malaysia* (Boston, 1967); G.P. Means, *Malaysian Politics (London, 1970);* and on its effect on economic policy issues see, e.g., Gayl D. Ness, *"Economic Development and the Goals of Government,"* in Wang Gungwu (ed.), *Malaysia* (London, 1964); Martin Rudner, *Nationalism, Planning and Economic Modernization in Malaysia.*

32. Ungku Aziz, *The Sub-Division of Estates in Malaya* (Kuala Lumpur, 1962) and "Land Disintegration and Land Policy in Malaya," *MER* Vol. 2 (1958).

33. Assistant Minister of Rural Development, *Federation of Malaya, Dewan Riayat (House of Representatives) Proceedings*, 23 February 1960. On government's response to the subdivision problem, see Rudner, "Malayan Rubber Policy," pp. 256-9.

34. Lim Sow Ching, *Land Development Schemes in Peninsular Malaysia* (Kuala Lumpur, 1976).

35. Barlow, *Natural Rubber Industry*, pp. 92-6. See also B.C. Sekhar, "Scientific and Technological Development in the NR Industry," *Malayan Rubber Review* Vol. 1 (1976), pp. 25-31.

36. Lim, *Economic Growth*, pp. 218-9.

37. C.T. Edwards, *Public Finances in Malaya and Singapore* (Canberra, 1970), pp. 211-47. Edwards shows (Table 50) that a low-income rubber smallholder pays some 35 percent of his income in tax payments, mainly in rubber export duty, whereas more affluent smallholders pay around a quarter, rice producers between 15 and 8 percent, and urban dwellers between 18 and 10 percent, at similar levels of income. See also A.H.H. Tan, "The Incidence of Export Taxes on Small Producers," *MER* Vol. 12 (1967).

38. Lim Sow Ching, "Towards and Equitable International Trade in Natural Rubber," *Malayan Rubber Review* Vol. 1 (1976), pp. 14-19 and 22-4.

39. On the Malaysian inflation of 1973-4, and its effects on economic activity, see, *e.g.*, Lim See Yan, "The Inflation Syndrome and Its Implications for Policy"; Ramesh Chouder, "Price Stability and Inflation in Malaysia"; Lajman Sirat, "Price Behaviour and Inflation in Malaysia"; H.G. Manur, "Inflation in Malaysia - Diagnosis and Prescription," all in Chee & Khoo, *Malaysian Economic Development and Policies.*

40. Lim, "Towards an Equitable International Trade in Natural Rubber," pp. 15 *et passim.*

41. Ursula Wasserman, "Commodities in UNCTAD: Rubber," and "Jakarta Natural Rubber Agreement 1976," both in the *Journal of World Trade Law* Vol. 2 (1978), pp. 287-9 and 289-90, respectively.

42. Subsequently, shortly after these lines were written, the producer countries decided, in January 1978, to defer for the time being the establishment of the projected buffer stock since natural rubber prices were currently on a rising trend (*Malaysian Digest*, 15 January 1978). However, preparations for the eventual introduction of the buffer stock and supply rationalization schemes reportedly continue under the aegis of the ANRPC Secretariat.

43 Lew Sip Hon, "A Case for an International Price Stabilization Scheme for Natural Rubber," *UMBC Economic Review* Vol. 12 (1976), pp. 18-25; Mr. Lew was Parliamentary Secretary for the Ministry of Primary Industries, Malaysia. See also Lim Sow Ching, "Towards an Equitable International Trade in Natural Rubber"; Dr. Lim is Head of the Rubber Economics and Planning Unit of the Malaysian Rubber Research and Development Board. Academic economists have, for their part, also accepted the UNCTAD doctrine: see, *e.g.*, Paul Chan Tuck Hoong and Lee Kiong Hock, "The New International Economic Order - Some Implications for Malaysia," *UMBC Economic Review* Vol. 12 (1976), pp. 18-24. This conceptual conversion to the UNCTAD doctrine of trade restriction, under the slogan of "New International Economic Order" is all the more remarkable in a country which had more experience with, and demonstrably suffered more from, such output restriction schemes in the past, and which currently enjoys manifest comparative economic and technological advantages in the production of natural rubber.

CHAPTER 8

TRENDS IN MALAYSIAN DEVELOPMENT PLANNING: Goals, Policies And Role Expansion

Since 1950 Malaya/Malaysia has experienced a succession of six five-year development plans. Over this period, planning emerged as the institutional centrepiece of national development strategy. Through the medium of planning, successive Malaysian governments defined and applied their economic, social and political development goals. The Malaysian mode of planning represented a particularly tractable instrument for the policy direction of an otherwise open, market-oriented economic system. Yet, planning experience had to cope with the usual constraints of underdevelopment, compounded in a way by Malaysia's historical legacy of exaggerated dualism and dependency. In addition, in the Malaysian case, planning had also to accommodate itself to the distinctive patterns of an intensely pluralistic society.[1] Malaysian planning was governed by a peculiar political process, in which the parliamentary system of government evolved into a dominant coalition pattern of governance.

It is necessary to distinguish between two distinct, if related, aspects of planning: the declared plan on the one hand, and the actual or realized plan on the other. Declared plans express the nominal policy preferences put forward on behalf of the governing authorities. The realized plan represents effective priorities in the authoritative allocation of planning resources. Comparison of the priorities declared and priorities fulfilled reveals the actual degree of commitment on the part of the political leadership to what policy goals. Performance of planning functions and resulting policy priorities may be traced through successive plans to reveal the evolving role of planning in relation to changing development goals, priorities and policies over time.

Review of Indonesian and Malayan Affairs, Vol. 14, No. 2 (1980).

Development planning in Malaysia underwent significant role changes during the past quarter century. While the magnitudes of expenditure increased with each successive plan, even more fundamental changes occurred in the functions of planning. These took the form of a role expansion of the planning institution. Up to the present, three distinct phases of role change in Malaysian development planning can be discerned, each extending over two plan periods.[2] In the first phase, covering the so called Draft Development Plan (DDP), 1950-51, and subsequent First Five-Year Plan (FYP), 1956-60, planning concentrated on the public sector only. The role assigned to planning remained narrowly confined to forward capital budgeting for government services. During the following phase, which included the Second FYP, 1961-65, and the First Malaysia Plan (FMP), 1966-70, the role of planning was extended to a more wide-ranging, pursuit of economic growth. The third phase has been characterized by the growth and redistributive goals expressed in the vaunted New Economic Policy (NEP).[3]

As a result, the Second Malaysia Plan (SMP), 1971-75, and the current Third Malaysia Plan (TMP), 1976-80, were given an instrumental role in the projected restructuring of the economic and social order. It would be noted, parenthetically, that mid-term reviews of plans were also published since 1964, assessing past progress and sometimes providing marked revisions of targets. These periodic role changes in Malaysian planning reflected essentially political events, wherein a changing configuration of power generated new claims on development policy.

The Structure of Planning

The institution of planning was first introduced into Malaya as a benign act of the latter-day colonial administration. The impulse for planning stemmed from without, having originated in the Colonial Development and Welfare Act 1945, providing for British grants-in-aid to "centrally administered schemes" for development in the colonies, including (once post-war rehabilitation was completed) Malaya.[4] Decisions on planning were vested exclusively in the colonial bureaucracy. However, as subsequent phases of planning became more comprehensive, their decision-making processes became increasingly differentiated and functionally specialized. The creation of specialized organs for the different levels of decision-making altered not just the organization but also the composition of authority over planning. As a result, the centre of responsibility tended to shift, as the role of planning evolved, away from purely bureaucratic control by Treasury toward a broader spectrum of administrative and political involvement in the making of development policy.

This structural transformation in planning was impelled by the dynamics of Malaysian politics. Most plan periods coincided with terms for parliamentary elections. The proximity to elections heightened the responsiveness of planning to political considerations. Political sensitivity had the effect of accentuating the tendency to treat planning as a tool of statecraft. Already at the outset, the DDP was influenced by Imperial and local political concerns: anxieties about post-war colonial legitimacy; the election of the Labour Party government in the U.K.; the outbreak of the Communist "Emergency"; and the stirrings of local nationalism. Movement towards self-government, leading up to the first General Election of 1955, cast the First FYP in the cauldron of decolonization. Following independence, the drive to consolidate the newly-created structure of nationhood, prompted by the elections of 1959 and 1964 and intensified by the Confrontation with Indonesia over the formation of Malaysia and the separation of Singapore, conditioned the Second FYP and FMP. Later, the 1969 elections and their aftermath of racial violence engendered a radically different style in Malaysian politics, as expressed in the NEP and translated into the SMP. NEP, continuing social unrest, and the prime ministerial succession of Datuk Hussein Onn, together impressed their political stamp on the TMP. Political pressures imposed a dual need for greater technical proficiency in planning, on the one hand, and for enhanced political control over planning, on the other.

The transition from a purely public sector role for planning, first to a growth and then restructuring role for planning, was marked by changing patterns of political and administrative involvement in the planning mechanisms. In the initial public sector phase, planning decisions remained vested in the bureaucracy, and centred on the Financial Secretariat. Not only were fiscal proficiency and policy prerogatives both concentrated in the financial bureaucracy, but bureaucratic ranks were still dominated by a colonial expatriate administrative class.[5] Planning decisions for the DDP reflected colonial financial priorities from among internal departmental proposals. Colonial bureaucratic authority was moderated but slightly by *ex post facto* consultation with an appointive Legislative Council.

Following the 1955 elections and the advent of representative government, an economic committee of the elected Executive Council was established. This provided a forum for ministerial superintendence over the management of economic policy. A small Economic Secretariat was set up under the direction of the (expatriate official) Economic Adviser, in order to advise and service this ministerial Committee. Planning decisions for the First FYP were taken at the Economic Secretariat level.[6] In formulating the First FYP, as with the previous DDP, the Treasury mediated between other departmental claims and higher ministerial aims. This structure of authority over planning tended to concentrate power, as well as technical competence, in the financial bureaucracy, allowing it effective control over economic management.

During the second phase, the structure of authority over planning was broadened by the creation of distinctive agency executive organs. Shortly after the adoption of the Second FYP, a National Development Planning Committee (NDPC) was created with a responsibility for plan formulation, development budgeting and progress evaluation. The NDPC constituted a bureaucratic co-ordinating body, composed of ranking officials of the several government agencies directly concerned with economic aspects of development.[7] Bureaucratic representation on the NDPC closely paralleled the ministerial composition of the cabinet Economic Committee. This correspondence reinforced the executive authority of the NDPC.

At the same time, the former Economic Secretariat was now reorganized and upgraded into an Economic Planning Unit (EPU), staffed with its own economic officers and attached—a measure of its stature—to the Prime Minister's Department. Serving as a technical bureau for the NDPC, the EPU undertook specialist staff work concerning planning technique and "high policy," meaning development strategy. Responsibility for the actual drafting of the FMP and subsequent plans, within the guidelines supplied, centred on the EPU. Meanwhile, certain ministries also set up their own departmental planning staffs, beginning with the Treasury itself, Bank Negara Malaysia (the central bank) and the Ministries of Agriculture and Co-operatives, and Education. The effect of these institutional innovations was to raise the technical proficiency of the planning apparatus. As well, the structural changes altered the balance of authority as between the financial bureaucracy and other public sector interests involved in planning at the departmental, NDPC and also Cabinet levels.

The third, present phase furthered the trend towards greater institutional specialization in planning procedures. Government administration acquired a positive rule in the operations of planning of the administrative authority structure. Specialized administrative organs were established to co-ordinate and supervise plan implementation. One of these, the General Planning Unit, was soon afterwards reorganized into a General Planning and Socio-Economic Research Unit (GPU), combining administrative and planning responsibilities as the social-developmental counterpart of the economic-developmental EPU. To complement the work of these centralized planning agencies, departmental-level planning staffs were set up in several additional individual ministries, notably Health, Transport, Works and Utilities, Power and Communications, and some of the statutory authorities as well.

Other hitherto neglected components of the Malaysian administrative apparatus have been incorporated in recent years, with greater or lesser coherence, into planning operations. The former State Economic Development Corporations were reconstituted and upgraded into State Planning Units. This, it was hoped, would serve to overcome federal-state discontinuities affecting land use and natural resources policies. Also, a Private Sector Consultative Committee was set up alongside the NDPC, to provide the large multifaceted business establishment with direct access to the planning institution. The wider involvement of departmental, regional and sectoral interests served to pluralize the structure of decision-making as planning became more comprehensive and change-oriented.

Since the 1969 crisis, a resurgent United Malays National Organization (UMNO) political leadership—the dominant force in the ruling coalition—has involved itself directly in the planning process. Indeed, the much vaunted NEP has been predicated on more assertive political control over the course of development.

In a major departure, in the wake of the 1969 crisis, the Director of Operations and later Prime Minister, Tun Abdul Razak, took to reorganizing responsibility for key development-relevant ministries around a cadre of trusted party and official associates holding shared policy perspectives. Indicative of this new trend was the creation of a magisterial (if short-lived) Department of National Unity, followed in 1974 by the transfer of the Finance portfolio— hitherto treated as belonging to the Malayan Chinese Association coalition partner—to UMNO's own hands. The political symbolism of this changeover was accentuated by its communal connotations. Ministerial involvement was now represented, actively and forcefully, in a cabinet-level National Economic Council (NEC) chaired by the Prime Minister. NEC directives on development policy were transmitted down through the NDPC to the EPU and lower level planning staffs, with the new Department of National Unity assuming a major role in formulating SMP goals and priorities. This unprecedented assertion of positive political authority over the planning process underscored the mobilization of government instrumentalities towards them to declared national objectives of the NEP.[8]

The sudden death of Tun Razak and the succession of Datuk Hussein Onn as Prime Minister may have affected leadership style, but did not impinge upon the exercising of political authority over the preparation of the impending TMP. Proposals for the TMP were initially mediated by special ministerial committees under the chairmanship of the Prime Minister or his Deputy, prior to consideration by the NEC and subsequent verification by Cabinet. Actual formulation of the TMP proceeded through specialized technical organs at the various levels and spheres of competence, all co-ordinated by newly instituted Inter-Agency Planning Groups under the direction of the NDPC and NEC. Basic decisions on plan strategy flowed from the highest ministerial level, and were accepted as the personal and ultimate responsibility of the Prime Minister.[9] The resulting TMP represented, therefore, a fully institutionalized expression of politically warranted development goals and priorities.

The emergent pattern of ministerial intervention in planning was symptomatic of a deeper politicization of economic policy issues since the promulgation of the NEP. The NEP legitimized radical demands for a restructuring of Malaysia's communally segregated economy and society, and galvanized a more pronounced development consciousness among the broadly based and already restless UMNO. This radical impulse was particularly notable among the UMNO Youth wing and the radical Islamic factions of the party. The upsurge of Malay activism over economic policy tended to exacerbate the strains of communal and class cleavages in the national body politic. Yet, NEP did place politics forthrightly in command of development planning, in marked contrast with the past bureaucratic management of Malaysian economic policy.

Planning Goals, Priorities and Commitments

The structural transformation of the planning apparatus was instrumental to policy changes bearing upon the direction of planned development. Malaysian planning, as a fiscal mechanism, allocates public capital expenditure authoritatively among prescribed objectives. The goals of planning may be distinguished according to types of policy objectives, whether concerned with economic output, social order, cultural values, or political purpose (i.e., administration, security, defence). Specific priorities are reflected in internal sectoral allocations of investment resources, e.g., for agriculture, industry, education, administration, etc. The overall allocation of development resources expresses the ranking of planning goals between purely economic objectives and alternative social, cultural or political goals.[10]

Initially, the role of planning related specifically to government sector development. The relatively modest fiscal appropriation presented in the DDP was subsequently revised and multiplied more than fourfold in the wake of the Korean War inflation. The original DDP allocation of planned expenditure between economic and social services in the proportion 73% to 27% shifted to 90% to 10% respectively, in the revised plan. In the event, actual DDP allocations indicated a realized economic-social capital expenditure ratio of better than 11:1. Highest priority went to the provision of public economic infrastructure, including telecommunications, electric power, roads, railway and port facilities, designed to service the established primary commodity export sectors. Altogether, public economic infrastructure type attracted well over half of total government investment during the plan period.

The subsequent First FYP called for substantially increased capital expenditure in real as well as money terms, with continuing emphasis on the government domain and its economic services. Nevertheless, certain alterations in plan priorities had become apparent. The transition to independence brought with it a general expansion of the bureaucratic machinery of statehood. While this political-administrative goal found expression in the First FYP, in the event personnel shortages effectively retarded the state-building process. Even so, government itself exercised a dominant claim on plan resources. The declared First FYP allocation of expenditure as between economic, social and administrative development goals of 69% to 19% to 12% shifted in practice in favour of a greater priority for economic and administrative infrastructure. Actual allocations were in the proportions 75% to 14% to 10%. Not only were social development targets on the whole downplayed, but nearly half of "social" investment actually consisted of concessional housing, typically of better standard, for government officials.

The second phase of planning highlighted this emergent growth role. A quantum leap in plan expenditures—a doubling of the prior level for the Second FYP and half again in the FMP—accompanied a new ordering of development goals. Social objectives in particular now obtained an enlarged share of developmental appropria-

TABLE 1
Malaysian Development Plan Targets and Attainments (M$ million current values).

	DDP 1950-55				First FYP 1956-60			Second FYP 1961-65		
	Plan	Revised	Actual*	%†	Plan	Actual	%†	Plan	Actual	%†
Total Public Investment	214.7	846.9	680.6	79.5	1,148.7	1006.7	87.7	2,150.0	2,651.7	123.3
Economic Sector	156.4	766.8	550.1	71.7	794.7	759.9	97.4	1,477.9	1,763.7	119.3
• Agriculture	46.5	189.4	155.6	82.2	265.6	227.5	85.6	543.3	467.9	85.9
• Infrastructure	109.9	577.9	394.5	68.3	513.3	520.3	101.4	905.6	1,236.7	136.5
• Industry	n/a	n/a	n/a	—	15.8	12.1	76.3	27.0	59.1	218.9
Social Sector	53.3	80.1	48.3	61.1	212.7	138.8	65.3	491.0	413.6	84.2
• Education	35.0	51.1	33.0	64.6	95.4	60.9	63.8	260.0	236.5	91.0
• Health	16.9	18.5	15.3	82.7	50.0	12.7	25.4	145.0	101.9	70.3
• Housing	3.0	10.5	n/a	—	67.3	65.2	96.8	80.0	69.4	86.8
• Other Services	3.4	n/a	n/a	—	n/a	n/a	—	6.0	5.8	96.7
General	n/a	n/a	82.2‡	—	141.3	108.0	—	181.1	474.4	261.9
• Administration	n/a	n/a	n/a	—	141.3	65.0	46.0	88.1	167.1	189.7
• Security	n/a	n/a	n/a	—	n/a	43.0	—	93.0	307.3	330.0
Price Deflator††	15% (est)				2% (est)			2.4%		

TABLE 1 (continued).

	First Malaysia Plan 1966-70						Second Malaysian Plan		
		Malaya			Malaysia			Plan	
	Plan	Actual	%†	Plan	Actual	%†	Malaya	Malaysia	Revised
Total Public Investment	3,713.6	3,610.2	97.2	4,556.9	4,242.9	93.2	5,868.1	7,250.0	10,255.6
Economic Sector	2,228.1	2,210.8	99.2	2,710.2	2,685.4	99.1	3,898.8	4,870.9	7,349.7
• Agriculture	900.2	911.2	101.2	1,086.6	1,114.1	102.5	1,570.9	1,920.8	2,368.9
• Infrastructure	1,218.2	1,162.6	95.4	1,539.1	1,430.0	92.9	1,763.4	2,366.5	3,372.6
• Industry	110.3	137.0	124.2	84.5	141.3	167.2	583.6	583.6	1,608.1
Social Sector	797.4	644.7	80.8	975.3	752.1	77.1	836.0	1,067.4	1,431.0
• Education	368.0	286.9	77.9	470.8	329.4	70.0	458.9	537.3	763.6
• Health	150.4	114.2	75.9	189.4	146.6	77.4	458.9	573.3	226.8
• Housing	194.8	188.0	96.5	209.7	206.8	98.6	149.7	195.9	240.0
• Other Services	84.2	55.6	66.0	105.4	69.3	65.7	56.3	120.6	200.6
General	687.5	754.7	109.8	865.4	804.9	93.0	1,133.4	1,311.7	1,474.7
• Administration	87.9	109.0	124.0	126.4	138.1	109.3	139.3	211.6	369.9
• Security	599.6	645.7	107.7	739.0	666.8	90.2	994.1	1,100.1	1,104.8
Price Deflator††	6.9%			n/a					

TABLE 1 (continued).

	Second Malaysia Plan (Actual est.)			Third Malaysian Plan	
	Malaya	Malaysia	%‡‡	Malaya	Malaysia
Total Public					
Investment	8,075.8	9,820.8	95.8	15,445.7	18,555.0
Economic Sector	5,771.8	7,100.3	96.0	10,475.5	12,665.1
• Agriculture	1,747.0	2,129.1	89.9	4,972.8	4,735.5
• Infrastructure	2,482.6	3,353.0	100.6	4,972.8	6,195.1
• Industry	1,542.3	1,618.2	100.6	1,600.8	1,734.5
Social Sector	797.4	1,347.7	94.2	2,511.2	3,099.1
• Education	368.0	675.8	88.5	1,282.6	1,671.3
• Health	150.4	173.9	76.7	327.1	377.1
• Housing	194.8	234.8	97.8	606.0	710.1
• Other Services	84.2	263.1	76.3	295.5	333.5
General	687.5	1,372.9	93.1	2,458.9	2,797.7
• Administration	87.9	348.7	94.3	418.9	597.7
• Security	599.6	1,024.2	92.7	2,040.0	3,200.0
Price Deflator††	27.2%	n/a			

*   Estimates.
†   Percentage fulfillment of Plan.
‡   Including government housing.
†† Based on rate of increase in consumer price index for previous quinquennnium.
‡‡ Percentage fulfillment of Revised Target.
Sources: *First Malaysia Plan*, *Second Malaysia Plan*, *Third Malaysia Plan*;
     M. Rudner, "The Draft Development Plan of the Federation of Malaya,
     1950-1955", *Journal of Southeast Asian Studies*, (March, 1972); M. Rudner,
     Nationalism, Planning and Economic Modernization in Malaysia, (Sage
     Publications, 1975); *Economic Report, 1975-76*.

tions. Planned expenditures were allocated 69% for economic targets and 23% for social targets in the Second FYP, reaching 60% economic and 21% social in the FMP, with the remainder being devoted to general administration and security. Also during this phase, plan objectives were explicitly related (with greater or lesser sophistication) to anticipated investment activities in the private sector. Planning evolved towards a more wide-ranging and better integrated public investment role in promoting economic growth and social improvement. However, the pursuit of development goals remained inhibited somewhat owing to the military requirements of the Confrontation with Indonesia.

The combination of goals adopted in the Second FYP and FMP emphasized the expansion of both employment opportunities and

related social facilities, as means of raising domestic income levels. New policy directions became apparent in the actual allocations of plan investment. Goal priorities were allocated 67%
economic, 16% social, 18% general governmental (12% for security) in the Second FYP; and 61% economic, 18% social, 21% general
governmental (18% for security) for peninsular Malaysia under the
FMP (all Malaysia: 65%, 18%, 19%), respectively.

Sectoral allocations underscored the goal priorities implicit in
this phase. While economic infrastructure still continued to obtain
the largest share of public capital, the two successive plans tended
also to enhance the economic growth priorities of government investment in agriculture, industry and, significantly, education. Policies
towards agriculture enunciated as part of the Second FYP, and continued in the FMP, aimed at increasing rural employment and productivity through substantially expanded public expenditure on new land
settlement schemes for cash crops and smallholdings rubber replanting, as well as irrigation for padi. Despite early lags, agricultural development eventually attracted over a quarter of realized FMP public
investment. Moreover, a co-ordinated and deliberate effort was made
beginning with the Second FYP to extend roads, public utilities and
social services into the rural areas. At the same time, the plans directed government investment to a considerable and unprecedented
extent towards industrial diversification. As this policy unravelled
under the FMP, the largest share was earmarked along essentially
ethnic lines, in effect for the promotion of commercial skills and
enterprise among Malays.[11] Yet a major provision was also made
for concessionary finance and facilities for the development of
manufacturing generally, in support of an ostensibly labour-intensive, import-substitution industrialization policy.[12]

The development of education was treated as a crucial factor
pertinent to each and all of the economic, social and administrative goals of this phase of planning.[13] Both the Second FYP and SMP
provided for a succession of fundamental reforms to post-primary
schooling. The National School policy introduced in 1961 inspired
a rapid expansion of the secondary education level during the Second FYP. This was intended to foster national integration while
meeting the manpower requirements for administrative and social
development. Curricular and institutional reforms designed to
generate scientific, technical and vocational human resources for
industrialization were taken up in the FMP. Actual rates of public investment in education accelerated to a peak at 9% of the Second
FYP, declining slightly to 8% of the FMP. Of course, total expendi-

tures had increased substantially in each successive plan. Meanwhile, other popular social services such as health also attracted historically high allocations of development expenditure.

The seeming complacency of a public investment approach predicated on linear and cumulative growth was suddenly shattered by the explosion of social tensions and racial violence following the 1969 elections. Previous directions in development planning subsequently succumbed to political challenges culminating in the NEP.

The introduction of the NEP meant a radical revision of development goals and priorities. Planned capital expenditures reached new heights in this third phase: the original SMP provided for a 70% increase over actual FMP expenditure, which was raised again to double that, in real terms, in the mid-term revision of the SMP. Then the TMP followed with a further 5% increase in real expenditure planned. Since the NEP was predicated on redistributing incremental resources along ethnic and (secondarily) income lines, leaving existing interests intact, this growth in public investment also marked a redirection of developmental resource allocations at the margin. The proclaimed NEP intention of bringing about a restructuring of the economy, so as to yield enlarged Malay shares of national income, occupational status, and ownership of assets, made for an enhanced SMP emphasis on economic goals, with particular respect to industrial development. This change in policy direction, reversing the past decline in proportional allocations to economic objectives, became even more pronounced following the mid-term review of SMP administrative and social targets.

Actual SMP allocations of public investment adhered to these revised priorities accentuating essentially economic goals. Over 72% of total (estimated) public capital expenditure went for economic objectives, while the social sector obtained just under 14%—a proportion reminiscent of the earlier First FYP. However, fundamental changes in the direction of development were revealed by the altered sectoral allocations of plan resources. Public investment in agriculture stood virtually constant in real money terms since the previous plan. This amounted to a proportionate decline to less than 22% of actual SMP. Conversely, the real rate of direct government investment in industry (including commerce), designed to foster Malay enterprise and the promotion of industrialization generally, escalated more than sixfold.

The portion of SMP public capital expenditure actually devoted to industrial targets attained an historical peak at 16.5% of the total, or over 19% for peninsular Malaysia alone. Indeed industry attracted a much greater allocation of actual SMP expenditure than all social development objectives together. SMP capital expenditure for social development barely exceeded the level of the previous FMP in real terms, with severe reductions in health and public housing items. The pattern of SMP allocations clearly highlighted the economic restructuring role assigned to NEP-inspired planning. Implementation now tended to downplay the priorities hitherto attached to agriculture and social development and instead placed emphasis on incipient industrialization as the commanding strategy of the NEP.

While adhering to an industry-centred strategy, the successor TMP has nonetheless moved towards redressing some of the imbalance among other economic and social objectives. TMP concern to ameliorate conditions of rural and urban poverty induced significantly higher appropriations for agriculture and education in particular, as compared to the previous plan. Planned public investment in agriculture and education regained their earlier relativity. However, the overall trend manifested in TMP allocations has been consistent with the current strategy. The role of development planning continued to emphasize accelerated industrialization as a means of restructuring ethnic and also class relations in the context of economic growth. Meanwhile, both the SMP and TMP continued to direct large proportions of their available resources, ranging between 10% and 12%, to internal security requirements of a smouldering insurgency.

Patterns of plan fulfillment reveal the extent of official commitment to originally proclaimed development goals. Following the poor overall performance of the first phase of planning, the Second FYP and subsequent plans achieved generally higher rates of overall fulfillment. For the colonial authorities, planned developmental expansion of the government sector remained subordinate to other, basically custodial policy concerns, including the building-up of sterling reserve balances. Even after the transition to independence, the conservative legacy in public finance inhibited the performance of the First FYP. In later phases of planning, the conservative canons of economic management began to give way before the political imperatives of development.

Development planning had undergone a metamorphosis, emerging as an institutionalized policy mechanism related to the twin goals of nation-building and economic modernization. An interlude of political complacency allowed the performance of the FMP to slip somewhat. Still, the mounting political urgency of devel-

TABLE 2
Malaysian Development Plan Sectoral Allocation (percent).

	DDP			First FYP		Second FYP		First MP	
									Malaya
	Plan	Revised	Actual*	Plan	Actual	Plan	Actual	Plan	Actual
Economic Sector	72.8	90.6	80.8	69.2	75.5	68.8	65.5	60.0	61.2
• Agriculture	21.6	22.4	22.9	23.1	22.6	25.5	17.7	24.2	25.2
• Infrastructure	51.2	68.2	57.9	44.7	51.7	42.1	46.6	32.8	32.2
• Industry	n/a	n/a	n/a	1.4	1.2	1.2	2.2	3.0	3.8
Social Sector	27.2	9.4	7.1	18.5	13.8	22.8	15.6	21.5	17.9
• Education	16.3	6.0	4.8	8.3	6.0	12.1	8.9	9.9	7.9
• Health	7.9	2.2	2.3	4.3	1.3	6.7	3.8	4.1	3.3
• Housing	1.4	1.2	n/a	5.9	6.5	3.7	2.6	5.2	5.2
• Other Services	1.5	n/a	n/a	n/a	n/a	0.3	0.3	2.3	1.5
General	n/a	n/a	12.1	12.3	10.7	8.4	17.9	18.5	20.9
• Administration	n/a	n/a	n/a	12.3	6.4	4.1	6.3	2.4	3.0
• Security	n/a	n/a	n/a	n/a	4.3	4.3	16.1	16.2	17.9
TOTAL	100.0	100.0	100.0	100.0	100.0	100.0	100.0	100.0	100.0

TABLE 2 (continued).

	First MP (Continued)		Second MP			Second Malaysia Plan*		Third Malaysia Plan	
	Malaysia		Malaya	Malaysia					
	Plan	Actual	Plan	Plan	Revised	Malaya	Malaysia	Malaya	Malaysia
Economic Sector	59.6	63.3	66.4	67.2	71.6	71.5	72.3	67.8	68.3
• Agriculture	23.2	26.3	26.8	26.5	23.1	21.6	21.7	25.3	25.5
• Infrastructure	33.9	33.7	30.0	32.6	32.8	30.8	34.1	32.1	33.3
• Industry	1.9	3.3	9.6	8.6	15.7	19.1	16.5	10.4	9.5
Social Sector	21.4	17.8	14.3	14.7	14.0	14.0	13.7	16.3	16.6
• Education	10.3	7.8	7.8	7.4	7.4	7.1	6.9	8.3	9.0
• Health	4.2	3.5	2.9	2.8	2.2	1.8	1.8	2.1	2.0
• Housing	4.6	4.9	2.6	2.7	2.3	2.3	2.4	3.9	3.8
• Other Services	2.3	1.6	1.0	1.6	2.1	2.8	2.7	2.0	1.8
General	19.0	18.9	19.3	18.1	14.4	14.5	14.0	15.9	15.1
• Administration	2.8	3.2	2.4	2.9	3.6	2.8	3.6	2.7	3.2
• Security	16.2	15.7	16.9	15.2	10.8	11.7	10.4	13.2	11.9
TOTAL	100.0	100.0	100.0	100.0	100.0	100.0	100.0	100.0	100.0

* Estimates

Sources: *First Malaysia Plan, Second Malaysia Plan, Third Malaysia Plan*;
M. Rudner, "The Draft Development Plan of the Federation of Malaya, 1950-1955", *Journal of Southeast Asian Studies*, (March, 1972); M. Rudner, *Nationalism, Planning and Economic Modernization in Malaysia*, (Sage Publications, 1975); *Economic Report, 1975-76*.

opment had by and large mobilized governmental commitment to planning and created a developmental imperative for economic management.

Variations in government commitments to the objectives of planning were indicated by differing sectoral rates of plan fulfillment. Economic objectives realized consistently higher rates of fulfillment than social objectives. Within the economic sector, infrastructure development targets from the First FYP onwards were either fulfilled or, more usually, over-fulfilled. Industrial targets likewise enjoyed a generally high level of fulfillment. By contrast, agricultural targets remained more or less under-fulfilled, except during the FMP. Indicative of the uneven contours of policy commitment was the almost routine under-fulfillment of social development objectives. Even though education performed comparatively well, it rated on average beneath the economic sector level. Other social targets experienced consistent and sometimes acute short-falls in public-investment. If housing recorded an untypically high fulfillment rate, this in fact reflected a mainly bureaucratic concern for accommodating government officials, an essentially administrative objective.

Part of the lag in social and administrative investment arose from difficulties in recruiting suitable personnel, at least in the earlier phases. But the long-run pattern implied a more fundamental policy predilection. A differential commitment towards the economic and social objectives of development was clearly manifest in the systematic pattern of plan fulfillment and under-fulfillment. This pointed to an underlying bias in the normative concepts being applied in Malaysian development planning.

The Normative Foundations of Economic Policy

Behind the role of expansion of planning lay politically engendered changes in the policy norms underpinning economic management. These norms derived from the social composition of political power. The value preferences and interests dominant in the political regime stipulate the norms that guide economic management and, in particular, defined which outputs are to be maximized, and which inputs minimized, through policy.

During the initial phase, when Malaya was still subject to colonial rule, the norms of planning were laid down by external Imperial institutions. Whereas in the past British economic management conceived of the colonial territories as part of a broader community of Empire, after the Second World War a narrower political perspective placed deliberate priority emphasis on maximizing the economic and social welfare of the U.K. itself.[14] No longer were Malaya and the other colonies included on equivalent terms in calculations of Imperial economic strategy, although, as overseas parts of the British trade and payments community, they were automatically embraced by its constraints.

Reflecting the influence of Imperial norms, the formulation and implementation of the DDP were expressly subject to overriding British concern for the accelerated accumulation of colonial budgetary and sterling area reserve balances. Locally, British interests sought the preservation of asset values built on the continuity of the existing structure of the Malayan economy, as the maximum and minimum objectives of policy. Although Malayan dependence on British policy perspectives terminated formally at the advent of self-government, economic management doctrine still remained subordinate to external metropolitical influences. The development strategy underlying the successor First FYP still reflected traditional normative preferences of an expatriate-dominated Economic Secretariat and Treasury, as legitimized by the report of the visiting World Bank Mission.[15] Moreover, Malayan economic management remained subject to external institutional checks on the use of foreign exchange and other official reserve balances, in accordance with the London Round Table Conference Agreement (1956) on independence.[16]

The inherited norms of public finance, which emphasized stability *a priori* in terms of continuing adherence to the sterling area financial regime, in effect confined Malayan development planning to a sort of post-colonial protective custody during this period of political transition.

Subsequent changes in the structure of Malaysian planning wrought new directions to development strategy. The creation of specialized bureaucratic planning organs as part of the second phase of role expansion coincided with the accelerated pace of "Malayanization" of the government service, reaching right up to the topmost echelons.[17] Through the NDPC and EPU, the new found power of this ascendant administrative class impressed its own normative perspectives onto economic management. Certainly the financial bureaucracy based on the Treasury, Bank Negara (central bank) and EPU continued to exercise a powerful influence on the economic policy doctrines being applied in development planning. Consultants from international organizations and Western bloc countries retained an expatriate presence in economic administration, to be sure. Be that as it may, beyond certain technical matters, where international advice was needed, ultimate control over policy decisions had passed into local Malaysian hands. By the third phase of role expansion, pre-eminent authority over development planning was now assumed directly by the national political leadership. Officialdom still maintained some professional or bureaucratic influence. However, the normative conception of development, its planning strategies and economic doctrines were now determined at the national political level.

Changes in the structure of authority over planning, and in the associated normative foundations of development strategy, were reflected in three critical and inter-connected spheres of economic management: the treatment of macroeconomic savings, or capital formation; avenues of public investment; and the accepted areas for state activity in the economy. Some modification to economic management techniques would perhaps have come about anyway owing to the accretion of experience and confidence. But there can be little doubt that the major evolutionary changes in the role and concept of Malaysian planning represented deliberate political acts.

The initial phase of planning presented few departures from the long-standing colonial norms governing capital formation. As hitherto, the assumptions and rules associated with colonial public finance gave overriding priority to the accumulation of external sterling reserve balances against Malaya's limited capacity for savings. Conventional thought on colonial development placed stress on financial "stability" as a policy prerequisite for attracting private capital inflows, the assumed mainspring for their economic growth. Such stability was typically identified with a strong financial reserve position in sterling. Until the mid-1950s, the colonial Malayan Currency Board still maintained its sterling reserves at a sacrosanct 110% coverage for the domestic money supply.[18] Past practice weighed heavily even on the successor monetary authorities. Inordinately high currency reserve ratios were still maintained after independence,[19] ostensibly to underwrite the historic exchange rate parity with sterling.

Official obsessions with reserve balances conditioned fiscal policy perspectives spanning the DDP and even the First FYP. Fiscal policy generally remained predisposed to the accumulation of budgetary reserves in sterling. Plainly the prior consideration of public finance during this phase was to safeguard government's revenue position against possible fluctuations. Colonial Treasury opinion went so far as to propound the building up of budgetary reserves to the equivalent of a full year's total federal government expenditure.[20] This reserves syndrome indeed went far beyond conventional conservative predilections for "sound" public finance or "balanced" budgeting. Malayan financial management, in fact, tended almost invariably towards surplus finance. Systematic surpluses on revenue account served to augment the government's external asset balances over this first decade of planning.

It is a sad comment on then-prevailing policy preferences that the recorded increase in fiscal reserves deposited abroad (mainly in Britain) exceeded, by a considerable margin, the concurrent shortfalls in planned investment incurred by the DDP and the First FYP (Table 3). This perverse bias in public capital formation was symptomatic of the conventions underlying colonial and transitional economic management: an obsession with reserves, on the one hand, coupled with simplistic expectations concerning foreign investment-led growth, on the other.[21] The fiscal policy predisposition towards surplus finance was, accordingly, bracketed along with a relatively low-key overall taxation effort.[22]

Normative constraints on public finance made planning in effect a device for colonial bureaucratic control of the Malayan economy. During this first phase, planned expenditures on economic and especially social objectives were regularly subject to curtailment, owing to what were in essence contrived budgetary stringencies. Official financial doctrine inspired financial policies that were, in the circumstances, even detrimental to the immediate investment requirements of domestic Malayan development. For while planned expenditure performance was systematically inhibited owing to these budgetary restraints, the concomitant penchant for surplus finance brought about a parallel growth of financial reserves held in sterling, adding to the already substantial transfer of public capital resources—at low and often negative returns— from Malaya to Britain.

The succeeding phases of planning altered the norms of public finance. In a striking departure from past conventions, the Second FYP replaced the earlier fiscal cult of reserves with a macro-economic conception of public finance. No longer was investment planning confined merely to available residual finance—"cutting one's coat according to one's cloth." Rather, the planning function now provided for a more ambitious and instrumental mobilization of financial resources directed at government-determined development objectives. Whereas official attitudes towards monetary policy remained patently conservative,[23] the role expansion of planning brought about a far-reaching transformation of prevailing norms of fiscal conduct, from the custodial revenue accounting of the past to a more positive style of investment finance.

The financial norms associated with the second phase of planning derived specifically from a Harrod-Domar economic growth model.[24] Planners now approached development finance by calculating the rate of investment required to generate the plan-warranted rate of growth based on an incremental capital-output ratio (ICOR). Foreign private investment was still regarded as the mainspring of the development process. An inflow of capital, it was assumed, would generate the growth of national income deemed necessary for achieving planned economic-output objectives, while maintaining intact the twin structural-maintenance objectives of institutional and price stability.

These output and order goals were translated into incremental growth targets, to be generated through the ICOR nexus by prescribed levels of investment. For the Second FYP, an overall growth rate of 22% was planned over the quinquennium, with the ICOR taken at 4, requiring an annual rate of investment of 18% of GDP.[25] This represented a one-third increase in the (net) investment rate compared to the previous plan phase, amounting to some two-thirds more in absolute money terms. Next, the FMP set a quinquennial growth target of 24% which, with an ICOR calculated anew at 3.9, called for investment at an annual rate of 19% of GDP.[26]

Official convention still considered private investment "the main dynamic element producing rapid economic growth."[27] Although planned public investment underwent a greater proportional increase in the Second FYP this was expected to taper off considerably by the FMP as private investment surged ahead as forecast. Private domestic and foreign investment were expected to provide the critical growth thrust in industry, construction, road transport, commerce and related trades. But private investment lay by and large outside the formal controls of the planning apparatus. At this stage, planning related to the non-agricultural private sector only through indirect means: through public investment in economic infrastructure. A public investment role of this type, it was assumed, would provide inducement and direction for private non-agricultural capital formation. The indirect linkage between public planning and private investment activity would, it was further assumed, suffice to realize declared growth targets.

In line with (or perhaps because of) this emphasis on overall growth, only scant consideration was given during these earlier two phases either to the impact of their respective growth formulae on the distribution of income and wealth or on ethnic participation patterns in the economy. Insofar as these development strategies related to social inequalities, prevailing doctrine assumed that the remedies would invariably follow upon such plan achievements as improved education and rural amenities, administrative provision for Malay "Special Rights"[28] and the broad "trickle down" effects of growth itself.

The complacency implicit from this development doctrine came under strong political challenge after the 1969 elections, with its aftermath of racial turmoil and social ferment. A shaken political and bureaucratic elite found itself impelled towards a radical reappraisal of the norms prescribing their development goals and priorities. A revised development strategy now accepted that "economic growth alone will not be sufficient" to realize the politically warranted "restructuring" of the economy.[29] Malaysian planning presently embarked upon a further phase of role expansion. This new role was predicated upon the NEP declaration which was distinguished by bold prescriptions of economic and social norms for restructuring society through development planning.

The planning techniques applied in the SMP and TMP expressed the capital requirements for a prescribed growth path utilizing some seeming ICOR calculus, though the precise methodology behind this exercise remains undisclosed. Indeed its technical aspects were obfuscated by the elaborate treatment of the "restructuring of society" strategy put forward in the so called Outline Perspective Plan, 1971-1990, appended to the NEP.[30] However, the main thrust of the NEP projected a planned growth process aimed at urgent economic goals including industrial expansion, agricultural modernization and full employment, blending in with specific social welfare goals pertaining to specific target groups, sectors and also regions. Somehow—the actual formula has not been indicated—this intended restructuring postulated a long-term average real growth rate of 8%. Probably of greater significance, however, were the three redistributive criteria applied to the social directives of growth: income maintenance above certain conventional poverty lines; ethnic proportionality in the social composition of economic occupations; and raising the Malay ethnic share of total asset ownership to 30% over a 20-year time scale.

By grafting these distributive principles onto the earlier ICOR-based approach, this third phase of planning presented an unconventional and syncretic strategy of contoured growth that was neither linear nor monolithic. Development planning proceeded, accordingly, in a radically interventionist direction, following the contours of declared "socio-economic" (as they were officially termed) objectives:[31]

1. Reducing the incidence of rural poverty through expanded labour mobility, including new land settlement and internal migration, and improved agricultural infrastructure;

2. Reducing the incidence of urban poverty through expanded employment opportunities and improved provision of social services, including low-cost housing;

3. Enhancing the "quality of life," particularly of the poor, through the expansion of education, health services, family planning facilities and housing;

4. Increasing the share of Malays and other "indigenous" peoples in mining, manufacturing and construction, and the share of non-Malays in agriculture and public services, towards eventual achievement of ethnic proportionality, by occupation, by the year 1990;

5. Raising the share of Malays and other indigenous peoples in the ownership of economic assets, aimed at achieving an eventual racial balance of 30% Malay-indigenous ownership, 40% non-Malay ownership (the remainder being foreign-owned) by 1990;

6. Fostering entrepreneurship among Malays and other indigenous communities so as to induce wider ethnic representation in the commercial and industrial capitalist class;

7. Encouraging and supporting private domestic and foreign investment activity, for ideological as well as practical purposes;

8. Promoting the further mobilization of human and other economic resources for development; and

9. Developing and expanding the social and physical infrastructure of the economy to effectively sustain the above objectives.

Yet, despite its political imperatives, this interventionist approach to restructuring the economy has not permeated evenly through all facets of public policy. Explicit redistributive norms now may be applicable in development planning, but certain other critical areas of economic and social management still remain under the influence of more conservative canons and institutional constraints. Even in development planning, those policy norms invoking redistributions of income and wealth are effectively circumscribed by the narrow criteria of poverty and race decreed by political authority.

Economic Management Under the NEP

The radical intervention espoused in the third phase of planning was predicated upon some deliberate administrative involvement in the mobilization and direction of economic and also social resources.[32] Since accepted planning techniques lacked any rigorous formulae for determining the capital requirements of their economic and social restructuring goals, the rates of capital formation presented by the SMP and TMP expressed apparently notional magnitudes and allocations. Whenever the application of other macroeconomic allocative techniques seemed inadequate for the purpose, the plans called for direct administrative intervention as and where necessary to realize their goals. The pressure of political determination on the limits of technical proficiency invokes a tendency towards a somewhat pragmatic problem-solving approach to plan implementation. This new flexibility in economic management, by way of coping with constraints affecting specific targets, enabled the administrative apparatus to better reconcile its characteristically custodial bureaucratic outlook to the more radical goal commitments of development planning.

The typically conservative canons of monetary policy were probably the least influenced by these new perspectives on economic management. Formally, at least, the historical institutional link with monetary tradition was finally severed in 1973. That year the Malaysian *ringgit* was unpegged and allowed to appreciate against currencies of its major trading partners.[33] For Malaysia, this marked a significant departure in monetary policy. Slight, controlled variations in exchange rates were now accepted as a means of defending domestic economic objectives (e.g., price stability) against exogenous pressures (e.g., international inflation). Yet the long-abiding ethos of monetary caution, in the very context of managing floating exchange rates, made the Malaysian monetary authorities inclined to uphold unusually full international reserve cover for their currency liabilities. International reserves symbolized stability and remain a paramount concern in the conduct of monetary policy.

Gross external reserves of Bank Negara, held mostly in foreign exchange and gold, had been allowed to decline to around 95-98% of a rapidly expanding domestic money supply (M1) in the later years of the (under-fulfilled) SMP. Subsequently this reserve ratio rebounded sharply to an extravagant 119% during the initial year (1976) of the TMP.[34] This denoted an extraordinarily high reserve ratio even for Malaysia. At the time, the international reserves of

Bank Negara alone could have sufficed to cover between five and eight months' total imports. Malaysia's monetary regime has adhered rigorously to its customarily strict canons of stability. The rules governing monetary policy, therefore, tended to differ from, and occasionally were at variance with, the norms of development mandated by planning.

By contrast with the monetary policy situation, the management of fiscal policy was rather more strongly influenced by development planning. To be sure, stabilization continued to figure prominently in short-run fiscal perspectives. Nevertheless, the overall trend in fiscal management has tended to focus on mobilizing public finance to meet plan targets. The impact of fiscal mobilization became notably apparent in an intensified taxation effort. Tax revenues as a proportion of GNP escalated in quantum leaps from around 10 to 13% during the 1950s, to the 14 to 16% range in the 1960s, to well over 20% since the 1970s.[35] Increased revenue capabilities made the government's budget into the single most important source of public capital formation during the Second FYP and FMP period. By the third phase, however, the government's current revenue account surplus remained almost constant, though declining proportionally and in real terms. The incremental revenue effort went instead towards meeting the expanded expenditure outlays incurred on account of the socio-economic development goals of this phase. The greater magnitudes and new purposes evidenced in the government's revenue effort demonstrates the adaptation of fiscal management to the expanded role assigned to development planning.

The impact of fiscal mobilization was also manifest in changed official attitudes towards the financing of development planning. Inherited norms of colonial public finance regarded deficit finance as anathema. Indeed, although the colonial government had occasion to resort to precautionary domestic and, less frequently, external borrowings in anticipation of possible budgetary deficits, these loans were more than offset during the DDP period by the growth of external budgetary reserves. Following independence, and particularly from the 1960s, governments came to accept deficit financing as a regular and integral component of development planning. In the earlier phases of planning, such deficits were financed for the most part through domestic borrowing from statutory funds (e.g., Central Provident Fund, Rubber Industry Replanting Fund), the banking system (including the Post Office, now National Savings Bank), insurance and other financial organizations. Domestic borrowing mobilized increasingly substantial capital resources, becoming the major single source of development finance for the third phase of planning. However, local borrowing capacity was limited by money market considerations and cyclical fluctuations, whereas the rapid escalation of planned development expenditure required deficit financing on a much larger scale from further afield.

Until recently, external sources of capital for development finance had been tapped only sparingly, and in ad hoc circumstances. Now from the late 1960s governments embarked on a systematic and expansive programme of external borrowing to satisfy the resource requirements of their expanded development role. By the third phase, burgeoning external borrowings contributed over a fifth of SMP public investment and were expected to provide nearly a third of the public development finance for the TMP. For all that the Malaysian external debt service ratio remained relatively low at 4% in 1975 and was forecast at 7% by 1980.[36]

As the role of planning and therefore, its capital requirements expanded, any residual savings gap in (deficit) finance was now made up by calling upon hitherto sacrosanct budgetary (as distinct from monetary) reserve balances. Already during the second phase, financial planning began to draw down accumulated budgetary reserves, albeit to a relatively minor extent. While high levels of budgetary reserves still continued to be regarded as important for "international confidence" and future needs, a subtle turnabout in the norms of public finance had nevertheless occurred.

Significantly, this normative transformation was very largely conditioned by political exigencies. Thus political factors behind the Second FYP made for a much greater readiness to tap budgetary reserves than the successor, more complacent, FMP. Under the NEP, the SMP anticipated only a "marginal" drawing on external budgetary assets.[37]

Yet in the course of its implementation, the political urgency of its socio-economic objectives led to a substantial running down of accumulated balances in order to sustain planned levels of investment. The combined revenue effort along with internal and external borrowing and reserves utilization brought about a dramatic increase in the rate of (gross) investment during the SMP to nearly 24% of GNP, surpassing the domestic savings ratio by a wide margin. Development finance was stimulated by a process of fiscal mobilization that overrode conventional normative and institutional constraints on public capital formation.

TABLE 3
Sources of Public Development Finance ($M million, current prices).

	1956-1960	%	1961-1965*	%	1966-1970	%	1971-1975‡	%
1. Public sector current surplus	487	35.5	1,140	39.3	1,814	41.7	1,768	17.9
2. Net domestic borrowing	606	44.2	1,089	37.3	1,751	40.2	4,505	45.2
3. Net foreign borrowing	124	9.0	184	6.3	457	10.5	2,100	21.1
4. Special receipts†	153	11.3	166	5.7	245	5.6	170	1.7
5. Change in government reserves††	-363	(-26.4)	325	11.2	85	2.2	1,408	14.1
Total Public Sector Development Finance	1,007	100.0	2,904	100.0	4,352	100.0	9,969	100.0

* 1961-63 Malaya; after 1963, Malaysia.
† Including foreign grants-in-aid.
‡ 1975: estimate.
†† (-) = increase.
Sources: *Second Five-Year Plan*; *Economic Reports*, 1973-4; 1975, 1975-76.

It is noteworthy that foreign grants-in-aid contributed relatively little to Malaysian public finance and tended to be mainly defence-related.

Role expansion also wrought significant normative changes to the definitions of "public investment" applicable through planning. At the outset, colonial planning disclosed a traditional dichotomy between capital expenditure on economic infrastructure as against social services. Economic infrastructure was deemed to be "actually productive in character" by virtue of the revenues generated. It was, therefore, distinguished conventionally as public *investment*.[38] Social services, however, though admittedly "desirable in themselves," were considered by the logic of colonial revenue accounting to represent merely "heavy consumers of public money" offering few immediate (economic) returns.[39] Expenditures on education, health, housing and other social facilities were accordingly treated like *consumption* items in public accounts. According to this reasoning, budgetary appropriations for these items of social *consumption* tended to reduce the quantum of public finance otherwise available for economic *investment*. This fundamentalist differentiation between economic *investment* and social *consumption* permeated the determination of development goals and priorities right through the initial phase of planning.

The custodial, revenue-biased, treatment of public investment was quite consistent with the colonial policy norms emphasizing an institutionally stable, socially orderly growth process. On the assumption that inadequate infrastructure inhibited such growth,

TABLE 4
Average Annual Rates
of Growth of Real Expenditure and Product (percent).

	1956-1960	1960-1965*	1966-1970	1971-1975†
1. Private Consumption	3.2	4.9	5.3	3.8
2. Public Consumption	2.9	12.5	9.4	9.0
3. Private Gross Fixed Capital Formation	10.4	5.1	9.6	7.2
4. Public Gross Fixed Capital Formation		27.6	1.9	17.6
5. Gross Domestic Product at Factor Cost	3.7	5.8	5.5	7.4

TABLE 4a
Savings and Investment Ratios (Cumlative).

	1966-1960	1960-1965*	1966-1970	1971-1975†
6. Domestic Savings as % of GNP	n/a	18.1	17.8	21.7
7. Gross Investment as % of GNP	12.0	18.5	15.8	23.9

* Malaya to 1963; Malaysia after 1963.
† Estimates
Source: D. Lim, *Economic Growth and Development in West Malaysia*, (OUP, 1973).

colonial Malayan planning strategy postulated that revenue-generating public investment in the modern infrastructure of transport, telecommunications and public utilities would create pre-conditions for attracting foreign private capital inflow into primary export expansion, whose spread effects should raise national income without unduly upsetting established institutional arrangements. DDP investment, therefore, highlighted "productive" infrastructure and short-run, "early returns" to revenue.[40]

In practice, however, government pricing policies tended to provide user subsidies on modern, export-oriented infrastructure, despite its declared revenue accounting "principles." Meanwhile, the application of these same principles tended to discourage public investment in economic developments having longer gestation periods.

Although the DDP had labelled social services "conditions precedent to progress," their development was treated like items of mere public consumption, contingent upon what revenues could currently "bear."[41] Colonial fiscal authorities insisted adamantly on "cautious" capital appropriations for social services, in order to avoid pre-commitments to popular expectations and to avoid exposure to downward fluctuations in government revenues.[42] That this tended to tie the pace of Malayan social development to vagaries of the world market for rubber and tin seemed inevitable, or else immaterial, to the colonial economic management. Ironically, the retardation of social development relative to the country's level of economic attainment severely limited any prospective spread effects arising out of post-war growth.

The transition to elected government paved the way to new criteria for public investment. Already in the second phase of planning, public investment was effectively redefined to embrace economic and social objectives important to the emergent nationalist political leadership. Changes to the criteria for public investment unfolded along two dimensions of policy, in particular, concerning agricultural and educational developments.

Agricultural policy innovations introduced by the newly elected government signalled a dramatic increase in public capital appropriations for smallholder rubber replanting, on the one hand, and for irrigation, roads and other rural infrastructure for the rice sector, on the other. The scale and allocation of public investment in agriculture indicated, as regards rubber, considerations of long-run income creation. As regards rice, the new policy reflected politically meaningful considerations of ethnic Malay welfare. Income effects—both its creation and distribution—were thus incorporated in the operational definition of public investment with respect to agriculture, alongside the traditional revenue accounting still applicable elsewhere under the First FYP.

Consideration of the income effects in planning afterwards became more general in the second phase of role expansion. Public investment was now related directly to national income, writ large. Benefits and costs of (public) investment in income-creating activity were henceforward assimilated through appropriate ICOR calculations into plan allocations of resources. Whereas public investment generally was evaluated according to these "economic" criteria, a special "strategic" political weighting was introduced especially to offset otherwise inferior ICOR calculations for rice agriculture.[43]

As for education, post-independence policy reforms introduced a new social perspective into public investment. The newly elected Alliance government treated education as its main policy instrument of nation-building.[44] With the introduction of the national school policy in 1957, public expenditure on education now came to be considered as a form of "investment" in the country's political "future."[45] However, fiscal doctrine did not as yet relate education to economic goals, as distinguished from social or political develop-

ment objectives. It was only after the accelerated retirement of expatriates from the government service during the late 1950s, coming
at a time of increasing demands on development administration,
that attention was called to the manpower constraint inherent in
Malayan underdevelopment. Scarcities of educated and technical manpower underscored the economic relevance of education.
By the 1960s planning had become cognizant of the value of education to the economy: "The traditional system of education is
[now] being reorientated to achieve not only the objectives of nation-building and universal literacy, but also the economic goals of
the country."[46]

The role assigned to education policy in development strategy
was reflected in claims on plan resources.[47] Capital spending on
education continued to show a substantial increase—relatively as
well as absolutely—during the Second FYP. Allocations of financial
resources to education were expressly committed to the national
policy target of near-universal primary school enrolment. After
1965, post-primary education underwent a reorganization designed
to meet anticipated industrialized labour market requirements. The
FMP explicitly characterized education as being directly pertinent to
economic short-run growth as well as longer-run development.[48]

Plan expenditure on education was now redefined in fiscal
cost/benefit terms, ahead of other social services, as "investment"
in human capital formation. Current educational expenditure levels
remained politically and socially unassailable. However, incremental appropriations to and within education were allocated
henceforward on a quasi-economic basis using internal rates of return as an ICOR proxy.

With the public finance of education thus governed by economic manpower considerations, an unwitting cleavage
emerged between these new educational investment criteria and
the social expectations enshrined in development planning.
Ironically, just when prevailing policy norms signalled a higher
marginal propensity to invest in education, the FMP emphasis on
essentially economic, manpower-related investment criteria
for educational investment tended to keep *social* objectives
proper outside the maintenance of development finance.

The third phase presented a somewhat more syncretic conception of public investment, corresponding to the economic and social facets of its proclaimed restructuring goals and relating to
specific target groups. Moreover, the political imperatives attached
to the composite socio-economic objectives of planning in effect

pluralized the investment criteria applicable to public finance. Official conceptions of economic investment acquired a broader developmental perspective, embracing not only income effects but also social considerations of racial balance and poverty.

It is significant that the most pronounced normative changes had occurred in the role-definition of social investment. Thus, the TMP treated the development of social services as a form of "infrastructure" component of economic development directly relevant to the objectives of the NEP.[49] Public investment for specified social services such as education, training or low-cost housing, was linked expressly to the "real income" requirements of particular target groups. Social development emerged with its own implicit investment criteria, relating the expansion of education, health services, family planning facilities and housing, in particular, to both human resources development and upgrading Malaysia's "quality of life."

To administer the inter-related economic and social components of investment, the third phase role expansion highlighted certain development programmes where administrative proximity to target groups might be expected to compensate for somewhat indeterminate formal investment criteria. The efficacy of public investment allocations tended to be evaluated not so much in terms of income maximization pure and simple, but more in the context of administrative problem-solving related to the socio-economic objectives of planning.

Planning and the Private Sector

Plan relationships with the private sector of the economy constituted a third area of normative change. During the initial phase, planning was construed narrowly as a forward capital budgeting device for public sector services in support of an overwhelmingly private, primary export-based market economy. Growth, in the colonial view, was expected to arise out of private capital inflows, primarily from the U.K., into Malaya's traditional export sectors: rubber and tin. It therefore remained for planning to meet the anticipated infrastructural needs of expected levels of export activity.

Later, in the second phase, planning acquired a somewhat more positive role as a public sector stimulator of private investment. Without detracting from either private enterprise or market operations, planning embarked on direct large-scale public investment in peasant agricultural modernization, rubber and rice, along with pacemaking investment in economic and social infrastructure. This style of indicative planning was supposed to lend direction and provide stimulation for economic expansion, while relying on private investment as the actual engine of growth.[50]

With the introduction of the NEP, political demands propelled development planning towards a progressively more interventionist relationship to private sector economic activities. Certainly the private sector came within the purview of socio-economic restructuring. Government reiterated its welcome to private, especially foreign, investment. However, private enterprise was expected to conform to operating guidelines derived from the NEP.[51] As planning acquired a more interventionist policy role, conventional fiscal instruments were augmented by affirmative administrative measures in support of declared economic and social objectives. Under the SMP and TMP, intervention in the private economy took three main forms: the enactment of regulations intended to promote the objective of ethnic Malay employment in the modern business sector; government acquisition of equity capital in private companies on behalf of the ethnic Malay community, "in trust" (ostensibly for eventual resale to individual Malay capitalists once these came forward), to foster the intended ethnic balance of ownership; and the creation of government business enterprises, sometimes in competition with private firms, in pursuit of particular ethnic-commercial objectives.[52]

TABLE 5
GDP by Industrial Origin (percent).

	Malaya				Malaysia			Average Annual Growth Rate 1970-1975
	1960	1965	1970	1975*	1967	1970	1975	
1. Agriculture, Forestry, & Fishing	40.5	31.8	34.3	33	32.5	33.0	30	5.9
2. Mining & Quarrying	6.1	8.9	6.8	4	6.3	5.7	4	0.0
3. Manufacturing	8.6	10.4	16.6	20	11.2	13.2	14	10.9
4. Construction	3.0	4.1	3.8	5	4.1	3.8	5	8.1
5. Electricity & Water	1.5	2.3	3.2	3	2.4	2.5	3	10.4
6. Other Services†	40.3	42.5	35.3	34	43.5	41.5	44	8.7
TOTAL	100.0	100.0	100.0	100	100.0	100.0	100	7.4

* Estimates.
† Including transport, communications, trade, banking, insurance, dwellings, and public administration.
Sources: *Third Malaysia Plan; Economic Reports 1973/74; 1975; and 1975/76.*

Changes in the norms and policies of planning testified to changes in the goals of economic management. The first phase of planning stressed the primacy of essentially *custodial* goals. In the next phase, planning emphasis shifted in favour of economic *output* defined in terms of income growth. Further changes in the third phase of planning witnessed the emergence of radically combined *output* and *order* goals. Planning strategy now assimilated income-creating and redistributive policies, aimed at specified economic and social targets. But while economic management became committed to development planning, the NEP-inspired criteria for "restructuring" society were still constrained by politically determined boundaries of ethnicity and poverty. It is noteworthy that specifically *cultural* goals, pertaining to the societal values as such, remained by and large outside the concern of development strategy. The pattern of goal changes that occurred related instead to a reallocation of planning resources; from preoccupation with structural continuity and then growth to the present restructuring of growth. This process of goal change gave expression to the role-expansion of planning, from an agency of social control into an instrument of social change.

Politics and the Economic Rationale of Planning

Outside the Communist sphere, Malaysia is one of the countries most attached to development planning. It is noteworthy that this Malaysian affinity for planning certainly did not stem from socialist convictions; nor from the zeal of economic nationalism or disappointment with the market economy. Quite the contrary, Malaysia's involvement with development planning occurred within the framework of a market-oriented and open, predominantly private enterprise economy governed by an innately conservative political elite. The role(s) assigned to planning in Malaysia eschewed the archetypal command model, virtually as a matter of course. Nevertheless, Malaysian planning has been significantly more interventionist than any mere *dirigiste* model might imply.

What began originally as simple forward budgeting on the part of the colonial administration evolved after independence into a politically increasingly interventionist problem-solving approach to development planning. The essence of this approach, which has emphasized coping with resource complaints affecting the realization of politically determined development goals that accompanied successive phases of planning, accentuated the importance of this problem-solving approach. Planning acquired a central institutional position in the formulation and application of Malaysian development policy.

Like most, if not all, countries that plan, Malaysia has come to settle on a five-year horizon for its planning. The DDP sponsored by the colonial administration provided for a longer-term public investment programme. But five years later, the transition to self-government led to a new plan being formulated in its place. As from the (unpublished) First FYP of 1956, five years became the accepted time span for Malaysian planning operations.

Over the next 15 years, each successive plan was conceived separately and individually within its own quinquennium. Beginning with the introduction of the SMP, however, this five year time frame has been placed into the longer-run context of a 20-year strategy projection. This so called "Perspective" Plan provides an outline of certain target values to be pursued through planning during the period 1971-1990. Meanwhile the effective horizon for the planning of current policy continues to be five years. Apart from the convention of five-year planning, however, there seems to be little real economic justification behind this particular time frame. Rather, the rationale would appear to be found in its political convenience.

As already noted, the sequence of planning has tended to coincide with the sequence of Malaysian parliamentary elections. Except for the early election called in 1978, which took place mid-term through the TMP, all other general elections were followed in short order by the introduction of successive plans. The influence of elections on governmental behaviour was manifest in the tendency to adjust its development policies to respond to the ebb and flow of electoral support. In reciprocal effect, this electoral responsiveness of planning served to bolster the dominance of the incumbent ruling coalition. Planning became, in effect, a political resource contributing to the maintenance of the existing party regime.

The reciprocal influence of electoral politics on planning did not produce in Malaysia the election policy cycle experienced in some other countries.[53] Vote catching behaviour has had some bearing on public expenditure decisions and their timing, most notably on the eve of elections.[54] But to the extent that the magnitudes involved remained relatively small, the attendant opportunity costs and distortions in resource allocations have been of not great import. Nor has the macro-economic impact of electioneering finance been notably de-stabilizing. Indeed, the very dominance of Malaysia's ruling coalition afforded it the capacity to eschew the more blatant sort of vote-loss-minimizing fiscal conduct. Malaysian party politics were thus able to avoid a de-stabilizing election policy cycle while pursuing a more-or-less responsive form of economic management.

It would be inappropriate to describe parliamentary politics simply as a constraint or limiting factor on economic management. Rather, elections and party politics ought to be viewed as legitimate political mechanisms through which society's social welfare function obtains representative and authoritative policy expression.

If electoral politics had comparatively little effect on current budgetary practices, far greater significance may be attached to the influence of elections upon the ensuing determination of goals and priorities in development planning. Basic elements of planning, such as the definition of objectives, the allocation of development resources among them and the choice of policy instruments for plan-implementation were sensitive to political demands articulated through the party system and ultimately arbitrated by the election mechanism. The Malaysian experience demonstrates a predisposition among dominant coalition forms of government to translate their electoral responsiveness into new departures in development strategy. Behind such responsive initiatives, and shaping their normative underpinning, rests what may be defined as a "conservative social welfare function," derived through the political process and manifest in development planning.

From the outset of self-government in Malaysia (then the Federation of Malaya), the norms of public policy were conditioned by the emphatically communal character of the body politic. The ethnic-communal contours of the political party system imbued the parliamentary process with what has been termed a consociational style of governance.[55] The dynamics of consociational politics accentuated the effective authority of the ethnic power elites, representative of the communal parties forming the dominant coalition. It was there, at the elite level, that inter-communal consensus was attained through political bargaining. Consociational elite consensus established the norms that shaped society's social welfare function.

Not surprisingly, the social welfare function associated with Malaysian consociational politics displayed distinctly conservative properties, indicative of communal elite values. The conservative inclination of such a social welfare function is manifest in its tendency to avoid policy prescriptions that may have the consequence of reducing real incomes or asset value of *any* significant segment of the political community.[56] A social group becomes significant in this sense by virtue of its connection with political authority. The ultimate test of any policy initiatives derived from a conservative social welfare function is its political acceptability.

In Malaysia, consociational political consensus engendered a conservative social welfare function that provided for the economic and social "advancement" of the Malay ethnic community, the core component of the ruling Alliance-based coalition, while preserving the "legitimate interests"—usually understood to include real income levels and assets—of the non-Malay (notably Chinese and Indian) communities.

Regionalism denoted another important parameter of the conservative social welfare function. Malay ethnicity embodies an inherent sense of identification with their respective Malay States. The interlocking "racial" (to use the official Malaysian terminology) and regional-state patterns of Malaysian consociational politics imbued the conservative social welfare function with intrinsically communal characteristics.

This communalism imbued plan-formulation and ensured policy implementation with a particular sensitivity to ethnic and regional interests. Explicitly economic interests formed along horizontal social class or industrial-sectoral lines, therefore, tended to be segmented by and subordinated to a hierarchy of communal norms prescribed by this conservative social welfare function.

Such inherent conservatism and intrinsic communalism impressed themselves on Malaysian development planning. Certainly, abrupt redistributions of income or assets found no sanction in consociational political consensus. Rather, it was *incremental* national income that was to be allocated through planning. While the growth impulse predominated, evolving political norms redirected the allocation of planning resources towards changing goals and priorities consistent with this communally conservative social welfare function. Planning emerged as the institutional fulcrum for managing this development strategy, promoting redistribution in the wake of growth.

As the role of planning expanded to cover broader areas of domestic economic activity, this in turn exposed plan performance all the more to pressures from the world economy. The Malaysian economy has been kept especially "open" to international trade and finance. Although the contribution of exports to Gross National Product has declined since the colonial era, it still remained around the 40 to

45% level through the late 1970s. Indeed, Malaysia must rank among the most open economies given to planning. Instead of fostering economic insularity, the expanding role of Malaysian planning increased the need to cope with international market forces, particularly as these affected export-oriented industrialization.

Until very recently, planning limited itself to comparatively crude predictions of future international trends. Lately, however, the impact of prolonged international recession in the mid-1970s on planned private capital inflow and on export demand for manufacturers impelled a reassessment of the international linkages of planning. A deliberate effort is currently being made to take systematic account in the formulation and application of development strategy of relevant trends in the international economy. It remains to be seen how and to what extent the uncertainties of the world economic environment can be integrated into a coherent, albeit "open," planning mechanism for the pursuit of domestic development goals.

Planning now constitutes an agency of developmental change, notwithstanding its essentially conservative mainsprings. Yet the greater the planning commitment to mobilizing society's resources, the more likely its attendant policy thrust would tend to cut across the communal and conservative assumptions underlying the prevalent social welfare function. Certainly the unprecedented resort to legislative and administrative sanctions to give effect to NEP objectives during the third phase of planning, as exemplified by the Industrial Co-ordination Act, signified a deviation from long-standing policy norms. Planning came to touch upon sensitive entrepreneurial and communal nerves. As a result, domestic private investment has reportedly lagged behind TMP expectations. Among the Malays, incipient intra-communal tensions over religious values and social direction, exacerbated by shockwaves from the Iranian Revolution, have challenged the normative foundations of the NEP.[57]

Development strategy, though responsive to the electoral will, nonetheless came into conflict with communal-based attitudes, values and institutional interests opposed to the secularizing, modernizing, and distributive thrust of planning. As the role of planning expanded, its increasingly interventionist strategies provoked intensified political reactions over the normative and allocative implications of development.

ENDNOTES

1. On the structure and institutions of the Malaysian economy, see, e.g., T.H. Silcock & E.K. Fisk, eds., *The Political Economy of Independent Malaya* (Canberra, 1963); David Lim, *Economic Growth and Development in West Malaysia 1947-1980* (Kuala Lumpur, 1973); Stephen Chee & Khoo Siew Mun, eds., *Malaysian Economic Development and Policies* (Kuala Lumpur, 1975); Gayl D. Ness, *Bureaucracy and Rural Development in Malaysia* (Berkeley, 1967); and Martin Rudner, *Nationalism, Planning and Economic Modernization in Malaysia* (Beverly Hills, 1975).

2. For recent studies of Malaysian development planning, see Martin Rudner, "The Draft Development Plan of the Federation of Malaya, 1950-55", *Journal of Southeast Asian Studies (JSEAS)* Vol. 3 (1972), and *Nationalism, Planning and Economic Modernization in Malaysia*; Milton Esman, *Development and Administration in Malaysia* (Ithaca, 1972); David Lim, "Malaysia", in Yip Yat Hoong, ed., *Development Planning in Southeast Asia: Role of the University* (Singapore, 1973); Gayl D. Ness, *op. cit.* and "Economic Development and the Goals of Government", in Wang Gungwu, ed., *Malaysia* (London, 1964); and C.T. Edwards, *Public Finances in Malaysia and Singapore* (Canberra, 1970), esp. pp. 34-46.

3. On the background and purpose of the New Economic Policy, see R.S. Milne, "The Politics of Malaysia's New Economic Policy," *Pacific Affairs* (1976); Colin MacAndrews, "The Politics of Planning: Malaysia and the New Third Malaysia Plan," *Asian Survey* (1977).

4. *Colonial Development and Welfare* (London: HMSO, 1945), Cmd. 6713, para. 10. See also Rudner, "The Draft Development Plan," pp. 63-67.

5. Ness, *Bureaucracy*; R.O. Tilman, *Bureaucratic Transition in Malaya* (Durham, NC, 1962).

6. Federation of Malaya, *Report on Economic Planning in the Federation of Malaya in 1956* (Kuala Lumpur, 1957), pp. 2-5.

7. At this phase the NDPC was composed of senior officials of the Bank Negara Malaysia (Malaysian central bank), the Treasury, Ministry of Commerce and Industry, Ministry of National and Rural Development, Department of Statistics, representatives from Sabah and Sarawak, and the Economic Planning Unit, under the chairmanship of the Personal Secretary of the Prime Minister's Department. On the NDPC and its terms of reference, see the Federation of Malaysia, *First Malaysia Plan 1966-70* (Kuala Lumpur, 1966), pp. 90-91.

8. Federation of Malaysia, *Second Malaysia Plan, 1971-1975* (Kuala Lumpur, 1971), p. 113.

9. "My Cabinet colleagues and I have personally directed the preparation of the [Third Malaysia] Plan up to its final stages": Prime Minister's Foreword, Federation of Malaysia, *Third Malaysia Plan 1976-80* (Kuala Lumpur, 1976), pp. v and 264.

10. The analysis used here corresponds to Ness, *Bureaucracy*, except that his "cultural" and "mixed economic-cultural" goals are here treated as a "social" goal, relating to specifically human developments in the planning context. This paradigm for goal determination is derived in turn from A. Etzioni, *Comparative Analysis of Complex Organizations* (New York, 1967).

11. During the period 1966-1970 M$13 million was appropriated to the re-organised *Majlis Amanah Ra'ayat* (MARA—Council of Trust for Indigenous Peoples) for the provision of loans and technical assistance to Malay business and,

additionally, the newly established Bank Bumiputra allowed a M$134 million line of credit to Malay enterprises: *Second Malaysia Plan*, pp. 15-16.

12. Ibid., p. 15.

13. Martin Rudner, "Education, Development and Change in Malaysia," *South East Asian Studies* (1977).

14. Ida Greaves, *Colonial Monetary Conditions* (London, HMSO, 1954), Col. No. 10, p. 87; and Martin Rudner, "Financial Policies in Post-War Malaya" The Fiscal and Monetary Measures of Liberation and Reconstruction," *Journal of Imperial and Commonwealth History* (1975), pp. 326 *et passim*.

15. International Bank for Reconstruction and Development, *The Economic Development of Malaya* (Baltimore, 1955).

16. *Report of the Constitutional Conference, 8 January—6 February 1956* (London, HMSO, 1956), Cmd. 971.

17. R.O. Tilman, *Bureaucratic Transition*, and Gayl D. Ness, "The Malayan Bureaucracy and its Occupational Communities: A Comment on James de Verra Allen's 'The Malayan Civil Service, 1874-1941'," *Comparative Studies in Society and History* (1970), pp. 179-187.

18. See Sir Basil Blackot, *Report of the Commissioner Appointed by the Secretary of State for Colonies to Enquire into the Question of Malayan Currency, Straits Settlements Paper No. 78 of 1934*, where a reserve ratio of 15% was recommended, though this would reduce in practice to 110% cover; see also A. Hazelwood, "Colonial External Finance Since the War," *Review of Economic Studies (1953-4);* Rudner, *"Financial Policies in Post-War Malaya,"* esp. pp. 326-328, and "The Draft Development Plan", p. 72 *et passim*. On the Colonial Currency Board mechanism, see Greaves, *Colonial Monetary Conditions;* F.H.H. King, *Money in British East Asia*, (London, HMSO, 1957); and Sir Sydney Caine, "Malayan Monetary Problems," *Malayan Economic Review* (1958).

19. Edwards, *Public Finances*, pp. 295-307.

20. Financial Secretary, *Federation of Malaya Legislative Council Proceedings*, 21 November 1951 (Henceforth: *L.C. Proc.*). This was stated to "always" have been the target of the Financial Secretariat.

21. See T.H. Silcock, "General Review of Economic Policy", in Silcock & Fisk, eds., *Political Economy*.

22. Edwards, *Public Finances*, pp. 46-55 and Table 9 on Malayan taxation effort and government revenues.

23. For a survey of the guiding principles of Malaysian monetary management, see Bank Negara Malaysia, *Money and Banking in Malaysia* (Kuala Lumpur, 1979).

24. David Lim, "Malaysia," pp. 84-93. The Harrod-Domer model postulates a rate of growth, $g = S/K$, where S is the rate of saving, equals investment, and K marginal or incremental capital-output ratio.

25. *Second Five-Year Plan*, para. 75.

26. *First Malaysia Plan*, pp. 46-49, 61.

27. Ibid., para. 117.

28. See Gordon P. Means, "'Special Rights' as a Strategy for Development: The Case of Malaysia," *Comparative Politics* (1972).

29. *Third Malaysia Plan 1976-80*, para. 164.

30. Ibid., chap. 4.

31. Ibid., para. 193. Emphasis in original.

32. R. Thillainathan, "Inter-Racial Balance in Malaysian Employment and Wealth: An Evaluation of Distributional Targets," *The Developing Economies* (1976).

33. Malaysian *Ringgit* exchange rates, subject to a managed float since June, 1973, have been adjusted on the basis of a trade weighted average of exchange rates of Malaysia's ten major trading partners.

34. Ministry of Finance, Malaysia, *Economic Report 1976-77* (Kuala Lumpur, n.d.).

35. Edwards, *Public Finances*, pp. 46-55, esp. Table 9. *Third Malaysian Plan*, pp. 242-243.

36. *First Malaysia Plan*, para. 175.

37. *Second Malaysia Plan*, para. 236.

38. *Draft Development Plan*, chap. 1, para. 12.

39. *The Colonial Empire 1939-1947* (London, HMSO, 1947), Cmd. 7167, para. 107.

40. *Draft Development Plan*, chap. 11, para. 58(b).

41. *Report of the Standing Committee on Finance, Federation of Malaya, Legislative Council Paper No. 70 of 1954,* pp. 4-5.

42. Ibid., p. 8.

43. *First Malaysia Plan*, para. 249.

44. Rudner, "Education, Development and Change in Malaysia"; Francis Wong & Ee Yiang Hong, *Education in Malaysia* (Hong Kong, 1971); Chai Hon-chan, *Education and Nation-building in Plural Societies: The West Malaysian Experience* (Canberra, 1977).

45. Minister of Education, *L.C. Proc.*, 11 December 1958.

46. *First Malayan Plan*, para. 491.

47. Martin Rudner, "The Economic, Social and Political Dimensions of Malaysian Education Policy," in Kenneth Orr, ed., *The Appetite for Education in Contemporary Asia* (Canberra, 1977); *Second Malaysian Plan*, para. 97.

48. *First Malaysian Plan*, paras. 37, 42-3, 180.

49. *Third Malaysia Plan*, para. 198 (9).

50. *First Malaysia Plan*, para. 117.

51. *Third Malaysia Plan*, paras 146-7.

52. Ibid., paras. 164-5.

53. On the electoral policy cycle and its impact on economic management, see C. Duncan MacRae, "A Political Model of the Business Cycle," *Journal of Political Economy* (1977).

54. R.S. Milne & K.J. Ratnam, "Politics and Finance in Malaya," *Journal of Commonwealth Political Studies* (1965).

55. On the application of the consociational concept of pluralist democracy to Malaysia, see Arend Lijphart, *Democracy in Plural Societies* (New Haven, 1978), and R.S. Milne & Diane K. Mauzy, *Politics and Government in Malaysia* (Singapore, 1977).

56. The concept of a conservative social welfare function as a determinant of the norms of policy is set out by W.M. Corden in *Trade Policy and Economic Welfare* (Oxford, 1974), esp. p. 107.

57. Vide. Tham Seong Chee, *Malays and Modernization* (Singapore, 1977).

CHAPTER 9

CHANGING PLANNING PERSPECTIVES OF AGRICULTURAL DEVELOPMENT IN MALAYSIA

Malaysia's planning organization has become the institutional centrepiece of that country's development effort. Indeed, Malaysia ranks as one of the non-Communist developing countries where planning is most highly institutionalized. Malaysian planning evolved as an effective policy mechanism for directing the authoritative allocation of public resources towards declared developmental objectives.[1] Despite this attachment to national planning, Malaysia remains a staunchly market-oriented, open, and predominantly private enterprise economy. Nevertheless, as the role of planning expanded, private sector activity became increasingly subject to policy interventions predicated upon the politically determined goals of development planning.

Rubber and, to a somewhat lesser extent, tin have constituted the main sources of Malaysian economic growth over recent decades.[2] Although the contribution of rubber planting to Malaysian Gross Domestic Product (GDP) has in fact declined from around a quarter during the 1950s to about 10% in the mid-1970s, rubber exports still yield between a fifth (in 1975, a year of poor prices) and a quarter (in 1976, a better year) of value to GDP, which implies an even more significant total export earnings.[3]

Rubber did not constitute in Malaysia a narrow enclave-type export sector. Malaysian rubber planting succeeded in generating a network of supply and demand linkages with other sectors of the economy. A substantial portion of rubber export earnings have consequently been retained through domestic accelerator and multiplier effects.[4] Furthermore, rubber export duties and associated company taxes continue to finance a significant proportion of government expenditure, including the increasingly comprehensive scale of development planning.

Modern Asian Studies, Vol. 17, Pt. 3 (July, 1983).

Annual average real rates of growth of Malaysian Gross Domestic Product accelerated from the 3 to 4% level of the 1950s to over 5.5% during the 1960s, and reached 7.5% over the first half of the 1970s; meanwhile, a reducing rate of population increase during this period resulted in a credible improvement to average real income per capita.[5]

While rubber has made a major contribution to Malaysia's growth performance, its policy behaviour reveals a three-tier pattern of dependency: Malaysian development has been and still is heavily dependent on rubber export earnings; rubber export earnings are in turn dependent on continuing policy support for technological and entrepreneurial innovation for improved productivity; yet, the conduct of policy has come to reflect a style of governance dependent politically on conservative, entrenched interests in the rubber economy itself.

Economic historians of Malaysia have recounted the deleterious impact of past administrative bias in the allocation of resources between rubber estates and smallholdings on productive efficiency and ensuing economic developments.[6] In a somewhat different vein, and referring to agriculture generally, recent writings on the social history of Malaysia and elsewhere have underscored the effects of constraints deriving from landlord-peasant conflict upon agrarian modernization.[7] Be that as it may, the earlier structural distortions in the Malaysian rubber economy virtually disappeared once the termination of colonial rule deprived the largest, mainly British-owned, estates of their former patrons. It is noteworthy that Malaysian rubber planting is virtually free of the familiar landlord-peasant tensions afflicting the political economy of agriculture.

Rice cultivation ranks after rubber as the second most important sector of Malaysia's economy by share of both employment and land utilization. However, the level of income generated by rice agriculture has fallen consistently and significantly below that of most other occupations.[8] Peninsular Malaysia seems not to possess any comparative advantage in the production of rice. Yet, notwithstanding its manifest impoverishment, the cultivation of rice has long been identified as the occupational symbol of a stable, traditional rural Malay community. Under the colonial economic regime, rice agriculture was segregated from, and insulated against, the emerging market economy. A deliberately subsistence rice economy evolved as a Malay occupational cocoon, protected by administrative regulation and traditional sanctions and intended to preserve the established agrarian order along with its cultural values.[9]

Well before the advent of planning to Malaya (as it was before 1963), government policy appeared much more interventionist concerning the rural economy compared to the virtually laissez-faire urban and commercial situation. Historically, the British colonial administration exercised a dual set of regulatory controls over the rural Malayan economy. One component controlled access to and utilization of its factors of production, notably land and other factor inputs as well, while related controls regulated the marketing of primary products (by means of export permissions, levies, quotas or tariffs). These controls had an especially pronounced impact on agriculture, though tin mining and forestry were likewise affected. The thrust of such interventions tended to differentiate in policy treatment between different commodity groups and classes of producers, in accordance with colonial biases concerning agricultural structures and roles.[10]

Colonial agricultural policy thus provided for the differential treatment of rice cultivation as an insular, specifically Malay, subsistence peasant economy set apart from the cash crop sectors like rubber, while within the rubber sector itself differential policies applied as between estate and smallholding producers.[11] Differential—and in that sense, discriminatory—access to policy resources engendered the communal insularity and its identification with occupation and economic deprivation that were later to trouble Malaysian nation-building.

The Evolution of Development Planning

Malaysian development planning has evolved through three successive evolutionary phases of institutional role expansion.[12] In the initial, colonial phase, the role of planning was confined to the government sector, as such. The First Five-Year Plan (FYP) was introduced in 1956 as a colonial development legacy to the newly elected, soon-to-be independent government. This unpublished plan constituted merely an outline of public capital expenditure foreshadowing the extension of governmental departmental activities during the transition to independence. Colonial-style public sector planning had its precedent in Malaya in the so called Draft Development Plan (DDP) of 1950-53.[13]

The second phase of planning was represented by the Second FYP of 1961-65, and successor First Malaysia Plan (FMP) of 1966-70. The planning technique adopted for this second phase related planned public investment to targeted rates of growth of national output.[14] Planning now acquired an expanded fiscal policy role in the promotion of growth. By the third phase, however, the proclamation of a New Economic Policy (NEP) directed subsequent planning towards a more radically interventionist role. Development goals were no longer denominated simply in terms of aggregate growth. Rather, the promotion of economic growth under the Second Malaysia Plan (SMP), 1971-75, Third Malaysia Plan (TMP), 1976-80, and Fourth Malaysia Plan FoMP), 1981-85, had to be reconciled with NEP-inspired commitments to "restructuring" society in accordance with specified "socio-economic" development objectives.[15] The role of planning expanded to embrace the promotion of income redistribution as well as just growth, involving social as well as purely economic development.

This process of role expansion in planning was impelled by political events. It followed that the sequential phases of planning were also marked by shifts in the locus of authority over development policy, which in turn reflected the changing constellation of political power in independent Malaysia. During the initial phase of colonial-style planning, responsibility for the formulation and management of development policy, like all other matters pertaining to public finance, was vested in the Treasury. At the time, the influence of expatriate colonial officialdom was still paramount, especially among the planners of the Economic Secretariat attached to the Ministry of Finance.

Financial officialdom's hold over development policy weakened as planning entered the second phase of role expansion. In the event, the new growth promotion role incidentally implied organizational changes making for wider departmental participation in the planning process. Treasury control was diluted accordingly. Not only was bureaucratic authority over planning pluralized, but technical responsibility for planning was now assigned to a reconstituted Economic Planning Unit which, symbolically, had been removed from Treasury auspices and relocated in the Prime Minister's Department. Broad development goals promulgated at ministerial level would henceforward override the fundamentalist revenue-accounting outlook of Treasury in planning.

The elections of 1969 and their violent aftermath prompted a far-reaching reassessment of development strategy. A New Economic Policy was proclaimed, which imputed a more radically interventionist "restructuring" role to planning.[16] As Planning took on this expanded role, the high-echelon political leadership became increasingly directly engaged in the formulation of plan policy. Ministerial-level involvement in detailed planning decisions for the SMP and even more so for the TMP, though almost without precedent, was certainly clear-cut and authoritative. This trend towards ministerial participation in plan formulation is symptomatic of a deepening politicization of development policy issues since the promulgation of the NEP. The political imperatives attached to NEP-inspired development were such that responsibility for planning could no longer be left just to the planners. The involvement of Malaysia's political power elite with planning gave high-level expression to the impact of the NEP on the resources of government. NEP placed development planning emphatically at the command of the Malay political leadership.

Changes to the institutional format of planning, its authority structure and role in the economy, were indicative of more basic changes in the underlying strategic perspectives of development. The dynamics of change were exemplified by the transformation of official attitudes towards the agricultural economy and rural development generally, as expressed through planning. Political factors may have generated the momentum for change, but its thrust was revealed in changing attitudes and policies manifest in the sequence of plans. Continuity and change, tensions and bias in the perspectives of planning can be discerned along three analytically-distinct dimensions of policy making: in perceptions of the agricultural situation in relation to the national economy; in the definition of development goals; and in the selection of strategies determining the priorities and direction of policy. The analysis of perceptions, goals and policies that follows relates to planning for the rubber and rice sectors of Malaysian agriculture, primarily. These are illustrative of the interplay of policy perspectives and planning roles concerning the industrial-crop and foodcrop facets of an agricultural economy under development.

The Political Economy of Agricultural Development

Official perceptions of the underdevelopment situation reflected political circumstances. Colonial planning had its origins in the twin traumas of wartime and post-war decolonization. Responsibility for the domestic economic development of individual colonial territories was formally accepted for the first time by Great Britain itself in the initial Colonial Development and Welfare Act adopted during the year of crisis, 1940. The Act represented a landmark measure of post-war promise no less than wartime experience. In 1945, the post-war British Labour Government rendered assistance under the Act contingent upon the colonies' introducing "centrally administered schemes" for promoting development. In Malaya, however, the application of this new development approach was deferred until after the costly post-war reconstruction and rehabilitation of the economy was completed. By then, however, a menacing Communist insurgency, whose threat was made more potent by the recent revolution in China, compelled an unsettled colonial administration to react with the urgent introduction, still in draft form, of its prototype development plan. This DDP was afterward swept up in the Colombo Plan concept of a developmental antidote to Communism.

In the event, Malaya's accelerated progress towards self-government by the mid-1950s prompted a penultimate review of development programmes prior to decolonization. Already before the country's first general election, an International Bank for Reconstruction and Development (World Bank) mission had been invited to inquire into Malayan (and also Singaporean) economic conditions and prospects. Its report[17] set out the pattern of development that was subsequently formulated into the planning strategy of the newly elected Alliance government. Meanwhile, basic guidelines for the future management of the economy were laid down in the financial talks accompanying the London Constitutional Conference of 1956 that settled the terms of Malayan independence. At these talks, it was accepted that the emphasis would have to be placed on the overall primacy of "financial stability" in independent Malayan economic management. This perspective left its imprint on government as well as on Treasury. Economic and social development were subordinated explicitly to budgetary conservatism and to the continuing struggle against Communism.

To be sure, the elected Alliance government did put its political weight behind development programmes deemed vital to its nation-building effort. The most notable instance concerned education, which acquired a particular urgency related to the government's newly designed national education policy.[18] As a rule, though, government departments had to submit their respective capital expenditure proposals for the coming quinquennium, and it was Treasury that decided the allocation of finance for the First FYP. Economic and development policy prescriptions remained very much the province of a financial bureaucracy dominated, still, by expatriate colonial officialdom and subject to its custodial attitudes.

The First FYP included both rubber and rice agriculture among its "highest" priorities for development. But this notional "first priority" did not mask the long-standing colonial differential perception of the agricultural economy. On the one hand, the development of the rubber sector was perceived—albeit narrowly—in essentially revenue terms. That economic perspective focused on the need to reduce costs of production. Government's major concern was that Malayan natural rubber, "the country's greatest single industry *and source of revenue*," be able to meet any prospective challenge of cost competition from the synthetic product. The economics of rubber production, defined in terms of costs, were treated accordingly as the "overriding" development issue confronting the economic future of Malaya.[19] The development of rice agriculture, on the other hand, was still perceived more in the light of general policy pronouncements favouring foodcrop self-sufficiency and peasant welfare, rather than as a function of economic policy proper.

The First FYP treatment of the rice sector was cautious and unambitious. Indeed, the problems of rice agriculture were conventionally regarded to be particularly intractable because of cultural and institutional conditions compounding the economics of underdevelopment.[20] Yet the First FYP did go some way to modify the rice policy obsessions of the colonial past. Whereas rice cultivation retained its unique cultural attraction among Malays, it was no longer perceived as an insularized subsistence economy identified with the stability of the Malay agrarian order.[21] Likewise, the latter-day colonial rhetoric of rice "self-sufficiency" was now translated into more restrained, longer-run aspirations for greater import substitution to the extent justified by relative cost considerations. Indeed, the implied criterion for prospective structural adjustment in the Malayan economy under the First FYP was comparative advantage, a criterion that overshadowed even long-standing anxieties about Malaya's continued dependency on international trade in a few specialized commodities.

With regard to agriculture, the First FYP envisaged no substantial structural changes within the rice and rubber sectors of the economy. As it was, policy-makers were caught quite unawares by the major incident of structural change during this plan period, i.e., the rapid subdivision of marginal rubber estates during the late 1950s.[22] The development strategy applied to this first phase of planning assumed virtual continuity of the existing agrarian order and its institutions. Structural impediments such as poverty, inequality, or exploitation were perceived rather in the classical liberal light as "traditional" conditions which would be overcome through the eventual spread effects of economic modernization. The role imputed to development planning in the context of an agrarian status quo emphasized maximization of levels of current output from the inherited structure. Current output attainments, rather than levels of agricultural income as such, or its distribution, formed the indicator of policy performance in this early phase of planning.

Implementation of the First FYP, in the event, was greatly circumscribed by the prevailing norms of fiscal conduct. For, even after the transition to independence, the colonial budgetary heritage continued to stress revenue accounting as the bottom line of economic management during this earliest phase of development planning.[23]

The general election of 1959 led to a significant expansion of the development role of planning in the subsequent Second FYP. Compared to the 1955 elections, the 1959 election results indicated a threatening erosion of electoral support for the ruling Alliance party on both communal flanks.[24] By way of responding to the communal challenge, the returned Alliance government moved to buttress its appeal to ethnic accommodation by invoking a strategy for national integration, a strategy built around material values. Later, the outbreak of the Confrontation with Indonesia lent further impetus to this strategy. In keeping with the turn of events, development planning acquired a broader politico-economic role. National income accounting displaced the former strict revenue accounting among the criteria of economic management. Economic growth therefore became a political imperative of this second phase of planning.[25]

The development strategy adopted in the Second FYP and its successor FMP had its conceptual origins in the ruling Alliance Party's ideological predilection for an equilibrium approach to growth. It was conventionally assumed that established institutional arrangements represented an equilibrium condition for the economy, in which poverty denoted a kind of low-level equilibrium trap. The postulated remedy lay in bringing about an accelerated rate of investment within the existing institutional framework, generating a linear and cumulative process of economic growth leading to a higher-level equilibrium condition.

Behind the official prognosis for equilibrium growth loomed, however, the more threatening spectre of Malaya's economic vulnerability. The Second FYP alluded in passing to fundamental structural weaknesses of the Malayan economy. These were reiterated and given greater stress in the FMP: rapid population growth pressing upon the available resource base, particularly in the agricultural economy; "the depressed situation and land hunger of large numbers of people in the rural areas"; "over-specialization and excessive dependence" of the economy on a rubber sector exposed to the vicissitudes of the world market and deepening competition with synthetic; and inadequate development of the country's human resources.[26]

As well, the FMP hinted also at "institutional shortcomings" affecting the agricultural economy, in particular. However, the development doctrine applied to this phase of planning emphasized employment creation and output expansion.[27] This reflected the accepted strategy seeking a stable, equilibrium path to the growth of national income.

The employment-growth promoting role assigned to the Second FYP and FMP tended to revise, though not eliminate entirely, the differential status of rubber and rice in agricultural development planning. While differing public investment criteria were still applied in planning for the two sectors, their perceived growth prospects had now converged on pessimism. This despondency reflected a real sense of foreboding.

Natural rubber faced intensified competition with increasingly substitutable synthetics, at declining world market price trends through the 1960s. If rubber planting was still deemed "viable and productive," the FMP concluded that it no longer offered "especially bright prospects for future growth of national income and employment."[28] Rubber replanting would continue especially on smallholdings, and new planting with high-yielding rubber would go ahead on land settlement schemes where soil conditions were unsuitable for alternative cash crops. But it was clear that in the official view rubber planting was losing—if it hadn't already lost—its former economic advantage.

Planning for the rubber sector adhered, therefore, to a basically defensive, income loss minimizing tactic. The formulation of rubber policy under the Second FYP and FMP was designed to "minimize" the adverse effects on national income of continued deterioration in rubber's terms of trade through offsetting improvements to overall productivity.[29] Replanting and new planting targets set out in these plans were conceived in a way that tended to subordinate the developmental requirements of the rubber sector as such to income-maintenance at the aggregate, national level. Meanwhile, public investment priorities for development planning were to be redirected towards alternative, supposedly more advantageous economic activities where the prospective employment creation and income effects were perceived to be greater.

Parenthetically, however, it should be noted that despite deteriorating terms of trade, Malaysia's rubber economy still had to bear a disproportionate share of the burden of public finance, including other-directed development expenditures.[30] Rubber export duties were restructured in 1979, but still constituted a regressive levy on peasant producers' incomes and capital formation.

Plan policy concerning the rice sector during this second phase likewise resembled a holding operation, so to speak. Certainly those in authority, politicians and planners, were by now cognizant of the impoverishment of rice agriculture and the prevalence of land hunger.[31] As a result, the Second FYP proclaimed a "much more ambitious" output growth target for rice production compared to rubber.[32] When translated into policy provisions, however, the line taken still conformed to the parameters of past strategy. Magnitudes may have increased with each successive plan, but still the direction of planned expenditure on rice agriculture kept by and large to the conventional infrastructure triad of irrigation, roads and rural social services.[33]

By increasing investment in rural infrastructure, government apparently hoped to facilitate expansion of domestic rice production to keep pace with expected growth in consumption. At least this would hold the rice import ratio constant, while providing some measure of agricultural income maintenance.[34] Yet any such improvement to rice productivity was implicitly predicated upon preservation of the established agrarian order. There was little sentiment for agrarian reform in planning, nor among the landed classes that constituted the power elite in the politically-dominant United Malays National Organization (UMNO). The dominant conception of agricultural "development" was predicated on the traditional agrarian economy rendered, somehow, more prosperous. Rice agriculture was perceived as if in a low-level albeit equilibrium situation, which required only improvements to rural infrastructure to stimulate output growth without inducing institutional changes that may encroach upon vested interests.[35]

Admittedly there was an awareness by this time that existing land tenure conditions and other institutional and attitudinal impediments had deleterious effects on peasant cultivators' incomes and productivity.[36] However, the prescribed corrective measures fell far short of reform. By way of responding to perceived structural constraints, the FMP provided for the extension of further lines of concessional agricultural credit through a newly constituted Bank Bumiputra, (Indigenous Peoples' Bank) as well as through rural co-operative societies, and for the creation of a Federal Agricultural Marketing Authority (FAMA). Though signalling a more interventionist approach to the agricultural economy, the establishment of these government instrumentalities was directed more particularly at remedying specific structural deficiencies affecting agricultural credit and marketing, without aiming at broader structural changes.

Agricultural planning perspectives in this second phase reflected a conceptual prism shaped by official fears of subversion, alongside vested interests and ideological predilections favouring essentially custodial social doctrines. The development prognosis accepted by the Alliance government projected an image of a property-owning agrarian democracy rooted in a stable and satisfied peasantry. Little was it realized that the policies put forward as part of this development strategy could tend, ironically and inadvertently, to widen inequalities between the returns to rice and to rubber, between poorer and better-off strata of peasantry, between those with and those without access to new agricultural technologies, and between agricultural and non-agricultural income levels.[37] Movement towards a more redistributive policy intervention had to await the third phase of planning.

Development strategy came in for a fundamental reassessment in the wake of the 1969 elections and subsequent race riots.[38] Political events seemed to reinforce the view that government management of the economy should minister to nation-building. Only, henceforward, the doctrine of nation-building would be radically altered in favour of resurgent Malay claims for ethnic proportionality in the allocation of modern economic resources, along with continued Malay pre-eminence in control of political power. While non-Malays were accepted as belonging to Malaysia, according to this revised nation-building doctrine, Malaysia was to belong most assuredly to the Malays.

The more radical ethnic political imperative for a social-reconstructionist style of development found expression in the NEP. Forming an outline of future economic strategy, the NEP prescribed a "two-prong" approach to "restructuring" society through development planning (which was, in turn, integrated into a looser, 20-year Perspective Plan, so called).[39] One prong consisted of policy interventions intended to bring about eventual proportional involvement of

Malays (and other indigenous peoples) in the modern sectors of the economy. The second prong promoted the eradication of poverty by means of policy interventions designed to augment lower-level incomes generally and generate additional employment opportunities, irrespective of race. Planning thus embarked on a third, more interventionist phase of role expansion involving a two-dimensional redistribution of income and of economic functions.

The policy interventions and economic redistribution stipulated for the third phase of planning revolved around a core concept of "balance" and "imbalance."[40] Malaysia's development predicament was now perceived as a problem of "balance," or in its absence, the presumed "imbalances" between the "modern" and "traditional" segments of the economy. These imbalances were attributable to structural discontinuities in modernization, and were held accountable for inter-sectoral inequalities in income, communal insularity in employment, and ethnic disparities in the ownership and control over assets of production. Imbalances were perceived both within and among the rural, urban and government sectors. In the rural sector itself there was perceived imbalance between the traditional forms of subsistence (single crop) rice cultivation and obsolescent rubber smallholding, where Malays were concentrated and predominant, and the modern forms of commercial (double cropping) padi farming and high-yielding rubber planting.

Unlike the former preoccupation with equilibrium growth and the presumed low-level equilibrium trap, the current phase concern for balance lends a somewhat optimistic prognosis to development strategy. For inter-sectoral imbalances can presumably be rectified by the application of appropriate policies fostering the spread of economic modernization.[41] The interventionist and redistributive policies introduced in the third phase of planning envisaged an expanded, modernizing role for the SMP and TMP, which was continued in the FoMP.

This modernizing role was to function internally and externally to the traditional agricultural sectors. Planning effort was now directed towards the modernization of traditional technologies in the retarded agricultural (and also non-agricultural) sectors themselves. However, planning also aimed at promoting factor mobility, notably labour and land use, from traditional to modern segments of the economy. Economic modernization, in the current planning perspective, is specifically concerned with rectifying inter-sectoral imbalances, and not so much with intra-sectoral, socio-economic inequalities. Indeed, the TMP conceded that the modernizing strategy might even tend to accentuate existing income inequalities at least in the short run, until its benefits might become more widely spread.[42] Anyhow, a more abrupt redistributive policy would have been unacceptable ideologically and politically. Instead, the modernization strategy for the third phase of planning has been predicated on ethnic re-deployment and income redistribution in the wake of growth.

Although urban and manufacturing development attracted much attention in this third phase of planning, the modernizing strategy had particular applicability with regard to the traditional sectors of the rural economy. Contemporary planning for rural development focuses on the modernization of agricultural production so as to close the gap between agrarian and urban productivity, while aiming for closer linkages between the agricultural sectors and the expanding commercial and industrial economy. Yet, because of varying states of "imbalance" ascribed to the two main rural sectors, planning has imparted differing policy approaches to the modernization of rubber and rice agriculture. Modernization of the rubber economy was already fairly well advanced as a result of past replanting and new planting with high-yielding varieties. Rice agriculture, however, still remained with minor exceptions a laggard, subsistence occupation. If the further modernization of rubber production entailed, in essence, a downward spread of available technologies, rice agriculture for its part required a more fundamental and thorough going modernizing transformation.

In the event, these divergent needs for modernization yielded rather paradoxical patterns of policy behaviour as between the two sectors. Around the mid-1970s, rubber policy began to indicate a curious ambivalence. By comparison, the transformation of traditional subsistence agriculture remained a consistent goal of development policy.

Any lingering doubts about the long-run viability of natural rubber planting had dissipated by the late 1960s. As a result of productivity gains owing to replanting and new planting with high-yielding materials, the SMP concluded with new-found optimism that natural rubber "could continue to strengthen its competitive position" against synthetic rubber.[43] Planning for the third phase of role expansion apropos the rubber sector followed the lines of policy laid down earlier. Emphasis in the SMP continued to be placed on replanting, in particular on the predominantly Malay-owned smaller plots with low-grade stands, and on accelerated new planting on land development schemes. Government involvement in land development now extended beyond the original FELDA settlement schemes, to include additional types of fringe rehabilitation schemes (FELCRA) and co-operative block planting schemes (RISDA).[44]

A key marketing innovation of the late 1960s was the introduction of block rubber factories for processing smallholders' latex into technically specified Standard Malaysian Rubber (SMR).[45] Provision was made in the SMP for setting up government-sponsored local processing centres in designated districts in the hope that these might serve to stimulate higher output from smallholdings while increasing their net returns.[46] These expanded policy interventions, upon which the modernizing strategy was predicated, steered the SMP towards a greater redistributive role in the rubber economy.

The TMP continued to follow this modernizing strategy, but retreated somewhat from the underlying commitment to rubber sector development. Although the long-term economic viability of natural rubber was no longer in question, official perspectives of the rubber economy were beginning to shift. The catalyst was provided by the trauma of global recession in 1974. Rubber prices had collapsed, inflicting a severe 1970-style deflation-cum-cost inflation on the Malaysian rubber economy.[47]

Typically it was the smaller, predominantly Malay, traditional segment that was hardest hit by this crisis.[48] Reacting to resulting unrest, government introduced a National Crash Programme to regulate producers' activity and output, as a means of stabilizing the downward movement in prices and maintaining rubber incomes. Such direct administrative intervention in the rubber economy was without precedent for Malaysia since the regulatory schemes of inter-war years. Its reappearance, albeit in extremis, paved the way for official espousal of the interventionist doctrine sponsored by the United Nations Conference on Trade and Development (UNCTAD) for the creation of a so called "New International Economic Order" (NIEO).

With remarkable swiftness, remarkable because of their attachment hitherto to open market economic principles, the Malaysian political leadership and officialdom have become enthusiastic converts to the NIEO precept of governmental intervention to control international trade in commodities like, inter alia, natural rubber.[49] Malaysian academic economists likewise expressed virtually uncritical acceptance of the NIEO doctrine.[50] This conversion of Malaysia's economic-managerial élite to the perspectives of the NIEO seems all the more remarkable in a country which has had substantial historical experience with, and suffered demonstrably from, such international commodity restriction schemes in the colonial past.[51] It is indeed surprising that this protectionist outlook could have such strong appeal in a country which currently enjoys manifest economic and technological advantages in the production of natural rubber. Yet, Malaysia has emerged nevertheless as the leading force behind the recently formed Association of Natural Rubber Producing Countries (ANRPC), and the foremost proponent of stabilizing international trade in natural rubber.[52]

The shift in official policy perspectives represented more than just attitudinal changes, for it was grounded in social changes arising out of developments in the rubber economy. The prospect of governmental intervention to control trade in rubber certainly conformed to the vested interests of the already modernized segment of rubber planters. The modernizing strategy gave rise to a substantial new strata of dominant peasant planters, distinguished by their relatively larger and high-yielding stands, and enjoying close ties with political authority.[53] Any policy regulation of production under a trade stabilization agreement would invariably serve to protect the privileged economic position acquired by dominant peasants and estates, against unrestrained competition from smaller peasant producers.

The ascendance of NIEO doctrine tended to eclipse the original planning commitment to modernizing the traditional rubber sector. In a striking policy reversal, the TMP made substantial cutbacks compared to the previous plan's commitments to all three main policy instrumentalities for the spread of modernization— rubber replanting, new land settlement, and the establishment of additional SMR processing centres. The pace of rubber modernization was to decelerate under the TMP in the interests of upholding the current terms of trade.

In November 1976, the member countries of ANRPC—Malaysia, Indonesia, Singapore, Sri Lanka and Thailand—concluded an International Natural Rubber Agreement on Price Stabilization. This Agreement, covering the 85% ANRPC share of world natural rubber output, included a supply rationalization mechanism. In the event of downward pressure on prices, ANRPC is bound to adjust domestic output in each country to the level warranted by its export entitlements. As the leading producer and proponent of the scheme,

Malaysia had to accept a relatively lower entitlement by way of underwriting the Agreement.

The prospect of intervention in the international rubber trade thus took on a perversely retrogressive redistributive turn. Any resort to export entitlement quotas to restrict output would invariably inhibit further modernization and new entry into production, while the accrual of economic rents would tend to diminish the efficiency of those beneficiaries of the restrictive policy, i.e., the dominant peasants and estates.

In the meantime, other producer countries remaining outside the Agreement (notably India, Liberia, Nigeria, the Philippines and Papua New Guinea) now producing around 15% of world output, would be likely to expand production to capitalize on the situation. Malaysia's comparative advantage in rubber production would thus be in jeopardy. To be sure, implementation of supply restrictions under the Agreement may confer certain immediate gains upon the short-run balance of payments, on export tax revenues and on economic rents of established planters (though distributed in a way that would bolster the dominance of already privileged classes of producers). But like its predecessors of the 1920s and 1930s, the workings of a restriction scheme would threaten the Malaysian rubber economy with structural stagnation and eventual decay.

In 1979, the earlier ANRPC-based Price Stabilization Agreement was extended under the aegis of the UNCTAD Integrated Programme for Commodities into an International Natural Rubber Agreement (INRA). This was the first of the UNCTAD-fostered international agreements for stabilizing world market prices of major primary commodities through the operations of a buffer stock mechanism financed out of a common fund and reinforced by the prospect of supply management. Although when INRA was concluded, the market price of rubber actually exceeded the agreed ceiling, by 1982 the world recession drove prices below the floor level. With buffer stocks failing to sustain prices, some producer interests began to call for supply restriction to bolster INRA.

As under the previous Price Stabilization Agreement, Malaysia has tended to assume itself the reserve, or swinging producer among ANRPC, analogous to the Saudi Arabian role in the Organization of Petroleum Exporting Countries (OPEC). Yet, very real differences militate against the seeming analogy. For, unlike Saudi Arabia, Malaysia is but a comparatively poor developing country. Moreover, unlike petroleum, natural rubber is not a geophysical resource endowment, but simply a plantation industry that can be readily replicated elsewhere. The prospect of a return to international regulation of the rubber export trade was accepted explicitly in the TMP. However, any policy of export restriction would run counter to the modernizing thrust of current development strategy. Clearly, the developmental imperative has given way to a more custodial perspective on rubber policy.

While the FoMP returned to the encouragement of accelerated investment in rubber planting, "in view of its attractive prospect in the future," policy remained committed to the protectionist quest after regulated output levels and prices.[54]

Though rubber policy wavered, the modernization goal still had policy precedence from the perspective of rice agriculture. The role of planning in rice agriculture provided for continuation of the major policy programmes of the past, but with even greater poignancy. Long-standing policy concern to improve rural economic infrastructure and social services accordingly underwent a significant variation in emphasis. Lifting rural living standards was of course important per se, however, consideration was now given to better integrating the agrarian and urban economies so as to override traditional insularity and draw under-employed Malay resources into the modern sector. Plans for the extension of irrigation facilities likewise became more focused. Rather than extend into scattered new padi areas, the current irrigation programme concentrates on designated schemes where double-cropping might be facilitated.[55] It had been originally expected that rice output would increase on account of SMP agricultural programmes to reach 90% of Malaysia's consumption requirements. As a result of the world food crisis of 1972-73, this objective was raised to full rice self-sufficiency.[56] By 1980 Malaysia had reached 80% self-sufficiency in rice.[57]

The third phase of planning led to an interventionist role also in rice production and marketing, notably through pricing. An expanded distributive role was embarked upon by the SMP with the establishment of a National Padi and Rice Authority (LPN) and a Farmers Organization Authority (FOA). Intended as an administrative superintendent over the production, processing and marketing of padi and rice, the LPN was given a specific mandate to determine "a fair and stable" price for these commodities.[58] Subsequent administrative interventions sought to manipulate agricultural prices, and thereby incomes, as a means of promoting modernization. Thus, expanded lines of concessional agricultural credit were offered through a specially created agricultural bank, Bank Pertanian, and through rural co-operatives operating under the aegis of FOA. A subsidy of urea fertilizer represented another form of rice incentive favourable to modern, market-oriented agriculture. FAMA also introduced regulatory controls over market intermediaries, and in some areas itself engaged in processing and marketing activities in conjunction with FOA outlets, bypassing commercial channels.[59]

Apart from institutional intervention, government also embarked upon direct regulation of agricultural pricing. A guaranteed minimum padi price mechanism had long existed as a residual safeguard of agricultural incomes in the last resort. However, with effect from the SMP, the guaranteed minimum price turned into a deliberate and positive instrument for manipulating domestic agricultural terms of trade, in tandem with a more protectionist rice import policy.[60] This use of the guaranteed minimum price was supposed to reassure the spread of double-cropping. Admittedly, the new regulatory approach to rice prices would also have to be sensitive to other claims on prices policy, especially from urban consumer and export interests.[61] Still, in a radical break with past policy norms, governmental regulation of pricing has now been officially acknowledged to be the key to modernizing rice agriculture and achieving the planned level of self-sufficiency. As well, a positive treatment of the guaranteed minimum price could raise the overall level of economic welfare in traditional agriculture. The modernizing strategy embarked upon in the third phase of planning transformed agricultural development perspectives from mere output maximization to the realm of an incomes policy proper.

Planning Perceptions and Role Expansion: An Overview

Far-reaching changes in agricultural policy perspectives accompanied the role expansion of Malaysian development planning.[62] Such changes in perspective may be summarized along several dimensions of planning.

1. The Scope of Coverage: In the initial phase, planning covered certain limited public sector activities, with the salient extensions into rural development being rubber replanting and the inauguration of FELDA on the one hand, and irrigation and drainage schemes on the other. By the third phase, the scope of coverage had broadened substantially to cover most facets of production, processing, and marketing of both rubber and rice. Policy intervention in pricing remains prospective rather than actual as regards rubber, except for the short-lived Crash Programme, while for rice the TMP withdrew to somewhat "more flexible" considerations of consumer as well as producer interests. Be that as it may, agricultural market and pricing mechanisms now come clearly within the pruview of planning and potential policy control.

2. The Economic Functions of Government: The role expansion of planning involved not just an extension of the coverage of policy, but furthermore entailed a broadening of the economic functions performed by government. In the initial phase, government confined its functions to the provision of a stable, orderly and conducive economic environment which might attract private capital inflow to supplement domestic private capital formation and together generate growth. The second phase witnessed the emergence of a governmental savings-investment promoting function directed at fostering the growth of the rubber economy in particular. By the third phase, government became involved in a range of economic activities, including savings-investment, marketing, and management functions directed according to comprehensive, modernizing plans. These changing economic functions were exemplified by the expanded role of established government departments and by the creation of new specialized functional agencies (e.g., RISDA, Bank Pertanian) along with the revitalization of already established statutory authorities (e.g., FELDA, FAMA, FELCRA).

3. The Degree of Policy Control: In the initial period, with the coverage of policy being limited and confined to custodial functions, government control over private economic activity remained essentially reactive. As the coverage of policy extended and its economic functions grew broader, relationships between public authorities and private sector activities were effectively altered. Even in the rural sectors, private economic activities became increasingly subject to positive controls, symbolized by the economic-administrative responsibilities vested in specialized agencies such as FELDA, RISDA, LPN, FELCRA, FAMA. Land ownership and tenure, virtually alone among economic activities, remain exempt from policy constraints, at least in areas of existing agricultural settlement.

4. Differential Treatment of Export Promotion and Import Substitution: The initial phase of planning persisted with the earlier colonial policy distinction between the export-oriented rubber sector and the subsistence rice sector of the Malayan agricultural economy. The former was treated as an economic asset to be promoted, whereas the latter had been relegated to the status of an economic liability, in effect. From the third phase of planning, export earnings potential was no longer the sole nor even the predominant criterion of development policy. Under the influence of NEP, the politically warranted needs for Malay economic and social advancement on the one hand, and for the eradication of poverty on the other, imposed their own criteria on planning. Traditional subsistence agriculture now acquired the modern dynamics of an import substitution policy. Most remaining attitudinal dichotomies between the rice import substitution and rubber export promotion policies paled into insignificance before the political imperatives of economic modernization.

5. Strategic Concepts of Planning: The economic strategies guiding development planning underwent modification in conjunction with the role expansion. Economic conceptions of "maximization" and "minimization" evolved from a first phase emphasis on maximizing government revenues and minimizing expenditures; to the second phase concern for maximizing income growth albeit within much the same cost-minimization rules. Subsequently, the NEP invoked a radically new redistributive development strategy for the third phase of planning. The current rules of maximization stress not just income growth, but also the redistribution of incremental income along lines dictated by ethnic and social development criteria. Cost minimization rules have had to be adapted accordingly. Plan strategy is to minimize not only immediate economic costs, but furthermore the opportunity costs of ethnic insularity and social impoverishment. Thus, the operational definition of output maximization has become increasingly relativistic over successive phases of planning, highlighting physical output, then income, then a particular income distribution; while the definition of cost minimization was likewise transposed from simply costs to government, to economic costs, to social opportunity costs.

If cost-benefit criteria for planning were thereby made "softer," in the sense of less definitive, they incidentally became more relevant to felt public needs. This represented a change in economic management method, first from mere revenue accounting to economic accounting, and then to the current approach to ethno-economic accounting.

ENDNOTES

1. Martin Rudner, "Trends in Malaysian Development Planning: Goals, Policies and Role Expansion," *Review of Indonesian and Malayan Affairs* Vol. 14 (1980); Milton Esman, *Administration and Development in Malaysia* (Ithaca, 1972).

2. Lim Chong Yah, *The Economic Development of Modern Malaya* (Kuala Lumpurs, 1967); John T. Thoburn, *Primary Commodity Exports and Economic Development: Theory, Evidence and a Study of Malaysia* (London, 1977).

3. Federation of Malaysia, Ministry of Finance, *Economic Report, 1976/77* (Kuala Lumpur, 1976), pp. 29-41;—, *Economic Report, 1978/79* (Kuala Lumpur, 1978), pp. 51-68; V.V. Bhanoji Rao, *National Accounts of West Malaysia, 1947-1971* (Singapore, 1976), esp. pp. 80-81.

4. J.T. Thoburn, "Exports and Economic Growth in West Malaysia," *Oxford Economic Papers* Vol. 25 (1973), pp. 89-91.

5. David Lim, *Economic Growth and Development in West Malaysia* (Kuala Lumpur, 1973), p. 127.

6. P.T. Bauer, *The Rubber Industry. A Study in Competition and Monopoly* (London, 1948); J.H. Drabble, "Malayan Rubber Smallholdings in the Inter-War Period. Some Preliminary Findings," *Malayan Economic Review* (*MER*) Vol. 23 (1978), pp. 61-72 and "Peasant Smallholders in the Malayan Economy: An Historical Study with Special Reference to the Rubber Industry," in James C. Jackson & Martin Rudner, eds., *Issues in Malaysian Development* (Singapore, 1979), pp. 71 *et passim*; Martin Rudner, "The State and Peasant Innovation in Rural Development. The Case of Malaysian Rubber," *Asian and African Studies* Vol. 6 (1970).

7. Lim Teck Ghee, *Peasants and their Agricultural Economy in Colonial Malaya 1874-1941* (Kuala Lumpur, 1977); Martin Rudner, "Agricultural Policy and Peasant Social Transformation in Late Colonial Malaya," in Jackson & Rudner, eds., *Issues in Malaysian Development*, pp. 7-61.

8. Federation of Malaysia, Ministry of Finance, *Economic Report 1975/76* (Kuala Lumpur, 1975), pp. 104-5; David Lim, *Economic Growth*, pp. 234-45; Akimi Fujimoto, "Land Tenure and Rice Production: Implications for Land Reform in Malaysia," *Kabar Seberang* No. 7 (1980), pp. 42-4; John Purcal, *Rice Economy: Employment and Income in Malaysia* (Honolulu, 1971).

9. Ding Eing Tan Soo Hai, *The Rice Industry in Malaya, 1920-1970* (Singapore, 1963); Lim T.G., *Peasants*; Rudner, "Agricultural Policy and Peasant Social Transformation."

10. See Charles Hirschman, "Sociology," in John A. Lent, ed., *Malaysian Studies: Present Knowledge and Research Trends* (DeKalb, IL, 1979), pp. 8-29.

11. Martin Rudner, "Malayan Rubber Policy: Development and Anti-Development during the 1950s," *Journal of Southeast Asian Studies* (*JSEAS*) Vol. 8 (1976).

12. Rudner, "Trends in Malaysian Development Planning"; David Lim, "Malaysia," in Yip Yat Hoong, ed., *Development Planning in Southeast Asia: Role of the University* (Singapore, 1973).

13. On economic planning in Malaya during the colonial period, see Martin Rudner, "The Draft Development Plan of the Federation of Malaya," *JSEAS* Vol (1973), and *Nationalism, Planning and Economic Modernization in Malaysia. The Politics of Beginning Development* (Beverly Hills, 1975), esp. Ch. 4; Lee Soo Ann, *Economic Growth and the Public Sector in Malaya and Singapore 1948-1960* (Kuala Lumpur, 1974); C.T. Edwards, *Public Finance in Malaya and Singapore* (Canberra,

1970), Ch. 2. For a survey of public financial institutions and their roles during this period see P.J. Drake, *Financial Development in Malaya and Singapore* (Canberra, 1969).

14. D. Lim, "Malaysia," pp. 120 *et passim*.

15. Federation of Malaysia, *Second Malaysia Plan 1971-75* (Kuala Lumpur, 1971); R.S. Milne, "The Politics of Malaysia's New Economic Policy," *Pacific Affairs* Vol. 49 (1976), pp. 235-62.

16. *Second Malaysia Plan 1971-75*, chap. 1; Federation of Malaysia, *Mid-Term Review of the Second Malaysian Plan* (Kuala Lumpur, 1973), chap. 4; Milne, "The Politics"; Rudner, "Trends in Malaysian Development Planning"; Colin MacAndrews, "The Politics of Planning: Malaysia and the Third Malaysia Plan," *Asian Survey* Vol. 17 (1977); Ungku A. Aziz, "Footprints in the Sands of Time—The Malay Poverty Concept Over 50 Years From Za'aba to Aziz and the Second Malaysia Five Year Plan" and C.L. Robless, "The Feasibility and Internal Consistency of the New Economic Policy," both in Stephen Chee & Choo Siew Mun, eds, *Malaysian Economic Development and Policies* (Kuala Lumpur, 1975).

17. International Bank for Reconstruction and Development, *The Economic Development of Malaya* (Baltimore, 1955).

18. On education policy and development in Malaysia, see Martin Rudner "Education, Development and Change in Malaysia," *South East Asian Studies* Vol. 15 (1977); Charles Hirschman, "Political Independence and Educational Opportunity in Peninsular Malaysia," *Sociology of Education* Vol. 52 (1979); Tham Seong Chee, "Issues in Malaysian Education: Past, Present and Future," *JSEAS* Vol. 10 (1979); Chai Hon-Chan, *Education and Nation-building in Plural Societies: The West Malaysian Experience* (Canberra, 1977); O.D. Hoerr, "Education, Income and Equity in Malaysia," in David Lim, ed., *Readings on Malaysian Economic Development* (Kuala Lumpur, 1975).

19. Federation of Malaya, *Report on Economic Planning in the Federation of Malaya in 1956* (Kuala Lumpur, 1957), p. 4.

20. On this point see Hirschman, "Sociology," esp. pp. 18-25; B.K. Parkinson, "Non-Economic Factors in the Economic Retardation of the Rural Malays," *Modern Asian Studies* Vol. 1 (1967); William Wilder, "Islam, Other Factors and Malay Backwardness: Comments on an Argument," *Modern Asian Studies* Vol. 2 (1968).

21. Martin Rudner, "Malayan Quandary: Rural Development Policy Under the First and Second Five-Year Plans," *Contributions to Asian Studies* Vol. 1 (1971).

22. Ungku Aziz, *The Subdivision of Estates in Malaya* (Kuala Lumpur, 1962); Rudner, "Malayan Rubber Policy," esp. pp. 256-9.

23. Gayl D. Ness, "Economic Development and the Goals of Government," in Wang Gungwu, ed., *Malaysia* (London, 1964); Edwards, *Public Finances*, pp. 58-60; Rudner, *Nationalism, Planning and Economic Modernization in Malaysia*, chap. 3.

24. R.S. Milne & K.J. Ratnam, *The Malaysian Parliamentary Election of 1964* (Singapore, 1967).

25. Federation of Malaysia, *First Malaysia Plan 1966-70* (Kuala Lumpur, 1966), para. 35; Gayl D. Ness, *Bureaucracy and Rural Development in Malaysia* (Berkeley, 1967).

26. *First Malaysia Plan*, paras. 2, 45, 46, 47.

27. Ibid., paras. 280 (iii) and 281 (v).

28. Ibid., para. 19; Malaysian academic economists shared this pessimism about the future of natural rubber: David Lim, *Economic Growth*, pp. 13 *et passim*.

29. Federation of Malaya, *Second Five Year Plan 1961-65* (Kuala Lumpur, 1961), para. 55; *First Malaysia Plan*, para. 22.

30. Edwards, *Public Finances*, pp. 214-47; Simon Bell, "The Tax/Subsidy Policy of the Malaysian Government towards Rubber Producers in Peninsular Malaysia," *Kabar Seberang* No. 7 (1980).

31. *Second Five Year Plan*, para. 45; T.B. Wilson, *The Economics of Padi Production in North Malaya, Pt 1* (Kuala Lumpur, 1958).

32. *Second Five Year Plan*, para. 55.

33. Ibid., para. 56; *First Malaysia Plan*, chap. 7; Rudner, "Malayan Quandary."

34. *Second Five Year Plan*, para. 55.

35. Rudner, "Malayan Quandary."

36. *First Malaysia Plan*, para. 280.

37. *Second Malaysia Plan*, chaps. 2 and 3.

38. Ibid., para. 1. See also Milne, "The Politics."

39. *Second Malaysia Plan*, para. 2; Federation of Malaysia, *Third Malaysia Plan, 1976-1980* (Kuala Lumpur, 1976), chap. 4.

40. *Second Malaysia Plan*, chap. 2.

41. Ibid., paras. 21-8; *Third Malaysia Plan*, paras. 187, 203; Federation of Malaysia, *Fourth Malaysia Plan 1981-1985* (Kuala Lumpur, 1981), paras. 487-96.

42. *Third Malaysia Plan*, para. 33.

43. *Second Malaysia Plan*, para. 379.

44. Lim Sow Ching, *Land Development Schemes in Peninsular Malaysia* (Kuala Lumpur, 1976).

45. Colin Barlow, *The Natural Rubber Industry. Its Development, Technology and Economy in Malaysia* (Kuala Lumpur, 1978), esp. pp. 172-4.

46. George Cho, "The Location of Development Centres for Rubber Smallholders in Peninsular Malaysia," in Jackson & Rudner, eds., *Issues in Malaysian Development*, esp. pp. 101-5.

47. See Lim See Yan, "The Inflation Syndrome and its Implications for Policy"; H.G. Manuyr, "Inflation in Malaysia—Diagnosis and Prescription"; Ramesh Choucher, "Price Stability and Inflation in Malaysia"; all in S. Chee & Choo Siew Mun, eds., *Malaysian Economic Development and Policies*.

48. Lim Sow Ching, "Towards an Equitable International Trade in Natural Rubber," *Malayan Rubber Review* Vol. 1 (1976).

49. Ibid. Dr. Lim was then Head of the Rubber Economics and Planning Unit of the Malaysian Rubber Research and Development Board. See also, Federation of Malaysia, *Economic Report 1978/79* (Kuala Lumpur, 1978), esp. pp. 35-6; and Lew Sip Hon, "A Case for an International Price Stabilization Scheme for Natural Rubber," *UMBC Economic Review* Vol. 12 (1976)—Mr. Lew was Parliamentary Secretary to the Minister of Primary Industries; and Tan Siew Sin, former Minister of Finance and currently Financial Consultant to the Government, cited in *New Straits Times*, 11 April 1979.

50. See, *e.g.*, Paul Chan Tuck Hoong & Lee Kiong Hock, "The New International Economic Order—Some Implications for Malaysia," *UMBC Economic Review* Vol. 12 (1976).

51. The impact of inter-war international rubber export restriction schemes on the Malayan rubber economy is reported in P.T. Bauer, *The Rubber Industry*, and in "The Working of the Rubber Regulation," *The Economic Journal* Vol. 54 (1946), pp. 391-414, and in "Malayan Rubber Policies," *Economica* Vol. 14 (1947), pp. 81-107; Barlow, *Natural Rubber Industry*, pp. 58-73; Drabble "Peasant Smallholders in the Malayan Economy."

52. Ursula Wasserman, "Commodities in UNCTAD: Rubber," and "Jakarta Natural Rubber Agreement of 1976," both in the *Journal of World Trade Law* Vol. 2 (1978); Martin Rudner, "Development Policies and Patterns of Agrarian Dominance in the Malaysian Rubber Export Economy," *Modern Asian Studies* Vol. 15 (1981).

53. Rudner, "Development Policies and Patterns of Agrarian Dominance," *loq. cit.*; D.W. Fryer & J.C. Jackson, "Peasant Producers or Urban Planters?" *Pacific Viewpoint* Vol. 7 (1966).

54. *Fourth Malaysia Plan*, para. 697.

55. *Second Malaysia Plan*, para. 415.

56. Ibid., paras. 934, 955.

57. *Fourth Malaysia Plan*, para. 699.

58. *Second Malaysia Plan*, para. 433.

59. Ibid., paras. 430-1.

60. Ibid., para. 435; D. Lim, *Economic Growth*, pp. 239-44.

61. *Third Malaysia Plan*, para. 955.

62. See Martin Rudner, "Trends in Malaysian Development Planning: Goals, Policies and Role Expansion," *Review of Indonesian and Malayan Affairs* Vol. 14 (1980).

CHAPTER 10

AGRICULTURAL PLANNING AND DEVELOPMENT PERFORMANCE IN MALAYSIA

The evolution of Malaysian agricultural policy since independence in 1957 gave expression to changing official attitudes, social interests, and public expectations concerning rural development. As the dominant perspective changed, new planning norms and development goals were imputed to agricultural policy. These new policy directions were evident in the shifting pattern of resource allocation for the agricultural sector over successive Malaysian development plans.

Planning constituted the institutional centrepiece of the Malaysian development effort. Although Malaysia maintains a market economy, planning has served as a significant and increasingly comprehensive instrument of economic management. Malaysian development planning has undergone three successive historical phases of role expansion: an initial forward-budgeting phase represented by the colonial-style First Five-Year Plan (FYP), 1956-60; a second public investment phase denoted by the Second FYP, 1961-65, and First Malaysia Plan (FMP), 1966-70; and a third, more broadly interventionist phase inaugurated by the New Economic Policy (NEP) and carried forward in the Second Malaysia Plan (SMP), 1971-75, Third Malaysia Plan (TMP), 1976-80, and the current Fourth Malaysia Plan (FoMP), 1981-85.[1]

It is important to distinguish between the two distinct, albeit connected, facets of planning, i.e., the declared plan and the realized plan. Planned allocations of (public) development expenditures represent a declared plan, whereas the ensuing actual allocations of capital investment constitute the realized plan. The

Contemporary and Historical Perspectives in Southeast Asia, ed. Anita Beltran Chen, (Ottawa: Carleton University Printshop for the Canadian Asian Studies Association, 1985).

declared plan denotes formal policy preferences. The realized plan specifies the effective goals and priorities fulfilled. A comparison of the expenditure patterns, declared and realized, reveals the degree of real policy commitment on the part of planning authorities to which goals. Moreover, by tracing the patterns of declared and realized development allocations over successive plans, it is possible to discern the evolving trend in public policy commitments as the role of planning expands.

In examining the role of Malaysian planning in agricultural development, certain difficulties are encountered in determining the aggregate allocations of plan expenditures for the agricultural and rural development are readily identifiable, to be sure. However, the agricultural and rural component of other general developmental appropriations are less easily accountable. No agricultural-rural assignment of general plan expenditures on economic or social development is available. Analysis of planning trends for agricultural development must therefore confine itself primarily to the specific agriculture and rural development appropriations, being aware that these represent only a portion of the aggregate allocation for agriculture and rural society in planned development.

TABLE 1
Public Investment
and Growth, 1956-60 (percentage).

	Average Annual Real Growth Rate GDP (1)	Investment Ratio† (2)	Public Investment Ratio‡ (3)	Average Annual Growth Rate of Public Investment (4)	Public Investment as Proportion of Gross Capital Formation (5)
1956-60*	4.1	12.6	2.7	(12.3)	21.4
1961-65	5.1	16.8	7.3	24.0	43.4
1966-70	5.4	17.0	6.0	1.9	35.3
1971-75	7.1	24.7	7.9	17.6	31.9
1976-80	8.6	26.2	8.8	9.3	33.2
1981-85††	7.6	26.4	6.1	0.9	27.9

* 1956-60 Peninsular Malaysia only.
† Investment Ratio: Gross investment/GNP.
‡ Public investment ratio: Public investments/GNP.
†† Plan forecasts.
Sources: Bank Negara Malaysia: *Money and Banking in Malaysia*, (1979);
V.V. Bhanoji Rao, *National Accounts of West Malaysia, 1947-1970*,
(1976); First Malaysia Plan; *Second Malaysia Plan*; *Third Malaysia Plan; Fourth Malaysia Plan.*

Phases and Trends in Planning

The functions of Malaysian development planning served to accelerate as well as direct the rate of investment, private and public, in the economy. Plan expenditures have been financed for the most part out of increased domestic savings, mobilized through government revenues and public borrowing.[2] Public capital formation in particular emerged as a significant factor in the growth of investment in Malaysia since 1950. Gross capital formation as a proportion of Gross National Product (GNP) rose by more than a quarter, in real terms, on annual average between the first and second phases of planning, and by half again between the second and third phases.

TABLE 2
Malaysian Development Plan Targets
and Fulfillment (M$ million, current values).

	1FYP			2FYP		
	Plan	Actual	Fulfill-ment	Plan	Actual	Fulfill-ment
Total Federal Public Investment	1,148.7	1,006.7	87.7	2,150.0	2,651.7	123.3
Economic Sector	794.7	759.9	97.4	1,477.9	1,763.7	97.4
• Agriculture & Rural Development	265.6	227.5	85.6	543.3	467.9	85.6
Other Economic*	529.1	532.4	100.6	932.6	1,295.8	100.6
Social Sector	212.7	138.8	65.3	491.0	413.6	65.3
Administration	141.3	65.0	46.0	88.1	167.1	46.0
Security	n/a	43.0	—	—	—	—

	FMP		
	Plan	Actual	%
Total Federal Public Investment	4,5563.9	4,242.9	93.2
Economic Sector	2,710.2	2,685.4	99.1
• Agriculture & Rural Development	1,086.6	1,114.1	102.5
Other Economic*	1,623.6	1,571.3	96.7
Social Sector	975.3	752.1	77.1
Administration	126.4	138.1	109.3
Security	739.0	666.8	90.2

TABLE 2 (continued).

	SMP			
	Plan	Revised Plan	Actual	% Fulfill-ment
Total Federal Public Investment	7,250.0	10,255.4	7,415.1	72.3
Economic Sector	4,870.9	7,349.7	4,956.4	67.4
• Agriculture & Rural Development	1,920.8	2,368.9	1,793.5	75.7
Other Economic*	2,950.1	4,980.7	3,162.9	63.5
Social Sector	1,067.4	1,431.0	1,286.7	89.9
Administration	211.6	369.9	149.9	40.5
Security	1,100.1	1,104.8	1,022.0	92.5

	TMP			FoMP
	Plan	TMP Actual†	% Fulfill-ment	Plan
Total Federal Public Investment	18,555.0	21,201.9	114.2	39,329
Economic Sector	12,665.1	13,590.8	107.1	22,764
• Agriculture & Rural Development	4,735.5	4,672.4	98.6	8,358
Other Economic*	7,929.6	8,898.4	112.2	14,406
Social Sector	3,099.1	3,636.0	117.3	6,388
Administration	597.7	465.3	77.8	805
Security	3,200.0	3,529.8	110.3	9,372

(1) Percentage fulfillment of Revised plan targets.
* Including mineral resources, commerce and industry, transport and communications, energy and public utilities, and feasibility studies.
† Estimate.
Sources: *First Malaysia Plan, Second Malaysia Plan, Fourth Malaysia Plan*; *Economic Report, 1975-76;* M. Rudner *Nationalism, Planning and Economic Modernization in Malaysia*, (Sage Publications, 1975) and *Trends in Malaysia Development Planning*.

These quantum leaps in Malaysia's investment ratio occurred, significantly, in the initial quinquennial period of each successive planning phase. This coincided with the introduction of the Second FYP and SMP, which inaugurated these new phases of role expansion. The rates and magnitudes of public investment under these plans escalated accordingly. Private investment activity tended to expand along with plan expenditure. The public component of Malaysian gross capital formation therefore remained relatively steady at 38 to 40% of the total.

Public investment within the planning framework constituted an important generator of Malaysian economic growth. Investment on the part of the public sector had comprised only about 4% of Malaysian GNP during the first phase of planning, escalating to the 6% level during the second phase, and reached the 8% level relative to a much higher all-Malaysia GNP in the third phase of planning.

The annual average real rate of growth of GNP for peninsular Malaysia increased from under 2% during the post-war years 1947-1956 to around 4% in 1956-60, stimulated by the First FYP. Growth increased to 5% during the decade 1960-70 corresponding to the second phase of planning and accelerated to an average annual rate of 7-8% over the SMP-TMP decade, 1971-1980. Not only was aggregate growth performance affected, but planned alloca-

TABLE 3
Proportional Allocations of Plan Expenditures, (1956-60) (percent).

| Plan Headings | Phase 1 | | | Phase 2 | | | |
| | 1FYP | | 2FYP | | FMP | |
	Plan	Actual	Plan	Actual	Plan	Actual
Agriculture & Rural Development	21.4	22.6	24.5	17.7	23.9	26.3
Economic Infrastructure	41.3	51.7	42.1	46.6	33.8	33.7
Industry & Commerce	1.3	1.2	1.3	0.2	2.5	3.3
Social Development	17.1	13.8	22.8	15.6	20.8	17.7
General Government	11.4	7.2	4.1	6.3	2.8	3.3
Security & Defence	7.5	3.5	11.3	11.6	16.2	15.7
TOTAL	100.0	100.0	100.0	100.0	100.0	100.0

| Plan Headings | Phase 3 | | | | | |
| | SMP | | TMP | | FoMP | |
	Plan	Revised Plan	Actual	Plan	Est. Actual	Plan
Agriculture & Rural Development	26.5	23.1	21.7	25.5	22.0	21
Economic Infrastructure	40.6	32.9	34.2	33.6	26.8	23
Industry & Commerce	8.0	15.7	16.5	9.5	15.3	13
Social Development	14.7	13.9	13.7	16.6	17.1	16
General Government	2.9	3.6	3.6	3.2	2.2	2
Security & Defence	18.6	10.8	10.4	9.5	16.6	24
TOTAL	100.0	100.0	100.0	100.0	100.0	100.0

Note: 1FYP, 2FYP refer to Peninsular Malaysia, later plans to Malaysia.
Sources: As Table 2

tions of public investment also led to an extension and expansion of capital formation to hitherto underdeveloped sectors of the Malaysian economy.

Trends in Planning for Agriculture and Rural Development

As the rate of planned public investment was stepped up, the specific allocation for agriculture and rural development tended to fluctuate over successive plans and between declared and realized plans. Each new phase of planning provided for increased proportional allocations of planned development expenditures to agriculture and rural development. Agriculture and rural development obtained 21.4% of planned First FYP expenditure, rising to the 24% level in the next phase Second FYP and FMP. The declared level of public development expenditure accelerated sharply in the third phase, as did the specified share allocated to agriculture and rural development, to around a quarter of planned public investment. The progressively greater share of declared plan resources allocated to agriculture and rural development represented a planning response to the political challenges precipitating each new phase. These phased leaps in declared capital allocations signified the economic tribute paid through planning to the political imperatives of agricultural and rural development.

While political motives impelled the plans inaugurating each new phase to make substantially larger provision for agriculture and rural development, the return to political complacency in subsequent plans in each phase evinced a contraction in declared agricultural and rural allocations back to historical relativities.

Realized plan performance indicates that the actual conduct of agriculture and rural development policy has been somewhat more restrained than the intentions declared. Actual expenditures on agriculture and rural development, to be sure, recorded substantial real money increases with each successive plan. Public investment in agriculture during the First FYP was well up on the standards of the post-war colonial administration.[3] This was followed by further cumulative increases, by 75% under the Second FYP, by a further 95% under the FMP, and again by over 90% under the SMP. The annual average rate of growth of public capital expenditure on agriculture and rural development increased in real money terms, compounded, of about 10% during the First FYP, over 11% during the Second FYP and nearly 13% during the FMP, easing to around 6.5% during the SMP.

The actual share of public investment allocated to agriculture and rural development remained more or less stable over the successive phases of planning, however. Agriculture obtained 22.6% of actual First FYP public capital expenditure. This declined to 17.7% of the Second FYP, due to personnel and material constraints on rural development administration, but then rose to over 26% as these were overcome by the time of the FMP. Taking the two plan periods together, the proportional allocation of realized public capital expenditure on agriculture and rural development during this second phase of planning ranged between 22 and 23% for peninsular Malaysia and Malaysia as a whole, respectively. During the subsequent third phase of role expansion, the actual share of agriculture and rural development in actual plan expenditure decreased to under 22% during the SMP and TMP.

Historically, Malaysian planning showed considerable variation between the originally declared and actually realized allocations of public investment to agriculture and rural development: greater in the First FYP, lesser in the Second FYP, greater again the FMP (though lesser overall for the second phase as a whole), and substantially less in the third phase SMP and TMP.

The extent of these variations between declared and realized public investment allocations pointed to an uneven planning commitment to agriculture and rural development. The degree to which intended targets were fulfilled or under-fulfilled can serve as a useful indication of the intensity of policy commitment to the particular planning objective. Agricultural investment reached only 86% of its First FYP target.

While the considerably expanded Second FYP experienced a similar shortfall, this was due more to administrative bottlenecks affecting rural development performance than to any lack of policy resolve. Indeed, once rural administrative capacity improved, the subsequent FMP agriculture and rural development expenditure backlog was made up. Yet, taking the second phase of planning as a whole, the policy commitment to agriculture and rural development still remained under-fulfilled. On aggregate, just 97% of planned second phase public investment in agriculture and rural development had been realized, even less in real money terms. During the third phase of planning, the SMP and TMP rates of agricultural plan fulfillment declined to around 90%. The apparent erosion of planning commitments to agricultural and rural development at the very outset of the third phase of role expansion bodes ill for the future prospects of realizing NEP expectations.

The rate of plan fulfillment for agriculture and rural development tended to lag behind the performance of other important spheres of Malaysian development planning. The shortfall in plan performance was particularly pronounced relative to other economic sector programmes. Levels of plan fulfillment were generally higher for economic infrastructure, e.g., transport, communication and utilities, than for agriculture and rural development, except during the FMP and SMP. Industry and commerce became leading beneficiaries of the second and third phases of plan role expansion, consistently over-fulfilling its planning targets and so out-distanced agriculture and rural development. The only sector to experience generally lower levels of plan fulfillment was social development (particularly health and community services), at least until the NEP raised its effective priority for the third phase.

The actual rates of direction of public investment indicated the effective ranking of priorities in Malaysian planning. Opposing trends towards the over-fulfillment of urban and industrially-oriented expenditure targets, on the one hand, in contrast with under-fulfillment of agricultural and rural targets, on the other, signified an explicit re-ordering of public investment priorities. The resulting patterns of actual plan expenditures tended to diverge from that originally declared.

Actual patterns of public investment tended to enhance the shares of economic infrastructure and of commerce and industry ever since the second phase of role expansion, while diminishing the shares of agriculture and rural development (except during the FMP). A gap in policy commitments thus arose between plan formulation and plan implementation. The political factors that shaped the emergent role of planning in agriculture and rural development did not carry over with the same degree of commitment to real policy priorities.

The Distribution of Public Investments in Agriculture and Rural Development

The growth of public investment in Malaysian agriculture and rural development also involved significant shifts in investment targets. As public investment activity increased, the attendant role expansion of planning served to channel development resources towards hitherto neglected and newly innovative agricultural applications. Historically, the scope of public investment in colonial Malayan agriculture remained severely confined as to economic purpose and breadth of coverage. Towards the end of the colonial period, the aims of public investment in agriculture underwent a significant broadening. Faced with the gathering obsolescence of Malaya's rubber acreage, government-sponsored rubber replanting schemes for estates and smallholdings was introduced in 1952.[4] The advent of self-government in 1955 inspired a widening scope for agricultural investment in the ensuing First FYP. This trend towards more extensive government intervention in the rural economy led to a further broadening of the agriculture investment outlook of subsequent plans.

Drainage and irrigation have remained, for some time, important items of public investment in Malaysian agriculture. In pre-war Malaya and for years afterwards, public investment in irrigation for padi cultivation represented a kind of token tribute to the grail of rice sufficiency.[5] But by the late 1950s, this self-sufficiency goal paled into the realm of public rhetoric.

Under the Second FYP, agricultural development strategy aimed somewhat less ambitiously at enhancing local employment opportunities in the rice sector, as an antidote to the undesirable urban drift of Malay population.[6] Emphasis was placed on improving irrigation facilities on already cultivated areas, with only minor provision being made for extensions to additional new lands.[7] This approach signified a retreat, in effect, from the proclaimed self-sufficiency and employment creation goals attached to earlier policy, reflecting something of the pessimism prevailing at the time in official perspectives concerning agricultural planning.

Public investment in irrigation and drainage was to undergo yet another change in direction with effect from FMP, and again later plans. Beginning with the FMP, expenditure allocations for irrigation aimed at enlarging the cultivable area, facilitating off-season ("double") cropping, and improving padi yields.[8] The emphasis of agricultural policy had switched in favour of comparatively large-scale integrated irrigation (and later also drainage) schemes. Two very large irrigation schemes, the Muda scheme, complete in 1974, and the Kemubu scheme, completed the next year, were followed by several more modest scale, integrated regional irrigation schemes. As the planning approach to the hitherto dominant item of agricultural investment, irrigation and drainage, became more rationally defined in economic, or benefit-cost terms, paradoxically its planning priority effectively declined.

The NEP perspective on income growth and the restructuring of society saw the relative importance of irrigation and drainage eclipsed by other more economically efficient items of agricultural investment pertinent to this third phase of planning. It is ironic that the investment criteria applied in conjunction with the emergent modernization goal served to diminish the planning priority of those irrigation and drainage facilities required to raise the productivity of specifically the poorest strata of Malay peasantry.

Trends in public capital expenditure reflected the fluctuating priorities of irrigation and drainage in agricultural development planning. Actual expenditures rose from M$38 million under the First FYP to over M$108 million in the Second FYP, and rose again to over M$328 million (for peninsular Malaysia; M$342 million on an all-Malaysia basis) in the FMP. Then, in line with changed NEP priorities, SMP expenditures on irrigation and drainage declined in real money terms, but virtually doubled again in the TMP following incidence of agrarian unrest in the mid-1970s.

Plan performance concerning expenditure for irrigation and drainage tended to oscillate along with the underlying policy commitments. Irrigation and drainage expenditure targets in the First FYP remained under-fulfilled by more than a third. Subsequently, the heightened policy commitment to irrigation and drainage works in the rural development strategy of the Second FYP and FMP led to the actual over-fulfillment of both their target allocations.

The altered priorities for public investment postulated by the NEP implied a lower degree of planning commitment, and a concomitant level of target fulfillment in the SMP. Incidents of agrarian unrest in the mid-1970s led to a considerably expanded planned allocation for irrigation and drainage under the TMP; subsequent expenditure performance lagged well behind.

Similar fluctuations became apparent in the actual proportions of plan expenditures allocated to irrigation and drainage. The share of public investment devoted to irrigation and drainage rose from 3.8% of the First FYP to 8% of the FMP, but fell back to the 2% level under the SMP and TMP.

Rubber replanting with high-yielding varieties constituted the other major area of public investment in Malaysian agriculture that had been inaugurated already in (late) colonial times.[9] If natural rubber shared with rice a pessimistic official prognosis, during the 1960s at least, rubber replanting represented an economically worthwhile form of public investment activity nonetheless. Indeed, investment in replanting performed a dual function in the rubber economy.

Rubber replanting was necessary anyway for asset renewal in a plantation economy otherwise prone to obsolescence, as well as for the spread of technologically advanced high-yielding rubber varieties (or alternatively for re-deployment into other high-value cash crops, e.g., palm oil) among producers.[10] Financial resources for rubber replanting schemes have been derived since their introduction, from an earmarked levy, or cess, or rubber exports. Proceeds from this cess are divided into two replanting funds, for the estate and smallholding subsectors respectively, on the basis of their proportional contributions. Each replanting fund had its own appropriations mechanism. Estates acquire automatic reimbursement of their contributions to their fund upon proof of replanting, however smallholders must apply and qualify for replanting grants.

Over the years, the value of these smallholder replanting grants was stepped up from time to time, to compensate for inflation but also to induce wider peasant participation. Despite this, actual expenditures from the smallholding replanting fund tended to lag behind receipts. This had a redistributive effect of turning the smallholding replanting fund into a regressive form of taxation. The socially regressive impact of the established institutional mechanism weighed especially heavily on the typically smaller, inferior grade of holdings operated mostly by poor Malay peasants. The deleterious consequences were further exacerbated by consistent expenditure shortfalls and reduced policy commitments for rubber replanting.

Even as the replanting scheme expanded in scope over successive plans, its financial appropriations recorded an irregular and oscillating pattern. Actual expenditure on replanting declined from M$153 million under the First FYP to M$131 million under the Second FYP (peninsular Malaysia only), then grew to M$168 million under the FMP before contracting to only M$145 million under the SMP and rising again to M$198 million under the TMP. Actual expenditure on replanting fell short of planned expenditure in every plan except for the FMP, by 14% under the First FYP, 21% under the Second FYP, 17% under the SMP, and 70% under the TMP. Financial allocations for replanting as a proportion of total public development expenditure fell dramatically, from 15% of the First FYP to 5% of the Second FYP, and again to 4% of the FMP and 1.6% of the SMP, and down to just 0.8% of the TMP.

The Baling peasant demonstrations of 1974 had impelled a considerable increase in the financial provision for replanting under the TMP, in an invigorated effort to modernize the laggard traditional segment of poor rubber smallholders. However, the return to political complacency witnessed a reduction in expenditure actually committed. The FoMP for 1981-85 kept its allocation for rubber replanting at the same reduced level.

The earlier public investment emphasis given to irrigation and drainage and rubber replanting tended to diminish as planning priorities adjusted to newer policy claims on rural development expenditures. In particular, the transition to self-government led to agricultural land development emerging as a major new area of public investment.[11] A Federal Land Development Authority (FELDA) was set up in 1956 to undertake responsibility for the establishment of integrated new land settlement and new planting schemes were also introduced in order to satisfy peasant hunger for additional lands for plantation crops.

Public investment in the newly initiated FELDA schemes reached M$16.7 million, or just over 1.5% of total appropriations during the First FYP. As land development policy emerged as an increasingly prominent feature in the political and economic perspectives of planning, this rate of investment accelerated accordingly. More and varied new land planting schemes were developed, with capital allocations growing in quantum leaps to M$130 million in the Second FYP, then to M$309 million in the FMP, and again to M$952 million in the SMP, reaching M$2752 million the TMP. The land development allocation in the FoMP was substantially higher still, between 1976 and 1980.

The growing salience of land development in agricultural development policy is indicated by the rapidly expanded proportional share of plan expenditures devoted to FELDA and other new planting schemes. Whereas the initial capital allocation for land development stood at 1.5% of total First FYP expenditure, the Second FYP allocated 5%, the FMP 8.6%, the SMP 11.6% and the TMP 13% of their respective outlays to land development. Land development became the largest single item of public investment in agriculture and rural development. Planned expenditure targets tended to be fulfilled to a comparatively high degree, underscoring the extent of policy commitment to land development.

Public investment in land development displayed considerable structural flexibility and organizational adaptability as the role of planning expanded. At the initial stage, public finance for land development under the First FYP and Second FYP was confined to FELDA and its tightly organized settlement schemes devoted to rubber planting. Later on, oil palm was accepted as an alternative cash crop on which to base land development. From the mid-1960s, the organizational format taken by land development policy became more flexible as well, in response to emerging demands and perceived needs.

While the lion's share of land development finance during the FMP and SMP was still being directed to FEDA, over 68% and 63% respectively, clearly the trend was towards a more differentiated approach. By the TMP, over 37% of land development funding was being channelled to alternative programmes such as the Rubber Industry Smallholders Development Authority (RISDA) block new planting schemes, Federal Land Consolidation and Rehabilitation Authority (FELCRA) projects, public estates managed by the several State Economic Development Corporations, and joint public sector private ventures. In the successor FoMP, FELDA attracted only just over half of the total land development appropriation in real money terms a reduction from the actual allocation under the previous plan. The growing acceptance of different forms of publicly sponsored land settlement highlighted the more comprehensive scope of Malaysian planning. Carried forward by role expansion, agricultural development policy shifted direction from a narrow concentration on a single organizational mode, FELDA, to a multiple policy effort for rational problem-solving through land development.

Two other agricultural areas for public investment acquired some new prominence as the role of development planning expanded. Although agricultural credit and marketing had been accepted as a colonial administrative responsibility, albeit a limited one, public finance for the purpose was maintained merely at a minimal level.[12] Notwithstanding official rhetoric favouring the promotion of rural co-operative credit and marketing, which were conventionally considered to be particularly appropriate to the Malay peasant condition, actual policy commitments remained inadequate and, indeed, ambiguous even after independence.[13] Thus, the Second FYP appropriated M$20 million for agricultural credit and marketing, but merely M$1.3 million of this was actually expended. By the mid-1960s, intensified government concern over rural economic stagnation prompted a more positive interventionist approach to agricultural credit and marketing. Some M$30 million of FMP funding was allocated for agricultural credit institutions and the newly established Padi Marketing Board, plus an additional M$2.6 million for newly established rubber processing centres. By the third phase of role expansion, public capital expenditure on agricultural credit and marketing (including rubber processing) had expanded to over M$139 million under the SMP, and reached M$269 million under the TMP. The FoMP envisaged another massive leap in public-sector involvement in agricultural credit and marketing, having budgeted more than M$761 million for the several specialized organizations engaged in these operations.

The style of government intervention in the agricultural economy altered as the role of planning expanded and the pattern of public investment in rural development underwent change. During the colonial (post-war) period and initial phase of planning, public investment in agriculture emphasized improvements to existing agrarian assets, mainly through irrigation and drainage and the original rubber replanting scheme. Because of laggard expenditure performance and the investment criteria that were then applied, this early approach tended to widen agrarian inequalities between those enjoying access to policy benefits, who thus modernized their operations early on, and the disadvantaged majority who were left behind in traditional and impoverished modes of production.

During the subsequent phases of planning, government intervention extended to an increasingly extensive development of Malaysia's agricultural resources. Rates of agricultural investment accelerated as government policy encouraged the spread of modernization within the existing agricultural frontier, and its extension through land development.

Traditional agrarian conditions were transformed as a result of public intervention stimulating private economic activity. The Malaysian style of government intervention was restrained, in as much as it neither undercut private activity nor encroached on landownership. Yet its role in mobilizing and directing agricultural investment through planning led to a deepening and broadening of capital formation for rural development within the established institutional framework.

Agricultural Development Performance Under the New Economic Policy

The completion of the TMP in 1980 marked the half-way point in the 20-year time frame for the New Economic Policy. Malaysian agriculture recorded a real average annual growth rate of 4.3% during the 1970s, the period of the SMP and TMP.[14] This growth performance was somewhat below the rate of 5.4% targeted in the Outline Perspective Plan for the New Economic Policy. The marginal revenue product of Malaysian agriculture was severely affected by the world economic recession of 1974-75, by adverse weather conditions prevailing during the second half of the decade, aggravated by greatly depressed world market conditions at the end of the decade. The share of agriculture in the Gross Domestic Product of Malaysia declined from 30.8% in 1970 to 22.2% in 1980.

Agricultural employment continued to expand nevertheless, as real income grew. About 21% of new employment opportunities were created by the agricultural sector. Agricultural employment grew by an average rate of 1.9% per annum over the decade, compared with the projected rate of 1.3%. Labour productivity in agricultural occupations thus increased. However, rapid development elsewhere in the economy produced a shift in the structure of employment, with agriculture's share of total employment decreasing proportionately (though not absolutely) to 40.6% in 1980, compared to over half in 1970.

As a result of the sustained growth of agricultural incomes and rising productivity, the incidence of poverty in the agricultural sector declined from the 68% level in 1970, to the 46% level in 1980. Despite the marked improvement, progress was much slower than expected in the Outline Perspective Plan for the New Economic Policy, which had envisaged a decline in the incidence of poverty in the agricultural sector to the 49% level after the first decade. The incidence of poverty remained intractably high in certain subsectors such as padi, mixed agriculture and fisheries.

In the padi sector, several large drainage and irrigation based projects for integrated agricultural development were completed during 1971-80. These included the Muda, Kemubu and Besut projects, which together contributed some 57% of total padi production in Peninsular Malaysia. Average yields per hectare improved by over a third in the Muda scheme, by 60% in Kemubu, and by almost 90% in the case of Besut, during the course of the decade.

Apart from these integrated schemes, investment in drainage and irrigation under the SMP and TMP led to the improvement of some 68,000 hectares of land for both single and double cropping of padi. This represented a 67% achievement of the land area target. The area of padi land under irrigation increased by some 70% over the decade. In addition, some 99,500 hectares of established farming land, and 205,800 hectares of new land settlement areas were provided with improved drainage facilities. These improvements to drainage enabled planting and intercropping with more remunerative crops, as well as enhancing tree crop production.

During 1971-80 over 10,300 hectares of rubber and padi were rehabilitated by FELCRA in Peninsular Malaysia. The rehabilitation effort involved the improvement of agricultural holdings through the introduction of modern agricultural practices, and the provision of basic infrastructure and support facilities. Most of these programmes were directed towards less successful land schemes developed by various state governments. FELCRA also launched three pilot projects for the rehabilitation and consolidation of existing village holdings aimed at maximizing production and increasing incomes.

Rubber replanting lagged behind target during the period. A total of 302,900 hectares were replanted with rubber and other crops, compared with a target of 393,000 hectares. The overall rate of replanting decreased significantly towards the end of decade. Despite the introduction of differential replanting grants for very small holdings of under 4.1 hectares, most of the replanting under RISDA-sponsored programmes took place on larger holdings. Very small peasant producers remained reluctant to replant, even in face of obsolescence, for fear of losing their income stream.

New land development extended over 866,000 hectares during the decade, representing 97% of the target figure. FELDA was responsible for developing over 43% of the total, with the remainder having been undertaken by FELCRA (6%), RISDA (4%), state government agencies (33%), and joint ventures and/or the private sector (14%). Of the 455,000 hectares developed under the aegis of federal land development agencies (i.e., FELDA, FELCRA, RISDA), 150,700 were planted with rubber, 282,900 with oil palm, and the remainder with sugar cane, cocoa, coffee, and padi. FELDA land development schemes resettled 42,200 families; FELCRA resettled 16,600 families and 4,100 youths in its fringe and youth schemes, respectively; and the various state schemes benefited 9,288 families. The number of poor agricultural households was 582,000 in 1970, and reduced to 443,000 by 1980.

The first decade of the New Economic Policy witnessed an expanded role for government in the provision of agricultural credit, processing and marketing facilities. Bank Pertanian Malaysia started operations in 1970 and contributed substantially to agricultural credit requirements. Between 1971 and 1980 Bank Pertanian approved loans amounting to M$642 million, of which 27% went to padi producers, and 21% to plantations. Bank credit facilities tended to favour better-off peasants, small companies, and plantations in particular. RISDA provided credit to medium-size smallholdings (over 4.1 hectares) to supplement their replanting grants and sustain incomes. Very little of this public sector credit was accessible, in fact, to poor, very small, peasant producers.

Government intervention in the padi sector provided producer subsidies and income stabilization. Since its establishment in 1973, the Farmers' Organization Authority supplied fertilizers, agri-chemicals, and planting materials under its subsidy programme amounting to M$53.5 million. The establishment of the Lembaga Padi dan Beras Negara (Padi Marketing Board - LPN) under the SMP replaced the Federal Agricultural Marketing Authority as the agency responsible for the marketing of the rice and padi, and expanded its activities in the provision of drying, processing complexes were set up to enlarge LPN milling capacity to meet the processing requirements of the major drainage and irrigation project areas. By 1980, the LPN had come to operate sufficient drying capacity to serve over 28% of padi production, and had milling capacity equal to 15% of domestic Malaysian output. While expansion of the public sector role did not supplant private operations entirely, the activities of the LPN in particular in the areas of intensive agricultural development did provide important leverage for government policy in managing the rice economy.

The LPN's role in the market enabled government to intervene in the domestic producers' prices for padi and rice. Government's price support scheme for padi was administered through the LPN as its buying agent. The padi and rice purchasing and stockpiling activities of the LPN helped to stabilize domestic supplies and prices in face of fluctuating international market conditions. Production of padi increased during the decade from 1.4 million tonnes in 1970 to 1.9 million tonnes in 1980. Drought conditions prevailing at the end of the decade lowered output in the last two years. The area under padi increased by over 11%, and over half (56%) of the total acreage was under double-cropping by 1980. Average yields per hectare improved by about a fifth. The gap between domestic supply and rice consumption diminished progressively. Malaysia's rice self-sufficiency level increased from 78% in 1970 to 92% in 1980.

In the rubber sector, the Malaysian Rubber Development Corporation, which was set up in 1971, established 15 factories during the SMP period, with a combined capacity of 110,000 tonnes, benefiting 75,000 smallholders. RISDA established over 1,900 smallholder development centres serving some 47,000 smallholders. Two factories for producing Standard Malaysian Rubber (SMR) and another two latex concentrating plants were opened by FELDA. These processing operations were, however, essentially supplementary to well-established and generally efficient private sector role in the processing and export marketing of natural rubber. Rather, the main thrust of government intervention was directed at rubber incomes and investment policy.

In an attempt to stabilize producers' incomes and encourage investment in rubber, government increased the smallholders replanting grant and restructured its rubber export duty at the end of the decade. The relatively high prices for natural rubber that prevailed during the second half of the decade had not induced sufficient additional investment in rubber replanting and new planting to meet forecast world demand. Laggard investment was attributed to the onerous burden of rubber export taxation on smallholders' income, and on the seeming unwillingness of smallholders to forego immediate gains for the longer-run risks of replanting. The increased replanting grant did stimulate replanting activity, which was subsequently bolstered still further by the introduction of revised rubber export duties in 1979. Very small peasant holdings, however, still lagged behind in replanting. The overall area under rubber remained steady at 2.1 million hectares, mainly as a result of the continued expansion of the smallholding sector, particularly in FELDA schemes, which offset the tendency of larger estates to diversity towards other cash crops.

Malaysian rubber output grew at an annual average rate of about 2.3%, from 1.2 million tonnes in 1970 to 1.6 million tonnes in 1980. This improvement was due mostly to the expansion of small holding acreage and the overall gains in yields. Yet growth in production lagged behind the projected rate of 2.8% warranted by the New Economic Policy.

Malaysian government efforts to maintain producers' prices and output growth extended also to the international arena. Malaysia actively promoted international agreement on an integrated commodity scheme for natural rubber in order to achieve stability of income and production growth over what was expected to be an upward market trend. An International Natural Rubber Agreement, based on a Rubber Stockpile Scheme was concluded towards the end of the decade, at Malaysia's initiative, ironically just when the world recession was about to dampen demand for rubber. Falling prices subsequently crashed below the lower intervention point of the initial Agreement, notwithstanding the accumulation of substantial buffer stocks. Attempts at achieving export income security through international commodity agreements carry a double jeopardy, in that such schemes are vulnerable to increased market penetration on the part of unassociated producer countries at times of rising markets, while they threaten efficient associated producers with export regulation and output restriction at times of declining markets. The history of previous international rubber agreements amply demonstrates the risks of regulation, restriction, and substitution to the long-term competitive position of the Malaysian rubber economy.[15]

ENDNOTES

1. Martin Rudner, "Trends in Malaysian Development Planning: Goals, Policies and Role Expansion," *Review of Indonesian and Malayan Affairs* Vol. 14 (1980) pp. 48-91.

2. Ibid., pp. 74-80; See also, C. T. Edwards, *Public Finances in Malaya and Singapore* (Canberra, 1970).

3. Martin Rudner, *Nationalism, Planning and Economic Modernization in Malaysia* (Beverly Hills, 1975); *David Lim, Economic Growth and Development in West Malaysia* (Kuala Lumpur, 1973).

4. Martin Rudner, "Malayan Rubber Policy: Development and Anti-Development During the 1950s," *Journal of Southeast Asian Studies, (JSEAS)* Vol. 7 (1975); Colin Barlow, *The Natural Rubber Industry: Its Development, Technology and Economy in Malaysia* (Kuala Lumpur, 1978).

5. Martin Rudner, "The Malayan Post-War Rice Crisis: An Episode in Colonial Agricultural Policy," *Kajian Ekonomi Malaysia* Vol. 12 (1975); E. K. Fisk, "Malaysia," in R. T. Shand, ed., *Agricultural Development in Asia* (Canberra, 1969).

6. Federation of Malaya, *Second Five-Year Plan 1961-65* (Kuala Lumpur, 1961), para. 26.

7. Federation of Malaysia, *First Malaysia Plan 1966-70* (Kuala Lumpur, 1971), p. 325.

8. Ibid., para. 326; Lim, *Economic Growth*, pp. 234-45.

9. Martin Rudner, "The State and Peasant Innovation in Rural Development: The Case of Malaysian Rubber," *Asian and African Studies* Vol. 6 (1970); Lim Sow Ching, *Land Development Schemes in Peninsular Malaysia* (Kuala Lumpur, 1976); Colin MacAndrews, *Land Settlement Policies in Malaysia and Indonesia* (Singapore, 1978).

10. Syed Hussein Wafa, "Strategies and Programmes of Land Development in Malaysia," and Harcharan Singh Khera, "The State and Peasant Innovation in Rural Development: The Case of Felda Oil Palm Schemes," both in Stephen Chee & Choo Siew Mun, eds., *Malaysian Economic Development and Policies* (Kuala Lumpur, 1975).

11. Rudner, "The State and Peasant Innovation in Rural Development"; MacAndrews, *Land Settlement Policies*; P. P. Courtenay "Some Trends in the Peninsular Malaysian Plantation Sector 1963-1973," in James C. Jackson & Martin Rudner, eds., *Issues in Malaysian Development* (Singapore, 1979).

12. Martin Rudner, "Agricultural Policy and Peasant Social Transformation in Late Colonial Malaya," in James C. Jackson & Martin Rudner, eds., *Issues in Malaysian Development*; Leo J. Fredericks, "Free Enterprise and the Co-operative Movement in Malaysian Economic Development," *The Developing Economies* Vol. 12 (1974).

13. Vide. Martin Rudner, "Malayan Quandary: Rural Development Policy Under the First and Second Five-Year Plans," *Contributions to Asian Studies* Vol. 1 (1971). On the wider policy trends during this period see Donald R. Snodgrass, *Inequality and Economic Development in Malaysia* (Kuala Lumpur, 1980).

14. Data for agriculture and rural development performance in this section is derived from the *Fourth Malaysia Plan 1981-85* (Kuala Lumpur, 1981), chapter 15.

15. On the recently concluded International Natural Rubber Agreement and its risks for the Malaysian rubber economy, see Martin Rudner, "Development Policies and Patterns of Agrarian Dominance in the Malaysian Rubber Export Economy," *Modern Asian Studies* Vol. 15 (1981), esp. pp. 99-105, and "Changing Planning Perspectives on Agricultural Development in Malaysia," *Modern Asian Studies* Vol. 17 (1983). For a more sanguine view of the prospects, see Richard Stubbs, "Malaysia's Rubber Smallholding Industry: Crisis and the Search for Stability," *Pacific Affairs* (1983). On Malaysia's historical experience with international rubber agreements, see J. H. Drabble, *Rubber in Malaya, 1876 - 1922: The Genesis of the Industry* (Kuala Lumpur, 1973); P. T. Bauer, *The Rubber Industry: A Study in Competition and Monopoly* (London, 1948); Colin Barlow, *Natural Rubber Industry.* See also J. H. Thoburn, *Primary Commodity Exports and Economic Development: Theory, Evidence, and a Study of Malaysia* (London, 1977).

CHAPTER II

COLONIAL EDUCATION POLICY AND MANPOWER UNDERDEVELOPMENT IN BRITISH MALAYA

The introduction of modern education in British Malaya followed as a by-product of colonial rule. Colonial administration carried in its wake considerable European investment in trade and primary industry along with a substantial influx of Chinese and Indian immigrants to the new towns, tin mines and rubber estates. If the indigenous Malay agricultural community lay largely outside these economic developments, they were at least due special political treatment by virtue of the principles of protectorate and indirect colonial rule upon which the British rationalized their presence in Malaya. Thus, even more than other instruments of colonial policy, education was obliged to give expression to Britain's differential commitments to the Malays on one hand, and to alien Chinese and Indians on the other, while at the same time ensuring an adequate supply of educated manpower for government service and the commercial economy. The education systems that emerged during the colonial period reflected this divergence of goals between differential communal commitments and manpower training, where ethnic pluralism was very largely coterminous with the dualistic pattern of economic development.

Before the coming of the Europeans, Malay education centred on village schools operating at low levels of institutionalization.[1] No significant centre of Islamic theology, or schools of thought, arose in peninsular Malaya. At the same time, alien communities resident in Malaya operated their own educational establishments in their native languages. Schools set up by Chinese and Indian traders, whose settlement in Malaya dated from the 18th century and earlier, were run essentially as Malayan adjuncts of their respective

Development Studies and Colonial Policy, eds. Barbara Ingham and Colin Simmons (London: Frank Cass & Co. Ltd., 1987).

homelands' education systems. When the Portuguese conquered Malacca in 1511, a school was opened for local Eurasians under Roman Catholic auspices. By the turn of the 19th century, the Malayan education system had already been crystallized along lines linking ethnicity to language, culture and religion, with each group's schools enjoying autonomy in management and curriculum.

Early Colonial Education Institution-Building

English education began in Penang in 1816 as a result of efforts by the Church of England and with financial support from the East India Company, then responsible for administering British outposts in Malaya. In 1823 Sir Stamford Raffles, founder and administrative architect of Singapore, endowed on behalf of the East India Company the establishment of an English school for all races in the new settlement of Singapore—some 23 years before annual education grants were offered in England.[2] While English schools operated with official sponsorship and finance in the British-ruled Straits Settlements of Penang, Malacca and Singapore, Chinese and other vernacular schools were left to themselves. From the very beginnings of British rule in the Straits Settlements, the structure of education was therefore divided according to linguistic and communal streams having separate organization, financial provision and orientation. The pattern for the next 150 years of education institution-building was thus set.

Despite Raffles' parting injunction that "education must keep pace with commerce in order that its benefits may be assured and its evils avoided," subsequent progress in educational development in 19th century Singapore proved almost painfully slow. Neither the colonial administration nor the newly established mercantile communities were prepared to underwrite the expansion of schooling. Following the extension of British rule through the Malay peninsula, Christian missionary societies spread from the Straits Settlements to open English-language schools in the main towns of the Malay States.[3] Faced with a rapidly expanding demand for English-educated clerks and subordinate staff for both government service and business, local administrations also set up a small number of government-financed English schools in the Malay States of Perak and Selangor during the 1880s and 1890s.

Meanwhile, traditional Malay education underwent a radical structural and secularizing transformation under the impact of "indirect" colonial rule.[4] Many village Malays viewed with suspicion sponsored secular-oriented vernacular schools. The emergent

Westernized elite, on the other hand, expressed a preference for more extensive instruction in English and "European" subjects (e.g., mathematics) among the Malays. The colonial authorities, for their part, conceded that there existed a considerable appetite for education among the Malays, but characteristically declined to divert additional public funds from investment in economic infrastructure to the social services.[5]

Chinese- and Indian-language schools in Malaya developed according to the private capacities of their respective communities. In spite of the fact that Chinese constituted nearly half the non-European population of the Federated Malay States (FMS) at the turn of the 20th century, except in rare instances, state administrations declined all responsibility for vernacular education other than in Malay. The official attitude maintained that the Chinese and Tamils, as transients in Malaya, did not merit public finance for their own language schools. This line of argument was reinforced by a declared fear that vernacular education for non-Malays would strengthen racial barriers and inhibit social integration.[6] Denied government finance, the Chinese proceeded to build up their own vernacular primary and later school systems throughout Malaya, financed by voluntary contributions not all of which came from upper income groups. Some of these Chinese vernacular schools were organized and managed by individuals, some by groups, most charged fees and virtually all were China-oriented in curriculum.

The structure of education administration reflected this irregular pattern of institution-building. Even after federation each of the Malay States enjoyed near autonomy in the conduct of education policy. The education policies of the FMS treated schooling essentially as a matter of administration rather than as a programme of public instruction. This was by way of contrast with the Straits Settlements of Singapore, Malacca and Penang, where from 1901 a professional Director of Public Instruction effectively controlled the colony's education system. In 1906, the FMS and Straits Settlements Departments of Education were merged under a single professional Director of Education based in Singapore.

Since the greater part of Malay schooling was located in the Malay states, the vernacular system obtained few direct benefits from this administrative reorganization compared to the Straits Settlements-centred English Schools. Then in 1916, the continuing deterioration of standards in Malay vernacular schools impelled the government to appoint an Assistant Director of Education (Malay) with special responsibility for Malay schools in the FMS and Straits Settlements. With education administration as with much else, the Chinese were left to fend for themselves.

The Education of an Anglophone Elite

From 1903 the policy of the colonial administration was to "encourage," through government subsidies, private philanthropic organizations to undertake the provision of English schooling. Although this policy relieved the colonial governments of a considerable portion of the direct costs of education, and especially English schooling, the latter still received favourable financial treatment compared to other language streams. Thus, in 1937 the Straits Settlements government directed 71.4% of its education budget towards English schooling, notwithstanding the considerably greater enrolment in vernacular schools. Similarly, the FMS in that same year allocated 48.3% of its public expenditure on education to English schools alone. This distribution was typical of government spending for education in all the pre-war Malay States and Straits Settlements.

Judged by conventional criteria, the overall quality of English schooling was much superior to that of the other vernacular streams. Only the English stream offered opportunities for local post-secondary education at Raffles College and at the Straits Settlements and Federated Malay States Medical School (1905), later renamed the King Edward VII College of Medicine. A proposed merger of both these institutions into a university college with British affiliation, as a first step towards establishment of a Malayan university, was aborted by the Japanese conquest of Malaya in 1942. Yet, by virtue of curriculum, language of instruction and organizational linkages, access to higher and professional education in pre-war Malaya remained very largely limited to graduates of the English stream.

Though designed to create a Westernized, English-speaking cadre of government officers and clerks, English education was definitely not seen as an agency for broader social modernization. Indeed, on the contrary, British colonial administrators had early on warned against any general provision of English schooling. In the words of Frank Swettenham, then Resident of Perak, the most advanced Malay State:

> One danger to be guarded against is to teach English indis-
> criminately. . . I do not think it is at all advisable to attempt to give
> the children of an agricultural population an indifferent knowl-

edge of a language that to all but the very few would only unfit them for the duties of life and make them discontented with anything like manual labour.[7]

For the first four decades of the 20th century FMS education policy sought to strike a balance between the provision of sufficient English schooling to satisfy urban manpower and colonial administrative needs, while avoiding unwanted social changes among the local population. Though open to all ethnic groups, English education remained very restricted in the number of school facilities and enrolments.

Government ambivalence towards the provision of English education was especially pronounced with respect to the Malay community. English education among Malays remained a prerogative of scions of Rulers and chiefs, for whom special provision to learn English had been made, and for the few others able or willing to overcome imposing cultural-religious barriers to attend alien, infidel schools.[8] In order to avert possible "economic dislocation and social unrest," government policy deliberately limited the provision of English education for Malays, despite the colonial commitment to enhance Malay participation in administration.[9] Yet, English had become a virtual prerequisite for entry even into minor government service posts, thereby excluding the great majority of Malays.

Veiled criticism by the Rulers of the Malay States of the low level of Malay participation in administration led, in 1905, to the establishment of an English-language residential grammar school, based on the British model. The Malay College at Kuala Kangsar was originally conceived as a training school for Malay boys from any social class for public service, but shortly evolved into the educational preserve of Malay royalty and aristocracy—the "Malay Eton."[10] Enrolments at Malay College remained constant at about 150 boys of gentle birth, and generous financial provision was made to provide offspring of the traditional Malay ruling class with a proper preparation for entry into the higher-level cadres of the colonial bureaucracy.

The post-World War I trade recession led the colonial administration to try to economize on expatriate salaries by further extending the English education of the Malays. In 1924, the first two English schools were opened in non-urban Malay districts. This departure from past policy of concentrating English education in the towns encountered serious misgivings on the part of British education officials in Malaya, including R.O. Winstedt, then FMS Director of Education. The Malay aristocratic elite was similarly apprehensive lest English schooling in the rural areas undermine traditional values and disrupt the peasant social order.[11] Nevertheless, fiscal requirements dictated education policy, and further led to improvements in English-language instruction in Malay vernacular schools. These measures brought about a considerable increase in Malay enrolment in English schools and in their rate of participation in government service in the 1930s, though both remained predominantly non-Malay in ethnic composition.

If English education and its attendant employment opportunities still remained beyond the reach of most Malays, it did not touch the bulk of Malayan Chinese population. Although English school fees were not high—indeed these covered but a fraction of their total cost to government—they were well beyond the means of most poor Chinese. At the same time, many Chinese were antipathetic towards English schooling and its bureaucratic orientation, preferring instead their own Chinese traditions. English education appealed mainly to the locally born, urban, middle-class segment of the Chinese community, who tended to regard English schools as a means of obtaining colonial good graces as well as entry into government service and the professions. Of the 91,534 Chinese children enrolled in schools in British Malaya in 1938, only 27,064 attended English schools, a small proportion of their eligible school age group.[12]

Along with a minority of Malayan Chinese, English education also attracted the better-off segment of the other major non-Malay immigrant community, the Indians (and Ceylonese) who had been brought to British Malaya during the early expansionary period to meet the personnel requirements of government departments. Together with their Chinese counterparts these "middle class" Indians comprised the great majority of English school enrolment in British Malaya through the 1920s and 1930s.

The deliberately narrow provision of English-medium education for urban and upper-income groups limited its developmental impact upon Malayan society as a whole. Rather than functioning as an agency for social integration, modernization and development, English schooling served instead to create a privileged Westernized, English-speaking elite geared to administrative office-holding and the free professions. This anglophone product of the English-language education stream was set apart from the bulk of Malayan society, culturally divorced from the vernacular population and alienated from its social, economic and political environment.[13] It was this cultural gap between the elitist anglophone caste and the vernacular masses which contributed, as much as anything, to the social distance that characterized ethnic and class relations in pre-World War II British Malaya.

Malay Schooling for Rural Poverty

The development of the Malay-medium school system up to the outbreak of the Pacific War gave expression to the fundamental ambivalence of colonial policy towards the Malays. British administration was committed to promoting participation of the Malay ruling class in the colonial government, but was *pari passu* concerned to preserve intact the fabric of traditional Malay society. To reconcile the contradictory educational implications of these divergent goals, Malay education was divided between English and vernacular streams. The former served as an agency of elite socialization and recruitment, while the latter formed an instrument of agrarian social control and Malay cultural preservation.

Malay vernacular education was intended to contribute to moral and physical betterment, without distracting the Malay peasantry from their traditional agrarian preserve. Intellectual creativity was to be confined to traditional rural horizons:

> The aim of the Government is not to turn out a few well-educated youths, nor a number of less well-educated boys, rather it is to improve the bulk of the people, and *to make the son of the fisherman or peasant a more intelligent fisherman or peasant than his father had been, as a man whose education will enable him to understand how his lot in life fits in with the scheme of life around him.*[14]

Colonial policy towards Malay vernacular schooling was generally welcomed by British commercial interests as a device for teaching indigenes the "dignity of labour" while avoiding "trouble" through "over-education."[15]

The early expansion of Malay vernacular schooling was haphazard and slow. Vernacular school facilities were generally meager, the quality of instruction poor, the curriculum of little relevance to peasant needs. Many Malay parents were in any case unwilling to send their children, especially girls, to secular, albeit Malay-language schools sponsored by an alien colonial government. Efforts at educational reform introduced by R.J. Wilkinson, Federal Inspector of Schools (1903-06), led to a temporary invigoration of Malay schooling.[16] However, the subsequent period witnessed a general deterioration in Malay education, notwithstanding a continued growth in enrolments.

The crisis in Malay education prompted a reversion to a more explicitly conservative policy. The newly created post of Assistant Director of Education (Malaya) was assigned to R.O. Winstedt, who thereupon visited Java and the Philippines to examine the vernacular and "industrial" education provided by their respective "native schools." What he saw impressed Winstedt as to the prospects of excluding purely "academic" subjects from the vernacular curriculum and emphasizing instead such "practical" arts as basketmaking and horticulture. The stress was always on "the dignity of manual labour."[17]

The education reforms introduced at Winstedt's instance institutionalized the "rural bias" in Malay vernacular schooling. Whereas access to English education would continue to be limited to a select privileged few, the bulk of the Malay population were to be educated in rural-oriented Malay-language elementary schools. The number of years of elementary schooling was reduced, and renewed emphasis was placed on manual and agricultural subjects. Basket-making became virtually the symbol of the "new" Malay education policy.

Although the rural bias in Malay education presented an illusion of reform, in effect it deprived the rural Malays of the substance of educational progress. To be sure, Winstedt desired to reorient vernacular schooling away from the type that "merely produced boys who think they ought to be clerks but are insufficiently educated."[18] But his "rural bias" implicitly denied the very desirability of intellectual pursuits. The conservative thrust of Winstedt's reforms committed the Malay vernacular school system to the training of peasants for subsistence agriculture, and little else.[19] This benign custodial outlook in education tended to reinforce the prevailing colonial presumption that the Malay peasantry should be retained, and improved, in their traditional kampung environment and saved from the disruptions of modernization.

A major feature of this educational policy reform was the establishment of a proper teacher training college for the Malay vernacular stream. The Sultan Idris Training College (SITC) was opened in 1922. Like its aristocratic counterpart, the Malay College, SITC drew its students from throughout British Malaya, and subjected them to the unifying experience of an English mode of education. Yet, there were fundamental differences in enrolment and socialization patterns between the two. While the Malay College educated the scions of the Malay ruling class for careers in the English-speaking, urbane world of the civil service, SITC trained the sons of peasants, and fishermen to return to Malay-language village schools. The Malay College produced an Anglicized elite of administrators, SITC nurtured a distinctively Malay intelligentsia.[20]

The spread of Malay education under colonial auspices fomented a resurgence of the (non-governmental) religious school network. Then as now, Islam played a major role in the definition of Malay culture. At the turn of the century, Cairo-educated religious reformers, the "Young Faction," set up new-style *medrashas* as part of their quest to purify Islam and render it compatible with contemporary social developments.[21] Borrowing from Egypt and the West, the curricula of these *medrashas* attempted a synthesis of modern secular knowledge and the fundamental principles of Islam. Students were drawn to *medrashas* from both town and country, teachers came from intensely nationalist Java as well as from the Arab world, while numbers of graduates went on to Cairo for higher education. From the *medrashas* came forth a counter-Malay elite, whose intellectual affinities with Egypt and Java shared the current anti-colonialist, pan-Malay mood.[22]

Opinion among this nascent nationalist counter-elite was highly critical of the vernacular education offered Malays in government schools:

> We do not deny that education is necessary for freedom, but we do not believe that education which is given in countries under colonial rule can contain the seeds of freedom. The knowledge that is given to peoples under foreign influence has no purpose other than to impoverish their intellects and teach them to lick the soles of their masters' boots.[23]

While the *medrashas* enjoyed a rapid expansion up to 1913, the reformist views of the "Young Faction" encountered resistance from the Malay communal establishment. By way of reaction, the Malay establishment wielded its religious and communal authority in favour of government vernacular schools. The "rural bias" of Malay vernacular education came to reflect the shared vested interests of Malay aristocracy and colonial control.

By the late 1930s enrolments in Malay vernacular schools had expanded more than 15-fold over the 1900 figure and exceeded 100,000. Nevertheless, this represented fewer than a fifth of the eligible school-aged Malay population of British Malaya. So far as the mass of rural Malays was concerned, the educationally sound principle of instruction in the vernacular language became a negative and intellectually stultifying experience. In its way, colonial education policy may have reflected a genuine feeling of solicitude for Malays. But Malay language education did not acquire either a development goal or a "higher" cultural-maintenance goal, such as preserving an Oriental culture or even containing European influence. Rather, vernacular schooling for Malays aimed expressly at keeping the peasantry in their station, while teaching the disciplines of industry, punctuality and obedience to authority. This was a static, mundane, even anti-developmental conception of education. Indeed, the establishment and success of the elite Malay College constituted a confession of failure of the purely vernacular stream. In its social conception and economic utility, Malay vernacular schooling constituted an immobilizer of roles and entailed a veritable "education for poverty."[24]

Immigrant Education and Cultural Irridentism

The education of the Chinese and Indian populations of British Malaya, apart from those few having access to English schools, remained almost entirely outside the responsibility of colonial government policy. Several attempts were made by the colonial authorities during the 1920s and 1930s to modify Chinese and Indian schooling in terms more compatible with British Malaya. Official concern was directed at the content of the vernacular curricula, and especially their orientation towards overseas states and nationalisms. Yet, there was no question of accepting public responsibility, especially financial responsibility, for Chinese and Indian education.

Most privately and communally established Chinese schools originally followed a traditional pedagogical regime imported from Imperial China. The Chinese Revolution of 1911 found strong support among the Malayan Chinese, and it was not unnatural that the revolutionaries' zeal for educational reforms extended to their overseas compatriots.[25] With the beginnings of the National Language movement in China, *kuo yu* (Mandarin) came to be adopted as the language of instruction in most overseas Chinese vernacular schools as well. This facilitated adoption of a curriculum focusing exclusively on the culture, geography and history of China, frequently with a strong republican and nationalist bent. To British officials in Malaya, Chinese education sounded of subversion, pure and simple.[26] Moreover, the arrival of radical left-wing teachers and school managers from China brought many Chinese vernacular schools under Communist influence.

The Republican Government of China retained an abiding interest in Overseas Chinese education.[27] To forestall any loss of cultural identity among Chinese emigrants, the Chinese authorities endeavoured to integrate Overseas Chinese schooling into Nationalist Chinese education policy. Chinese government inspectors were dispatched to inspect Overseas Chinese schools, administrative procedures were laid down, textbooks prescribed, annual reports to Nanking requested and a regular system of grants-in-aid instituted. The overall effect was to institutionalize the China-orientation among Chinese vernacular schools in British Malaya, as elsewhere.

An increasingly radical and anti-Western Chinese nationalism, transmitted through vernacular schools, moved the colonial administration from indifference to concern over the education of Malayan Chinese. After taking office as Governor of the Straits Settlements and High Commissioner for Malaya in 1929, Sir Cecil Clementi set about "Malayanizing" the Chinese community and severing their allegiance to China. The Malayan Kuomintang (Chinese Nationalist Party) was banned (May 1930), and those Chinese leaders and others considered unassimilable, were deported.[28] At the same time the colonial authorities concluded that Chinese educational socialization patterns were at the core of the problem, so that the brunt of the Malayanization campaign was to be borne by an incipient schools policy.

A proposal was put forward for the abolition of Chinese vernacular schools and their replacement by so called "National Schools" which would be government financed and free to all communities, and in which the language of instruction would be Malay. No Chinese content whatsoever was to be provided in the curriculum. Most Chinese perceived this National School proposal as a direct threat to their cultural heritage and social status. Strenuous objections against forced assimilation to what most Chinese considered to be an inferior and economically retrogressive Malay language and (peasant) culture forced the government to abandon the proposal. An alternative suggestion for universal and free education in English was stillborn, only to be resurrected again in the 1950s.

In the absence of genuinely national norms for Malayan education, the emergent schools policy offered financial inducements in order to bring under control Chinese vernacular education. Chinese schools were given direct grants-in-aid per pupil enrolled from the 1920s, on condition that they accept government inspection and supervision. Most Chinese schools initially declined government aid and attendant control, preferring their independence. However, the Depression of the 1930s drove many schools to apply for government grants, so that by 1938 well over half those receiving a Chinese vernacular education in the FMS and Straits Settlements were enrolled in aided schools. Although motivated primarily by political rather than educational considerations, the limited provision of financial aid, coupled with inspection and supervision, denoted the beginnings of a positive government commitment towards the education of Malaya's Chinese.

Government aid to eligible Chinese schools pertained only to the FMS and Straits Settlements. None of the five Unfederated Malay States (UMS) accepted responsibility for Chinese-language education, even though Johore alone had over 10% of total Chinese school enrolment in 1938. School enrollments among Malayan Chinese reached approximately a third the eligible age group before the Second World War. Enrolments in Chinese schools in the FMS and Straits Settlements in 1938 (91,534) greatly exceeded the total enrolled in English Schools (26,974). The Chinese school network in British Malaya offered both primary and secondary level instruction, with access to higher education available back in China. Notwithstanding the colonial authorities' effort to Malayanize education through limited grants, the institutional orientation of Chinese education in effect insularized Chinese-educated manpower within the traditional occupational structure and cultural perspectives of the immigrant community.

Vernacular education for Indians in Malaya was rather less acutely political. FMS authorities looked favourably upon Tamil-language schooling as a means of promoting a needed immigration of Indians for Malaya's expanding plantation industry. A Labour Code enacted in the FMS in 1912 compelled rubber estates with 10 or more children of school age to provide and staff free vernacular schools for their Indian labour force. Government subsidies were available for this purpose. The comparatively few Indian schools located in towns obtained limited direct government grants. This arrangement assured the Indian population, most of whom lived on rubber estates, at least a rudimentary elementary education in their vernacular.[29] No facilities existed in British Malaya for post-primary schooling in Tamil or other Indian languages. Indian vernacular education remained intellectually deprived, with little potential for genuine manpower development. Rather, it served more as a palliative for the immigrant manual labour force.

Education and Development in British Malaya

Education in British Malaya evolved distinctive institutional forms, marked by the following characteristics:

1. The propensity of each community, Chinese, Indian and Malay, to have recourse to its own language schools. With few exceptions, there was little crossover between language streams. The only language stream attended by all communities were the English schools, so that inter-ethnic educational integration was effectively limited to an anglophone elite.

2. The tendency of each language stream to provide its own pattern of educational socialization according to its particular institutional outlook. English education was directed towards creation of a class of officials grounded in anglophone thought and values. By way of contrast, Malay vernacular schooling reflected colonial feelings of solicitude for Malays, but aimed at preserving their traditional peasant condition. Chinese schools, for their part, maintained a strong China-orientation, while Indian schools were expressly intended to make immigrant Tamil labourers feel "part of India." Divergent patterns of educational socialization, reflecting differential occupational and normative orientations, in effect reinforced the identification of ethnicity and language with economic role and social stratification.

3. The policy of encouraging the private running of schools made for a minimal level of curricular commonality and educational integration in British Malaya. Private schools constituted a major part of the school system in all language streams, except for the Malay. Public expenditure on education seldom exceeded 1.5% of total revenues, and government grants to schools were generally limited and haphazard. The virtual autonomy of private schools in British Malaya created powerful vested interests in the institutional status quo which militated against efforts at educational reforms.

4. The divided structure of authority over education in British Malaya made for regional as well as communal linguistic inequalities in the provision of school facilities. Administrative responsibility for education was fragmented among the governments of the Straits Settlements, the four Federated Malay States individually and in federation, and the five Unfederated Malay States. Public responsibility for and support of education varied in the different jurisdictions. The resulting unevenness of educational development engendered deficient standards of manpower development.

The character of education in British Malaya constituted a divisive factor, serving to reinforce existing communal and social barriers. Later colonial policy initiatives were to founder upon these discontinuities in education institutionalization.

Public expenditure on education reached 1.5% of total FMS revenues by 1902. This budgetary proportion was seldom exceeded up to the Second World War. This low fiscal priority for education, characteristic of colonial education policy, made for a correspondingly low level of educational development for British Malaya. Educational retardation was indicated by the relatively low rate of school enrolments before the war, less than a quarter the total eligible age group.[30] The result was a comparatively low rate of literacy among adult (age 15+) Malayans of all communities, only 41% for males and a mere 7% of females in 1931.[31] While the problem of illiteracy was doubtless compounded by immigration, this widespread underdevelopment of human resources and its segregation along ethnic-linguistic-occupational lines underscored the educational impoverishment of colonial Malaya.

The Japanese conquest of Malaya in 1942 signalled the beginning of the end of colonial dominion over education, as over other public institutions. British rule was no longer incontestable. In education, English and Chinese language schooling were terminated by the Japanese occupation, and Japanese substituted. Malays were given expanded opportunities in administration, reinforcing their nationalist aspirations.

The political turmoil following the post-war British return to Malaya had a further unsettling effect on the existing education system.[32] Malay resistance to British plans for a reconstructed Malayan Union, labour unrest culminating in a Communist-led insurgency ("The Emergency"), and the Communist revolution in China all had an impact on social expectations and demands on education policy on the one hand, and on governmental determination to utilize education policy as an instrument of social control on the other.

In 1949, leaders of the ethnic communities and the British administration accepted the notion that Malaya required an educational system which had an integrative, national focus, while being responsive to the country's ethnic and linguistic pluralism. The following year, the government commissioned an inquiry into Malay education, which went beyond its term of reference to make far-reaching recommendations on education policy generally.[33] These recommendations would have had the effect of reconstituting Malayan education around English and, in a limited way, Malay-language schooling, while disestablishing Chinese and Tamil. This served to plunge education into the vortex of ethnic politics in Malaya.

Whereas the recommended policy changes found favour in the colonial administration, they received little support from the Malays, who were concerned about the subordination of Malay-language schooling to English. The Chinese and Indians, however, were bitterly opposed. Indeed, the education question galvanized the Chinese to political action as never before. In response, the government invited a second inquiry into Malayan Chinese education. Its report recommended that education in Chinese be continued with public support, but that a new curriculum be designed to give Chinese-language schooling a Malayan orientation.[34] (No official inquiry was launched into Tamil education, though the Indian community proceeded to submit its own report and recommendations to the administration.) The result was an effort at compromise. The colonial government proposed to establish a "national" education system which would be publicly financed and offer plural language schooling around a common, integrative curriculum; however, English would remain the educationally dominant stream. This compromise solution pleased neither ethnic nor nationalist sentiments, and in the event fell victim to the budgetary stringencies resulting from the trade recession of 1954.

The building of a national education system in Malaysia had to await the election of the country's first government in 1955 and its transition to independence. That story has been told elsewhere, suffice to note here that the educational reforms introduced beginning in 1956 have contributed significantly to Malaysian economic and social development.[35] Yet, the education system inherited by the elected, independent government suffered from the legacy of structural deformity, diffuse scholastic standards, and chronic under-investment. Enrolment ratios which underwent a brief spurt immediately after the war regressed during the last years of colonial rule.[36] At the end of the colonial period Malaysia was still acutely under-educated in relation to the country's level of economic attainment. This lag in educational development was to leave its imprint on high-level manpower constraints, on social and ethnic inequality, and on regional disparities for some time afterwards.[37]

ENDNOTES

1. On the organization of education in pre-colonial Malay society, see R.O. Winstedt, *Malaya and its History* (London, 1956), pp. 130-1, and Chai Hon-Chan, *The Development of British Malaya, 1896-1909* (Kuala Lumpur, 1964), pp. 226-7.

2. This school underwent a long series of changes in organization and function until 1903, when it was made into a government sponsored secondary school, renamed Raffles College in 1928. According to Winstedt, the history of Raffles College was "an epitome of the stumbles and falls of education in Malaya": *Malaya and its History*, p. 132. See also E. Wijeysingha, *A History of the Raffles Institution, 1823-1963* (Singapore, 1963).

3. On early British contact with the Malay States and the transformation of British interest from non-intervention to protection, see Chai Hon-Chan, *Development of Education*, pp. 1-37; Willian R. Roff, *The Origins of Malay Nationalism* (New Haven, 1967), Chap. 1; K.G. Tregonning, *The British in Malaya* (Tucson, Arizona, 1965); F.A. Swettenham, *British Malaya, An Account of the Origin and Progress of British Influence in Malaya*, rev. ed. (London, 1948).

4. Rex Stevenson, *Cultivators and Administrators. British Educational Policy Towards the Malays 1875-1905* (Kuala Lumpur, 1975).

5. Cf. Sir Frank Swettenham, *Report on the Protected Malay States for 1892*, C. 7228, p. 26: "What we spend on education at present is too small a proportion of our revenue, but until the railways under construction are completed, I fear we cannot greatly increase the expenditure on other services."

6. *The System of Education in the Federated Malay States*, p. 11. Whatever the merit of this latter argument in principle, the failure of the colonial adminmistration to provide adequate English (or Malays) school facilities for all non-Malay children and its tolerance of privately financed non-Malay education places doubts on its validity. Note that in 1902 the Conference of Residents agreed to the provision of vernacular education in Tamil "with the object of making the FMS, from the point of view of the Indian immigrant, an outlying part of India" (Ibid., p. 11). Expedience, the need to encourage immigrant labour for the expanding plantation industries, triumphed over principle.

7. *Annual Report for Perak for 1890*, C.6576, p. 18.

8. Cf. High Commissioner, *Federal Council Proceedings* (Kuala Lumpur, 1920), p. 1365.

9. R.O. Winstedt, *Education in Malaya* (London, 1924). The phrase "economic dislocation and social unrest" was to become the conventional slogan in official publications for rationalizing the denial of English education to the Malay community-at-large.

10. As early as 1905 the Resident of Perak was able to note that "This school is exclusively for boys of gentle birth" (*Annual Report of Perak for 1905*, p. 12).

11. *Federal Council Proceedings* (Kuala Lumpur, 1924), p. B57.

12. According to the 1931 Census of Malaya, covering the FMS, UMS and Straits Settlements, there were some 417,000 Chinese in the age group 5-14 years; see T.E. Smith, *Population Growth in Malaya* (London, 1952), pp. 12-13. Tables VIII, X.

13. For a discussion of the attitudes towards education of English-speaking elites in colonial and post-colonial societies, and their general resistance to the expansion of English educational opportunities, see D. Adams & R.M. Bjork, *Education in Developing Areas* (New York, 1969), pp. 94-7.

14. *Annual Report on the Federated Malay States for 1920*, p. 13. Emphasis added.

15. *Federal Council Proceedings* (Kuala Lumpur, 1915), p. B67.

16. For a study of Wilkinson's attitudes towards Malay schooling and his resultant educational reforms, see Roff, *Origins of Malay Nationalism*, pp. 130-5.

17. *Report by Mr. R.O. Winstedt, Assistant Director of Education, Straits Settlements and FMS, on Vernacular and Industrial Education in the Netherlands East Indies and the Philippines, Straits Settlements Legislative Council Proceedings, Council Paper No. 22 of 1917* (Henceforth: *Winstedt Report on Vernacular Education*), pp. C96-118.

18. Ibid., p. C118.

19. Winstedt's policies have been subject to considerable debate. For a favourable view of the "new world of vision...opened to the Malay," viz. gardening and basket-making, see, e.g., J.S. Nagle, *Education Needs of the Straits Settlement and Federated Malay States* (Baltimore, 1943), p. 142, while Roff, *Origins of Malay Nationalism*, pp. 139-41 provides a detailed critique of Winstedt's "rural bias." Winstedt's antipathy to Malay intellectual development did not prevent him from building a personal reputation as a scholar of Malay literature and history.

20. For a detailed study of Malay schooling and elite creation see Roff, *Origins of Malay Nationalism*, chap. 5, esp. pp. 142-3.

21. On the "Young Faction," or *Kaum Muda*, and their rivalry with the established religious theoarchy, the *Kaum Tua*, see William R. Roff, "Kaum Muda—Kaum Tua: Innovation and Reaction Amongst the Malays," in K.G. Tregonning, ed., *Papers on Malayan History* (Singapore, 1962), pp. 162-5; Gordon P. Means, "The Role of Islam in the Political Development of Malaysia," *Comparative Politics* (1969), 273-4.

22. On the role of the *medrashas* in the formation of an anti-colonialist, Pan-Malay elite, see Roff, *The Origins of Malay Nationalism*, p. 66.

23. Tengku Abdullah Ahmad, "Apa Kah Faedah Merdeka," (What is the Advantage of Freedom?) *Serual Azhar* (October, 1924), pp. 492-3, cited in Roff, *The Origins of Malay Nationalism*, pp. 89-90.

24. Cf. Gunnar Myrdal, *Asian Drama* (London, 1963), pp. 1737-41.

25. On Malayan Chinese and the 1911 Revolution see L.E. Williams, *Overseas Chinese Nationalism. The Genesis of the Pan-Chinese Movement in Indonesia 1900-1915* (Glencoe, Illinois, 1960), p. 171; Png Poh Seng, "The Kuomintang in Malaya, 1912-1941," *Journal of Southeast Asian History* (1961), 6-9.

26. Victor Purcell, *The Chinese in South-east Asia* (London, 1965), p. 280.

27. Shortly after re-establishing a united China in 1928, the Kuomintang regime convened a National Education Conference. This indicated a departure from the past practice of Chinese governments which ignored the education of Overseas Chinese. Instead it took upon itself the task of ensuring that all Chinese everywhere obtain a national education. The conferences resolved that Sun Yat-sen's Three Principles be made the philosophical underpinnings of Overseas Chinese education. Cf. Ch'en Ta, *Immigrant Communities in South China* (New York, 1940), pp. 157-60; Yoji Akashi, "The Nanyang Chinese Anti-Japanese and Boycott Movement,

1908-1928," *International Conference on Asian History* (Kuala Lumpur, 1968), Paper No. 4, p. 25.

28. Over a half million Chinese labourers were repatriated during the early 1930s, ostensibly because of the lack of employment resulting from the Depression. However, demands by Chinese that the unemployed be allowed to settle in Malaya's abundant virgin land and plant rice, thus using their agricultural talents and saving on the country's import bill, went unheeded. Vide. Robert Elegant, *The Dragon's Seed: Peking and the Overseas Chinese* (New York, 1959), pp. 59-61.

29. On Indian education in British Malaya see J.N. Parmer, *Colonial Labour Policy and Administration* (New York, 1960), pp. 124-5.

30. International Bank for Reconstruction and Development, *The Economic Development of Malaya* (Baltimore, 1955), p. 440 (henceforth: *IBRD Report*); and Smith, *Population Growth*, pp. 12-13.

31. UNESCO, *World Illiteracy at Mid-Century*, Monographs on Fundamental Education, Vol. 9 (Paris, 1957), p. 63.

32. On post-war turmoil in Malaya see Martin Rudner, "Financial Policies in Post-War Malaya: The Fiscal and Monetary Measures of Liberation and Reconstruction," *The Journal of Imperial and Commonwealth History* (1975) and "The Political Structure of the Malayan Union," *Journal of the Malaysian Branch, Royal Asiatic Society* (1970); James de V. Allen, *The Malayan Union* (New Haven, 1967); Michael R. Stenson, *Repression and Revolt: The Origins of the 1948 Communist Insurrection in Malaya and Singapore* (Athens, Ohio, 1969); Anthony Short, *The Communist Insurrection in Malaya, 1948-1960* (New York, 1975).

33. Federation of Malaya, *Report of the Committee on Malay Education* (Kuala Lumpur, 1951), known as the Barnes Report, after the chairman of the Committee, L.J. Barnes of the University of Oxford.

34. Federation of Malaya, *Chinese Schools and the Education of Chinese Malayans: the Report of a Mission invited by the Federation Government to Study the Problem of the Chinese in Malaya* (Kuala Lumpur, 1951), known as the Fenn-Wu Report after its co-chairmen, Dr. William P. Fenn of the United States and Dr. Wu Teh-yao, a United Nations official.

35. On the development of education in independent Malaysia, see Chai Hon-Chan, *Education and Nation-building in Plural Societies: the West Malaysian Experience* (Canberra, 1977); R.O. Tilman, "Education and Political Development in Malaysia," *Yale University South-east Asian Studies*, Reprint Series No. 27; Francis Wong & Ee Yiang Hong, *Education in Malaysia* (Hong Kong, 1971); Martin Rudner, "The Economic, Social and Political Dimensions of Malaysian Education Policy," in Kenneth Orr, ed., *Appetite for Education in Contemporary Asia* (Canberra, 1977).

36. The enrolment ratio, that proportion of the eligible age group actually enrolled in schools, was estimated to have reached a peak of 63% for the colonial period in 1951 (vide. Member for Education, *Federation of Malaya, Legislative Council Proceedings*, 19 Sept. 1951), and subsequently declined steadily to only about 58% by 1954 (*IBRD Report*).

37. Charles Hirschman, "Educational Patterns in Colonial Malaya," *Comparative Education Review* (1972) calls attention to the long run effects of colonial education policies on ethnic imbalances, social inequality and regional disparities in independent Malaya. On independent Malaysian education policy and development strategies see Martin Rudner, "Education, Development and Change in Malaysia," *South East Asian Studies* (1977).

CHAPTER 12

EDUCATION, DEVELOPMENT AND CHANGE IN MALAYSIA[1]

The creation of a modern, national, integrated institution of education in Malaysia was a post-colonial undertaking. The conception of education in British Malaya had been narrowly confining, both socially and scholastically. Indeed, through to the end of the colonial period, education was segregated into separate and disjointed linguistic-ethnic streams: English, Malay, Chinese and Tamil, with impoverishment of resources their common lot.[2] Following the Second World War there had occurred a dramatic rise in enrolments; however, ongoing organizational discontinuities and constraints resulted in a downward trend in enrolment ratios during the last years of colonial rule.[3] The advent of representative government in 1955, and independence in 1957, marked a point of departure for the modernization of educational institutions and policies. Over the period of independence, education has been systematically assimilated, by stages, with government's emerging goals of national development.

The study of the performance of education systems presents certain methodological difficulties. It is often convenient to portray educational trends by devising input-output tabulations for particular denominators, or variables, e.g., enrolments, expenditures, etc. However, a degree of caution must be exercised in their interpretation, lest logical fallacies intrude through the application of "closed" systems analysis to essentially "open" institutions like education. Education cannot be logically isolated from the context of society, from external normative and social influences.[4] This chapter will, therefore, treat the development of the Malaysian education institution as a system, in relationship with the multiplexity of attitudinal, his-

South East Asian Studies, Vol. 15, No. 1 (June, 1977).

torical and cultural factors affecting the country's economic, political and social life.

The Evolution of a National Education Institution

Among the priority issues tackled by the inter-communal Alliance Party government following its victory by an overwhelming majority in the country's first general election (1955), was the reform of education policy. Shortly after assuming office, the government appointed a special parliamentary committee under the then Minister of Education, Dato (later Tun) Abdul Razak, to consider the reconstitution of Malaya's fragmented colonial educational system along more integrated, national lines. The mandate for the Razak Committee charged is with:

> Establishing a national system of education acceptable to the people of the Federation as a whole which will satisfy their needs and promote their cultural, social, economic and political development as a nation, having regard to the intention of making Malay the national language of the country whilst preserving and sustaining the growth of the language and culture of other communities.[5]

The criterion of acceptability enabled the Razak Committee to combine diverse ethnic and modernizing values into a formula for education institution-building. The ensuing legislation of 1957 set the process in motion. The new policy crystallized in an education institution linguistically plural in form, integrally national in content, Malay in its symbolism and developmental in its purpose. Given the enthusiasm of independence, it appeared as if the Alliance formula had indeed succeeded in sublimating the primordial racial controversies of the recent colonial past.[6] But not for long.

The Alliance leadership presumed, with a simplistic utilitarian faith that was to become characteristic of their political style, that the benefits of dynamic growth would serve to overcome latent dissensions in society. Hence, the very rapid expansion of primary school enrolments seemed to demonstrate widespread acceptance of the linguistic and cultural elements of the 1957 reforms among the main ethnic blocs, Malay, Chinese and Indian (Tamil). However, the extent of the consensus achieved did not preclude further dispute over the attendant social, economic, and political functions of the new education policy, as it unfolded. During the 1960s, education was to become, in effect, a policy surrogate for issues of high strategy concerning the direction of national development. For Malaysia, the emergent education system acquired a special significance as an instrument for, and expression of, politically determined goals.

The initial thrust of the 1957 policy reforms focussed on the primary level of education, and particularly on the historically sensitive matters of language and curriculum. In reshaping the heterogeneity of the past, primary schooling was reconstituted into an educationally integrated whole having linguistically separate parts: so called "Standard schools" in which the main language of instruction was Malay, and "Standard-type" schools in which the medium was English, Chinese (*Kuo-Yü*) or Tamil. All Standard-type schools provided compulsory instruction in Malay, the constitutionally-ordained National Language; similarly, English was a compulsory subject in all schools.[7]

Thus the Razak policy distinguished between linguistic usage and language status, admitting pluralism in the media of primary instruction while conferring educational primacy onto English as the international language, and Malay as the National Language. Moreover, all Standard and Standard-type schools were to use a common curriculum and syllabus. Indeed, the notion of common educational content was the pivot around which the Razak policy turned. The uniformity of educational content comprised the institutional cement that bound linguistic pluralism to national norms of educational enculturation.

Standardization of the primary school curriculum was significant not just for enculturation, but also with respect to patterns of socialization in education. Historically, each of the language streams had its own instructional orientation and, through this, its particular social bias. The English medium followed the grammar school type; Chinese schooling was directed at recreating the literati of the classical tradition of China; Malay education was perceived early on in terms of a fossilized, agrarian, peasantry; while the Tamil school was geared to its constituency of an immigrant plantation and urban *lumpenproletariat*. Just as the English and Chinese schooling reflected their respective literary traditions in educational socialization, the Malay and Tamil curricula connoted education for social stabilization, at best, or economic impoverishment, at worst. Following the Second World War some initial but not very definite steps were taken to modernize the vernacular schools' curricula. This process was carried to fruition by the 1957 policy reform. In line with the new policy, the grammar school outlook of English-medium education was now extended to all Standard and Standard-type schools. Public education conceived as plural in form and national in content, became also literary-academic in orientation.

Secondary education received a somewhat more ambivalent treatment under the 1957 policy. The Razak Committee, for its part, had called for the institution of a new, assimilated "National-type" secondary school network having English as its medium of instruction. The purpose was to bring about the desired linguistic-cultural synthesis at higher rungs of independent Malaya's education system. Serving all communities, this assimilated secondary level would blend anglophone manner with communal accommodation, after the style of the contemporary alliance ruling elite. In order to encourage existing Chinese and English secondary schools to conform to the new model, the government for the first time offered full financial support for National-type secondary education. At the same time, privately maintained schools were permitted to continue operating and even qualified for partial grants-in-aid. By pursuing a dual policy of supporting both continuity and change in secondary schooling, conflict was avoided or postponed, though at the price of failure to give momentum to the new directions in post-primary institution-building.

Paradoxically, the successful implementation of the Razak Committee recommendations at the primary school level shifted the focal point of public controversy onto the more ambiguous secondary education policy. As numbers of pupils passing through the Standard and Chinese and Tamil-medium Standard-type schools increased during the late 1950's, the English language basis of National-type secondary education posed an increasingly frustrating bar to their advancement.[8] Although the issue appeared still to be linguistic, language in fact represented an education policy mechanism regulating pupil progression and, ultimately, access to social status and roles. Bitterness over education language obstacles to social mobility was sharply manifest in the relative success of the more communal-oriented Malay and non-Malay opposition parties in the 1959 general elections. The returned, but shaken, Alliance government felt impelled to take stock of its education policies, for which a review committee was set up under the new Minister of Education, Abdul Rahman Talib.

Whereas the initial Razak Committee formulations comprised, in essence, a formula for inter-communal accommodation, the policy review undertook an exercise in social and cultural engineering. Responding to perceived challenges from their communal flanks, the Alliance leadership came to treat post-primary education instrumentally as an antidote to the incubation of counter-elites. The Rahman Talib Committee accordingly confirmed the post-1957 pattern of primary schooling, and set about harnessing secondary level education to the imperative of elite formation in the Alliance image. However, since the Alliance had not yet formulated any coherent social doctrine of its own, the policy review fell back on ethno-linguistic differentiation, as between Malays and non-Malays, as the basis of post-primary educational reform.

The reversion to a dualistic approach to secondary education underscored the divergent enculturation and socialization goals pertaining to Malays and non-Malays. Malays were to be satisfied of the status of the National Language in education, and assured of their vernacular avenue to upward mobility. Their post-primary education could continue in Malay. As regards non-Malays, it was deemed necessary to extend English-language National-type education as a means of inculcating Chinese and Indians with attitudes and values considered suitable. For, English education was regarded as making non-Malays acceptable for co-option to the elite, in the oligarchic tradition of Anglo-Malay colonial condominium, perpetuated, in a cultural sense, in the anglophone Chinese-Malay independence partnership.

The separate acculturalization and socialization patterns introduced into secondary education bore the seeds of future conflict among the second generation elites of the different communities. Later in the 1960s, government reacted by shifting back to a unitary post-primary model, though the future basis of institutional assimilation would be the National Language exclusively (albeit gradually).

In the meantime, the conclusions of the policy review were given formal legislative sanction in the 1961 Education Act. Henceforward, all publicly financed secondary schooling had to be conducted in two official languages only, either Malay or English, though Chinese or Tamil could still be taught only as subjects. Malay secondary education was free, while government-aided English secondaries had to levy tuition fees. English and Malay also became the joint languages of public examination both for entry to, and graduation from, secondary education. To facilitate the linguistic transition on the part of pupils from Chinese and Tamil Standard-type primaries, a special one-year Remove Class was instituted prior to secondary level. Otherwise, those Chinese middle schools that had hitherto qualified for partial grants-in-aid were now obliged to transform themselves into English or Malay-medium

National secondaries, or else remain unassisted, private enterprises. The reaction of Sinophone Chinese to the 1961 enactment was predictably bitter, and many middle schools refused to comply until financial pressures compelled most to conform to the new policy standard. In doing so, all chose conversion to National-type schools, as a matter of course. While the Malay medium achieved formal parity for purposes of secondary education, it was not without irony that the new policy thus served the expansion of English-language secondary education, when even tended to attract pupils from the Malay stream.

At this stage there was no suggestion that the grammar school tradition of Malayan education be altered. As during colonial times, the quality of secondary schooling was still strongly identified with literary-style academic education. Popularization and functional differentiation of a post-primary education were characteristically impugned and dismissed for allegedly devaluing scholastic standards. It was in this light that the policy review fixed an arbitrary ceiling on the pass rate from primary to secondary level at 30%, based on past colonial practice. This then became the criterion for educational planning in the Second Five-Year Plan (1961-65).[9] For the overflow, quasi-vocational educational alternatives were set up, in distinct subordination to the grammar-style mainstream, and limited in scope and intent.[10] The prevailing obsession with grammar school education not only circumscribed the development of post-primary institutions, but, even more significantly, also restricted the capacity to cope with functional specialization. Officialdom preferred to blame public prejudice for the unpopularity of technical and vocational schooling, though responsibility can be traced directly to the grammar school cult fostered and supported by the education authorities themselves.

The third stage of education institution-building evolved out of economic considerations, which induced a further reform of secondary-level education towards a greater consonance with development strategy and planning. The expansion and extension of the old grammarian format led, by the middle 1960s, to an education policy gap between large and growing numbers of primary school leavers, and emerging as semi-educated unemployed, concurrent with a shortage of middle and higher calibre professional, technical and vocational skills. Educational shortcomings had become a limiting factor in economic development. Concern over the country's lagging economic performance prompted the Alliance government, following the 1964 general election, to inject manpower planning considerations into the education policy component of the First Malaysia Plan, 1966-70. In the event, this manpower planning concept denoted the primacy of development goals even over entrenched educational values, and paved the way for far-reaching changes in the internal organization and orientation of secondary education.

The reforms introduced with effect from 1965 divided secondary schooling into two stages, separated by selection and differing in curriculum. At the lower secondary stage, admission was non-selective, open, and the three-year programme offered a so called "comprehensive" curriculum combining academic, technical and crafts subjects. Post-primary selection was thus deferred, and the dead-end "secondary continuation" and "rural trade" categories abolished. Upper secondary schooling still remained selective, but was now separated educationally and organizationally into parallel academic technical, vocational and teacher training streams.

Agricultural subjects were incorporated in the "comprehensive" curriculum and, after 1969, agricultural science was offered as an Upper Secondary (both academic and vocational) alternative. A pre-university "Sixth Form" was similarly divided into arts, science and technical streams. This institutional realignment of Malaysian education connoted a new policy conception in moving towards the rationalization of levels and types of post-primary schooling in relation to the manpower requirements of the economy.

Although the immediate introduction of open-admission, comprehensive education resulted in an acknowledged fall in standards, especially in the academically weaker Malay-medium stream, this was now accepted, in the manner of "positive thinking," as the unavoidable short-run of social adaptation for eventual economic development.

The tertiary level of education was to experience at this stage a similar process of institutional reform and innovation. The country's first institution of higher learning, the University of Malaya (founded in Singapore, 1949, Kuala Lumpur Division, 1957; separation and autonomous university status, 1961), was conceived as an English academy for the scholastic elite, which defined its social composition and educational purpose. Pressures of events (the combination of language politics, educational reforms and social trends during the 1960s) brought about the official adoption of English-Malay bilingualism at the University of Malaya by mid-decade, followed by the establishment of the Malay-language Universiti

Kebangsaan Malaysia (National University of Malaysia) in 1970. Along with the termination of the English social and linguistic monopoly came a broadening of the scope and structure of higher education. Within the conventional universities of the English model, the sciences and technocratic professions were given increasing prominence, a trend reflected in the new foundation set up in Penang in 1969, subsequently renamed Universiti Sains Malaysia (Malaysian University of Science). The early 1970s also witnessed the establishment of new types of functionally specialized tertiary institutions geared to high-level manpower requirements of particular communities in their quest for economic development. These included the university-status Universiti Teknologi Malaysia (Malaysian Technological University) and Universiti Pertanian (University of Agriculture) operating in Malay; and the MARA Institute of Technology and Ungku Omar Polytechnic offering professional and sub-professional courses in technical and administrative subjects, in Malay and English, respectively. Additionally for non-Malays, English-medium pre-university and sub-professional studies were also available at the Tunku Abdul Rahman College. Malaysian education still retained a scholastic bias, to be sure, evidenced in the schools' preoccupation with preparing candidates for university, rather than intermediate employment opportunities. Yet, the emergence of an academically and functionally differentiated tertiary structure underlined the policy trend towards aligning education institution-building more closely with manpower planning for economic development.

The next stage of educational reform witnessed a revival of the language question, this time as part of the political search for symbols of national identity. As the constitutionally prescribed 10-year term for reviewing its National Language provisions approached in 1967, the communal controversy over future language rights surfaced with renewed passion and extended, by implication, to education as well. Language politics revolved around the increasingly forceful efforts of the newly emergent, modern, Malay-educated elite, with certain factional backing from the United Malays National Organization (UMNO), senior partner of the Alliance. Together, these ultra-nationalist components of Malay political life endeavored to consolidate the National Language status of Malay and therefore ensure its social rewards. An artful Alliance compromise had the National Language Act, 1967, proclaim Malay the "sole official language" while reserving the use of other language for education and certain other public purposes. The long-standing inter-communal *modus vivendi* was preserved more or less intact, but the ultra-nationalist core of Malay demands remained unsatisfied.

Malay ultra-nationalism now turned against the rival and non-domiciled English-language education stream. Partly to mollify the fervor among Malays, and partly as a gesture towards the National Language objective of the Act, the Education Ministry decreed the juxtaposition of Malay language teaching upon four minor subjects in the first three grades of English-medium primary schools, with effect from 1968. Whereas the Malayanization of the English stream had originally been thought of as a quiet and gradual process, the pace of change was ultimately to be dictated by political events.

The challenge to Malay political primacy apparent in the 1969 general election results and culminating in racial violence,[11] propelled Malay nationalism towards a more strenuous reassertion of the Malay norms of statehood. As a result, the conversion of English schools to the Malay language was accelerated and progressed on the basis of a detailed timetable, subject by subject, year by year, scheduled for completion by 1983. Thereafter, English would no longer have the status of a mainstream language of public instruction. This would leave Malay as the only educational language ranging over the primary, secondary and tertiary levels. Standard-type schools in the Chinese or Tamil media were as yet unaffected by the conversion timetable. However, they would in any case be reduced to the status of peripheral, virtually terminal primary school languages when Malay became the exclusive medium of post-primary education.

That the target of linguistic Malayanization was English-language schooling—rather than Chinese or Tamil—pointed to the current political anxieties of the UMNO leadership, the dominant element in Malaysia's ruling Alliance. Earlier Malay suspicions about non-Malay loyalty gradually abated, a tribute to the efficacy of the Razak education policy. They were replaced by a new sense of political rivalry over national status questions. The cataclysmic events of 1969 indicated to Malays that the newly emergent, nationally educated, non-Malay elite had yet to be induced to accept the established political equation for allocating power. Thus, the conversion of the English stream was calculated to foster shared educational experiences in elite formation, while ensuring that this enculturation process was steeped in Malay linguistic and national symbols. The extension of Malay political norms through the education system to non-Malays conveyed a double sense of belonging: that non-Malays belong to Malaysia, while Malaysia belongs to the Malays.

It is noteworthy that these developments pertained mainly to the territories of peninsular Malaysia, the former Malaya, and only to a lesser degree to the eastern Malaysian States of Sabah and Sarawak. By constitutional agreement, the administration of education in Sabah and Sarawak has remained under state jurisdiction (though federally financed). Policies therefore have differed somewhat from those pursued by the federal government in peninsular Malaysia. Lately, however, there has been a marked trend towards conformity with the national system.

The building of a national education system in Malaysia had to treat the fundamental problems of language, culture, social change, economics, and politics, which confronted society. Yet, educational institution-building did not reflect haphazard or ad hoc arrangements. At each stage it constituted the outcome of considered policy. These policy solutions were designed to cope with the complexity of social issues involving education, in accordance with the multiple goals of government. Outside the administration, an active public interest exercised its influence as both a stimulus and constraint on policy, and it is significant that the stages of education institution-building were broadly coterminous with general elections. Education policy evolved from an object to an integral subject, or instrument, of national policy-making, producing radical changes in educational organization and orientations in the process.

The "Supply" of Education

Expenditures on education govern the quantum of educational resources placed at the disposal of society at any given time. Historically, education in British Malaya was subject to complex financial treatment, with private and state and central sources participating in its provision each according to its own lights. The shift from considerable private to predominantly public finance of education was matched by the increased predominance of the central authorities, even more than the constitution obligated. Adapting public finance to assume the cost of education institution-building involved the redefinition of certain conventional economic attitudes, budgetary principles, allocative priorities and administrative goals.

Changes in official attitudes and assumptions regarding the economic utility of education heralded the changes in actual policies concerning the public finance of education. In British Malaya education was commonly viewed as a positive thing, for its humanistic value as well as for its role in elite formation. Yet, this same attitude disclosed certain negative assumptions about the economics of education. Colonial officialdom tended to see education as a purely social service, something good and desirable but offering few direct economic returns.[12] Education finance was therefore treated as a consumption item in public accounts, which implicitly depleted the financial resources available for investment in economic growth.

It was symptomatic of the character of colonial rule that those groups allowed to participate in colonial administration generally shared this attitude towards education, especially the influential British business interests who regularly insisted that "non-productive" social spending be "cut according to the cloth" of residual finance. They were allied to a traditional Malay elite on the defensive against rural social change. Even those who pressed for the expansion of educational finance, mainly professionals, trade unionists and rural Malay spokesmen, did so on the basis of social service and social welfare criteria rather than in broader development terms, by implication validating the conventional assumptions. One notable exception was the newly ascendant UMNO leadership of Tunku Abdul Rahman, who from the unofficial side of the colonial Legislative Council very early advocated mass education as a lever for Malay economic, social and political advancement.[13] Nevertheless, for the dominant colonial power elite there remained the dichotomy between education as a social service, however worthy its social or cultural objectives, and the hard economics of public finance.

The transition to elected government did not result in a frontal assault on inherited economic doctrine. Rather, the new Alliance government's inclination towards identifying education instrumentally with its emergent national goals served, in effect, to infiltrate an altered conception of education into public finance. With the introduction of the 1957 national school policy, public expenditure on education now came to be redefined as "investment" in the country's political "future."[14] Still, conventional economic philosophy had not yet conceived of education as being functionally related to economic, as distinct from social or political, development objectives. This was to come later, after it became increasingly apparent during the early 1960s that inadequate human resources constituted a limiting factor for economic planning. The government's development imperative thereupon absorbed education policy and turned it towards economic ends: "The traditional system of education is (now) being reoriented to achieve not only the objectives of nation-building and universal literacy, but also the economic goals of the country."[15] This marked a revision of the policy conception of education, from a mere social (or political) service to a manpower approach centred on human capital formation for economic development.[16]

The re-evaluation of educational finance, from budgetary liability to economic resource, signified a cognitive change in the precepts of public accounting, as well. Public financial perspectives shifted over from narrow revenue accounting to broader national and later social accounting.[17] While it may be tempting to explain this movement on the basis of improved government financial capabilities over time, actually the essence of the change was more in fiscal priorities. Thus, during the late colonial period restrictions were applied to expenditures on education at the same time as substantial reserve balances were being accumulated in London. By contrast, the development plans of the 1960s called for greatly expanded public expenditures on education, even at the expense of running down reserves, and borrowing. It has not been so much government's ability to afford education, as its willingness, prompted by decisions in the political sphere and articulated through changes in attitudes, that determined the provision of educational finance.

The First Five-Year Plan (FYP), introduced in 1956 by the newly-elected Alliance government, provided for a considerable expansion of public spending on the capital projects of government departments and authorities over the quinquennium.[18] Highest plan priority was assigned to projects related to the export and nascent industrial sectors, while implementation of the new national school policy received second priority. Yet, Education Ministry proposals for some M$128 million in capital investment were nevertheless pruned by the Treasury's Economic Secretariat, under the direction of expatriate colonial financial officials, to less than half that amount. But even that constituted a threefold increase, in real terms, over public capital expenditure on education during the previous five-year period. Subsequent plans were to greatly increase the magnitude and scope of public investment, while successive changes in the priorities and machinery of planning influenced education's share.[19]

The much enlarged sums involved in the Second FYP, 1961-65, were similarly devoted mainly to the development of the state apparatus, especially those parts dealing with "economic" or "productive" undertakings. The education target was addressed to the objects of the then-current policy review. Educational objectives were expressed rather simplistically in terms of crude enrolment and demographic relationships. Overall planning perspectives remained fundamentally unaltered, although this Second FYP hint at social accounting contained the germ of a new ingredient for education planning.

The next plan, termed the First Malaysia Plan (FMP), 1966-70, emphasized the mobilization of investable resources for accelerated economic growth, and in so doing treated education as a factor for human capital formation. Later, social and economic criteria for education planning were brought together and refined in the Second Malaysia Plan (SMP) of 1971-75, with reference to its radical goal of "restructuring" society along more "balanced" lines of economic attainment between Malays and non-Malays.

The Third Malaysia Plan (TMP), 1976-80, aimed at a strategy of overcoming poverty among all "races" (in the official terminology).[20] Objectives of employment, social mobility and economic nationalism thus rendered education into an integral component of planning for development of the economy.

This evolving planning role for education had a zigzag effect on the ratio of educational investment under the plans. Capital appropriations for education increased absolutely over the successive quinquennia, to be sure. The relative proportion of total public investment devoted to education grew in the earlier, departmentalised Plans, from 8% of the First FYP to 12% of the Second FYP. There followed a decline, paradoxically, under the broader, macroeconomic Malaysia Plans (peninsular Malaysia figures in brackets) to 11.6 (10.3)% in the FMP, and again to 7.4 (63.)% in the SMP, rising with the higher priority for social development to 9.4% of the midterm revision of the SMP and stabilizing at 9.1 (8.4)% of the TMP.[21] The closer integration of education into macro-economic planning was more than merely a gesture in the direction of popular social services. Indeed, the more integrated approach to educational planning led also to increased public investment "downstream" from the education system, in employment-related industrial developments.

In the event, developmental priorities were allocated somewhat differently by actual patterns of public finance, compared to the original plans. Malaysian planning experience discloses regular and significant divergence in the sectoral distribution of public investment between original plans and their implementation. On the whole, economic and administration-security planning targets were achieved, and usually over-fulfilled, while social sector objectives remained chronically under-fulfilled.

Education shared the social sector shortfall, though the degree of plan under-fulfillment depended on the place of education in the current development strategy as well as government motives and commitment. The First FYP achieved only 62% of its education expenditure target, slightly less than the social sector average, displaying the discontinuities between education planning and public finance. Subsequently, development strategy become more consistent in the Second FYP, so that its education target was 91% fulfilled, a level unprecedented for the social sector. Afterward, the shift in emphasis from fiscal outlays to structural reforms in the FMP saw the rate of plan fulfillment drop to 70%, far inferior to the 77% social sector average (all-Malaysia figures; rates for peninsular Malaysia were 77.9 and 80.8%, respectively). Education plan fulfillment rose again under the renewed urgency of the SMP to 88% of the revised mid-term target, compared to 94% for the social services generally and 95% for public investment overall.[22]

The ratio of (public) investment in education to total public investment under the plans experienced a similarly chequered trend. Between the First and Second Five-Year Plans the ratio increased from 6 to 9% as the policy focus shifted from the primary to the secondary level, and commitments entered high gear over the Rahman Talib policy review. The ratio reduced to 7.7% (peninsular Malaysia: 7.9%) of the FMP, but climbed again to 8.7% (9.5%) in response to the ethnic restructuring goals of the revised SMP.

Objective difficulties exacerbated the effects of policy and administrative ambivalence. Arguably, a good part of the persistent shortfall in public investment in education represented scarcities of suitable resources, pedagogical and other, especially at the more specialized secondary and technical levels and in East Malaysia. The accelerated expansion of education in recent years telescoped the normal gestation period for resource creation, inevitably causing bottlenecks for further expansion and refinement.[23] These scarcities retarded educational investment even when funds were available, though misallocations of actual investment (e.g., the lags

TABLE 1
Malaysian Development Plan Targets 1956-75 (M$ million).

	First FYP		Second FYP		First Malaysia Plan			
					Est.			
	Plan (1)	Actual (2)	Plan (3)	Actual (4)	Plan* (5)	Actual* (6)	Plan (7)	Actual (8)
Total Public Investment	1,148.6	1,007.0	2,150.0	2,651.7	3,153.6	3,610.2	4,556.9	4,242.9
Economic Sector	780.4	760.2	1,477.9	1,763.7	2,228.7	2,210.8	2,710.2	2,685.4
Social Sector	277.9	138.9	491.0	413.6	797.4	644.7	975.3	752.1
• of which Education	95.4	60.9	260.0	236.0	368.0	286.9	470.8	329.4
General Administration & Security	90.4	108.0	181.1	474.4	687.5	754.7	865.4	804.9

	Second Malaysia Plan				Third Malaysia Plan	
	Plan* (9)	Actual* (10)	Plan (11)	Actual (12)	Peninsular (13)	Malaysia (14)
Total Public Investment	5,868.2	8,075.8	7,250.0	10,255.4	15,445.7	18,554.9
Economic Sector	3,898.7	5,771.9	4,870.9	7349.7	10,475.5	12,665.1
Social Sector	836.0	1,132.6	1,067.4	1,431.0	2,511.3	3,092.1
• of which Education	370.1	765.6	337.0	963.8	1,296.9	1,691.3
General Administration & Security	1,131.3	1,171.3	1,311.7	1,474.7	2,458.8	2,797.6

* Peninsular Malaysia-Malaya only.
Sources: *Report on Economic Planning in the Federation of Malaya in 1956*; First Malaysia Plan; *Second Malaysia Plan*; *Treasury Report, 1975-76*; *Third Malaysia Plan*.

in teacher training) compounded the inadequacy of the educational resources base over the long run.

The allocation of public investment within the education system, among the different levels and types of schooling, spelled out the goals and perspectives attached to government's "supply" of education. A detailed breakdown of expenditures for the earlier period of planning is not available. However it may be inferred that the First FYP invested comparatively heavily in the expansion of primary education in order to realize the policy objectives propounded by the Razak Committee. This was eased under the Second FYP, by which time the policy review had redirected the emphasis towards National-type secondary education. Subsequently, the integral manpower approach adopted in the FMP brought about a further reallocation of internal investment priorities in education (Table 2).

Post-primary education now absorbed over three-quarters of actual public investment in education over the 1966-70 quinquennium, with the bulk going to the secondary (51.9%) and university (12.6%) levels. Even so, the secondary school investment target remained under-fulfilled almost by half, while for the much vaunted technical type (secondary) schools the investment shortfall amounted to nearly 65%. Teacher training suffered an even more severe investment lag, ironically in view of the pronounced shortage of qualified teaching staff for the schools. By comparison the universities did relatively well in Malaysia, as elsewhere, having attained over 80% fulfillment by way of attracting a disproportionate—in terms of enrolments, at least—share of realized public investment.

This distribution of education investment continued in the SMP. Despite the nominal over-fulfillment of the secondary school target, its actual allocation of real investment resources, discounted for inflation, had scarcely been augmented over the quinquennium. The actual distribution of education investment superimposed, in effect, its own pattern of institution-building onto the original policy scheme.

TABLE 2
Internal Distribution of Development Expenditure
by Level of Education, Peninsular Malaysia, 1966-1975.

	First Malaysia Plan			Second Malaysia Plan		
	Plan (1)	Est. Actual (2)	% Fulfill-ment (3)	Revised Plan (4)	Est. Actual (5)	% Fulfill-ment (6)
Primary school	54.6	48.5	88.8	87.4	80.2	91.8
Secondary school	188.7	100.7	53.4	133.2	138.0	103.6
Technical school	30.8	10.8	35.1	34.0	25.7	75.6
University	30.0	24.4	81.3	235.4	198.5	84.3
Teacher training	28.5	9.7	34.0	9.0	3.6	40.0
Higher Technical	—	—	—	7.7	6.6	85.7

Notes: Figures do not total the agregate given in Table 1, due to the omission of training and other programmes financed under the 'Education and Training' item in the plan.
Sources: *Second Malaysia Plan*; *Third Malaysia Plan*.

The ensuing balance of investment in education represented an effective demotion of the priority of secondary schooling, and teacher training most of all, in favour of enhanced tertiary level development. Although the disparity between plan and realization for secondary schooling was corrected in the SMP, the distributive balance remained much the same. Development emphasis on the elitist tertiary level discriminated against populist progression in secondary schooling, and (because of laggard investment in teacher training) tended to sacrifice the calibre of primary education. Yet, this operational redefinition of investment priorities seems to have occurred haphazardly, without regard for rationality in the development of educational resources. Such deviations from planned institutional priorities consequently lowered the efficiency of investment in educational development.

Internal rates of return attributable to the various levels and types of schooling provide a convenient indicator of the net marginal revenue product of education investment, together with attendant current outlays.[24] In his pioneering study of the returns to Malaysian education, made halfway through the FMP period, O.E. Hoerr[25] concluded that for peninsular Malaysia, at least, educational investment yields a comparatively high average revenue product, socially as well as privately (Table 3). Internal net social rates of return to all levels of education were judged favourably, compared to the officially determined public opportunity cost of capital, set at 10%.[26] In particular, secondary-level schooling demonstrated higher social and private returns than the primary or even university levels, well above the opportunity cost

TABLE 3
Internal Rates of Return to Education in Peninsular Malaysia, 1967-8.

	Cumulative			Marginal			Cumulative Social Benefit/ Cost Ratio at 10% Discount Rate
	Net Social (1)	Gross Private (2)	Net Private (3)	Net Social (4)	Gross Private (5)	Net Private (6)	(7)
Primary	8.2	29.5	12.9	8.2	29.5	12.9	0.82
Lower Secondary	11.9	45.5	17.0	15.6	61.5	21.1	1.06
Upper Secondary	13.6	52.0	17.6	15.3	65.0	18.9	1.28
'Sixth Form'	13.2	52.8	17.1	12.8	55.3	15.6	1.31
University (Domestic)	9.5	49.7	16.0	5.8	37.2	14.4	0.92

Sources: Hoerr, *Education, Income and Equity in Malaysia.*

of capital. This was so despite a relatively high unemployment rate among non-specialized, lower-secondary school leavers.[27]

In these circumstances, the high net returns to secondary education testified to the significant economic potential for suitably equipped middle-echelon manpower. Laggard investment in secondary education, and the application of strict selectivity rules above the comprehensive lower secondary level, would therefore seem to imply considerable opportunity costs in terms of incremental educational returns foregone.

Applying cumulative social benefit-cost ratios to the various levels of education, at a 10% social time preference rate, it appears that public expenditure on post-primary education was generally profitable. Although primary schooling produced social returns slightly below the opportunity cost of capital, these costs have come to be regarded more as indivisible investment in the substructure of educational capital formation, particularly after the introduction of open-access, comprehensive lower-secondary education. While the university ratio was, on average, marginally inferior to that of the secondary level, this may understate the contribution of the very remunerative professional and technical faculties, as well as the research and consultancy functions of universities.

On the whole, the comparatively advantageous social returns to education were exceeded by the respective private rates of return, which again proved especially favourable for secondary-level education. In his factoring of income flows, Hoerr has estimated that education may account for some 60% of unadjusted money incomes in Peninsular Malaysia, though this reduces upon adjustment for unemployment and labour-force participation rates in inverse relationship with levels of educational attainment.[28]

Education institution-building was also marked by a greatly increased ratio of (public) education expenditures to national income. The portion of GNP devoted to public education, indicated by total public sector expenditure (development and current) on formal schooling at all levels, grew from less than 2% at the end of colonial period to over 3% by the end of the First FYP, to some 4 3/4% at the end of the Second FYP, even considering adjustments for the formation of Malaysia. After a slight decline under the FMP, the ratio reached well beyond 5% of Malaysian GNP mid-way through the SMP.[29]

Pupil numbers had grown by a factor of three, yet the level of public expenditure on education per pupil enrolled rose almost threefold, in real terms, between 1955 and 1973 (Table 4).

TABLE 4
Public Educational Capital Formation, 1955-73.

		(1) GNP at market prices (M$ million)	(2) Total public expend- iture on education ($M million)	(3) (2) as percent of (1)	(4) (2) per pupil enrolled (1967 prices*)	(5) Average annual rate of growth of real (2)* (percent)
	1955	4,992	86	1.72	[111]	[20.4]
Malaya	1960	5,626	179	3.18	149	
	1963	6,362	283	4.44	215	15.7
	1965	[8,637]	411	4.75	260	3.9
Malaysia	1970	11,617	521	4.48	228	
	1973	16,634	947	5.69	310	11.3

* Retail price index (1967:190) pertains to peninsular Malaysia only, while
  aggragate expenditures apply to all Malaysia.
Sources: *Economic Reports, 1973-74, 1974-75; First Malaysia Plan; Second
          Malaysia Plan*, adapted.

Rates of expenditure reflected the intensity of government goal commitment for each stage of education institution-building or reform. For independent Malaysia, the most rapid rate of increase of educational expenditures occurred during the First and Second FYP and SMP periods. These plan quinquennia constituted particular stages of policy which emphasized the primacy of educational goals pertaining to the social and political systems. Developments in education were instrumentally related to certain compelling political objectives at each stage, which induced higher public financial priorities for the purpose. The rate of increase of public expenditure on education was lowest, in real terms less than the growth of enrolments, under the FMP.

There is some irony in that that period coincided with the primacy of educational goals relating to economic objectives, but with little or no political urgency attached. Official attitudes and policy had integrated education into economic development strategy at the time, without, however, ensuring the warranted capital and current commitments. In Malaysian practice, the realization of financial commitments derived more from political motivations than from economic purpose, per se. Economic ends may have provided a rationale for resource mobilization on behalf of education, however actual commitments depended on the political imperatives that effectively governed educational "supply" in relation to determined policy goals.

The "Demand" for Education

Enrolments reveal the effective social demand for education at each level for each type of schooling. Post-primary school in Malaysia is voluntary, i.e., not legally compulsory, and fee-paying, for the non-Malay population. Historically, only Malays were accorded free education, extended in the 1960s through to the secondary and tertiary levels. Primary schooling for non-Malays was made free in 1962 in "Standard-type" institutions, as a sweetener for the controversial secondary school reforms, though the colonial custom obliging government-aided secondaries to provide a margin of 10% free places for the (non-Malay) poor has been retained.

"Free" education, in the Malaysian usage, has meant free tuition only; and while conceding that children of poor families (Malay as well as non-Malay) have had difficulty meeting the attendant costs of schooling, government has pleaded financial stringencies for not making "free" education wholly free. Neither has government seen fit to make primary education compulsory. Instead, its policy has been to "assure" school places for all qualified children up to (from the 1970s) age 15. This facile substitution of assurances for compulsory attendance relieved government of the burden of providing for genuinely universal primary education, while shifting the onus of enrolment over onto society-at-large.

Nevertheless, the provision of places and extension of free and aided schooling produced a notable institutional change as the once strong private school sector declined to relative unimportance while incremental enrolment concentrated in public education.[30]

The total school population of British Malaya prior to the Second World War was to the order of 263,000 enrolled.[31] Enrolments subsequently increased sharply in post-war years, reaching over three-quarters of a million in Malaya alone by the middle 1950s (plus an additional 158,000 in Singapore). This accelerated growth of enrolments denoted a far-reaching change in public attitudes towards education.[32] To be sure, the surge in enrolments resulted in part from pent-up demand from the war years and difficult aftermath. Of greater long-run significance, however, was the wider recognition accorded the value of education, which, coupled with rising incomes, translated into an increasing public appetite for formal, secular schooling.

Expanded private demand for education was reinforced by its growing social utility, in as much as the post-war expansion of government service and economic developments generally produced broader employment opportunities for educated manpower. Unfortunately, the inadequate provision for education in colonial public finance restricted the capacity of existing educational facilities to cope with both the demand backlog as well as current demand from the rapidly increasing school-age population. Consequently, the ratio of primary-level enrolments out of the eligible age group actually declined during the first half of the 1950s, to approximately 58% in 1954,[33] notwithstanding the expansion of numbers.

Self-government led to institutional reforms and policy goals that gave rise to a dramatic upsurge in primary school intake. In order to maximize the effects of the Razak Committee prescriptions, the Alliance government declared its intention to accommodate all children of age 7+ who so desire in Standard or Standard-type primary schools by 1960. This output target explicitly acknowledged a likely fall in scholastic quality ("it is better to offer a slightly lower standard of education temporarily than no education at all").[34] Government even accepted the possibility of deficit financing in order to bring this about, a radical departure from the fiscal norms of the past.

Responding to government's commitment, Malayan primary school enrolments reached the one million mark in 1958, two years ahead of target. A good part of this sudden increase in fact consisted of over-age pupils whose schooling had been forcibly deferred. And yet there was no slack in enrolments as this backlog was made up. Demand for primary education now shifted in favour of more widespread and longer schooling on the part of the appropriate age groups. This was no doubt inspired by the favourable private rates of return current for primary and post-primary education, stimulated still further by policy innovations including the introduction of free primary schooling (for non-Malays) in 1962. Primary enrolments continued their rise, though the average annual rate of increase slowed down from 7.5% during the 1955-60 era to around 3%, equivalent to the rate of population growth, thereafter. The effect of this was to very nearly double the total primary school population of peninsular Malaysia between 1955 and 1973, to over 1 1/2 million enrolled.

Primary enrolments in the east Malaysian States of Sabah and Sarawak, where education was administratively separate from the federal centre, displayed an even more rapid growth rate arising out of their comparatively lower starting point. Nevertheless, apart from a rapid short-term increase immediately following the formation of Malaysia, the longer-run growth trend of primary enrolment in Sabah and Sarawak for 1964-74 scarcely bettered that for the earlier period of British rule, 1955-64 (Table 5).

TABLE 5
Primary-Level Enrolments, 1955-1973.

	Peninsular Malaysia			Sabah and Sarawak	
	Enrolment ('000)	Index (1955=100)	Enrolment Ratio* (%)	Enrolment ('000)	Index (195=100)
1955	776	100	58	92	100
1958	1,007	129	n/a	120	130
1960	1,125	145	86	142	154
1964	1,197	154	90	161	175
1968	1,371	177	91	250	272
1973	1,531	197	91	252†	317

* Enrolment Ratio: enrolment as a proportion of eligible age group for primary -level education.
† 1974
Sources: *Education Statistics of Malaysia 1937 to 1967*; *Educational Statistics of Malaysia 1969*; *Education in Malaysia 1974*; UNESCO Regional Office for Education in Asia, *Progress of Education in the Asian Region, a Statistical Review* (Bangkok, 1975).

More significant than mere numerical growth has been the real and very substantial improvement in the ratio of primary school enrolments to their eligible age groups in peninsular Malaysia (no data is available on enrolment ratios for the East Malaysian States). This ratio stood at about 58% in 1955, at the end of the colonial era in Malayan education. Increased enrolments accompanying the first stage of policy reform elevated the enrolment ratio to 86% five years later. Since a large but uncertain portion of the primary school population then consisted of over-age backlog, the effective ratio for the properly eligible age group was somewhat less than this aggregate figure indicated. Once this backlog was overcome, around the middle 1960s, the distortion disappeared. Growing demand for primary education among the currently eligible age group brought the effective enrolment ratio to 90% in 1964, stabilizing at just over 91% by the late 1960s, early 1970s. Primary education had become mass public education, though still not quite *universal* education.

Stabilization of the enrolment ratio at 90-91% implied, conversely, that about 9 percent of the eligible age group remained consistently outside the scope of formal primary education. These presumably comprised the socially remote and economically most disadvantaged segments of the population. Foredoomed by their lack of even elementary schooling, at a time of rising educational levels in the community generally, this hard core of national impoverishment represented the long-run social cost of the failure to utilize compulsory means of attaining universal primary education.

Along with higher enrolment ratios, a marked improvement has been recorded in the education of females, particularly in peninsular Malaysia. Female enrolments persistently lagged during the colonial period, despite the efforts of educators. Only 44% of Malaya's eligible female age group was enrolled in primary school, in 1953, compared to over 78% of the male group, with females constituting only 37% of total primary level enrolments as late as 1955.[35]

Under-enrolment of females gave way before the expansion of popular demand for education accompanying the policy changes after independence. The ratio of female enrolment grew to 89% of the eligible female age group by the late 1960s, so that slightly less than 49% of total primary-level enrolments consisted of girls.[36] That proportion remained virtually constant into the 1970s, for peninsular Malaysia. There was a greater imbalance in East Malaysia, although the female share of primary level enrolment had grown to 45% in 1973 from 40 percent a decade earlier.[37]

Higher female enrolment rates contributed, paradoxically, to the lowering of private and social returns to education especially at the primary level, where females were concentrated. This was because the female population, constituting now about half of primary enrolments, generally experienced lower rates of absorption into the labour force. And, among those absorbed, females, whatever their educational attainments, invariably suffered wage or salary discrimination. Nonetheless, the spread of education among the female population suggests the likelihood of increasing female participation and at higher-levels in the labour force in future. Moreover, the recent expansion of female enrolments contains the prospect of inter-generation transmission of the values being inculcated, with long-run effects on cultural attitudes and social behaviour.

The demand for education also revealed itself in vastly improved retention ratios for successive cohorts of primary schoolers.

Prolongation of primary education signified a real gain in sustained, effective enrolment. Previously, not only were the aggregate enrolment rates low, but pupil "wastage" was also inordinately heavy. Retention ratios for colonial Malayan primary schools as late as the 1950-55 period averaged a mere 32%.[38]

Between 1957 and 1962, the accelerated demand for primary education also took the form of greater continuity of schooling, boosting the retention ratio to over 80%. Then, with the introduction of free non-Malay primary schooling, the 1962 cohort experienced the retention of some 84% of its initial enrolment. (It is noteworthy that retention ratios for females were still lower than for males, 78% as compared to 88%). The improvement, though impressive, was still incomplete, so that it served ironically to accentuate the relative deprivation of the disadvantaged. Educational "wastage" on the current scale has tended to exacerbate the already existent social gap in the universality of primary education, particularly since the enrolments of those retained in the school system has become all the more "effective" educationally.[39]

The growth of primary-level enrolments disclosed variations in the demand for education in and among the four linguistic streams over the successive policy stages. Such variations denoted changes in "taste," or social preferences, for educational languages, tempered by the accent of government policy. The demand for English language education grew most rapidly during the last decade of colonial rule, though relatively high rates of growth of enrolment also occurred in the Malay and, to a lesser extent, Chinese streams (Table 6), despite adverse circumstances.

TABLE 6

Primary Enrolment Trends by Language Stream, Peninsular Malaysia.

Year	Malaya Stream No. ('000)	Index	English Stream No. ('000)	Index	Chinese Stream No. ('000)	Index	Tamil Stream No. ('000)	Index	All Streams No. ('000)	Index
1947	170.7	100	57.0	100	190.3	100	35.4	100	453.4	100
1956	392.0	229	135.9	238	291.2	153	48.2	136	867.3	191
1961	503.0	295	218.1	382	378.0	198	64.3	182	1,163.5	256
1966	576.0	337	275.8	484	352.5	185	76.7	217	1,281.0	282
1974	942.5	552	61.8	108	470.5	247	79.8	225	1,554.6	343

Source: *Education Statistics of Malaysia 1938-1967; Education in Malaysia, 1974.*

The education language reform of 1957 inspired increased rates of enrolment for the Chinese, Tamil and, to a lesser degree, Malay streams, even if incremental demand still favoured English by a wide margin. However, Chinese-medium primary schooling subsequently declined, absolutely as well as relatively, following the adoption of the national (Rahman Talib) secondary education policy. Most of the shift in enrolments went to the English stream. This preference for English education was ultimately reversed by the decision to gradually convert the English stream to the National Language.[40] From the late 1960s English enrolments therefore fell off suddenly and drastically. A small part of the demand shift reverted to the Chinese stream, which now terminated at the primary level. However, the main gains in enrolment were recorded by the Malay stream, which exclusively offered assured post-primary continuity of language. Malay stream enrolments thus accelerated during the second half of the 1960s and first half of the 1970s at nearly three times the rate for primary education as a whole.

Differential growth rates for the various streams, as policies unfolded, yielded a changing linguistic balance at the primary education level. After the first decade of reform, the linguistic balance showed a significant movement away from Chinese and towards English language education. Compared to 1956 (figures in brackets), by 1966 the Malay and Tamil-medium schools continued to attract a virtually constant 45% and 46% share, respectively, of total primary enrolments, whereas the English rose to 21.5% (15.6%) at the expense of a Chinese decline to 27.5% (33.6%). Eight years later, the evolution of educational language policy had engineered a dramatically altered linguistic distribution of enrolment. Over 60% of the primary population were now enrolled in Malay-medium schools, 30% in Chinese schools, 5% in Tamil schools, leaving a residual 4% in English schools, pending completion of their conversion to National Language Standard.

The displacement of English schooling by policy means led to a slight revival of Chinese-medium education, but more importantly to the emergence of Malay for the first time as the language of instruction for the majority of enrolments and on an increasingly multi-racial basis. This trend towards the de-communalization of Malay-medium education, as its share of primary level enrolment began to exceed the Malay proportion of the school population (Table 7), implied new meaning for the term, "National Language."

TABLE 7
Peninsular Malaysia: Enrolment
by Race and Level of Education, 1970-75 (thousands).

	1970					1975				
	Malay	Chinese	Indian	Others	Total	Malay	Chinese	Indian	Others	Total
Primary	759.0	511.7	142.1	8.5	1,421.4	875.9	550.0	151.7	9.1	1,586.9
%	53.4	36.0	10.0	0.6	100.0	55.2	34.7	9.6	0.5	100.0
Lower Secondary	193.0	146.9	36.3	2.2	378.5	305.7	198.5	54.3	2.9	561.4
%	51.0	38.8	9.6	0.6	100.0	54.4	35.4	9.7	0.5	100.0
Upper Secondary	43.6	38.8	6.2	0.7	89.4	101.4	54.1	10.4	1.1	167.1
%	48.8	43.4	7.0	0.8	100.0	60.7	32.4	6.2	0.7	100.0
Post Secondary	4.6	5.3	0.6	0.1	10.6	8.8	6.6	0.8	0.9	16.3
%	43.4	49.6	6.0	1.0	100.0	54.0	40.5	4.9	0.6	100.0

Source: *Third Malaysian Plan.*

Expanded primary enrolments, coupled to generally rising educational aspirations, exerted increasing demand pressure on access to post-primary levels of education. Transition ratios, indicating the actual proportions continuing through to higher levels of schooling, have remained relatively inflexible, however. Institutional and policy-inspired rigidities, largely eliminated at the primary level, remained to restrict the demand-responsiveness of post-primary education. These rigidities were not happenstance, but can be traced to the attitudinal legacy of colonial post-primary education policy.

British Malayan secondary education had been modelled on the archetype English grammar school, and was intended as preparation for higher administrative and professional roles. Strict selectivity was applied, and operated according to officially prescribed optimal (actually, maximal) transition ratios, in pursuit of elitist standards.[41] As a result, secondary-level enrolment ratios were kept comparatively low, at about 11% of the eligible age group at the end of the colonial period. Restricted orientation plus selectivity combined to ensure a strong upper class bias in these transition and post-primary enrolment ratios.

The narrow conception of post-primary educational purpose and constituency persisted also after self-government. Restriction was now justified by academic heritage. Obsessions with grammar-type schooling conditioned official attitudes towards post-primary continuation even at a time of reform in other areas. Hence, the old colonial ceiling on the ratio of entry into secondary-level education, at 30%, was reiterated by the Rahman Talib review committee and afterwards incorporated in the SFYP as its norm for post-primary educational planning. Overflow demand was to be separated out and diverted to quasi-vocational, terminal subsidiaries. Distinctly inferior both status-wise and educationally, these pseudo-differentiated alternatives failed to attract substantial enrolments. Aggregate secondary level enrolment increased more than fivefold during the decade since 1955, though relatively low transition ratios testified to the existence of considerable unsatisfied demand.

The secondary school reforms of 1965 aimed at reconciling traditional educational perspectives with the mounting pressures of demand. By the mid-1960s peninsular Malaysia's aggregate secondary-level enrolment ratio stood at 25%. With the introduction that year of open-access "comprehensive" lower-secondary schooling, enrolments at this level grew to encompass 60% of the eligible age group by 1974 (Table 8). Access to upper-secondary education, which now included parallel academic (arts and science), technical and vocational streams, remained selective still. Consequently,

TABLE 8
Peninsular Malaysian
Post-Primary Enrolment Trends and Ratios.

	1955		1960		1965		1973	
	No. ('000)	Ratio (%)	No. ('000)	Ratio (%)	No. ('000)	Ratio (%)	No. ('000)	Ratio (%)
Secondary Level								
Total Secondary	30.7	7	169.2	15	358.1	25	593.1	n/a
• Lower Secondary	—		—		354.5		469.2	80
• Upper Secondary	—		—				115.3	
• Technical Institutes	0.1*		0.5		0.8		2.2	25
• Vocational Schools	5.0*		7.9		8.4		6.4	
• Sixth Form	—		1.9		3.5		13.8	
Tertiary Level								
Teacher Training	1.0*		6.8		9.1		4.6	6.3
College & Institutes	0.2		0.5*		1.0*		10.4	
Universities	—		0.6		2.8		12.9	1.1

* Estimates.
Sources: *Progress of Education in the Asia Region; Educational Statistics of Malaysia 1938-1968; Education in Malaysia 1974.*

whereas enrolments in upper-secondaries increased steadily, the enrolment ratio for 1974 was still below 25%.

Further selectivity applied at the "Sixth Form" and college levels, such that their combined enrolment ratio reduced to 6.6%, and again at the university level, where the ratio stood at just over 1%, notwithstanding the great expansion of student numbers over the late 1960s, early 1970s.

Selectivity, in the recent Malaysian experience, amounted to more than just a test of educational achievement, inasmuch as the public examination mechanism was commonly wielded as an instrument for juxtaposing other policy objectives onto the education system. The differential impact of selectivity tended to be reinforced by institutional and policy constrictions that not only depressed levels of enrolment, but furthermore tended to distort the structure of demand for post-primary education. The National Language requirements built into the examination mechanism, for one thing, has tended to be particularly interdictive to those in the English or Chinese or Tamil streams with a propensity for scientific or technological studies.[42] Conversely, the utilization of fee discrimination, by which post-primary education was free for Malays and not for non-Malays, in effect tended to accentuate demand for the Malay-preferred humanistic subjects. Such measures worked to shift the composition of the (upper) secondary school enrolment proportionally away from technical, scientific, and vocational education, contrary to the intentions of the 1965 reform. Moreover, sub-professional tertiary training was given a strongly Malay bias in enrolment capabilities, limiting non-Malay access to, and therefore the manpower reservoir of, certain skilled occupations.

The effect was also felt at the tertiary level, in the general universities. There, the proportion of student population in the liberal arts actually increased during the decade since 1965, and the proportion of graduates even more so, to more than half[43] (Table 9). It is noteworthy that the balance would have been skewed in the other direction except for the concentration of Universiti Kebangsaan's mainly Malay enrolment in the humanities and, to a lesser extent, economics faculties. Indeed, it was symptomatic of ethnic educational propensities that Malays also predominated in the arts enrolment of the University of Malaya, while the composition of the scientific and technological faculties was overwhelmingly non-Malay, especially Chinese. If the newer technological universities and institutes are taken into account, the enrolment distribution emerged less emphatically

TABLE 9
Proportions of Tertiary Level
Enrolments and Graduates in Liberal Arts (percent).

	1965		1975	
	Enrolments	Graduates*	Enrolments	Graduates*
General Universities University of Malaya†	52.8	48.6	49.8	46.3
Universiti Ketangsaan Malaysia‡	—	—	81.5	84.7
Universiti Sains Malaysia††	—	—	42.8	63.2
Subtotal	52.8	48.6	53.8	54.4
All University Level Institutions	41.5	38.1	36.5	48.5

* First degree level.
† Facaulty of Arts, and Economics & Administration.
‡ Faculty of Arts, Islamic Studies, Malay & Culture, and Economics & Management.
†† School of Humanities, Comparative Social Sciences, Humanities with
  Education.
Source: *RIHED NEWS*, November 1974.

liberal arts, though it was precisely these institutions that suffered from laggard science enrolments at the upper-secondary level.

Policy and institutional constraints created a situation of qualified but unsatisfied excess demand for higher levels of education, only part of which found expression in the outflow of students to universities abroad, amounting to more than double the domestic university population.[44]

The availability of educational facilities remains imbalanced between urban and rural areas, notwithstanding the great strides taken since independence. Primary education has been made widely available in the kampungs, to be sure, though there exists some discrepancy between more-developed and less-developed regions. However, the distribution of secondary-level facilities has been rather less favourable (Table 10). By the mid-1970s, rural areas had five times the number of primary schools, and more than twice the classrooms, taking into account lower population concentration, but far fewer secondary schools, and classrooms, than the urban areas. In the crucial areas of science education, rural secondary schools have disproportionately fewer laboratory facilities than their urban counterparts. Although residential secondaries and so called "Special Science" secondaries were established in each state in peninsular Malaysia, except Perak and Malacca, in order to improve the availability of science and technical schooling for rural

TABLE 10
Urban-Rural Distribution of Educational Facilities, 1975.

	Urban	Rural
Number of Schools		
• Primary	770	3,553
• Lower-Secondary	68	169
• Combined Lower-Upper Secondary	317	256
Number of Classrooms		
• Primary	9,707	22,170
• Secondary	7,236	5,931
Number of Laboratories		
• Secondary Level	1,316	865

Source: *Bulletin of the UNESCO Regional Office for Education in Asia*, June 1976.

Malays, the prevailing imbalances militated against any substantial rise in transition and science-technical ratios.

Educational patterns are still effectively differentiated as between urban and rural schooling, with the latter suffering sharper cut-offs between the primary and secondary levels, and having a more pronounced bias away from science training. Because of the linguistic-ethnic interweaving particular to Malaysia, these imbalances especially affected the Malay-medium stream. Consequently, Malay enrolments have been heavily concentrated in the non-science/non-technical courses, in effect continuing at the post-primary level the old educational-occupation separation by language and race.

The shape of Malaysia's "education pyramid" depicts the narrowing effect of confined transition and enrolment ratios at higher rungs of education system (Table 11). Broadly based at the primary level, the "education pyramid" tapered sharply at the secondary level and beyond, coming to a very narrow tertiary-level peak. To be sure, the introduction of open-admission "comprehensive" schooling in 1965 tended to broaden the lower-secondary range somewhat, but a tight bottleneck occurred nevertheless at the upper levels. The skew of the "education pyramid" indicated a small proportion of Malaysian enrolments at the tertiary level, relative to the country's socio-economic development, or compared to other countries in the Asian region or Latin America. With the distribution of educational opportunity so confined, the selector mechanisms invariably involved a large element of pre-selection

TABLE 11
Percentage Distribution of Enrolments at
All Levels, Malaysia and Selected Other Countries.

	Year	1st Level	2nd Level Lower/Upper	3rd Level
Malaysia	1965	78.1	21.2	0.7
Malaysia	1975	68.0	(23.3/6.5)	1.0
Asian Region	1965	75.0	22.0	3.0
Philippines	1964	79.4	14.8	5.8
Republic of Korea	1965	78.6	19.1	2.3
Singapore	1965	74.0	23.6	2.4
Taiwan	1965	75.1	22.1	2.8
Latin America	1965	82.0	16.0	2.0
Europe	1965	64.0	32.0	4.0
North America	1965	64.0	26.0	10.0

Sources: For Malaysia: *Educational Statistics of Malaysia 1938 to 1969*; Education in Malaysia 1974; Third Malaysian Plan; *Progress of Education in the Asian Region.*

along class and racial lines, in curious combinations. Differential policy treatment of Malays and non-Malays made for a reportedly significant degree of upward mobility of Malays from lower class backgrounds to higher levels of the education system; while, conversely, for non-Malays this distributive mechanism for educational advancement tended to reflect and reinforce existing patterns of social stratification.[45]

This distribution of enrolment among the various levels of schooling implied an allocation of education capital formation as between "broader" and "deeper" education-manpower relationships. Increased enrolments over time raised the quantum of schooling per

TABLE 12
Average Labour Force Educational Attainments
for Selected Countries (years of schooling per worker).

Malaysia (1965): 5.10	Indonesia (1965): 3.28	Japan (1960): 10.3
	Philippines (1965): 7.37	U.K. (1960): 10.2
	Singapore (1965): 6.12	U.S.A. (1960): 11.8
	Taiwan (1965): 5.71	

Source: R.M. Sundrum, 'Manpower and Educational Development in Eastern and Southern Asia', *Malayan Economic Review* (1971).

Malaysian worker from an average of less than four years in 1950, to over five by 1965.[46] Education capital formation had broadened, as the growing labour force was schooled to the primary level, and after 1965 increasingly to the "comprehensive" lower-secondary level. Yet, the sharply skewed "education pyramid," with its stunted progressivity at its post-primary (after 1965, post lower-secondary) levels, militated against any parallel deepening of the educational attainments of the labour force at large. Ordinary selectivity was furthermore confining as a result of implicit and explicit linguistic and racial barriers to educational advancement. The average educational attainment of the Malaysian labour force may have compared favourably to that of less-developed neighbours, but still ranked well beneath the needs of economic development.[47] (see Table 12).

Education and National Development: Some Topics for Consideration

Education systems function to define, transmit, and thereby allocate values in society. This ultimately allocative role serves to make certain scarce valued resources available to some, while denying them to others. Thus, institutional limits on the scope of participation in education, and the selection mechanisms for advancement through the system, operate to regulate access to social status and roles. Again, the prescribed content of education designates what attitudes, beliefs, expectations, information and skills are imparted through the agency of formal schooling. In Malaysia, the once oversized private and parochial school sector has since been supplanted by a national education institution, in which the allocative choices are matters of public policy. Thus, education policy has become more all-embracing and uniform throughout, but also more singularly authoritative. Some of the consequences for Malaysian economic, social, and political development are considered below.

Education and the Labour Market—Employment

The Malaysian labour market has long been characterized by the paradox of relatively high levels of "hard core" unemployment coincidental with shortages of manpower, at differing levels of skills and educational attainment. A 1962 survey of the labour force disclosed unemployment rates of 5.2% among males, and 7.9% among females.[48] For both males and females, the highest rates of unemployment were incurred by those with incomplete secondary

TABLE 13

Specific Unemployment Rates by Level of Education, 1962.

	Percentage Unemployed	
	Males	Females
No Education	3.1	4.3
Primary Level	5.3	12.8
Secondary Level		
• Forms I and II	9.4	31.7
• Forms III	10.9	29.3
• Forms IV	12.1	22.8
• Forms V	6.7	10.2
• Forms VI	9.5	21.9
Trade Schools or Technical Institutes	0.2	0.3
Teacher Training College	0.0	0.0
Technical College or Polytechnic	0.01	—
University	0.04	0.07
All	5.2	7.9

Note: Specific unemployment rate $= \frac{UiUi}{Ui+Ei}$ where Ui is the number unemployed and Ei the number gainfully employed at each educational level.

Sources: 'Report on Employment, Unemployment and Under-employment, 1962', Department of Labour and Industrial Relations and Department of Statistics, Kuala Lumpur, reproduced in *Report of the Higher Education Planning Committee*, 1967.

level education of the undifferentiated, grammar school type, followed by those with just a primary education (Table 13). By contrast, graduates of technical, vocational or professional streams suffered little or no unemployment, with many vacancies actually being left unfilled.

This relationship between education—or the lack of it—and unemployment has persisted following the 1965 reform introducing open-access "comprehensive" lower secondary schooling. Between 1970 and 1975 the rate of unemployment oscillated between 7 and 8% percent of the labour force. As in the past, the highest incidence of unemployment affected youth with low and non-differentiated educational attainments. Some 69% of registered unemployed (those for whom data is available) in 1975 were aged between 15-24 years, and about 83% had lower-secondary education or less.[49] Unemployment of those having reached the upper-secondary level continued to be most pronounced among the arts stream.

At the same time, education policy, with its selectivity and sharp cut-off at higher and more specialized levels, has not met the growing demand for executive, professional and technical manpower. In order to overcome constraints on development due to the lack of qualified manpower, Malaysia has continued to rely on the employment of expatriate personnel. Data for the mid-1960s indicate that expatriates filled a fifth of all high-echelon professional and technical positions, and were particularly strongly represented in the private sector. Meanwhile, a large proportion of professional and sub-professional posts, especially in the public sectors, re-

TABLE 14

Vacant and Expatriate-filled Positions, 1965 (percentage of total posts).

	Government Sector		Education System		Private Sector		Total	
	V (1)	E-F (2)	V (3)	E-F (4)	V (5)	E-F (6)	V (7)	E-F (8)
All Occupations	6.4	0.2	7.7	2.8‡‡	0.4	0.6	2.5	1.3
Professional*								
• Managers	17.1	3.0	27.1	3.3	0.9	28.8	6.1	20.1
• Technologists	20.7	8.0	—	—	4.2	43.6	12.9	21.3
• Teachers	—	—	24.3	17.0	—	—	24.3	17.0
• Others	16.0	4.6	33.3	22.2	4.4	24.4	12.0	10.3
Sub-professionals†								
• Junior managers/accounts	11.7	0.1	9.0	1.7	1.3	15.3	5.8	5.8
• Teachers	—	—	13.4††	7.6	—	—	13.4	7.6
• Technologists and Others	18.3	—	12.3	0.4	3.2	12.1	15.2	2.1
Skilled Labour‡								
• Teachers	—	—	2.2††		—	—	2.2	—
• Bluecollar	6.2	—	15.2		0.8	—	2.3	—
• Whitecollar	6.7	—	14.7		0.5	—	3.4	—
Semi Skilled/Unskilled								
• Bluecollar	2.8	—	13.7		0.3	—	0.9	—
• Whitecollar	7.0	—	18.2		0.3	—	4.4	—

* University or equivalent experience for managers.
† Training of one or two years beyond School Certificate.
‡ Education beyond Lower Certificate of Education Level, but less than subprofessional.
†† Arbitrary division.
‡‡ Including posts filled by local but unqualified personnel (allocative only).
V: Vacant; E-F: Expatriate-filled

mained vacant.[50] (see Table 14). This pattern of employment persisted into the 1970s.[51] Dependence on expatriate personnel for managerial and technical manpower tended to favour private enterprise and weaken public service recruitment, especially since the end of colonial service. Moreover, the extent of the expatriate stake in top-ranking occupations carried certain negative implications for the management of the Malaysian economy, more about which is discussed below.

Shortages of qualified manpower affected not only the professional and sub-professional ranks, but also the skilled and semi-skilled occupations requiring some level of post-primary training (e.g., beyond the Lower Certificate of Education). Access to their occupations was restricted by the racial and linguistic selectivity of post-secondary institutions. Insufficient supplies of appropriately educated and trained labour became a significant limiting factor in Malaysian economic activity. Successive development plans have blamed inadequacies of human capital, more than of capital funding for persistent shortfalls in plan implementation.[52]

Responsibility for the apparent discontinuity between schooling and employment opportunities may be traced in to the survival of the "grammar" cult in the next context of racial restructuring. The strong hand of the past in matters of educational content and selectivity rendered the institution of education rather less responsive to changing circumstances than warranted by the evolution of government policy towards education. Explicit and implicit racial and linguistic tests further confirmed the social scope of educational continuation. Thus, Malaysia's sharply cut-off "educational pyramid" produced too many school leavers with inappropriate training, and too few with sufficient education relative to social and market demands.

Education and the Labour Market—Insularity

Ethnic insularity in the labour market, characteristic of plural societies and tradition-bound economic expectations, has been a major impediment to manpower mobility and the reduction of inequalities in (Peninsular) Malaysia. Historically, colonial education policy contributed to and reinforced ethnic-linguistic occupational separation. Malay-language education had a "strong rural bias . . . adapted to the needs of the home (i.e., kampung village) environment."[53] Tamil schools on rural estates were similarly confining, and Chinese education—the only vernacular stream then extending beyond the primary level—preserved an essentially parochial purpose.

From 1957, the adoption of the national education policy, built around a common curriculum, overrode schooled insularity in favour of modernizing expectations. A last attempt by the independent Malayan government to uphold the traditional occupational orientation of at least a segment of the Malay stream, through the establishment of "rural trade" schools geared to the kampung economy, failed to gain popularity and was finally abandoned in 1964. Since then, Malaysian education has evinced a generalist and modernist occupational outlook for all language streams.

The metamorphosis was most pronounced in Malay-language education. In the past, only English schooling provided generalized access to higher echelon occupations, leading many avenue for Malay upward mobility was for "intelligent" pupils to transfer out of the Malay stream to the English. During the first decade of independence, English education still provided the widest latitude for occupational mobility, even though the policy reforms had rectified somewhat the educational insularity of the hitherto confining vernacular streams. In particular, the extension of Malay-language schooling through the post-primary levels, coupled to policies of ethnic sponsorship for Malays, brought about a radical transformation of Malay educational ambitions and social aims.

Upward mobility through the education system, and thereafter into occupational roles, by the late 1960s was more conspicuous for Malays than for non-Malays.[54] By the middle 1970s, Malays comprised more than half of post-primary enrolment, and had already increased their share to over 45% of professional, technical, managerial and administrative employment.[55] While this process was doubtlessly abetted by discriminatory preferences, policy expressions of Malay "special rights," the operational key was to be found in the transformation of Malay-medium education. At the post-primary levels, this Malay educational transformation produced a new technocratic class, of mainly peasant background, schooled in modern skills and values, and constituting a "second generation" nationalist elite. Even at the mass primary level, the modernization of Malay education doubtlessly contributed to the improved employment rates for Malays, in the face of deteriorating unemployment generally.[56]

The gradual conversion of English schools will eventually eliminate all institutional competition to the post-primary mobility and occupational utility of Malay-language education. On the other hand, the Chinese and especially the Tamil streams, being terminal at the primary level, offer rather less scope for upward or occupational mobility.

Ethnic occupational insularity, together with attendant inequalities of income distribution, have remained features of the Malaysian labour market. Of course schools were hardly to blame for these differentials, which had their origins in history and were perpetuated through class and communal relationships. However, education has served to transmit existing occupational bias, or else not correct it. Within the Malay stream, their generally inadequate facilities for science and technical instruction has resulted in a de facto concentration on grammar-style literary education. Malay occupational predilections have accordingly been towards administration and pedagogy, leaving the scientific and technological professions very much to English-educated non-Malays, particularly Chinese.[57]

This racial channelling declined somewhat during the 1970s, but is still pronounced. Although deliberate discrimination among schools is no longer practiced, the inevitable leads and lags in policy innovation has meant that certain segments of the school system benefitted sooner, or more, from development than others. Overall improvements notwithstanding, rural schools are generally inferior to urban, Tamil-language schooling has remained problematic, certain neighbourhood schools have been better equipped than others, while reputedly "elite" institutions continue to exercise undue claims on public educational resources.

Modernity and uniformity in education have not wrought full equality of opportunity among the different communities. In Malaysia, like in India and elsewhere in South and Southeast Asia, linguistic constraints on occupational mobility, arising out of particular educational styles or differences in the economic utility of languages, accentuate anew the insularity of gains wrought by discontinuous educational development.[58]

Education and Management of the Economy

The social composition of control over national economic affairs depends largely upon the manpower output of education systems. During the colonial period, top echelon administrative, managerial, professional and technical posts were mostly filled by expatriate British personnel. At the outset of independence, in 1955, only about a quarter of Division 1 positions in the federal public service was filled by Malayans.[59] Measures aimed at rectifying this situation and bringing the understaffed government bureaucracy up to full establishment strength hinged upon the supply of qualified, high-level manpower. Whereas "Malayanization" had been scheduled to proceed at a gradual pace after independence, in the event the public service endured rapid expatriate retirements, spurred by the terms of compensation, far in excess of the capacity of the education system to produce local replacements.[60] The resulting strain of understaffing hit government bureaucracy at precisely the time when political developments were generating increasingly urgent economic and social demands on public administration.

Remedy was sought in the expansion of civil service recruitment through the growth of education. Following independence, Malay-educated personnel were accepted for senior posts, hitherto exclusively English, and came to occupy an increasingly dominant position in government bureaucracy. This not only altered the language of administration but, even more significantly, its social composition and political-cultural outlook.

Despite the pressures of development, public service recruitment has remained ethnically and educationally restrictive. Senior administrative positions have not been open to non-Malays except on the basis of a 1 : 4 (non-Malay : Malay) quota, originating from the early 1950s, although the technical and professional branches are necessarily more open.[61] The effect of restrictive recruitment has been to limit the expansion of the government service to the output of higher educated Malays. Consequently, understaffing at the senior administrative and professional and technical ranks incurred opportunity costs in terms of potential development foregone.

Economic developments during the 1960s and early 1970s led to a dramatic expansion of both the private corporate sector and state commercial enterprise.[62] The accompanying growth in demand for business administration and technical-professional personnel could not be met by the Malaysian education system, with its literary bias and sharp cut-off points. Most locally recruited corporate personnel tended to be non-Malay, particularly Chinese, since Malays generally preferred and were given preference in government administrative service. The remaining shortages were made up by the large-scale employment of expatriates in top-echelon managerial and professional-technical posts (Table 13).

One adverse consequence of this has been the formation within the economic administration (private as well as public) of separate occupational communities of expatriates, non-Malays, and Malays, set apart by educational experience, social attachments, value orientations and organizational commitments. Differences among occupational communities at economic decision-making levels have occasionally given rise to goal conflicts which interfered with the effective administration of development policy.[63] The dilution of national political control over economic management tended to inhibit policy initiative and innovation, especially where established procedures, norms or interests were at stake. Indeed, this tendency for breakdown and discontinuity in development administration was tacitly abetted by the political leaderships customary aversion to organizational discord. Structural deficiencies tended to be tolerated and often perpetuated, therefore aggravating their negative influence on administrative efficiency.[64]

Tensions in economic administration touched on the raw communal nerves of the Malaysian body politic. Growing impatience with laggard developmental performance engendered a more radical nationalism especially among the emergent, Malay-educated, second-generation elite, reacting against the composition and frustrations of economic management. Yet, the tenor of Malay ultra-nationalist argumentation revealed a barely-disguised racialism and xenophobia injected into political debate under radical guise.[65] Advocacy of a racial redistribution of income and wealth obtained official respectability through the adoption of a "racial economic balance" as the ultimate target of public policy as from the Second Malaysia Plan.[66] However, the pursuit of Malay economic power, by way of "restructuring society and its economic balance," placed in jeopardy the delicately contrived balance of inter-communal support for the Alliance political formula, without really treating the root issue, i.e., the apparent failure of education policy to generate sufficient high-level human capital to extend the scope of Malayanization towards greater charge of, and a larger share in, the expanding corporate economy.

Education and Acculturalization, Socialization and Social Brokerage

As the most salient public institution touching all communities, English-language education, historically served as an agency for the creation of social brokers to mediate inter-communal relations in Malaya's plural society. While the vernacular streams appealed to their respective communities only, English education was uniquely multi-racial in its enrolment, and remained singularly well positioned by its post-primary structure for colonial elite formation.

English language grammar-type education became the accepted preparation for social recruitment to leadership roles in public administration and corporate enterprise during the colonial period, and for some time afterwards.[67] What emerged was a bi-cultural elite, composed of personages representing the various communities but socialized according to the share values of English grammar schooling. The education process was emphatically elitist in the double sense that leadership recruitment through English acculturalization and socialization patterns was very largely confined to communal elites, and made for the management of underlying social tensions through elite-level social brokerage.

The first generation Alliance party leadership exemplified this consociational type of inter-communal elite, highly stratified by communal social background and related by the common cultural denominator of English grammar education. Under their influence social brokerage crystallized into a distinctive Alliance style of political compromise. The efficacy of this form of political entrepreneurship required ongoing cohesiveness and exclusivity for the common mode of socialization and acculturalization. Otherwise, non-shared avenues of elite formation might emerge to challenge or else shatter the bonds among brokers and between elite patrons and communal clients.

The education policy reforms of 1957 and 1961, widely regarded as a tribute to the Alliance manner of social brokerage, ironically carried the seeds of its eventual challenge. The provision of a national standard of primary schooling in the Malay, Chinese and Tamil languages, and the extension of Malay-medium education through the secondary level, and later to the tertiary as well, effectively pluralized the former English-stream monopoly over educational acculturalization and socialization for economic and political leadership roles. The shared English educational experience diminished relative to the considerable expansion of enrolments in separate National and National-type schools during the 1960s. Except for the provision of a common curriculum, this trend towards the vernacular decreased the commonality of education and generated competing communal ("ultra") elites. Moreover, there emerged a deepening dichotomy between the ethnic mass, educated increasingly in their respective vernacular primary streams, and the established English-educated consociational elites still dominating the component parties of the ruling Alliance. An invigorated ethnicity, now inspired by vernacular educated, modernized communal counter-elites, appeared less amenable to accommodation by traditional patrimonial style of social brokerage.

Dissension within the Alliance coalition weakened its political capabilities at a time of growing stress and strain on political integration. Its two main constituent party organizations, the United Malays National Organization (UMNO) and Malayan Chinese Association (MCA) came under increasing assault from their respective communal counter-elites during the 1960s. Alliance appeal constricted accordingly, costing the coalition a margin of support in the 1969 general elections. The voting result projected a rise of ethnic parochialism, which challenged the terms of inter-communal accommodation fostered by the Alliance leadership consensus. A sudden breakdown in the Alliance leadership competence contributed to the aftermath of racial violence.

The political reconstruction that followed the 1969 crisis and emergency aimed at restoring the modicum of inter-communal cooperation and accommodation necessary for the functioning of a more-or-less "open," plural society. The policies effected emphasized a double blend of norms and patterns of social brokerage. On the normative level, Malays were assured of their national title and non-Malays of their legitimate interests, an authoritative allocation of national rights to Malays and civil rights to non-Malays that became legally sacrosanct. The long-run task of creating a new set of social brokers to reconcile ethnic interests in terms of these norms fell to Malay-language education. To be sure, education policy continued to tolerate Chinese and Tamil language National-type primary schools, to avoid antagonizing these communities. However the English stream is to be eliminated grade by grade up to 1982, leaving a Malay language monopoly over post-primary education. With Malay to become the exclusive mediator of shared acculturalization and recruitment to leadership roles, it was calculated that this would engender a multi-racial, Malay-educated elite better disposed to social brokerage among their respective ethnic interests, while rendering the terms of racial consociation more emphatically Malay.

Existing education policies and practice have not been wholly consistent with these new directions in elite formation and political entrepreneurship. Ongoing restrictions on entry to the upper secondary levels amount a deliberate constriction of the scope of shared educational enculturation. Malaysia's sharply skewed "education pyramid," in which only the post-primary levels were racially and educationally integrated, offers only a narrow platform for the intended creation of social brokers. The restricted effective level of national educational socialization is narrowed still further by the degree of cultural alienation between prospective social brokers and their communal reference groups, where primary school enrolment is largely—about a third—in educationally and ethnically segregated Chinese and Tamil streams. Even within the Malay-language stream now being transformed along racially integrated lines, the persistence of differential continuation patterns for Malays and non-Malays might tend to prejudice the emergence of a new consociational elite. Discordant lines of acculturalization and socialization accompanying education policy may bring about a situation where the passing of traditional patrimonial social brokerage entails in its wake ethnocentred class or religious confrontation.

The Search for National Symbols of Political Community

The political development of Malaysia points to the distinction between state-building and nation-building. Modern state institutions have been established and extended to cope with the demands of development. On the other hand, integrative, normative symbols of nationhood have remained relatively underdeveloped and weak.[68] Building a modern state apparatus where any prior sense of nationhood was absent required the formulation, virtually *de novo*, of a cultural matrix for binding a plural society into a political community and legitimizing its authority structure.

Formal enculturation in British Malaya had been left largely to educational institutions, with their diverse orientations. While independent Malaysia retained and even accentuated their acculturalizing role of education, stricter political direction was applied to the determination and transmission of social values through the school system. In taking on this political imperative, policies towards educational acculturalization had to contend with the competing and often times contradictory requirements of authority, as distinct from social acceptability, normative orthodoxy or tolerance, consistency or flexibility in application.

For much of Malaysia's modern history the dilemma was tacitly resolved by avoiding any positive definition of authoritative national values, and substituting instead the manipulation of surrogate symbols or, more emphatically, negative anti-symbols. Colonial education policy during the early 1950s promulgated the fostering of a "United Malayan Nation" as its political cultural goal, though without specifying the meaning of "Malayan," or "nation," or, indeed, the notion of "unity."[69] The vagueness of the concept relegated it to the sphere of platitudes, while in practice the colonial administration treated educational acculturation primary as a problem of Chinese orientations. As in other times and places, whenever political forces arose that could not be contained by established institutions, or controlled by settled customs, authority variously ascribed them to the intrigues of hostile strangers.

Recurrent efforts on the part of the colonial Education Department to convert Chinese education to the English-medium ("National" schools of 1952; "Standard-type" schools of 1954) elevated the educational language question to a test of loyalty. English language education became a symbol of orthodoxy, whereas linguistic pluralism, especially Chinese, was tainted with the anti-symbol of Communist sedition. Official sponsorship of English instruction and curriculum substituted for any formulation of genuine national focal points of Malayan allegiance. Instead, the emphasis on English educational symbols produced hostile reactions among Malay nationalists as well as Chinese, and plunged political culture into the maelstrom of language politics.

Malaya's newly elected Alliance government assumed power in 1955 confident in its political authority, having derived its legitimacy from a popular mandate coupled with British-style constitutional association with traditional Malay monarchical forms. Yet, the Alliance political formula preferred to avoid potentially divisive normative issues, relying instead on a pragmatic style of social brokerage to advance the cause of an emergent consociational democracy. That marked the treatment of education policy adopted by the Razak Committee. Its resolution of the contentious language issue balanced educational acculturalization on the twin principles of national identity and inter-communal acceptability. These points of reference for policy indicated little about the actual normative content of educational acculturalization. Rather, the acceptance of compromise was itself conceived as producing, over time, definite commitments to political community. Form served as a substitute for substance in the Alliance approach to national-building.

Meanwhile, in view of their own caution and ambiguity over the determination of positive national norms, the Alliance leadership continued to manipulate the double anti-symbols of communism and racialism so as to demarcate boundaries of legitimacy.

An educational curriculum oriented towards Malaya, and not towards other countries, may well have been a *sine qua non* of national education enculturation, but itself hardly sufficed to foster national identity. As a matter of fact, the continued predominance of essentially ethnic values in society was accentuated, rather than being sublimated, by the modern form of mass public education and the creation of new parochial elites.[70] The Alliance formula came under mounting attack from Malay "ultra" insistence on fundamentally Malay national norms on the one hand, and non-Malay "chauvinist" demands for recognition of normative pluralism on the other.[71] Reacting to the situation, government's education policy review, expressed in the Rahman Talib Committee Report, resurrected the national language symbol in educational acculturalization.

Thereafter for much of the 1960s, language politics dominated the issue of political culture.[72] Carried forward by its own momentum, the controversy over the language status of Malaysian political community flowed over into a dispute about political legitimacy. When the explosion occurred during the unsettled aftermath of the 1969 General Elections, the original Alliance consensus on political community and political legitimacy ranked among the first casualties.

The political reconstruction that followed laid down the norms for a reconstituted political culture, and codified these in the *Rukunegara*, Malaysia's so called "National Ideology."[73] In reply to the challenge, official ideology projected distinctively Malay values onto the main symbols of Malaysian politics: the Monarchy (Malay Rulers), the Established Religion (Islam), the National Language (Malay) and communal status (Malay "special rights"). While the "legitimate rights" of non-Malays were assured as hitherto, the more positivist definition of Malaysian political culture affirmed Malay custody over the norms of political community and political legitimacy. This invoked a subtle but nevertheless meaningful change in the terms of inter-communal partnership, insofar as non-Malays were now expected to subscribe to strictly Malay symbols of national identity. The inculcation of Malay national norms postulated a stronger emphasis on political acculturalization by means of education policy. Conversion of post-primary schooling to the Malay language, exclusively, implies a greater degree of cultural integration eventually. However, language is now just one, albeit salient, symbol of the Malay nationalist resurgence. Political means of acculturation will have to cope with the dilemma involved in forging particularistic norms into the nationalism of an otherwise plural society. In the meantime, UMNO has proceeded to extend its bloc of political consensus beyond the original Alliance to a broader National Front coalition, designed to make impregnable the Malay dominion over the Malaysian political process.

Any evaluation of the wider consequences of education policies must necessarily remain tentative, to be sure, owing to our inadequate time perspective. It is still too soon to discern the full influence of changes in Malaysian education since independence: the first cohort to embark on post-1957 national schooling finished its primary education in 1963, completed the secondary level not before 1970, and graduated university (bachelor's degree) only in 1973. This lengthy time sequence, the gestation period of education, suggests that the outcome of the education institution-building process of the 1950s and 1960s has yet to be wholly revealed.

ENDNOTES

1. The author expresses his appreciation to the Harry S. Truman Research Institute at the Hebrew University of Jerusalem for its support for research in Malaysia and Singapore; and to the Institute of Southeast Studies, Singapore, for a visiting fellowship and the privilege of using its facilities.

2. On colonial education policy and practice in British Malaya, see Charles Hirschman, "Educational Patterns in Colonial Malaya," *Comparative Education Review* (1972); Philip Loh Fook Sen, *Seeds of Separatism: Educational Policy in Malaya 1874-1940* (Kuala Lumpur, 1976); Rex Stevenson, *Cultivators and Administrators: British Educational Policy Towards the Malays, 1875-1906* (Kuala Lumpur, 1976).

3. Malaya's overall enrolment rate was given as 63 percent in 1951 (Member for Education, *Federation of Malaya Legislative Council Proceedings*, 19 Sept. 1951), declining to about 58 percent of the eligible age group by 1959: International Bank for Reconstruction and Development, *The Economic Development of Malaya* (Baltimore, 1955), pp. 142-77 (Henceforth: *IBRD Report*). See Part 3, below.

4. Vide. Gunnar Myrdall, *Asian Drama* (New York, 1968), pp. 1533-6 and appendix 3, section 2.

5. Federation of Malaya, *Report of the Education Committee* (Kuala Lumpur, 1956), p. 1.

6. On Malaysian education since independence, see e.g. Francis Wong & Ee Yiang Hong, *Education in Malaysia* (Hong Kong, 1971); R.O. Tilman, *Education and Political Development in Malaysia, Yale University Southeast Asian Studies, Reprint Series No. 27*; and International Association of Universities & UNESCO, *Higher Education and Development in Southeast Asia* (Paris, 1969).

7. Provision was made for the teaching of Chinese and/or Tamil (Malay already being compulsory) in English-medium Standard-type schools at the request of 15 or more pupils in any grade.

8. With effect from 1958, special Malay language classes were attached to otherwise English-medium National-type secondaries, but this was clearly a limited venture.

9. Federation of Malaya, *Second Five-Year Plan 1961-1965* (Kuala Lumpur, 1961), para. 157.

10. At the time there were only two technical secondary schools, and two junior trade schools in the entire Federation. Under the 1961 policy so-called 'secondary continuation" and 'rural trade" schools were established as dead-end quasi-vocational alternatives. They never gained popularity and were abolished only four years later when more substantial post-primary reforms were introduced.

11. On the Revival of communalist antagonisms in the 1969 elections, see Martin Rudner, "The Malaysian General Election of 1696: a Political Analysis," *Modern Asian Studies* (1970).

12. Vide. *The Colonial Empire, 1939-1947* (London, HMSO, 1947), Cmd. 7167, p. 107; see also Martin Rudner, "The Draft Development Plan of the Federation of Malaya, 1950-1955," *Journal of Southeast Asian Studies (JSEAS)* (1973), and Gayl D. Ness, *Bureaucracy and Rural Development in Malaysia* (Berkeley, 1967), esp. pp. 100-2.

13. *Legislative Council Proceedings*, 20 September, 1951.

14. Minister of Education, *Legislative Council Proceedings*, 11 December 1958.

15. Federation of Malaysia, *First Malaysia Plan, 1966-70* (Kuala Lumpur, 1966), para. 491.

16. Ibid., paras. 37, 42-3, 180.

17. Cf. Gayl D. Ness, *Bureaucracy*.

18. This Plan, so-called, was never actually published, but its particulars were made known in the *Report on Economic Planning in the Federation of Malaya in 1956, Legislative Council Paper 14 of 1956* (Kuala Lumpur, 1956). For a study of this plan and its place in Malaysian economic history, see Martin Rudner, *Nationalism, Planning and Economic Modernization in Malaysia* (Beverly Hills, 1975).

19. For an historical survey of planning in Malaya, see David Lim, "Malaysia," in Yip Yat Hoong, ed., *Development Planning in Southeast Asia: Role of the University* (Singapore, 1973), and Martin Rudner, *Nationalism, Planning and Economic Modernisation.*

20. Federation of Malaysia, *Third Malaysia Plan 1976-1980* (Kuala Lumpur, 1976), Prime Minister's Foreward, pp. v-vii.

21. If non-defence-related expenditure only be considered, the Peninsular share for education rose from 6.3 percent of the First Five-Year Plan to 12.6 percent of the Second, falling to 11.5 percent of the First Malaysia Plan and further to 7.6 percent of the Second, and rising to 10.3 percent of the Third.

22. *Third Malaysia Plan*, table 22-9.

23. Cf. *Second Malaysia Plan*, p. 231.

24. The internal rate of return to education is that discount rate that equates the discounted flow of education costs to the discounted flow of income benefits, and is the equivalent of the net marginal revenue product of education capital; vide. T. Schultz, "Capital Formation by Education," *Journal of Political Economy* (1960) and G. Becker, *Human Capital* (New York, 1960). On the limitations of education investment analysis, and Rate of Return models generally, see Stephen Merrett, "The Rate of Return to Education: A Critique," *Oxford Economic Papers* (1966), pp. 289-303.

25. O.E. Hoerr, "Education, Income and Equity in Malaysia," in David Lim, ed., *Readings on Malaysian Economic Development* (Kuala Lumpur, 1975). This remains

the only study of the returns to education capital in Malaysia, to date. The distinction between social and private rates of return reflect the usual differences in the education costs actually incurred by the state and private beneficiary, on the one hand, and discontinuities in the flow of benefits from education in "insulated" labour markets like Malaysia, on the other. Ozay Mehmet, "Manpower Planning and Labour Markets in Developing Countries: A Case Study of West Malaysia," *Journal of Development Studies* (1972), pp. 277-289.

26. This is the rate used by the Economic Planning Unit of Malaysia for weighing social preferences in public investment. Another rate for comparison would be the interest rate earned on overseas reserve balances accumulated owing to the long-standing Treasury "Reserves Syndrome." In 1969, yields on long-term U.S. and U.K. government bonds, as indicator of the Returns to Malaysian Official Overseas Reserves, ranged from 7.48 to 8.82 percent; Bank Negara Malaysia, *Annual Report and Statement of Accounts, 1970* (Kuala Lumpur, 1971), pp. 7-8.

27. Ibid., p. 91; *Second Malaysia Plan*, pp. 99-100.

28. Hoerr, "Education, Income and Equity," pp. 295-6.

29. The so-called "Karachi Plan for education in Asia," to which Malaysia subscribed, envisaged the expenditure of four to five percent of GNP on formal education by 1980 as the target date: UNESCO & ESCAFE, *Final Report, Meeting of Ministers of Education of Asian Member States Participating in the Karachi Plan, Tokyo, 2-11 April, 1962* (Bangkok, 1962). The "Karachi Plan" was adopted in 1959.

30. At the primary level in 1974, private schools, mainly Chinese, comprised one percent of all schools and enrolled a half percent of all pupils. At the secondary level private schools, mainly English, comprised 18 percent of all schools (excluding, however, technical and vocational schools) and enrolled just over seven percent of all pupils: Ministry of Education, *Education in Malaysia, 1974* (Kuala Lumpur, 1975), annex 2. It is pertinent to note that official data on Malaysian education refers to enrolments, rather than attendance. Since there is usually a gap between enrolment and actual attendance, especially in poor and rural areas, this reduces the usefulness of official statistics for measuring real educational attainments. However, the enrolment figures do provide, at least, an indicator of trends in social participation in education.

31. Figures in this paragraph are from the *IBRD Report*.

32. Lim Chong Yah, *The Economic Development of Modern Malaya* (Kuala Lumpur, 1967), p. 305.

33. *IBRD Report*, pp. 142 ff.

34. Minister of Education, *Federation of Malaya, Legislative Council Proceedings*, 15 November 1956.

35. *Federation of Malaya Annual Report, 1953* (Kuala Lumpur, 1954), p. 173; UNESCO Regional Office for Education in Asia, *Progress of Education in the Asian Region*, pp. 90-91, Table A8.

36. Federation of Malaysia, Ministry of Education, *Educational Statistics of Malaysia 1938 to 1967* (Kuala Lumpur, 1968), Tables 4-11.

37. *Education in Malaysia, 1974*, annexes 1, 3, 9.

38. Figures in this paragraph are from UNESCO, Regional Office for Education in Asia, *Long Term Projections for Education in Malaysia* (Bangkok, 1962), p. 13; and *Progress in Education in the Asian Region*, p. 111, table A15. These retention ratios apply to peninsular Malaysia only.

39. On Retention Ratios and the effectiveness of primary enrolment, see "The Problem of Educational Wastage," in *Bulletin of the UNESCO Regional Office for Education in Asia* Vol. 1 (1967).

40. The conversion of English primaries to the Malay medium, began in earnest in 1969 and was to be completed by 1975; the secondary level by 1980, sixth form by 1982.

41. The *IBRD Report*, p. 465, cites colonial Education Ministry sources for setting the education constituency for grammar-type secondary education at a maximum of 20 percent of the eligible age group. The optimal transition ratio was accordingly fixed at 30%.

42. *Third Malaysia Plan*, table 22-8. Some 2/3 of Chinese degree students were enrolled in science and applied science disciplines in 1975, compared to 27% of Malays.

43. Note that the Karachi Plan called for a 45:55 balance between arts and other subjects, and the science and technologies, by 1975.

44. While the Second Malaysia Plan forecast an enrolment of 12,800 in the technical and vocational streams by 1975, actual enrolments lagged a third behind this target.

45. Yoshimitsu Takei, John C. Bock, Bruce Saunders, *Educational Sponsorship by Ethnicity: A Preliminary Analysis of the West Malaysian Experience* (Athens, Ohio, 1973).

46. R.M. Sundrum, "Manpower and Educational Development in Eastern and Southern Asia," *Malayan Economic Review* (1971).

47. *Third Malaysia Plan*, chap. 8.

48. Federation of Malaya, Department of Labour and Industrial Relations and Department of Statistics, *Report on Employment, Unemployment and Under-employment 1962* (Kuala Lumpur, 1962).

49. The Treasury, Malaysia, *Economic Report 1975-76* (Kuala Lumpur, 1976), p. 90; *Third Malaysia Plan*, chap. 8.

50. See also Sundrum, *Educational Planning*, pp. 41-3.

51. The results of the 1973 Manpower Survey reproduced in the *Third Malaysia Plan*, table 8:11. Then, vacancies were reported for some 10.4% of Professional and technical posts, 8.6% of administrative and managerial posts, 7.1% of clerical, 6.3% of service, 1.7% of sales, 4.4% of production, 3.1% of agricultural posts.

52. *Third Malaysia Plan*, chap. 8.

53. *IBRD Report*, p. 449.

54. Takei & Bock, *Ethnic Sponsorship in Education*, pp. 8, 11, 12. This study, conducted in 1968-69, reports that almost 60% of Malays in secondary schools are of lower socio-economic origins, and enjoy greater upward mobility through the school system than do non-Malays. At the university level they found that 40% of Malay students come from lower economic strata, compared to a negligible number of non-Malays (p. 11). See also the *Third Malaysia Plan*, Statistics on Racial Enrolment at the Tertiary Level, Table 22-6.

55. *Third Malaysia Plan*, table 4-15, and para. 433.

56. The Ministry of Labour, *Labour Force Sample Survey* (Kuala Lumpur, 1972) indicated that Malay unemployment had tended to improve (1971 figures in brackets) to 6% (7.8%) while the Chinese remained steady at 7% and the Indian

worsened to 12.2% (11.1%). This confirmed trends reported in the *Socio-Economic Survey of Households, 1967-68*, showing that between 1962 and 1968 Malay unemployment fell from 6.1% to 5.8%, whereas for Chinese and Indians it rose from 6% to 6.9% and 10.3%, respectively.

57. IAU & UNESCO, *Higher Education and Development in Southeast Asia*, Vol. 2, pp. 366-7.

58. Myrdal, *Asian Drama*, Vol. III, pp. 1741-3.

59. High Commissioner, *Federation of Malaya, Legislative Council Proceedings*, 30 November 1955. A further 13% of Division 1 posts were unfilled.

60. Cf. Federation of Malaya, *Report of a Committee on the Malayanization of the Public Service* (Kuala Lumpur, 1956); R.O. Tilman, *Bureaucratic Transition in Malaya* (Durham, NC, 1961).

61. *The Colonial Territories 1953-54* (HMSO, London, 1954), Cmd. 9169, para. 111.

62. *Third Malaysia Plan*, para. 424.

63. On this point, and for examples, see Gayl D. Ness, "The Malayan Bureaucracy and its Occupational Communities," *Comparative Studies in Society and History* (1970), esp. p. 183; and Martin Rudner, *Nationalism, Planning and Economic Modernization in Malaysia*.

64. Cf. Milton J. Esman, *Development and Administration in Malaysia* (Ithaca, NY, 1972).

65. Probably the most well-known published work in this line is Mahathir bin Mohammed, *The Malay Dilemma* (Singapore, 1970). The book was banned in Malaysia, notwithstanding Dr. Mahathir's appointment in 1976 as Minister of Education and Deputy Prime Minister, and his subsequent elevation to the Prime Ministership.

66. *Second Malaysia Plan*, para. 20.

67. On the social and educational backgrounds of the early Alliance nationalistic leadership, see R.O. Tilman, "Policy Formulation, Policy Execution, and the Political Elite Structure of Contemporary Malaya," in Wang Gungwu, ed., *Malaysia* (New York, 1965).

68. The political cultural dimensions of political systems, and their development, has not been fully examined in the political science literature. Yet it is clear that there exists a critical symbiotic relationship between the authoritative network of norms and the performance of state institutions in the political system; cf. G. Almond & S. Verba, *The Civic Culture* (Princeton, 1963); L.W. Pye & S. Verba, eds., *Political Culture and Political Development* (Princeton, 1965); David Easton, *A Systems Analysis of Political Life* (New York, 1965); Carl J. Friedrich, *Man and His Government* (New York, 1965).

69. *Report of the Education Policy Committee, Legislative Council Paper 70 of 1952*, para. 7. The term originated in the Report of the Barnes Committee on Malay education, and was subsequently adopted without further elucidation in the 1952 Education Ordinance.

70. Cf. Walker Conner, "National-building nor Nation-destroying?" *World Politics* (1972), pp. 319-55.

71. Cf. Wang Gungwu, "Malayan Nationalism," *Journal of the Royal Central Asian Society* (1962), p. 321 and "Chinese Politics in Malaya," *The China Quarterly*

(1970), pp. 1-30; and R.O. Tilman, "The Socialization of the Chinese into Malaysian Politics; Some Preliminary Observations," *Studies on Asia* (1966).

72. Margaret Roff, "The Politics of Language in Malaya," *Asian Survey* (1967).

73. See R.S. Milne, "National Ideology and Nation-building in Malaysia," *Asian Survey* (1970).

CHAPTER 13

LABOUR POLICY AND THE DILEMMAS OF TRADE UNIONISM IN POST-WAR MALAYA

The Second World War marked a significant turning point in Malayan labour history. Hitherto, the main objective of labour policy had been to encourage an adequate inflow of immigrant workers for Malaya's expanding economy, with the Labour Department acting as "protector" of labour from the more obvious social and economic evils.[1] Such labour legislation as was enacted originated in the British Indian government's concern for the welfare of its expatriate labour force in Malaya. In 1940, however, the Straits Settlements passed a Trade Union Ordinance enabling labour organization for purposes of collective bargaining and economic self-betterment. Although no trade unions were actually registered prior to the Japanese conquest, the stage had now been set for the emergence of organized labour as a representative interest group.

When the British returned to Malaya after the war they found widespread dislocation in the economy, including a scarcity of able manpower and an acute shortage of virtually all consumption goods, especially rice. Guided by Colonial Office policy directives, the British Military Administration moved quickly to organize the deployment of available labour for the tasks of administration and reconstruction. To restrain inflation and force down costs, a rudimentary incomes policy was instituted fixing wages at pre-war levels.[2] At the same time, controls were applied to prices and marketing, but these soon broke down owing to severe shortages compounded by corrupt administration. Since the authorities persistently refused to accept post-war inflation as permanent, wages were never brought into line with prices. Consequently, the real burdens of reconstruction and post-war adjustment were effectively shifted onto labour. In a situation already pregnant with labour unrest, Communist-led trade union militancy not only jeopardized the regime's incomes policy but further threatened its overall political authority.[3]

Responding to the challenge, the newly established Malayan Union government took firm action to restore economic and political order. Up to then, the Malayan Communist Party had sought acceptance under the existing regime, as wartime allies of the British. Communist objectives were pursued vigorously, though through legitimate trade union and overt political activities. To be sure, an official inquiry into the labour situation, the Awberry-Daley Report, had concluded that "industrial grievances were very real." Nonetheless, colonial administrators still tended to regard trade unions as a disruptive factor in an otherwise compliant and docile labour market. Trade union activism, in such an environment, tended to be treated like "manifestations of evil and sedition."[4]

From early 1948 the government began to clamp down "to remove this incubus." "Subversive" political activities were suppressed, radical militants were deported back to Chiang Kai-Shek's China, and, in the end, trade union legislation was introduced to regulate union leadership, which had the effect of outlawing Communists.[5] Tension between the government and the Communist-led Pan-Malayan Federation of Trade Unions escalated until June 1948, when the Malayan Communist Party embarked on insurrection and the Emergency was declared.[6]

The events of summer 1948 brought to an unhappy close the post-liberation era of relative permissiveness in labour policy. Resolute federal action against Communist-influenced trade unionism had forced the disbanding of over half the country's trade unions, including the once pre-eminent Pan-Malayan Federation of Trade Unions. Suddenly more than half Malaya's hitherto organized labour force found itself de-unionized and abandoned, its leadership having fled to the jungle and insurgency. While hostilities opened up between the Malayan Communist Party and colonial authorities, the Malayan government began a timely and far-reaching re-appraisal of labour policy.

Trade Unionism

Official attitudes towards trade unionism in the wake of the recent turmoil were predictably ambivalent. The Trade Union Advisor (TUAM) to the colonial administration believed that interest in trade unionism persisted and that with encouragement there could emerge from the Emergency a solid and democratic trade union movement. Yet others, including a large part of the senior civil service, felt quite the contrary, holding past policy favouring trade unionism to blame for the Communist insurgency. Many accepted the Commissioner for Labour's view that Malayan workers were as yet incapable of differentiating between trade unionism and Communism, and advocated the deferment of any further promotion of trade unionism until the termination of the Emergency.

With the top-level colonial bureaucracy split over the issue of supporting or postponing labour organization, it was left to the High Commissioner to translate his own progressive outlook into policy. Coming down firmly on the side of the TUAM, High Commissioner Sir Edward Gent committed his administration to encouraging the development of "democratic" trade unionism. It was the official policy that the Emergency Regulations not be directed against legitimate labour activities. Yet, it remained to be seen whether such a selective approach to labour policy could be sustained in the unstable environment of an insurgency.

The remaining non-Communist trade union leaders, though hard pressed by the outbreak of the Emergency, found faith in the High Commissioner's position and the TUAM's role. But British business interests operating in Malaya expressed virulent opposition to the High Commissioner's approach. To them trade unionism was but an unnecessary complication in colonial business management, an irritant to "happy" paternalism and a sinister carrier of subversive influence.[7] British planting, mining, banking and mercantile groups appealed jointly for London to apply firmer measures against all manifestations of labour militancy. Their insistence that Malayan labour unrest was "in no sense due to dissatisfaction of the workers with the conditions of employment" [8] was not only tenuous but also constituted a not-so-subtle attempt to bring industrial relations under the Emergency Regulations. As a result of their appeals, Sir Edward was recalled for consultations. His death in an aviation accident en route struck a sad blow at trade unionism in Malaya.

Although Sir Edward Gent's successors proclaimed their adherence to the basic tenets of his labour policy, the mounting tensions of the Emergency exaggerated the strain of trade union policy. From the outset employer interests sought to curtail the activities of the TUAM and to postpone further labour organizing for the duration of the Emergency.[9] By late 1948, trade unionists had begun to complain of harassment by employers as well as by "people concerned with government" under the guise of the Emergency.[10] Continuing fears of Communist infiltration led, in 1949, to changed regulations. New trade unions were allowed only with Executive Council consent following police clearance of the leadership, and the TUAM was instructed henceforth to concentrate his efforts solely on consolidating existing trade unions.

Even though his activities were now severely curtailed, the TUAM was still able to resist attempts by certain government departments and employers to "crack down" and close all unions.[11] Anti-union activities, victimization of trade unionists, and sometimes class exploitation of hapless labourers continued and were abetted by an aura of fear inspired by the Emergency Regulations.[12] In these circumstances, trade union organizing virtually ceased.

With legitimate trade unionism largely suspect, fearful and consequently docile, and subject to periodic insurgent terrorism, the underground Communists were able to reassert their leadership over much of the labour movement. Official disenchantment with trade unionism grew so acute after the assassination of High Commissioner Sir Henry Gurney in October 1951, that the TUAM stood virtually alone in defence of organized labour.[13]

At the London Conference of Labour Department Heads in autumn 1951, strong emphasis was put on the need for industrial harmony if colonial export economies were to expand as planned. Trade unions were deemed acceptable only where industrial relations could be "directly improved" thereby, and expressly not for collective bargaining or the articulation of labour interests generally.[14] The revival of free trade unionism in Malaya was effectively relegated to the distant post-Emergency future.

For the present, the colonial Malayan Labour Department preferred to concentrate its energies on combating Communist influence among labourers. As a way of working around the problem, the Labour Department contemplated promoting the formation of so called panchayats, traditional local councils, as substitutes for genuine trade unions among Tamil plantation workers. Suggestions from the Indian Government Representative in Malaya, itself a legacy of Colonial paternalism, that communal Tamil trade unions be set up as a bulwark against Communism were firmly rejected as a matter of principle by the TUAM. As for the new High Commissioner, Sir Gerald Templer was himself quite indifferent to trade unionism except to warn of the action he would take against Communist infiltration into the movement.[15] Although the Colonial Malayan Government still insisted that the "main aim" of its labour policy remained the establishment of a system of industrial relations based on voluntary organization and consultation between the parties involved, there remained a distinct operational ambiguity between the encouragement given the consolidation of existing trade unions and the unwillingness to promote new unions.

Malayan trade union expansion between 1950 and 1955 was therefore slow and difficult. Trade unionists spoke of a "hidden fear" that inhibited labour organization. Blame was placed on elections, the Malayan Trade Union Congress (MTUC) decided to remain aloof in future and refused to become the industrial wing of the newly established Labour Party. Although the MTUC preferred to maintain political independence, its 1953 Delegates Conference went against government advice and created a political fund "in order to consolidate the workers' front." Fears of an excessive concentration of political influence in the MTUC prompted an amendment of the Trade Union Ordinance to ban the creation of political funds by trade union federations while allowing them for individual trade unions.

In the event, MTUC political efforts did little more than mirror its striking organizational weaknesses. For all the enthusiastic pronouncements of its leadership, the MTUC suffered from such financial, structural and administrative disabilities that it was barely capable of adequately performing its primary liaison function.[16] By 1954 the MTUC had become virtually moribund, and did not even hold its statutory Annual Delegates Conference. Indeed, the MTUC no longer even represented the majority of trade unions. Steps taken by the TUAM and leading trade unionists to resuscitate the MTUC, including the calling of a Conference in April 1955 attended by only 48 of its affiliated unions, led to a major restructuring of the national trade union congress after 1956.

Collective Bargaining

The restoration of the trade union movement, difficult as that was, was a far cry from instituting proper collective bargaining procedures in the highly individualistic, free-wheeling colonial Malayan economy. While readily admitting that collective bargaining was a necessary concomitant of effective trade unionism, colonial Malayan industrial relations suffered conflicts of interest compounded by goal confusion. For its part, the colonial government remained disinclined to encroach on private business interests in Malaya by actively promoting collective bargaining. Moreover any encouragement of wage negotiations would implicitly undermine government's own pursuit of an incomes policy aimed at wage stabilization.

There was some confusion in official circles about the goals of collective bargaining. Organized labour relations were conventionally regarded as the antithesis of, and antidote to, industrial disputes, so that collective bargaining was understood by many to exclude use of the strike weapon. This represented a refusal to accept the "government's weak-kneed trade union policy" and a "subtle form of victimization . . . at all levels."[17] Employers were accused of refusing to recognize trade unions and resisting creation of negotiating machinery. Despite the gradual, painful growth of union numbers and members, these still numbered well below their pre-Emergency peaks.[18] Moreover, the numerical growth was patchy in scope, and only the government services and rubber industry could be said to have been reasonably well-organized.

A promising though late start had been made in forming six national labour federations, yet most individual unions were small, poorly organized, financially weak and plagued by a dearth of capable leadership. However, the year 1955 witnessed a dramatic increase in trade union activity, occasioned in part by the Rubber Boom of that year, in part by a lessening of Emergency restrictions and in part by the "spread effects" of labour activism in neighbouring Singapore. Political circumstances generally had now turned more favourable to trade unionism, in view of Malaya's first General Election and the advent of self-government.

Even while struggling with the restoration of trade unions after 1948, the TUAM set out to organize a national trade union congress. Despite opposition from the civil service and employers on the grounds that the time was premature and that such an organization would be likely to succumb to Communist infiltration, the idea found favour with the High Commissioner. Added support was forthcoming from the British government, then determined to block a Communist-controlled World Conference of Trade Unions offensive in Southeast Asia. Following intensive efforts behind the scenes by the TUAM, a Malayan Trade Union Council (MTUC) was formally inaugurated with much fanfare in March 1950. To mollify the opponents to this approach, and there were many in official and employer circles, the MTUC was accorded no executive authority over affiliated unions, but was limited to serving as a liaison agency for the separate unions and as an aggregator of trade union interests. Government recognized the MTUC as a representative body for both organized and unorganized workers and granted it participation on all government organs where labour was represented, including the Federal Legislative Council. MTUC determination to participate in the political process reflected the belief that political pressure could secure what individual trade unions on their own part could not.

In 1951, the MTUC formally aligned itself with the Malay Nationalist leader Dato Onn bin Ja'afar's Independence for Malaya Party, a calculated gesture against the British-owned rubber estates and mines. After this Party's decisive defeat in the 1952 municipal legitimacy of industrial disputation within the framework of collective bargaining procedure was especially pronounced in the Labour Department, which specifically described its mission as "the securing of peace in industry generally." The role of the Malayan government in industrial relations reflected the ambivalence of colonial industrial relations policy.

Regular collective bargaining procedures, therefore, were slow to arise in the Malayan economy. Following the early failure of trade unions to achieve negotiated wage settlements, the TUAM embarked on a campaign to foster the spirit of collective bargaining through the creation of permanent negotiating machinery for various sectors of the economy. Again employer response was negative, even at a time of rising product prices. A proposed survey of wages and conditions in Malayan industry, a prerequisite for effective collective bargaining, was successfully resisted by employer interests. The colonial authorities declined to press the issue.

Continuing industrial friction in the wake of the 1951 Rubber Boom and the consequential inflation impelled the government to impress upon employers and employees the need for establishing a Joint Industrial Council for the rubber industry. Although the trade unions were receptive to the idea, the Malayan Planting Industry Employers Association (MPIEA) refused to commit the rubber estates to a permanent negotiation machinery. Instead, the rubber employers organization offered to set up a consultative framework together with the unions. In face of employer intransigence, government did not pursue the point. Neither MTUC demands for the establishment of Joint Industrial Councils to facilitate collective bargaining, nor the angry protestations of trade union representatives in the Legislative Council, could goad the government into action or shame employers into concessions. Only when the rubber unions came close to disintegrating in the wake of successive reductions was agreement reached to form a Joint Consultative Committee for the Plantation Industries in March 1955, persuaded perhaps by the impending General Elections.

The rubber employers' participation in a consultative arrangement did not mean their involvement in a systematic negotiating mechanism. The breakthrough in that direction occurred elsewhere. Two months later, in May 1955, a wider-ranging industrial relations mechanism was instituted in the Eastern Mining and Metals Company Joint Industrial Council, serving the tin processing industry. This marked the beginnings of a permanent collective bargaining machinery in the soon-to-be-independent Federation of Malaya.

In the absence of negotiating machinery before 1955, collective bargaining, where it existed, proceeded on an ad hoc basis superintended in the interest of industrial peace by Government. The pattern was set by the rubber industry, where in 1949, falling prices led the MPIEA to propose a wages cut. When this was opposed by the trade unions, the matter was sent to officially sponsored arbitration. Although the award was overtaken by events, henceforth deadlocked negotiations over wages following changes in the fortunes of rubber were automatically referred by the Commissioner for Labour to arbitration. Arbitration came to be regarded in official quarters as the ultimate instrument of its industrial relations policy. Colonial government authority and influence backed the awards.

Officially backed arbitration, together with Emergency constraints on strike action, went far to keep industrial peace. Yet, industrial wage tribunals could hardly substitute adjudication for collective bargaining proper. Since there exist no real judicial criteria for wages adjudication, arbitration tended to reflect conventional colonial economic norms favouring "venture" capital. Arbitrators' awards effectively moderated wage increases at the time of the 1950-51 Rubber Boom, but authorized substantial wage reductions in the subsequent slump.

It is hardly surprising, then, that rubber estate companies came to accept this form of industrial relations as an expedient tool for managing labour relations. On the trade union side, arbitration was denounced as a poor excuse for true collective bargaining. Continual resort to arbitration was taken as evidence of employers' unwillingness to come to terms with trade unionism. Labour frustration was compounded by their own weaknesses in leadership and organization.

This interventionist pattern of industrial relations clearly had a retarding effect on the development of a cohesive and spirited trade union movement. Indeed it very nearly led to the disintegration of existing unions. Government reliance on arbitration to override industrial disputes, though effective in imposing industrial peace, incidentally served to sap trade union spirits and weaken their ability to act in defence of their own interests. Thus, rubber workers unions accepted, more or less passively, four successive reductions in wage rates between 1952 and 1953. While officially recognized unions turned out this lack-lustre performance, underground Communists embarked upon a programme of militant, albeit illicit, industrial action and enjoyed some success in winning estate labour support.[19] Nevertheless, the government retained an abiding faith in the justice and beneficence of industrial arbitration. Official illusions about "the happy relationship which has prevailed between capital and labour in the Federation" remained intact.[20] Only one month later the bubble burst.

An MPIEA attempt to obtain another wage cut was, this time, strongly opposed by the rubber workers unions, and was referred as usual to arbitration. The arbitrator's award, published in January 1954, was immediately seized upon by employers to pay the reduced wage without even waiting for the final settlement, despite continuing trade union objections. In fact, the unions were much too weak and demoralized even to maintain internal cohesion, let alone offer effective resistance. So great was the loss of faith in industrial procedures that trade union leaders even asked government to set up a statutory Wages Council to fix wage rates for the rubber industry. It required superlative efforts by the TUAM and the International Conference of Free Trade Unions' representative in Malaya, aided somewhat by rising rubber prices, to restore trade union confidence to a point where a settlement with the MPIEA was reached which, though virtually identical to the Arbitration Award, had at least been "freely negotiated."[21] By the end of the year, trade union morale had improved, as individual unions merged into a National Union of Plantation Workers (NUPW).

The NUPW proved more prepared to act in pursuit of members' interests, and the request for a Wages Council was tacitly withdrawn. The traumatic experience of spring 1954, coming dangerously close to shattering trade unionism in the rubber industry, also motivated new thinking about collective bargaining procedures. This culminated in the establishment of the Joint Consultative Council for the Plantation Industries.

Government's position with regard to collective bargaining in private industry demonstrated the dilemmas of colonial politics at a time of post-war transition. Conflicting interests and objectives between improving the relative position of Malayan labour on one hand, and upholding the prerogatives of a colonial export economy on the other, injected a high degree of ambivalence into industrial relations policy. Certainly the TUAM and moral persuasion were used to promote trade unionism, but the government was not at all prepared to infringe upon its avowed "principle of self-government in industry" to take positive action to ensure conformity with its own objective of "good" industrial practices.[22]

Despite the professed support for arbitration, the government firmly rejected labour demands, originally inspired by an arbitrator's report, that wages and conditions of employment be included within the terms of reference of the (1954) Mission of Enquiry into the Rubber Industry. These were dismissed as matters for private negotiation rather than public investigation. Yet, indicative of the paradoxes affecting labour policy, the colonial government initiated a survey of wages in shops and restaurants wherein labour was acknowledged to be poorly organized, but refused to countenance pleas to inquire into working conditions in the transport industry despite the repeated requests of a weak trade union engaged in a bitter dispute. The union involved subsequently collapsed and died. Strikes (and lockouts) were legal, yet as late as April 1955 police were sent against strikers at a leading British company, Tonoh Tin Mines, to the consternation of trade union representatives on the Legislative Council. Inconsistencies in industrial relations policy and practice tended to diminish its acceptability among those who were supposed to conform to its terms.

Whitleyism in the Government Service

Industrial relations in the government service underwent a somewhat smoother transition to British-style Whitley Councils. Following the establishment of British rule in post-war Malaya, public service salaries were fixed by periodically special Public Commissions. This form of salary determination came under challenge from local personnel in particular, who demanded that proper collective bargaining procedures be introduced into the government service. Because of its avowed commitment to trade unionism, the colonial government agreed in 1949 to the formation of Government Joint Councils.

Soon afterwards, this decision was rescinded pending the outcome of a study of the implications of national-level Whitleyism for Malaya. As a concession to collective bargaining, the government offered to enter into "negotiations" with public service trade unions, provided they did not go beyond the accepted salary scales. Despite union pressure, the government refused to budge on this point, with the result that "collective bargaining" in the public service was reduced to a means of legitimizing salary structures already officially determined.

As a matter of principle, the colonial government had long taken care to avoid having its own position as Malaya's largest single employer exert pressure on private sector wages. Trade unions generally sought to make government a "model employer," establishing wage leadership for private employers to follow. The government categorically refused this role, and its unwillingness to even contemplate wage leadership prompted its insistence that officially determined salary scales be strictly adhered to. Only one exception was made, for expatriate senior civil service officers, whose unregistered "Associations" aroused much resentment among other legally constituted domiciled public service unions.[23] The latter, lacking access to genuine collective bargaining, turned, upon occasion, to their representation in the Legislative Council to try and wring concessions out of government, without success.

It was only after the Rubber Boom expired and inflationary tendencies ebbed that a British expert was summoned to Malaya in March 1952 to make recommendations on the establishment of Whitley Councils. Finally, in April 1953, two national Whitley Councils were inaugurated, one each for monthly- and daily-rated government personnel.

With the establishment of Whitley Councils, public service unions sought "categorical" assurances that government would never again take "unilateral action" on civil service wages, salaries and allowances outside the bilateral negotiating machinery. Although these assurances were indeed given, certain employer interests were slow to accept the new situation. Thus, in the 1953 Budget Debate, repeated demands were put forward by company representatives in the Federal Legislative Council for cut-backs in government salary levels, which evoked sharp reminders from both the government and trade unions that public emoluments were now arranged strictly by negotiation in Whitley Councils.

Although Whitley Councils were acknowledged to be functioning "quite well" public service unions complained of persistent delays in government responding to points raised in negotiations. However, if collective bargaining with government was a slow process, at least it was bargaining. Following lengthy and intensive negotiations, a landmark was reached in May 1955, when the first fruit of Malayan Whitleyism was presented to the Legislative Council for ratification. Here again employer forbearance on industrial relations seemed to mellow with the imminence of the General Election.

Labour Protection

With the decline in trade union membership following the suppression of the Communist-controlled labour movement, and in line with its inherent paternalism, the colonial Malayan Labour Department decided in late 1948 to introduce "clear and comprehensive legislation for the protection of all workers." A draft revised Labour Code was then prepared and circulated to rubber and tin employers associations, chambers of commerce and trade unions, and was extensively amended in the light of their recommendations. After having been evaluated by the International Labour Organization (ILO), the proposed "Employment Code" was readied for introduction to the Legislative Council.

At this point, in autumn 1949, the attention of the colonial administration shifted towards its capital investment programme, the so called Draft Development Plan. Consequently its much vaunted Employment Code was shelved, ostensibly for want of "finance."[24] In spite of pleas for its immediate implementation by trade unionists and their sympathizers, the Employment Code lay dormant for another three years.

By 1953, the government decided that trade unions were still too weak to ensure proper working conditions, and that "basic standards of (labour) protection" were necessary as a base point for future collective bargaining. The 1949 Employment Bill was therefore resurrected. Employers' reactions were instantaneous and virulent: they attacked the approach made to the ILO, and resented their not having been consulted over the Bill's final draft. Rubber and tin interests, in particular, objected strenuously to their being given specific social and employment responsibilities under the proposed ordinance. And indeed, the very principle of the Employment Bill was bitterly condemned by employers as a retrogression from trade unionism and collective bargaining back to "benevolent paternalism."

Trade unionists in turn accused employers of obstructing the creation of joint negotiating bodies, and admitting their own weakness, fully supported the setting of "minimum standards." If anything, the MTUC wanted even stronger legislation against employer power, despite the stigma of "protection." Faced with employer demands for further postponement and Labour pressure for immediate action, the government decided to refer the proposed legislation to a select Committee of the Legislative Council. This effectively removed the employment Bill from the mainstream of Malayan political life, and allowed the issue to remain cloaked by employer obstructionism for a further two years.

With slow deliberation and after some prompting from a government eyeing the imminence of constitutional change, the Select Committee finally settled on policy lines for a new employment Bill. It was with almost indecent haste that the federal government conveyed the new draft, one that was rather more favourable to employers, to the Legislative Council at its very last session of the pre-election era, in June 1955.

Under the proposed legislation, government itself assumed overall responsibility for protecting the status of labour, thus relieving employers of any obligations for housing and health services. Still neither the trade unions nor employers appeared content, and the resulting Legislative Council debate was heated and sometimes acrimonious. Once again there occurred the curious spectacle of employer interests arguing that wages and conditions of employment should be left to collective bargaining, while trade unionists demanded "realism" by way of statutory measures to accomplish what their weak voluntary organizations could not. The Employment Bill was at last passed into law after seven years in the making, at the closing stage of colonial administration in Malaya.[25]

Labour Relations in Post-War Malaya

The Second World War and its aftermath had a pronounced impact on labour policy and the formation of a trade union movement in British Malaya. As a result of the turmoil caused by the Japanese conquest and occupation of the Malayan peninsula, and the circumstances of the British post-war restoration, the previously existing political, economic and social orders came under profound challenge. Perhaps more than in any other sphere of public policy, the effects of the war engendered confrontation over the fundamental norms, policies and institutions of labour relations.

As in other economic and social policy spheres, the original objectives of post-war colonial labour policy were never fully realized. Much of the initial intent for trade unionism, Whitleyism, and labour protection remained unfulfilled by the mid-1950s, when Malaya became independent. If the closing decade of colonial rule succeeded in telescoping into a short period the establishment of new patterns for industrial relations, indeed their substance, seemed less than their form. Yet, while trade unions, Whitleyism and labour-protection were still in a rudimentary state, nonetheless a basic legal-institutional framework emerged which served as the main-stay of labour policy following the transition to independence.[26]

ENDNOTES

1. On the pre-war background to Malayan labour policy see J. Norman Parmer, *Colonial Labour Policy and Administration* (New York, 1960), and Charles Gamba, *The Origins of Trade Unionism in Malaya* (Singapore, 1962).

2. On post-war economic policy see Martin Rudner, "Financial Policies in Post-War Malaya: The Fiscal and Monetary Measures of Liberation and Reconstruction," *Journal of Imperial and Commonwealth History* Vol. 3 (1975). The objectives of incomes policy were to restrain general inflationary pressures in view of existing shortages; to restructure the costs of Malaya's export industries, mainly rubber, along pre-war lines; and to minimize the costs of military administration to H.M. Exchequer.

3. On the Communist trade unions and their post-war tactics see H. Z. Hanrahan, *The Communist Struggle in Malaya* (New York, 1956), chap. 4; Ruth T. McVey, "The Southeast Asian Insurrectionary Movement," in Cyril E. Black & Thomas P. Thornton eds., *Communism and Revolution* (Princeton, 1964), pp. 171 *et passim*; C. Gamba, *The Origins of Trade Unionism in Malaya*, esp. Chap. 7; and Michael Stenson, *Industrial Conflict in Malaya* (London, 1970).

4. Cf. S.S. Auberry & F.W. Daley, *Labour and Trade Union Organization in the Federation of Malaya and Singapore* (London: HMSO, 1948); Hanrahan, *Communist Struggle in Malaya*; Stenson, *Industrial Conflict in Malaya*; Major Edgar O'Ballance, *Malaya: The Communist Insurgent War* (London, 1966), p. 69; Anthony Short, *The Communist Insurrection in Malaya* (New York, 1975); Victor Purcell, *Malaya: Communist or Free?* (London, 1954, p. 42).

5. Federation of Malaya, *Labour Department Report, 1948* (Kuala Lumpur, Printer, 1949), p. 26.

6. The question as to who "started" the Emergency is still subject to debate. So far as the British administration was concerned, the MCP insurgency was a premeditated act of insurgency against a territory "directly associated with the Western Democracies" (*Federation of Malaya Annual Report, 1948* [Kuala Lumpur, 1949], Introduction). In this view, the Communist rebellion originated in instructions from Moscow transmitted at the International Students Union Conference held in Calcutta in February, 1948, where the decision to launch insurrectionary attacks throughout Southeast Asia was allegedly taken. Interestingly, Communist sources have denied that the MCP was prepared for armed struggle, and argued that the proclamation of the Emergency marked a premeditated assault by the colonial authorities on the MCP and progressive trade unions, catching them somewhat by surprise (G.L. Bondarevsky, "Crisis of the Colonial System," *National Liberation Struggle of the Peoples of East Asia, Reports Presented in 1949 to the Pacific Institute of the Academy of Sciences, USSR*

(Bombay, 1951). There is ample evidence to suggest that the MCP was indeed about to abandon its civilian struggle for an armed insurrection, but that the Colonial authorities succeeded in launching a pre-emptive, and in the event, decisive blow; see, e.g., Purcell, *Malaya: Communist or Free?*, p. 132 et passim, and McVey, "Southeast Asian Insurrectionary Movements," 'pp. 172-3, where the evidence is summarized.

7. Cf. Chairman Sir John Hay's address to United Sua Betong Rubber Estates Ltd. general meeting, 17 June 1948.

8. *Straits Times*, 24 June 19489. J.D. Mead, *Federation of Malaya, Legislative Council Proceedings*, 6 July 1948 (Henceforth: *L.C. Proc.*).

9. J.D. Mead, *Federation of Malaya Legislative Council Proceedings*, 6 July 1948.

10. M.P. Rajagopal, *L.C. Proc.* 18 November 1948.

11. Trade Union Advisor, Malaya to Charles Gamba, cited in *The Origins of Trade Unionism in Malaya*, p. 359.

12. On the impact of the Emergency on trade unionism in Malaya, see *Trade Union Advisor, Malaya Annual Report 1949* (Kuala Lumpur, 1949), p. 3; Federation of Malaya, Labour Department Annual Report 1953 (Kuala Lumpur, 1954), p. 17; Commissioner for Labour, Singapore, *Review of the Labour Situation* (Singapore, January 1949; and Gamba, *The Origins of Trade Unionism in Malaya*, pp. 360, 366-7.

13. It is significant that neither the Labour Department nor Trade Union Advisor saw fit to publish reports for 1950, 1951 and 1952 owing to "pressure of other work".

14. Cf. Minutes of Meetings, Conference of Heads of Labour Departments, London, 14 November 1951, Appendix C; Colonial Office, *Labour Administration in the Colonies*, Colonial No. 275, London 1951. It is interesting to note that whereas Malayan employer interests were represented at the Conference in the person of Sir Sydney Palmer, the trade unions were not. See also *The Economist*, "Protecting the Colonial Worker," (8 September 1951).

15. General Templer's first address to the Legislative Council ignored trade unionism. In response to the hard feelings resulting from this ommission, Sir Gerald agreed to address the Trade Union Conference at which he warned against their falling "under the spell" of Communist influence.

16. *Federation of Malaya Annual Report, 1954* (Kuala Lumpur, 1955), p. 73 on these points. A major weakness in the MTUC was the fact that its business was conducted in English, an alien tongue to most trade unionists.

17. Labour spokesman Enche Mohammed Yusoff Noor, *L.C. Proc.* 26 November 1953.

18. In 1947, there were reportedly over 300 trade unions with about 195,000 members in the Federation of Malaya, *Federation of Malaya Annual Report, 1947* (Kuala Lumpur, 1948), p. 10; by 1955, membership of officially registered trade unions reached 145,749: *Federation of Malayan Annual Report, 1955* (Kuala Lumpur, 1956), pp. 89-90.

19. See the *Report and Award of a Board of Arbitration on Plantation Wages, Legislative Council Paper 22 of 1951*, para. 17: "In an industrial arbitration no such (judicial) process is possible because there are no rules for wage fixing and coherent principles cannot be deduced from practice."

20. *Federation of Malaya Annual Report, 1951* (Kuala Lumpur, 1952) p. 35; *Federation of Malaya Annual Report, 1952*, p. 6; *Straits Times*, 8 September 1951, p. 8; and Gamba, *The Origins of Trade Unionism in Malaya*, pp. 373-5.

21. See, the *Federation of Malaya Annual Report, 1954*, p. 82 on the consequences of the 1954 arbitration award.

22. On the Government's view of its own role in industrial relations, see the Fed*eration of Malaya Annual Report,* 1954, p. 79.

23. *L.C. Proc.*, 2 July 1952. In reply to the trade unions' criticism of the expatriate officer's "Associations" as "non-registered trade unions," the Attorney-General retorted ingeniously that these Associations did not "habitually negotiate" and were therefore excused from registering. Nevertheless, other public service groups were sternly warned "in no uncertain terms" against failing to register as legally required.

24. Federation of Malaya, *Labour Department Report, 1949* (Kuala Lumpur, 1950), p. 4. See also Martin Rudner, "The Draft Development Plan of the Federation of Malaya," *Journal of Southeast Asian Studies* Vol. 3 (1972), pp. 63-96.

25. Although the colonial authorities rushed to enact the Employment Ordinance prior to the 1955 elections, the newly elected Alliance government was less eager to proceed with its implementation. Further amendments were introduced at the behest of employers, and the Employment Ordinance was brought into force only two years later, on the eve of Malayan independence.

26. *Vide.* Martin Rudner, "Malayan Labour in Transition: Labour Policy and Trade Unionism, 1956-63," *Modern Asian Studies* Vol. 7 (1973), pp. 21-45.

CHAPTER 14

MALAYAN LABOUR IN TRANSITION:
Labour Policy and Trade Unionism, 1955-63

Malayan labour and trade union policy at the eve of Merdeka (independence) bore the indelible imprints of past crises and uneven development. Prior to the Second World War trade unions were outlawed in British Malaya, where labour policy limited itself to protecting workers from the more blatant social and economic evils as a means of encouraging immigration of needed man-power.[1] By the end of the war and Japanese occupation, however, the hitherto transient Chinese and Indians had become trans-formed into a domiciled labour force, conscious of their organiza-tional power and prepared to defend their interests.

Initial post-war attempts at trade unionism under a predomi-nantly Communist leadership succeeded in partially upsetting the regressive incomes policy of the reconstruction period, but in doing so came to challenge the authority of an uneasy colonial regime.[2] Responding with vigorous counteraction culminating in the proclamation of the 1948 Emergency, the British authorities managed to break the communist hold over labour. Under the tu-telage of a Trade Union Advisor for Malaya (TUAM), the colonial gov-ernment proceeded to reconstruct a more compliant and docile trade union movement. This second attempt at trade unionism never exhibited real strength of enterprise and finally crumbled in spring 1955, under the weight of successive industrial defeats, offi-cial indifference and employer hostility.[3]

Out of the maelstrom of failure there arose in the early summer of 1955 a better organized, more experienced, more confident trade union leadership reflecting the crest of national self-aware-ness accompanying the advent of self-government. Yet the emer-gence of a new, national trade union movement encountered a

Modern Asian Studies, Vol. 7, Pt. 1 (January, 1973).

heritage of labour policy mingling suspicion with conservatism, guided by the dead hand of the recent past.

Labour policy and politics

With the advent of independence, Malayan labour policy was confronted by a crisis in role expectations. As a matter of form, the newly elected Alliance government reiterated its commitment to foster trade unionism "by every possible means."[4] This only begged the question as to the place of labour in national political and economic development strategy. Whereas labour relations historically involved mainly conflicts of interests between employers and unions, with government doing little more than fixing the rules of the game, after the emergence of an elected government, the major problem of labour policy became one of role definition. On one hand the independent government was determined to exercise control over economic policy in the interest of promoting its development agenda, while on the other, the trade unions sought to capitalize on the newly democratized political system for the advancement of labour interests.

The question first came to a head shortly after the 1955 General Elections, when the Malayan Trade Union Congress (MTUC), assuming the role of arbiter of democracy, ventured to criticize Malaya's delicately contrived constitutional arrangement and chastised the Alliance government for accepting an allegedly "half-baked Independence" from Britain. At about the same time, a series of strike actions were initiated in response to reduced estate wages resulting from falling rubber prices. Fearing what it perceived as an attempt to recreate the situation of 1945-48, the still-unsteady Alliance government issued a grave warning to the trade unions against using industrial unrest to threaten the political order.[5] In a challenging reply the President of the MTUC pointedly justified the quasi-political role assumed by the trade union movement: "If the Alliance . . . could boycott the Government and withdraw all its nominees to threaten the colonial administration, surely it is also a democratic right for the Trade Union Council to threaten a constitutional strike."[6] Yet, it was precisely this threat of politicized trade unionism that alarmed Alliance sensitivities. Without resolving its own ambivalence towards the role of labour, the Alliance government reacted to this situation by posing a distinction between "normal" and "abnormal" trade union activities, the former to be tolerated, the latter to bear the full weight of official opprobrium.[7]

One thing which greatly piqued the Alliance government throughout its first term in office was the feeling that the MTUC "always"
sided with the opposition against the government.[8] Refuting
charges of opposition party control over their movement, MTUC
spokesmen insisted that their representatives in the appointed portion of the Legislative Council sat purely as trade unionists and not
as Labour Party members: "It must be known that the trade union
movement in this country is free and independent. We cannot tolerate any interference especially from political parties."[9]

As the 1959 General Election drew on, a pressured Alliance appealed to the MTUC leadership to abstain from "politics" in return
for influence at court.[10] Shortly afterwards the MTUC leadership formally denounced the "political" activities of certain of its component unions, rejected Socialist Front overtures, and adopted an
ostensibly "neutral" stance vis-a-vis the incumbent Alliance administration. In agreeing not to challenge the Alliance politically, the
MTUC leadership issued a pointed reminder to government that
their new relationship, and the position of the trade union leaders
themselves, would depend very much on the "consequences" of
future labour policy.[11]

This understanding between the MTUC leadership and Alliance
effectively undermined the SF and deeply split the two arms of the
labour movement. SF bitterness over the newly forged MTUC-Alli-
ance relationship inspired their attack on the union leaders as
mere "stooges" of British colonialism in the past and of the Alliance government of the present. MTUC leaders were accused of
betraying labour interests to the "plantocracy" and government; of
informing on trade union activities to the American CIA; and of vio-
lating their self-proclaimed political neutrality by offering Alliance
ministers a platform to "do propaganda."[12]

When the Alliance rewarded the MTUC President with appointment to the Dewan Negara (senate), the SF strenuously denounced
him for having forsaken the labour cause, and charged the government with subverting the trade union movement through the dispensation of honours. Coming to the defence of the MTUC, the
Minister of Labour publicly praised it as a representative body of
free trade unions serving the best interests of the workers. Not entirely displeased with their relationship, government maintained
that it was "only right" in the "present stage" of trade union development that organized labour eschew party politics.[13] The MTUC
therefore sacrificed alignment with opposition parties for a tenuous
rapport with the political powers-that-be. This in turn brought

down the wrath of the SF upon the MTUC leadership, with challenges to its labour credo combined with vain threats to form a rival trade union federation.[14]

Fearful of the SF's gaining "political influence" over the trade union movement, the Alliance right wing, both the Malayan Chinese Association (MCA) and the United Malays National Organization (UMNO) asked that "politicians" be barred from trade union affairs.[15] While conceding the right of individual trade unionists to engage in politics, the government re-emphasized firmly and forthrightly that it would never countenance any attempt of the trade union movement to play a "political role."[16] So far as the Alliance government was concerned, any politicization of trade unionism would have raised the specter of reinforced left-wing opposition ranks.

No single factor conditioned the government's approach to organized labour so much as the Alliance's profound fear of Communist subversion of the trade union movement. According to the authorities, there were at the time of independence some 50,000 Communists conspiring to subvert Malayan institutions, with the trade unions an obvious and especially exposed target for subversive machinations. In face of this perceived threat, the government pledged itself to protect the trade unions from infiltration by Communists as well as by those acting "in furtherance of the objectives" of Communism.[17] Its weaponry would include the Emergency Regulations inherited from the colonial administration and, later, its own Internal Security Act. In brandishing these formidable statutory weapons the government offered "unequivocal" assurances that "no genuine trade unionists need have any fear when going about their legitimate trade union business."[18]

These reassurances notwithstanding, the MTUC declared itself firmly opposed to both Communist subversion and government repression, and expressed uneasiness that government protection might turn into suppression.[19] To alleviate this anxiety, the MTUC suggested the creation of an all-party anti-subversion committee, but the government declined to share its custody of national security.[20]

Obsessed by the threat of Communist infiltration, the federal government remained intensely suspicious of militant trade union activity, tending to equate activism with subversion. Shortly after independence four leaders of the militant and successful National Union of Factory and General Workers were arrested on the ground of "propagating communist methods and practices."[21]

The MTUC itself termed these arrests "a challenge to the democratic Trade Union Movement of Malaya."[22] Labour and opposition demands that a White Paper be published specifying the reasons for the detention of these trade unionists were solidly rebuffed by government, albeit with assurances that there was "nothing to fear."[23] The subsequent release of one of the leaders on condition that he abstain from trade union activities merely enhanced MTUC anxieties over abuse of the Emergency Regulations. Later attempts by the MTUC to have government explain the arrest of trade unionists under the Emergency Regulations and Internal Security Act were to no avail.

Indeed, so sensitive was the Alliance to possible Communist manifestations that even May Day demonstrations by registered trade unions were barred.[24] Denouncing the Alliance as an "enemy" of trade unionism, the SF accused government of arresting activist trade unionists, banning militant unions, including the National Union of Factory and General Workers, and refusing to allow the formation of a national trade union federation. While aggressive trade unions endured the heavy hand of government, docile unions and tractable leaders were not only accepted but even set on a pedestal.[25]

Alliance perception of the role of trade unions was related not only to its political anxieties but also to its strategy for economic development. So far as budgetary considerations were concerned, the federal government, as the largest single employer of labour in the country, shared a common interest with employers on wage matters. Moreover, in Alliance economic thought, wage stability was regarded as a pre-condition for the expansion of both the public and private sectors. By way of dignifying this thinking by reference to economic theory, the Minister of Finance maintained, in face of abundant evidence of export-led demand-pull inflation, that trade union cost-push pressure threatened an inflationary spiral imperilling fulfillment of the First Five Year Plan (1956-60).[26]

To forestall the prospect of heavy wage demands the federal government, shortly after independence, suggested a rudimentary "incomes policy" based on the exercise of restraint over the trade unions. Earlier, in an extraordinary statement, the Minister of Commerce and Industry had publicly chastised the trade unions for their activism and praised employers' resistance to their demands, to the applause of the Alliance-dominated Legislative Council.[27] It was a shocked and embittered trade unionist who retorted bitingly that government . . .

Openly criticized trade unions for resorting to legitimate industrial action in trade disputes and promised support for employers. Not a word was said about bad employers. Unions making demands were accused of taking orders from communists and subversive elements. Nothing could be further from the truth. The stark truth is that the average workers does not enjoy a reasonable standard of living.[28]

Still, the Alliance government expected "responsibility on the part of labour" in order to achieve "a high standard of industrial peace" deemed necessary to attract foreign capital to Malaya.[29] The comparative passivity of Malayan trade unions, for which government claimed responsibility, appealed considerably to overseas investors.[30] So far as the authorities were concerned, labour policy had become instrumental to other industrial and economic goals.

Government's primary means of control over organized labour was the Trade Union Ordinance. Introduced in spring 1959 after a year's deliberation in the National Joint Labour Advisory Council, the Trade Union Ordinance was intended as a "realistic" measure to bar subversion and ensure a modicum of industrial peace.[31] According to the Act, labour organization was limited to "similar" occupations or trades, so that omnibus federations were banned. Compulsory registration was continued with new restrictions imposed on leadership, organization and union administration. Government authorities were given substantial checks over trade union finance, including the power to investigate their internal affairs.

While the MTUC accepted the Trade Union Ordinance, 1959, as necessary "to ensure the workers' interests," it did admit to being "not happy" over "the restrictions on freedom of association embodied in it," particularly compulsory registration and government control over union leadership-selection, organization and management. Humbled by authority, the MTUC was left to plead pathetically that the new law be applied "with understanding and sympathy" so as not to harass established trade unions.[32] A demand that provision be made to have the Trade Union Ordinance also protect weak trade unions from exploitation by employers, and union organizers from victimization, was dismissed in deference to the official doctrine of "voluntary" trade unionism.

Castigating the MTUC for lending itself to "anti-labour legislation," the SF denounced the Trade Union Ordinance, 1959, as a violation of the principle of free labour organization and accused the Alliance of seeking to crush the trade union movement. Blaming the restrictions in the Trade Union Ordinance, 1959, for the fall in trade union membership since independence, socialist trade union-ists vainly implored government to relax its regulations over labour and abandon the "bogey" of communism now that the Emergency had ended. However, the Alliance government was quite unwilling to see the trade unions deviate from the instrumental role allotted them in federal labour policy.

Trade Unions and Industrial Relations

Continuing the colonial administration's approach to industrial relations, the newly elected Alliance government declared as its policy "to foster the development of healthy Trade Unions and to leave wages and working conditions to be settled as far as possible by voluntary negotiations and by agreement between the repre-sentatives of employers and workers."[33] Yet, the federal govern-ment could no longer remain remote from industrial relations, since in its own view the maintenance of industrial peace was a key factor in encouraging domestic and foreign capital investment. For the promotion of industrial peace, while remaining true to the principle of free collective bargaining, the Ministry of Labour set up an Industrial Relations Division designed to encourage the forma-tion of industrial negotiation machinery, to act as a conciliator in industrial disputes and to provide industrial courts. On the other hand, the government declared itself "not convinced" that compul-sory recognition of trade unions, imposition of industrial relations machinery, or obligatory arbitration, would lead to "sound, healthy and democratic" labour-management relations.[34]

As in the past the principle of voluntarism remained directed, in practice, against Malaya's nascent, still-weak trade union move-ment. However, as a concession to their penultimate concern for social justice, the Alliance government did reserve for itself the right to intervene where workers found it "impossible" to form "ef-fective" trade unions to prevent exploitation."[35]

Very few among Malaya's British-owned rubber estates and tin mines were truly reconciled to trade unionism and collective bar-gaining at the time of independence. Complaining that it was "not easy" to deal with labour "indoctrinated for many years by com-munistic theories," one leading planter informed the recently-elected Alliance that employers looked to government to re-establish "a peaceful Malaya" by getting rid of labour "violence and intimidation."[36] Some of the still prevalent ambivalence among employers was evident when the (British) Malayan Chamber of

Mines expressed a preparedness to negotiate with the trade unions to establish a joint Industrial Council about the same time as a leading miner charged "the so-called leaders of the trade unions" with "inexperience and irresponsibility" in manipulating labour "for their own ends or for political purposes."[37] Nor were employers above terming quite legitimate industrial action "communist-inspired," for political purposes of their own.[38] Even as late as 1960, a significant article appearing in the rubber estates' trade magazine, *The Planter*, and reprinted in the influential Association of British Malaya journal *Malaya*, could still describe "most" trade union leaders as being "bereft of ideas," nurturing "old slogans" and engaging in "cheap demagogy." [39] Labour activism was denounced as the work of "outside," implicitly communist agitators, and was said to inhibit foreign capital investment. In a cunning attempt to associate the government with employer resistance to trade union activism, strikes were depicted as "direct political" challenges to constituted authority. Such sentiments indicated clearly that employers still doubted the very legitimacy of trade union activity, the articulation of labour interests. This was hardly an attitude conducive to inspiring the mutual confidence required for amicable and effective industrial relations.

Neither did the trade unions obtain much support from the federal Labour Department in their quest for recognition. For one thing, Alliance government policy was resolutely against making the recognition of trade unions or establishment of joint negotiating machinery mandatory. Furthermore, expatriate officials were not altogether out of sympathy with British employers still (as late as the 1960s) viewing joint consultation with trade unions as "an invention of the devil": "One cannot blame all estate managers who refuse to institute joint consultative machinery. Some have bitter memories of experiments along these lines in the past and are not anxious to repeat the experiments."[40]

At the same time, trade union leaders were patronizingly dismissed by expatriate officials as "inexperienced" men incapable of realizing the "eventual result of their action." This apparent convergence of views between the top echelon of the Labour Department and employers seriously compromised the role of the Department in the promotion of voluntary industrial relations. Indeed, Labour Department officialdom quite correctly suspected the trade unions of undermining their historically paternal role towards once-docile immigrant labour force.[41]

Among the non-socialist political parties there was little enthusiasm for trade unionism. UMNO's right wing regarded "labour troubles" as symptomatic of the social tensions arising from the presence of non-Malays in the country, concluding disparagingly: "There are a lot of people in the country we don't need."[42]

Even the mainly non-Malay opposition Peoples Progressive Party (PPP), notwithstanding its rhetorical declarations favoring "trade unionism" and "the unity of workers," accepted the existing policy regime as being fully compatible with the advancement of labour interests ("they are not complaining"),[43] to the obvious delight of the Alliance. Indeed PPP-run Ipoh Town Council expressed concern that trade union activities might deter Hong Kong industrialists from investing in their industrial zone, and asked the federal government to "keep an eye on the trade unions."[44] While acknowledging the possible exploitation of labour in such ventures, the self-styled "Socialist-minded" PPP still insisted, with ostentatious support from Alliance MPs, that it was more important to attract industrial investment from abroad.

It has long been a conventional wisdom of the Malayan political center that industrial growth, even at the expense of trade union development, would eventually lead to a diminishing of social tensions arising out of economic injustice. Faith in industrialization was prejudiced against trade unionism.

The two great issues of industrial relations confronting the Malayan trade union movement remained the formation of joint negotiating machinery and the extension of union recognition to those sectors where this was not yet forthcoming. In addition to the two industrial councils established just prior to the 1955 elections, a further five joint councils were set up by the time of independence, all in public or municipal enterprises. Most private employers were still stubbornly resisting the introduction of institutionalized collective bargaining procedures in industry. Not even in the rubber industry were the trade unions entirely satisfied with their recently won concession of a joint consultative council:

> We believe in self-government and democracy. It is an insult to our intelligence to suggest that we cannot have democracy in industries. Industrial democracy demands not the setting up of joint consultative councils, but full-scale joint industrial councils in the various industries.[45]

Incapable of securing employer agreement on their own, the trade unions, in frustration, called upon government to set up joint industrial councils, especially for the mining and transport industries. This the federal government refused to do, in keeping with its espousal of "voluntary" industrial relations. In reply, trade unionists charged the authorities with failure to promote even voluntary industrial relations machinery, insisting that effective trade unionism required the establishment of joint industrial councils in all industries, at all levels. The absence of adequate negotiating machinery contributed to poor labour relations and was a cause for industrial disputes.[46] Whereas joint consultative bodies were set up for a number of smaller enterprises through 1963, none of the major industries had yet progressed to joint industrial councils.

The main struggle of the trade union movement during the 1950s and early 1960s was over the basic issue of recognition. "The main opposition to the growth of a free and independent trade union movement in this country is the reluctance on the part of some employers to accept trade unions as the normal industrial relations practice."[47] Although the larger British-owned firms were generally amenable to dealing with organized labour, despite their antipathies, many local Asian employers remained strongly averse to recognizing trade unionism and collective bargaining.

Employers did not hesitate to exploit labour's weakness.[48] Company tactics intended to stave off trade unionism ranged from the subtle to the nefarious. Trade union leaders found themselves driven to admonish certain "clever" employers against offering wage increases designed to thwart organization of their labour force and order them to deal with the trade unions directly.[49] Other employers resorted to a variety of stratagems including the formation of company unions,[50] exploiting regional unemployment to forestall trade unionism,[51] inclusion of (illegal) anti-union clauses in employment contracts,[52] intimidation and victimization of union organizers and members[53] and most iniquitous of all, manipulation of ethnic sensibilities to prevent labour unity.[54] Among the more blatant offenders, according to the trade unions, were bus companies, locally-owned rubber estates, especially on the east coast, the iron ore industry and Penang port contractors. Blame for this situation was placed by the SF squarely on Alliance shoulders and particularly on the Trade Union Ordinance, 1959. Government policy, it was claimed, prevented the formation of a strong federation of labour to extend trade unionism into areas where workers were weak and disunited.

The federal government did acknowledge that "certain" local employers did not yet recognize trade unionism, but still declined to consider legal compulsion. Instead, the Alliance preferred to rely on "education," and even industrial action, to impel reluctant firms toward collective bargaining.[55] So concerned was the Alliance to preserve the "voluntary" character of its trade union policy that when the National Union of Plantation Workers (NUPW) called on government to compel unwilling employers to implement the union check-off provided for even in the Employment Ordinance, the official refusal argued that rule-implementation should nonetheless be left to private settlement between the parties.

To facilitate voluntary industrial relations following the expanded SF vote in the 1959 General Election, the returned Alliance government supported the creation of a Malayan Commercial and Industrial Employers Consultative Association to meet with the MTUC and formulate agreed procedures for labour-management relations. Greatly increased trade union pressure through to the end of 1962 finally impelled the MCIECA to conclude a "gentlemen's agreement" with the MTUC to establish a mechanism for union recognition, to the relief—if not the delight—of the federal government.

The Alliance stand on industrial relations was not as consistently enlightened as it would have liked to believe. In rebuffing SF allegations of widespread anti-labour activities on the part of Penang Port contractors, the Minister of Labour argued somewhat naively that the existence there of "industrial peace" comprised a prima facie case for good industrial relations.[56] Yet, when the trade unions embarked in 1962 on a militant campaign to force the issue of recognition, the government reversed its original position and now warned labour against subjecting the "voluntary" industrial relations process to "strains," or else "sufficient safeguards" would have to be introduced.[57]

Malaya's nascent industrialization programme compounded government's ambivalence over labour policy. Upon inaugurating its Pioneer Industries scheme in 1957, the federal authorities declared that they expected the trade unions to act according to the "truth" that overseas investment "will need a higher rate of reward than would be appropriate in the case of conventional . . . ventures."[58] This constituted a blatant attempt by government to make labour shoulder a portion of the burden of industrialization through reduced wages. While agreeing that foreign investment warranted a "reasonable return," the trade unions vigorously demanded that government ensure the position of organized labour in its industrialization policy: "Let no foreign capital think that they could get cheap labour in this country; they must recognize that the trade union movement is a growing force and they are going to live in a community where trade unions have developed."[59]

Trade union admonitions against tolerating "cheap labour" certainly seemed extravagant, given the authorities' view that Malayan wages were already too high by Asian standards to attract industrial investment from abroad. A government subscribing to this view could hardly be expected to be punctilious in encouraging trade unionism among new industrial enterprises. Government was accused of ignoring the interests of labour in industrialization, and demands were put forward to have Pioneer Industry status made conditional upon recognition of trade unions. Even at the mid-1960s the MTUC and SF still complained that workers in Pioneer Industries were being denied the right to organize, and that their labour forces were subject to intimidation and deteriorating conditions of employment. Particular accusations of anti-union practices were directed against industrialists from Hong Kong and Taiwan.

The Alliance government's response to these complaints testified to its lack of urgency in trade union matters. While repeating the conventional platitudes in support of trade unionism, the federal authorities excused the Pioneer firms as "new" and maintained, in any case, that workers in these industries would require "some time before they can settle down in their work and then think of trade unionism."[60] Indeed, the government was far more concerned that the trade unions' own bid for recognition might disrupt "industrial peace" and so jeopardize the "stability" deemed necessary to attract foreign investment.[61]

Notwithstanding its ambivalent treatment of industrial relations, the Alliance government insisted on its readiness to intervene to prevent "exploitation" in cases where workers found it "impossible" to form "effective trade unions."[62] On the basis of this "effectiveness" criterion, and despite its principle of voluntary industrial relations, the Alliance government decided shortly after independence to launch a Court of Inquiry under the Wages Council Ordinance into the "unreasonably low" remuneration offered in retail shops. When the Court of Inquiry issued its report (*Legislative Council Paper 77 of 1958*) the government agreed to set up Malaya's first Wages Council for the retail trade, to the applause of the MTUC.

This federal government initiative in support of more equitable industrial relations fell subject to successive delays, however, leading the SF to accuse the Alliance and employers of deliberate obstructionism. The Wages Council for the retail trade finally became operational in December 1962, some four years after being set up.

In the meantime, the banning of the militant and effective National Union of Factory and General Workers resulted in clearly deteriorating working conditions in Penang Port. In 1960, the SF called for a Select Committee of the Dewan Ra'ayat (House of Representatives) to investigate alleged malpractices by labour contractors there. Replying to this opposition move, the government reluctantly assented to a Commission of Inquiry under the Wages Council Ordinance to report on conditions in Penang Port. Following their report (CMD 21/60), government agreed to set up a second Wages Council for Penang Port labour in 1961, but again displayed a remarkable lack of urgency in the implementation of this decision. Members were appointed only in 1962 and the Wages Council was still not operative by mid-1963.

Pointing to the slow progress of the Wages Council, the SF called upon the federal government to introduce a statutory minimum "living wage" to protect unorganized, "cheap" labour against exploitation.[63] The government, for its part, was quite unprepared to abandon its principle of voluntary industrial relations, supplemented in particular instances by Wages Councils, for a more direct involvement in industrial relations.

Incomes Policy, Wages and Collective Bargaining

The Alliance government's espousal of the "British" practice of leaving wage matters and conditions of employment to private settlement did not preclude its playing a major part in the formulation of an incomes policy. Aside from its concern to fit labour into its overall development strategy, the federal government was also Malaya's largest single employer of manual labour and as such, manifested an abiding interest in wage agreements for major industries. Although not going so far as to prescribe terms of employment for private industry, other no-less-effective techniques were frequently applied to impel conformity to government's general objectives for a rudimentary national incomes policy.[64]

One potent instrument of official intervention in wage bargaining was the Industrial Relations Department of the Ministry of Labour, which kept in close and constant touch with industrial negotiations. The Industrial Relations Department tendered advice and provided assistance to parties in collective bagaining, making available its good offices at times of disputes. However, the continuing practice of the Industrial Relations Department of meeting privately with employers before and during industrial negotiations, though loudly condemned by the trade unions, did enable the government to influence bargaining positions by moral suasion. And the widespread tendency of leading Alliance politicians, and even Ministers, to use their personal authority to impress settlements, ensured an outcome in line with government incomes policy. So disturbing was this trend that the MTUC had the National Joint Labour Advisory Council declare that apart from the Minister of Labour, no other ministers should intervene in trade disputes.

Government's approach to unemployment helped reinforce its national incomes policy. From the outset, the Alliance regarded unemployment simply as an aspect of population growth, to be resolved through economic expansion.[65] Paradoxically, this preoccupation with structural unemployment inhibited government from coping with cyclical or seasonal unemployment. If government aimed at "creating conditions" for industrialization as the "only solution to unemployment,"[66] then one of these conditions was the existence of no artificially maintained levels of employment or wages to impede industrial expansion. Industrialization, originally conceived as a means of absorbing unemployment, was thereby transformed into an overriding goal of policy. This course of events was particularly evident during the recessions of 1958-59 and 1961-62, when the federal government firmly refused either to adopt counter-cyclical fiscal measures to sustain employment levels or otherwise introduce programs to alleviate the impact of unemployment on the labour force.[67]

Whereas the MTUC and SF angrily demanded a full-employment policy, or at least payment of unemployment benefits, the Alliance preferred instead to create temporary relief work as a device for ensuring a continued availability of ready labour for Malaya's major industries once expansion began anew.[68] In the meantime, the unemployed were not eligible for welfare payments, except in extreme hardship cases.[69]

During the mid-1960s, a time of relatively bouyant economic conditions, the federal government admitted to a persistent 6 percent rate of unemployment while looking to expanded growth under the Second Five-Year Plan to solve the problem.[70] This deliberate subordination of short-term employment objectives to a long-run growth strategy implied the continued toleration of not-inconsiderable levels of structural, cyclical and seasonal unemployment. By virtually abdicating responsibility for current unemployment as a matter of policy, the federal government seriously weakened the leverage available to trade unions in collective bargaining. Indeed labour force rotation, drawing upon pools of unemployment, served as a potent employers' weapon against trade union activism.[71] Alliance employment policy went far to reconcile an ideological commitment to voluntary trade unionism with a development strategy based on low-level wage stability.

As the largest single employer of labour in the country[72] the federal government also influenced Malayan wage levels through its own wages structure. Though ostensibly a matter for collective bargaining in Whitley Councils, public service wages in fact became an instrument of national incomes policy. Politicization of Whitleyism actually began shortly after the election of the first Alliance government, in the initial euphoria of self-government. Then, following a Whitley Council deadlock, the MTUC brought its wage claim to the Legislative Council where the Chief Minister intervened to accede to a favorable settlement for "social improvement."[73] Soon afterwards rubber estates and other private industries followed suit with parallel wage increases.

Cabinet intervention in Whitley Council operations paved the way for increasing political control over public service wages. In 1957, the Official Side refused to even entertain a wages claim submitted to the Whitley Council, owing to a forecast budget deficit. Nor would the government consider going to arbitration. Despite efforts to force the government's hand in the Legislative Council, including warnings that failure to negotiate might undermine free trade unionism and lead to subversion, the issue stood. Public service wages had become less a subject for collective bargaining and more a phase of fiscal policy. Later, as a result of the 1958 recession, government imposed a wage freeze on the public service, suspending the Whitley Councils until mid-1959.

As the General Election of that year approached, the government relaxed a little and indicated its readiness to be "fair" with wage claims based on "efficiency and equity," but reserved to itself the right to refuse to entertain all claims deemed inconsistent with "the national interest."[74] Shortly before the election, however, a deadlocked wage claim was given over to a Commission of Inquiry which offered a moderate award and was accepted. Thereafter the government asserted its role as custodian of the "national interest," and the Whitley Councils virtually ceased functioning except to legitimize ministerial decisions on public service wages.[75]

Public service wages were now directly tied to the goals of fiscal policy and Alliance development strategy. The resulting near-stability in public service wage levels since 1956 was hardly without impression on private industrial relations.

Other measures employed by government to induce conformity to the incomes aspect of its development strategy included varying degrees of implicit as well as explicit coercion. One of the after-effects of the Emergency was a generalized fear and reluctance among workers to ventilate their grievances. The tendency of ministers to publicly castigate trade unions for their activism lent credence to this fear that labour militancy would be regarded as subversion. Indeed some unions, like the National Union of Factory and General Workers, which pursued a policy of militant industrial action, found themselves banned, ostensibly on purely technical grounds.[76] Despite a 1956 agreement reached at the instance of the MTUC with the recently elected Alliance government, police interference in industrial disputes still inhibited trade union freedom of action.[77] Following a number of incidents of policy involvement in strike breaking in the early 1960s, both labour interests and the SF roundly condemned the Alliance for placing its policy power at the disposal of employers: "What freedom of trade unionism is this?"[78]

Government labour policy created a climate of inhibition conducive to comparatively quiescent industrial relations over the independence period. Apart from 1956 and 1962, years of recession from the previous rubber booms, there occurred little exceptional strike activity. In 1956, declining rubber estate wages linked to falling rubber prices, at a time when government servants secured generous wage increases in the spirit of independence, impelled the NUPW to seek a guaranteed minimum wage at the 1955 peak level. Employers, unwilling to abandon the sliding scale which shifted onto labour a portion of the rubber cycle, rejected this demand and suggested arbitration. Recalling past experiences with arbitration, the Union refused, while a strike was ruled out for fear of provoking anti-union feeling among Alliance political leaders. Instead the NUPW chose to "go-slow." When employers responded with stringent "disciplinary tests," the National Union of Transport Workers threatened a nation-wide sympathy strike for the rubber workers. All the while the government guarded against employer victimization and Communist infiltration into the unions, but its repeated suggestions of arbitration were firmly turned down by the NUPW. In the end the employers gave in, and an agreement was reached within the Joint Consultative Council for the Rubber Industry in June 1956 for considerably improved benefits and wages.[79]

To be sure, some estates had called upon government to "tackle with firmness" the "irrational demands backed by threats" of the trade unions.[80] Yet there can be little doubt that the 1956 "go-slow" marked the coming of age of the NUPW as the vanguard of a more self-confident, more cohesive trade union movement, ready and able to act in its members' interests.[81]

The wage settlements of spring-summer 1956 proved to be the last significant increases in basic wage rates for six and a half years.[82] Continued pressure for higher wages was denounced by the Minister of Finance in May 1957 as "inflationary."[83] This view ignored the possible positive effects of a higher wages floor in highly cyclical export industries on Malaya's secular terms of trade and real national income.[84] As the 1958 recession took hold, unions found it increasingly difficult to persuade employers even to enter into negotiations, especially since widespread unemployment deprived them of effective leverage.

Even in industries possessing collective bargaining machinery, negotiations reached an impasse. In 1959 a thoroughly frustrated MTUC appealed for an ILO mission to come and investigate industrial relations in Malaya. It was a sad commentary on the state of Malayan trade unionism when, advocating the interests of a rubber constituency, a non-union Alliance MP pleaded on the floor of the Dewan Ra'ayat for government action to raise tappers' earnings. Between 1957 and 1960 membership in industrial trade unions had fallen off by a third, and only reached its previous peak at the end of 1962.[85]

The turning point in the post-independence fortunes of the Malayan trade union movement came with the railway strike of 1962-63. This dispute pitted an autocratic Railway Administration against a determined Railwaymen's Union of Malaya (RUM). It further exposed the weaknesses of Malayan collective bargaining procedure, as well as the vital instrumental role played by related interests, notably the federal government and labour movement at large. The origins of this dispute may be traced back to autumn 1959, when a railway strike following the unilateral imposition of longer working hours was averted only by last-minute intervention of the Prime Minister, and the issue submitted to a Court of Inquiry. In its report, the Commission under Justice R.D.R. Hill strongly criticized the "intransigent" Railway Administration for refusal to negotiate with the RUM, recommended the setting up of a joint Industrial Council as "a matter of urgency," and pointed to the anomaly that railway workers endured all the obligations og government servants but enjoy none of the benefits.[86] These recommendations were subsequently ignored by the government and railway management, and it was 18 months later before joint negotiating machinery was established for the Malayan Railways.

Then, in late 1962, the RUM demanded substantial improvements in wages and benefits, together with a change in status to that of government workers, all of which the Railway Administration turned down. A government attempt to break the deadlock by reference to arbitration was declined by the Union, for want of "confidence" in official good faith.[87] Taking up cudgels on behalf of RUM in the Dewan Ra'ayat, the SF moved a debate bitterly criticizing the Railway Administration for refusing to come to terms with "reasonable" union demands, and denouncing government for failing to compel the railways to settle.[88]

Fearing serious disturbances, other parties called upon the government to use its trump card, personal intervention by the Prime Minister, to impress a settlement. Unmoved, the Alliance insisted that any settlement must adhere to the budgetary limitations of federal fiscal policy.[89] Within this framework, the Minister of Labour tried to continue to seek "new channels" to break the deadlock. In fact, following a strike notice, the Railway Administration, with at least tacit support from the Minister of Transport, refused to meet with the union for 10 days in the vain hope of breaking the strike by threat of a lockout.[90]

Meanwhile, labour interests expressed "grave concern" at the possibility of government conscripting rail workers "for national purposes" under Article 6 of the Federal Constitution, to break the impending strike. In a dramatic declaration from the floor of the Dewan Ra'ayat the SF warned that labour would not bow to "intimidation and threats," but would break the law "if necessary" and plunge Malaya into industrial chaos rather than tolerate "undesirable and undemocratic" infringement of trade union freedom of action.[91] Deterred from taking Emergency measures by the strength of labour feeling, the federal government instead appointed a Court of Inquiry on 19 December, the eve of the strike.

The outbreak of the railway strike was greeted with enthusiastic resolve on the part of the Malayan trade union movement. Allied unions in the normally docile MTUC, notably the Transport Workers and Civil Service unions, initiated sympathy strikes and a go-slow in support of the railway workers. Terming the strike a "breakthrough" for labour, an ebullient MTUC Action Committee pro-claimed a "solidarity unique in the history of the Malayan trade union movement" as unions joined together in "fighting for the le-gitimate rights of the workers."[92] Indicative of the grave concern of British investors, the *Straits Times* expressed editorial fears that MTUC-organized sympathy strikes would provoke "an experiment in industrial and political intimidation."[93]

Following an unsuccessful attempt by Professor Ungku Aziz to mediate the strike, the federal cabinet finally met to offer "consid-erable concessions" to the railway men. It had then required both the personal intervention of the Prime Minister, and the key media-tion role of Professor Aziz to bring the strike to an end after 23 days. The RUM gained a "notable victory" over wages, union check-off, paid holidays, fringe and retirement benefits. The issue of gov-ernment status for railway workers was resolved in March 1963, when the federal government unilaterally transformed the Malayan Railways into a quasi-private parastatal corporation, to the chagrin of the RUM.[94]

The success of the railway strike in mobilizing labour in pursuit of its interests, even to the point of getting the government to bend, rekindled the flagging spirit of the Malayan trade union movement. Thus inspired, unions in many other sectors of industry embarked on industrial activism during the spring of 1963, and achieved revi-sion of obsolete wage structures as well as negotiated wage increases.[95]

Uneasy over this new militancy, the Alliance government scolded trade union leaders for whipping up emotion and practis-ing industrial brinkmanship.[96] However, by early summer, the looming Confrontation with Indonesia over the creation of Malaysia moved the Prime Minister to plead for deferment of an impending tin strike. Appeals to an embattled patriotism effectively dampened down trade union militancy, by the Alliance government otherwise failed to provide alternative avenues for labour to realize its indus-trial interests.[97]

Alliance emphasis on voluntary industrial relations extended to staunch unwillingness to legislate a national minimum wage. From the first, the MTUC expressed disillusionment that the elected gov-ernment persisted in refusing a minimum wage enactment. Later, the SF criticized the Second Five-Year Plan for omitting provision for a minimum wage, desired especially to protect labour earnings against commodity slumps. These demands were categorically re-jected by the federal authorities as inconsistent with the policy of collective bargaining. A national minimum wage was dismissed as a "threat" to those already earning above the minimum.[98]

Alliance antipathy towards administered wages did not preclude direct government action in particular cases. On at least two occasions government reacted to abnormally low wages disclosed in Parliament as being paid by east coast employers, and despite the absence of legal norms promised "appropriate action." Presumably, this was to be limited to intense political suasion. Since the labour force in both these instances was predominantly Malay, it is fair to assume that Alliance motive to act reflected communal interests, at least in part, as well as a sense of social justice.

One consequence of the federal policy of subordinating labour to broader considerations of national economic strategy was the comparatively stunted development of the Malayan trade union movement. By the end of 1962, only about a quarter of the non-peasant labour force was organized in trade unions.[99] Nor had the structure of trade unionism changed much since 1955. The planting and government unions were still the strongest, while manufacturing, mining and service unions remained weak. Most Malayan trade unions were small and ineffectual, since an MTUC plan to integrate this multiplicity into 14 national industrial unions had made scant progress.

As for the MTUC itself, its financial plight was at times so severe that it could not meet current obligations.[100] Communalism still pervaded the trade union movement, which was was predominantly Indian in its ethnic composition. Malays and especially Chinese workers were largely unrepresented. Of the Chinese trade unions, "many" declined affiliation with the MTUC alleging its domination by Indian unions, leaders and politicians.

Blame for this unsatisfactory state of trade union affairs was placed squarely on the Alliance's "colonial" labour policy by the SF.[101] Much of the bitterness and frustration pervading Malayan labour stemmed from a feeling of having been deprived of the fruits of independence:

> There is no point in saying that Malaya is a rich country. We all know that is is a rich country; but it is only rich for a few privileged classes, the haves; the vast majority of the have-nots of this country are still in the same plight as they were prior to independence.[102]

However, the dramatic industrial actions and gains of early 1963 alleviated some of this despair, and certainly helped restore trade union self-confidence in their capacity to act in the labour interest.

Certain changes had occurred over time in independent Malayan political and industrial relations that altered the original colonial framework for labour policy. The most significant of these was transformation of non-peasant labour from its previous status of disenfranchised, inarticulate ethnic minority groups into voter-citizens with increasingly well-defined interests. The railway strike showed the regenerated labour movement to be quite capable of utilizing its new-found power astutely, responsibly, and moreover, effectively. To be sure, conservative elements in the Alliance government might continue to regard trade unionism as something inevitable, rather than desirable, and would view organized labour with suspicion. Nevertheless, in the freer atmosphere following the 1948-61 Emergency, the trade union movement emerged as an active advocate of labour interests.

Even as the situation for trade unions improved, the Malayan labour movement did not manage to build a solid and effective base for itself in Malayan political life. This systemic weakness reflected in large part the peculiar ideological and ethnic inhibitions of labour politics in Malaya. On the one hand, the labour movement was tainted by its historical association with left-wing parties, despite apolitical protestations of the MTUC leadership. On the other, the MTUC's communal linkage with the ruling Alliance operated through the coalition partner with the least political leverage, the Malayan Indian Congress. Without effective political leverage, the Malayan trade union movement proved unable to secure substantial gains and benefits for organized labour. The weakness of labour's political base exposed Malaya's trade unions to new restrictive measures during the second Emergency over Confrontation with Indonesia (1963-66), restrictions that were subsequently institutionalized in the Industrial Relations Act of 1967.[103]

ENDNOTES

1. On pre-war British colonial labour policy and practice see J. Norman Parmer, *Colonial Labour Policy and Administration* (New York, 1960); Charles Gamba, *The Origins of Trade Unionism in Malaya* (Singapore, 1962), ch. 1; and International Labour Office, The Trade Union Situation in the Federation of Malaya, *Report of a Mission from the International Labour Office* (Geneva, 1962), esp. pp. 24-28.

2. For a history of early post-war labour relations and the rise of the Communist-led Pan-Malayan Federation of Trade Unions, see Michael R. Stenson, *Industrial Conflict in Malaya* (London, 1970); and Charles Gamba, *The Origins*, chap. 7. For official accounts of the problems of post-war trade unionism in Malaya, see

F.S.V. Donnison, British Military Administration in the Far East (London, HMSO, 1956), pp. 238, 312-13; and S.S Awberry and F.W. Dalley, Labour and Trade Union Organization in the Federation of Malaya and Singapore (London, 1948), col. 234. The aims and tactics of the Communist trade unions and the counter-measures adopted by the government have been dealt with by G.Z. Hanrahan, *The Communist Struggle in Malaya* (New York, 1956), ch.4; Alex Josey, Trade Unionism in Malaya (Singapore, 1954), provides a sympathetic left-wing treatment of contemparary issues of labour policy.

3. For a detailed treatment of labour policy and trade unionism during this period of colonial tutelage, 1948-55, see Stenson, *Industrial Conflict in Malaya* and Gamba, *The Origins*.

4. Yang di-Pertuan Agong Royal Address, *Federation of Malaya, Legislative Council Proceedings*, 4 December 1957, col. 35 11-12 (Henceforth: *L.C. Proc.*).

5. Chief Minister, *L.C. Proc.*, 14 March 1956 (Merdeka Debate), col. 897-8.

6. P.P. Narayanan (MTUC), *L.C. Proc.*, 14 March 1956 (Merdeka Debate), col. 912.

7. Minister of Commerce and Industry, *L.C. Proc.*, 12 July 1956, col. 1456.

8. Cf. *L.C. Proc.*, addresses by the Chief Minister, 14 March 1956, col. 898; and by the Minister of the Interior and Justice, 19 February 1959, col. 6525.

9. Enche R.A Abdul Karim (MTUC), *L.C. Proc.*, 9 December 1957, col. 3758.

10. Minister of Interior and Justice, *L.C. Proc.*, 19 February 1959, col. 6524.

11. P.P. Narayanan (MTUC), *L.C. Proc.*, 23 April 1959, col. 6768-9.

12. K. Karam Singh (Socialist Front), *Federation of Malaya, Dewan Ra'ayat Proceedings*, 21 June 1960, col. 1273-4 (Henceforward: *D.R. Proc.*).

13. Minister of Labour, *D.R. Proc.*, 4 December 1959, col 1120.

14. Cf. R.S. Milne & K.J. Ratnam, "Politics and Finance in Malaya," *Journal of Commonwealth Political Studies* (1965), pp. 192-3; and Lim Kean Siew (Socialist Front), *D.R. Proc.*, 4 December 1959, col. 1112-12.

15. Addresses by Dr. Lim Swee Aun, *D.R. Proc.*, 26 April 1962, col. 64; and Abdul Razak b. Haji Hussin (UMNO), 12 March 1963, col. 4051.

16. Asst. Minister of Labour, *D.R. Proc.*, 12 march 1963, col. 4051-3.

17. Cf. Deputy Prime Minister and Minister of Defence, *L.C. Proc.*, 18 June 1958, col. 4775; and 11 December 1957, col. 3987.

18. Minister of Labour, *L.C. Proc.*, 8 December 1958, col. 5641.

19. K.V. Thaver (MTUC), *L.C. Proc.*, 8 December 1958, col. 5624.

20. Addresses by P.P. Narayanan (MTUC), *L.C. Proc.*, 8 December 1958, col. 5617-18, and Deputy Prime Minister and Minister of Defence, col. 5635.

21. The official explanation offered to the Legislative Council for these arrests claimed that the four trade unionists were "guided and advised" by militant, Communist-influenced Middle Road trade union leaders in Singapore; that they possessed "Communist" books and books having "Communist association"; and that they kept "Communist and worker's songs": Deputy Prime Minister and Minister of Defence, *L.C. Proc.*, 9 December 1955, col. 3788-9. The NUFGW was later banned.

22. K.V. Thaver (MTUC), *L.C. Proc.*, 7 December 1957, col. 3626-7.

23. Cf. *L.C. Proc.*, 7-9 December 19577: addresses by K.V. Thaver (MTUC), col. 3626-7; P.P. Narayanan (MTUC), col. 3719; and Minister of Labour, col. 4180.

24. The reason given for the ban on public May Day celebrations was that Communists would try to manipulate such labour symbols "to put over ideas which tend to sow dislyalty and to instill in the workers revolutionary ideas and violence": Deputy Prime Minister and Minister of Defence, *L.C. Proc.*, 1 May 1958, col. 4719.

25. Cf. Charles Gamba, "Malayan Labour; Merdeka and After,' *India Quarterly* (1958), p. 219.

26. *L.C. Proc.*, 7 May 1957, col. 2629.

27. *L.C. Proc.*, 16 November 1956, col. 2350.

28. K.V. Thaver (MTUC), *L.C. Proc.*, 12 November 1956, col. 1859-60.

29. Addresses by the Minister of Commerce and Industry, *L.C. Proc.*, 8 May 1957, col. 2738; and Minister of Labour, 23 April 1959, col. 2738, and col. 6763-4.

30. Chairman U.A. Granthan report to the Chartered Bank Ltd. annual meeting, 4 April 1962.

31. Minister of Labour, *L.C. Proc.* 23 April 1959, col. 6763-4. For a discussion of the provisions of the 1959 law and its impact on trade unions, see the ILO, *The Trade Unions Situation in the Federation of Malaya*, pp. 52-72.

32. K.V. Thaver (MTUC), *L.C. Proc.*, 23 April 1959, col. 6764-5.

33. High Commissioner, *L.C. Proc.*, 31 November 1955, col. 144.

34. Minister of Labour, *L.C. Proc.*, 12 December 1957, col. 4180-2.

35. Ibid.

36. Chairman Sir John Hay report to Kamuning (Perak) Rubber and Tin Co. Ltd. general meeting, 16 November 1955.

37. Cf. W.M. Warren report to Malayan Chamber of Mines annual meeting, 11 July 1956; and J.H. Rick report to Tronoh Mines Ltd. annual meeting, 16 November 1956.

38. J.H. Rick report to Tronoh Mines Ltd. annual meeting, 16 September 1955. In fact the strike referred to followed arbitrary dismissals of workers and their replacement by non-unionized labour. See also report by E.R. Turner to Malayan Mining Employers Association annual meeting, 27 May 1959.

39. V.D. Nair (manager, Prang Besar Rubber Estate), "The Strike Weapon is Outmoded," in *The Planter*, reprinted in *Malaya* (November, 1960), pp. 30-1.

40. R.G.D. Houghton (Commissioner for Labour to 1960), "The Big Task Ahead for Malaya's Rubber Industry," *Straits Budget*, 25 May 1960.

41. The former office of the TUAM was merged with the Department of Labour after 1957 into a new Department of Labour and Industrial Relations; however, personnel changes at the top proceeded slowly and, in any event, old ideas died hard.

42. Enche Abu Bakar, *L.C. Proc.*, 15 March 1956, col. 1050-1.

43. D.R. Seenivasagam (PPP), *D.R. Proc.*, 9 January 1962, col. 2458-9.

44. Cf. D.R. Seenivasagam (PPP), *D.R. Proc.*, 13 December 1962, col. 2883-4.

45. Enche R.A.Abdul Karim (MTUC), *L.C. Proc.*, 8 December 1955, col. 727.

46. V. David (SF/MTUC), *D.R. Proc.*, 30 November 1959, col. 607-8; 22 April 1960, col. 231.

47. K.V. Thaver (MTUC), *L.C. Proc.*, 3 December 1955, col. 349. On union weakness in establishing themselves as partners in industrial relations see ILO's *The Trade Union Situation in the Federation of Malaya*, pp.81-4.

48. Cf. *The Trade Union Situation in the Federation of Malaya*, pp. 75-9.

49. P.P Narayanan (MTUC), *L.C. Proc.*, 8 December 1955, col. 731.

50. V. David (SF/MTUC), *D.R. Proc.*, 30 November 1959, col. 609.

51. Addresses by Enche Abdul Karim, L.C. Proc., 8 December 1955, col. 727-8; and Enche Abdul Hamid, 23 April 1959, col. 6770-1.

52. Tan Phaock Kin (SF), *D.R. Proc.*, 24 January 1962, col. 3692.

53. President Yeoh Guan Leong, address to All-Malayan Estate Staff Union Conference, 25 September 1960 (*Straits Times*); and V. David (SF), *D.R. Proc.*, 21 April 1961, col. 211-12.

54. Cf. V. David (SF/MTUC), *D.R. Proc.*, 24 February 1960. col. 1901-13; and John Emmanuel, NUPWDeputy General Secretary, press statement in Ipoh, 24 April 1960: *Straits Budget*, 4 May 1960, p.7.

55. Assistant Minister of Labour, *D.R. Proc.*, 19 December 1962, col. 3458.

56. Addresses by V. David (SF/MTUC), *D.R. Proc.*, 24 February 1960, col. 1901-3; and Minister of Labour, col. 1914.

57. Minister of Labour, *D.R. Proc.*, 18 December 1962, col. 3382.

58. Economic Adviser, *L.C. Proc.*, 13 December 1957, col. 4250.

59. P.P. Narayanan (MTUC), *L.C. Proc.*, 8 December 1955; 31 July 1958.

60. Asst. Minister of Labour, *D.R. Proc.*, 30 November 1959, col. 1862.

61. Cf. Yang di-Pertuan Agong Royal Address, *D.R. Proc.*, 23 May 1963, col. 221.

62. Minister for Labour, *L.C. Proc.*, 12 December 1957.

63. V. David (SF/MTUC), *D.R. Proc.*, 26 June 1962, col. 941-3, 945-6.

64. Minister for Labour, *D.R. Proc.*, 3 December 1955, col. 398.

65. Cf. addresses by the Minister of Commerce and Industry, *L.C. Proc.*, 11 July 1956, col. 1335; and by the Prime Minister, *D.R. Proc.*, 30 November 1959, col. 657-8.

66. Addresses by the Minister of Commerce and Industry, *L.C. Proc.*, 31 July 1958, col. 4942-3; and by the Minister of Labour, *D.R. Proc.*, 4 December 1959, col. 1106.

67. Government refused to collect even simple unemployment figures ostensibly because of the dispersal of population (Minister of Labour, *D.R. Proc.*, 25 November 1959, col.186) and it was only in 1962 that Malaya undertook a comprehensive employment survey.

68. See Minister of Labour, *L.C. Proc.*, 17 March 1958, col. 4339-41 on this point.

69. Relief projects of limited scope and scant success were initiated in certain urban centres, but not in hard-hit tin and rubber areas for fear of redeploying labour away from their normal employers.

70. Prime Minister, *D.R. Proc.*, 23 May 1963, col. 126.

71. *Vide*. V.D. Nair, "The Strike Weapon is Outmoded," p.30. See also SF complaint on this practice: Lim Kean Siew, *D.R. Proc.*, 4 December 1959, col. 110.

72. Out of a total labour force of 2,126,182 in 1957, some 119,000 were in government service (excluding the armed forces, municipalities and public enterprises). This compared to 614,000 in the rubber industry. On the position of government-sector unions in the Malayan labour movement, see *The Trade Union Situation in the Federation of Malaya*.

73. Addresses by the Chief Minister, *L.C. Proc.*, 14 March 1956, col. 1020-1; and Economic Adviser, 9 December 1957, col. 3772.

74. Minister of Finance, *D.R. Proc.*, 25 November 1959, col. 124-6.

75. Thus the Official Side lacked authority to make any "major" decisions involving "a lot of money," which had to be referred to the Cabinet; Cf. Prime Minister, *D.R. Proc.*, 29 November 1959, col. 1699.

76. The NUFGW accounted for about a quarter of the man-days lost in 1956, and brought about substantial improvements in wages and working conditions using strikes as a ready weapon: *Federation of Malaya Annual Report 1956* (Kuala Lumpur, 1957), p. 81. The union was banned in 1957 for late submission of its annual statement to the Registrar of Trade Unions.

77. P.P Narayanan (MTUC), *L.C. Proc.*, 15 November 1956, col. 2256-7.

78. Cf. K. Karam Singh (SF), *D.R. Proc.*, 25 April 1960, col. 534; 28 April 1960, col. 835; 21 June 1960, col. 1272-3. In the strike at the Seremban Rubber Estate, police were accused of "most villanious" practices including arrests of strike leaders, assaults on picketers, attempts to ensnare strikers by tendering "sinister advice," attempts to "smuggle" strike-breakers into the estate in a police vehicle, and refusal to detain "armed thugs" hired by management, when reported by strikers. At least one major emplyer confessed reliance on police support in using strike-breakers to break strikes: J.H. Rick, report to Tronoh Mines Ltd. annual meeting, 16 November 1956.

79. The sliding scale wage rate geared to the price of rubber was retained, however. On the "go-slow," see *The Colonial Territories 1956-57* (Lomdon, HMSO, 1957), Cmd. 195, para. 868; and Charles Gamba, *The National Union of Plantation Workers* (Singapore, 1962), chap. 6.

80. Cf. A.E. Mullay report to Consolidated Salack Rubber Estates Ltd. annual meetings, 30 October 1956, and P. B. Coghlan, report to Anglo-Asian Rubber Plantaions Ltd. Annual meeting, 4 December 1956.

81. According to the *Federation of Malaya Annual Report 1956*, p. 82, the trade union situation in the rubber industry had now come "to resemble the situation which exists in the beeter organized industries in Britain." See also *The Trade Union Situation in the Federation of Malaya*, pp.40-2

82. This refers to basic wage rates and does not take account of cyclical fluctuations in rubber wages geared to commodity prices. The latter tended downwards from 1958 to 1960, re-bounded slightly during the boom of 1960 only to fall back to previous levels in 1961 and 1962. Other wages remained virtually constant throughout. On annual wage trends in Malaya, see the Colombo Plan, *Annual Reports of the Consultative Committee*, 1959 to 1963.

83. *L.C. Proc.*, 7 May 1957, col. 2629.

84. Raul Prebisch, first Secretary-General of the United Nations Conference on Trade and Development, argued that the failure of primary-exporting economies to achieve permanent higher wage levels during prosperity exposed them to deteriorating real terms of trade over the trade cycle, and results in an increasing gap between developing country primary producers and the industrialized economies that do secure higher wage levels: Raul Prebisch, "The Economic Development of Latin America and its Principal Problems," in *Economic Bulletin of Latin America* (February 1962), pp. 1-6. This thesis was incorporated in the official report of the Secretary General to UNCTAD, *Towards a New Trade Policy for Development* (New York, 1964), chap. esp. pp. 14-17.

85. Membership in Malayan industrial trade unions declined From 88 unions with 177,900 members at the end of March 1957 (*Federation of Malaya Annual*

Report 1957 p. 60) to 126,000 at the end of 1960 (*Federation of Malaya, Official year Book 1962*, p.179), and rose somewhat to 171,000 at the end of 1962 (Federation of Malaya, Official Year Book 1963. The number of unions was then 90.

86. Justice R.D.R. Hill, *Report of a Commission of Inquiry*, February 1961.

87. Cf. V. David (SF/MTUC), *D.R. Proc.*, 10 December 1962, col. 2618-20. The unions lacked confidence not only in arbitration, but in the government's readiness to implement awards with which it disagreed.

88. Cf. *D.R. Proc.*, 10 December 1962, col. 2615-47.

89. Deputy Prime Minister, *D.R. Proc.*, 10 December 1962, col. 2634. The SF retorted that the provision of cheap public services should be borne by the Treasury and not by the low-paid labour.

90. *Straits Times*, 15 January 1963.

91. V. David (SF/MTUC), *D.R. Proc.*, 10 December 1962, col. 2621-4.

92. *Straits Times*, 2 January 1963.

93. *Straits Times*, 2 January 1963.

94. The RUM had long demanded government servant status for railway workers, based on the Railway Ordinance of 1948. However, the Attorney General in 1951 issued an interpretation that railwaymen were not entitled to recognition as government servants, and this remained the basis of subsequent policy. Both the Hill Count of Inquiry (1961) and the Barakbah Court of Inquiry (1963) felt that the railwaymen merit the privileges of government servants. The transformation of the Railways into a corporation with effect from January 1964 ended the matter once and for all, although the RUM bitterly denounced the move and signified its intention to take the case to the High Court: *Straits Times*, 9 May 1963.

95. On wage and productivity gains in early 1963 see the Colombo Plan, *Annual Report of the Consultive Committee 1963* (London, H.M.S.O, 1964), Cmd. 2529. p. 155.

96. Minister of Labour to National Union of Commercial Workers Conference, *Straits Times*, 28 May 1963.

97. Following deferment of the tin strike, the All-Malayan Mining Industries Staff Union asked the prime Minister to intervene to compel a settlement in an industry long-resistant to collective bargaining (*Straits Times*, 12 August 1963).

98. Assistant Minister of Labour, *D.R. Proc.*, 9 February 1961, col. 5299-300.

99. For an evaluation of Malayan trade unionism at the end of 1962 see the *Report of the Registrar of Trade Unions 1962*. See also *The Trade Union Situation in the Federation of Malaya,* pp.33.

100. K.V. Thaver, MTUC General Secretary, Ipoh, 9 October 1960 (*Straits Times*).

101. G. Abraham, President of the Penang Port Commission Employees Union, Penang, 23 November 1960 (*Straits Budget*, 30 November 1960, p. 10).

102. V. David (SF/MTUC), *D.R. Proc.*, 20 December 1962, col. 3605-6.

103. For a survey of developments in Malaysian labour policy after 1963, see M.A. Raza, "Legislative and Public Policy Developments in Malaysia's Industry Relations," *The Journal of the Developing Areas* (1969), pp. 362-71.

MALAYSIAN DEVELOPMENT IN RETROSPECT AND PROSPECT |

Malaysia has come a long way in its development over three and a half decades of independence. According to most indicators, at the time of the transition to independence in 1957 the country's economy, social organization and political system still suffered from many of the traditional afflictions of a poor and deficient society. Even after a decade of post-war rehabilitation and progress, the machinery of government was still fragile, the democratic political leadership untested, and the Communist insurgency remained rampant, while ethnic divisions weakened the national fabric, human and social inequities abounded, with the economy chronically depressed and structurally constrained.

Comparative figures on Gross National Product (GNP) per capita can offer a contextual indication of Malaysia's development performance since that time. Thus, in 1950 Malaya's GNP per capita of US$350 was broadly similar to that of Ghana, or Morocco or Paraguay.[1] Indeed, the challenge of development for Malaya was generally considered to be more problematic, its economic and social constraints more intractable, its outlook less promising, than, for instance, Ghana's. From the 1960s, however, Malaysia managed to put in place development plans, policies and programs that fostered accelerated economic growth, coupled with a significant reduction in the overall incidence of poverty.[2] There was no magic formula; Malaysian planning and policy-making evolved through experimentation and institutional learning in an open and responsive political system, and this resulted in an enhanced national capacity to design and implement development programs. By 1991, the most recent year for which comparative data are available, Malaysia's per capita GNP reached US$2,520 in current money values, compared to US$400 for Ghana, US$1,030 for Morocco and US$1,270 for Paraguay.[3] This represented a level of economic attainment surpassing that of several Central European countries, including Bulgaria, the former Czechoslovakia and Poland.

Like other exercises in historiography, country studies of development typically focus on structural change over time. Only rarely do they address the detail of policy analysis—the political impetus, competing demands, alternative visions, and dilemmas of administration that impact so markedly on the development of government programs. By combining a macro-level of policy analysis with a micro-level of policy detail, the articles in this collected volume recapitulate the empirical dynamics of Malaysian development experience.

The Role of the State in Development

The World Bank report submitted on the eve of Malaya's transition to independence conveyed a cautious optimism about the country's economic growth potential. At the same time it also expressed a mild pessimism regarding the development policies that might be expected from the soon-to-be-elected government.[4] The policy issues and constraints identified in the report were subsequently addressed through the development planning paradigm adopted by the country's first elected government in 1956. Successive development plans were to undergo important paradigm shifts and role expansion during the decades to follow, however planning has remained the institutional centrepiece of Malaysia's development effort.

The collection of articles included in this volume provides an historical perspective on Malaysian development processes. Each article examines in detail a signal event in Malaysia's development experience. Taken together, they highlight the strategic paradigms and policy dynamics that shaped the formative era of Malaysian development effort. Among the key issues addressed in these articles are development planning, public finance and macroeconomic management, agriculture and rural development, education, and labour relations.

A review of Malaysia's historical experience reveals the extent to which development initiatives emanated from the central government, from the political leadership and from the bureaucratic managers, notwithstanding the governing elite's intuitive attachment to market principles, to private enterprise, and to international openness. The primary tasks of development involved state-building and public sector institution strengthening. The creation of an institutional capacity to formulate and deliver policy initiatives enabled the new state to vastly expand its role in the management of development processes.

The creation of a national planning institution, centred on the Economic Planning Unit, was of signal significance. Other institutional initiatives highlighted in this collection of articles include the establishment of Bank Negara Malaysia, the Federal Land Development Authority (FLDA), the Rural Industry Smallholders Development Authority (RISDA), Federal Land Consolidation and Rehabilitation Authority (FELCRA), the Rubber Industry (Replanting) Board, the Malaysian Industrial Development Authority (MIDA), and the Wages Councils. By strengthening its institutional capacity to plan and deliver development programs, the government in effect increased its control over structures of authority, over the mobilization and allocation of financial resources, over production, and over the sources and dissemination of information.

Policy development thus involved two elements of state power: (a) a functional power to promote certain kinds of economic and social activity, through rules, regulations, taxes and subsidies, and (b) a structural power to determine the shape and composition of economic and social sectors through their institutional framework. The effective exercise of these powers contributed to an expanded role for the state in the promotion of development objectives. As a result, the government apparatus emerged as the most modern, most capable structure in Malaysian society. Along with this expanded government capacity to manage development programs came a more extensive control over economic, social, and technological forces, and a determination to channel these to advantage.

The Shifting Development Paradigm

The evolution of Malaysian policy-making reflected parallel changes in prevailing concepts and definitions of development. These changes in the developmental agenda denoted, in effect, shifts in the underlying paradigms of economic and social thought. Unlike other multi-party political systems, shifts in the dominant policy paradigm in Malaysia did not result from changes in the party in power. Rather, Malaysia's single-party dominant system tended to adapt to electoral swings and other political challenges by modifying its own goals and objectives along with the underlying policy metaphor. According to the articles in this volume, politically driven paradigm shifts impacted upon the most conspicuous areas of the national policy agenda: development planning, macroeconomic management, public finance, education, and agriculture and rural development.

The policy paradigm that dominated during the late colonial era accentuated the economy and its growth. Development was defined in terms of economic growth, so that all other developmental goals (e.g., poverty alleviation, human resources development) were expected to wait until budgetary resources grew sufficiently to justify expenditure in these areas. Emphasis was placed on "sound" macroeconomic management, so called, a fiscal approach grounded on revenue-accounting. In the oft-cited phrase, government was expected to "cut its coat according to its cloth," trimming its growth objectives to its limited revenue base.

The elected government of independent Malaya soon embarked on a subtle but significant shift in the dominant policy paradigm. The articles describing this period and process indicate that the economy still dominated the prevailing policy paradigm, however other initiatives had now become part of the growth agenda. Thus, government spending on education, infrastructure, and agricultural modernization escalated in response to political expectations, and was now redefined as investment in development. To be sure, this growth impulse only related to those social and infrastructure developments that could be considered as contributing to the growth of the national economy. Be that as it may, it was clear that the inherited revenue-based paradigm had given way to a growth-driven policy paradigm. It was a mark of this paradigm shift that independent Malaya was even prepared to resort to deficit financing in order to sustain the policy commitment to a more broadly defined growth objective.

The next major paradigm shift noted in these articles occurred with the introduction of the New Economic Policy (NEP) in 1971. The traumatic race riots of 13 May 1969 impressed upon a shaken government that sheer growth could not enable Malaysia to overcome the tensions and constraints inherent in an economically dualistic, socially and ethnically disparate society. A new policy paradigm promulgated in the NEP elevated ethnic restructuring and poverty alleviation to primacy among the goals of Malaysia's development effort. Economic growth was now considered instrumental to the pursuit of these two "prongs" of the NEP.

The NEP paradigm determined the agenda of Malaysian development planning for a 20 span, 1971-91, covering the Second, Third, Fourth and Fifth Malaysia Plans. During this period, the twin prongs of the NEP had a far-reaching impact on policy actions and institutional interventions. The role of government in the economy and in society expanded markedly, justified by reference to the policy imperatives of the NEP paradigm.

As with all such policy paradigms, the development agenda set out in the NEP implied its own boundaries and inherent limits to government action. The analysis contained in several articles indicates how the NEP focus on ethnic restructuring (and to a somewhat lesser degree on poverty alleviation) entailed less attention, or inattention, to other important development issues. Policy areas which did not sit so comfortably with the dominant paradigm, like agricultural land policy, health policy, labour policy, social welfare policy, or environment policy, tended to suffer from indifferent treatment in development planning. They also received low priority in implementation.

At the level of development goals, the preoccupation of the NEP paradigm with inter-ethnic redistribution derogated from other parameters of social equity. In effect the ethnic redistribution goal displaced other, broader social equity concerns based on income or need. Nor were social equity considerations given primacy even within ethnic parameters. Various articles indicate how certain ethnic-oriented policies favoured relatively better-off individuals within the target community disproportionately, thus having a socially regressive impact generally.

A reduction in the incidence of poverty did take place in Malaysia, to be sure, thanks to the second prong of the NEP.[5] Yet, the share of national income going to the poor generally, and to poor ethnic communities like Indians and the indigenous Orang Asli, has diminished.[6] Under the NEP formula for ethnic restructuring, the gap between rich and poor within the various communities widened significantly.

Empowerment and Participation

The studies in this volume demonstrate how Malaysia's development dynamic was associated with a broadening of the boundaries of empowerment and participation. Empowerment involved access to political power, and related to the exercise of influence over decision-making authority in order to realize certain interests or objectives. Participation involved access to public sector resources, the results of policy decisions, to enhance individual or community well-being.

Colonial limitations on empowerment resulted in policies skewed against the interests of certain Malayan producer groups and against the well-being of large segments of Malayan society. Several articles on the late colonial period describe this happening in public finance, in the rubber producing sector, the rice-growing sector, in education, and in labour relations. The empowerment of Malayans through the devolution of political authority to an elected, representative government was decisive in transforming Malaya's policy orientation. Empowerment rendered government more responsive to the public interest, and engendered a development impetus for policy.

Studies indicate that elections have served as an important mechanism for empowerment. Even though Malaysia has evolved a single-party dominant political system, electoral politics continue to have an important function. The governing coalition, the Alliance and its successor the Barisan Nasional, remains highly sensitive to political responses of the public conveyed through the electoral process. Political swings revealed in election results have often been a harbinger of change in the metaphor and direction of government policy. Development policy initiatives, in particular, have tended to reflect government responses to electoral politics, as the ruling coalition sought to pre-empt opposition campaigning or counteract swinging voter sentiment.

As noted in several articles, the process of empowerment through elections also wrought a shift in the locus of authority over development policy. During the colonial period effective control over public finance, and theretofore over macroeconomic management and development policies, remained vested in the financial bureaucracy. With the advent of elected government, macroeconomic management was pluralized through the involvement of other departments in development planning. Likewise, overall responsibility for policy was transferred from the bureaucracy to the political leadership. Under the NEP, Malaysia's political leadership became increasingly assertive and accountable for development policy, with its accountability being validated through elections. The Malaysian bureaucracy, for its part, retained its professional prerogatives, which included advisory, reporting, and planning functions along with responsibility for the effective implementation of development programs and policies.

The emergence of a development goal in Malaysian public policy was accompanied by a proliferating network of governmental institutions dedicated to managing key economic or social programs. This proliferation of specialized institutions allowed the state apparatus to exercise more particular control over specific sectors of Malaysia's economy and social services, and their development. By virtue of this enhanced institutional capacity to manage and direct development activities, government also acquired the means to combine economic control with social control. This exercise of dual control was highlighted in some of the articles on agrarian dominance, on the one hand, and on trade unionism on the other. At the same time, the establishment of dedicated institutional mechanisms lent a sharpness and clarity to the delivery of development programs.

Just as state-building thus extended the outreach of development policy, so it broadened *pari passu* the scope of public participation in development programs. This broader participation was especially significant for peripheral groups in Malaysian society. The spread of economic and social infrastructure, education, agricultural investment and rural development, and their impact on hitherto disadvantaged marginal groups is treated in several articles. Expanded access to public sector resources meant wider participation in development activities along with a broader distribution of basic human needs. Participation represented a kind of proxy for redistributing some of the benefits of economic growth, in circumstances where incomes were themselves growing increasingly inegalitarian.

This is not to suggest that access to public sector resources was always equal to all comers. The national political consensus provided that Malaysian public policy under the NEP, and even beforehand, discriminated affirmatively on the basis of ethnicity in favour of Malays, albeit without intending to retract the existing interests of non-Malays. As well, certain more implicit, but no less significant, patterns of differentiation became associated with other economic and social policies. These implicit socio-economic differentiators were typically embedded in the design of programs, and served in effect to allocate certain benefits to some while denying them to others.

Several of the articles call attention to the socially regressive impact of this type of policy differentiation. Some programs provided differential benefits for different target groups. Sometimes these differentials imposed severe opportunity costs onto the disadvantaged groups. Historically, Malaysia's rubber replanting programs tended to discriminate against smaller peasant planters, jeopardizing their competitive position as low-cost producers. Another pattern of differentiation was apparent in programs which tended to channel a disproportionate share of available resources to more advantaged beneficiaries. Thus, in education, public expenditure tended to favour higher education rather than lower levels of schooling. This was tantamount to providing a large implicit subsidy to offspring of better-off families. Social groups that were not explicitly targeted in the dominant paradigm, like the Indians, indigenous East Malaysian bumiputra communities, and Orang Asli, tended to be least favoured in access to public policy resources.

The National Development Policy and Sixth Malaysia Plan, 1991-95

In 1991 Malaysia introduced its Sixth Malaysia Plan (SiMP), 1991-95, an initial expression of a new National Development Policy (NDP). The adoption of the NDP, following a process of domestic consultation, heralded a new strategic framework for Malaysian planning and development policy. The NDP is intended to serve as the successor policy paradigm to the former NEP, whose targets had been framed over a 20 time horizon, ending in 1991. Malaysian planning and policy formulation is to be guided by the NDP towards the so called "Vision 2020" target of newly industrialized country (NIC) status by the second decade of the 21st century.

The strategic thrust of the NDP emphasized a more "balanced" concept of development. The NDP goal of balance is expected to affect planning objectives between economic growth and social equity; allocations of public sector resources among various sectors of the economy; support for regional and urban-rural developments; and the promotion of scientific and technological progress, on the one hand, and the technical requirements of Malaysian industrial development, on the other. More generally, the NDP seeks to foster a better balance between the growth impulse and environmental sustainability.

The SiMP, the first operationalized expression of the NDP, aims to achieve a balance between its growth objective, as such, and other dimensions of the national development effort. Plan priorities relate to (a) diversifying the country's industrial base, (b) improving its human resources development capabilities, (c) upgrading its technological base, and (d) reducing inter-sectoral and regional imbalances. Growth projections for the SiMP period anticipate that the Malaysian economy will expand at an accelerated rate of 7.5%. Most of this growth is expected to derive from increased levels of private and public sector investment, coupled with technological improvement and productivity gains. The balanced development heralded by the SiMP envisages the creation of a better integrated structure for the Malaysian economy as a step towards the NIC agenda postulated by Vision 2020.

The balanced approach promulgated in the SiMP reaffirmed a further paradigm shift affecting the role of government in the economy. Whereas the balanced development goal is grounded on industrial diversification, the Plan perceives the private sector as the engine of its industrial strategy. To generate the resources required for growth and redistribution, the government proceeded to introduce an incentives framework designed to stimulate private sector investment activity. The prescribed role of government, according to the Plan, remains actively interventionist in promoting the desired balance of objectives, in raising scientific and technological standards, and in reducing targeted disparities. While this apportionment of roles between the public and private sectors is hardly entirely new to Malaysia, as a matter of practical policy, it does imply a renunciation of the more extensively interventionist normative imperative associated with the former NEP. The role changes prescribed in the SiMP revealed a shift in the dominant paradigm adopted under the NDP.

Lessons Learned

As Malaysia proceeds with implementation of its NDP inspired Vision 2020, it is relevant to recall some of the lessons learned from the country's development experience. Malaysia's historical experience in development is surely pertinent to planners and policymakers. Other stakeholders, whether international development agencies, national institutions, or the private sector, would also find that experience to be of interest. The lessons learned should be instructive for students of development in Malaysia and elsewhere as well.

At this point it may be in order to summarize two salient analytical lessons learned from these studies of Malaysia's historical experience in development planning and policy. One lesson relates to the importance of interdisciplinary analysis for evaluating policy developments. A policy-centred approach to the analysis of development requires an interdisciplinary melding of political, economic, and social analytical methodologies to explain the motivations, processes and outcomes of policy-making.

A second analytical lesson stresses the importance of addressing development policies and experiences at the macro- and micro-levels of analysis. Most studies of development policy concentrate on trends at the macro-level of national or international economic, social or political phenomena. Trends at the national or international levels of development certainly warrant analysis and evaluation. Nevertheless, a complete appreciation of the dynamics of development policy can only be obtained by also taking account of events and constraints operating at the micro-level of analysis. An analysis of activities at the level of the issue area or the individual sector can contribute important detail to the evaluation of policy development. The articles in this volume demonstrate such a top-down, bottom-up and multi-disciplinary approach, in which a micro-level focus on the detail of policy-making proceeds within the overall context of macro-level trends.

Malaysia's development experience acknowledges that poverty need not persist, that economic growth and development can be managed by policy means, but that the process of development may itself spawn inequalities and liabilities. Policy analysis can contribute positively to development efforts by deriving lessons learned from experience, and utilizing these to monitor and evaluate current objectives and performance.

ENDNOTES

1. David Morawetz, *Twenty-five Years of Economic Development. 1950 to 1975*, (Washington, DC, 1977), Table A1.

2. World Bank report on *The East Asian Miracle. Economic Growth and Public Policy* (New York, 1993), esp. Overview and Chap. 1.

3. Data from World Bank, *World Development Report 1993* (New York, 1993), Table 1.

4. International Bank for Reconstruction and Development, *The Economic Development of Malaya* (Baltimore, 1955), pp. 33, 38-41.

5. *The East Asian Miracle*, *op. cit.*, esp. pp. 28-32.

6. Ozay Mehmet, *Development in Malaysia. Poverty, Wealth and Trusteeship* (London, 1986).

MARTIN RUDNER: LIST OF PUBLICATIONS

BOOKS AND MONOGRAPHS:

(Editor) *Society and Development in Asia, Asian and African Studies*, Vol. 6 (1970), Jerusalem, Israel Oriental Society, 1970.

Nationalism, Planning and Economic Modernization in Malaysia. The Politics of Beginning Development. Sage Research Papers in the Social Science, Studies in Comparative Modernization. Beverly Hills, Calif.: Sage Publications, 1975.

(Editor, with James C. Jackson) *Issues in Malaysia Development.* Southeast Asia Publications Series No. 3, published for the Asian Studies Association of Australia by Heinemann Educational Books (Asia) Ltd, Singapore, 1979.

(Editor) *Canada Malaysia Towards the 1990s.* Kingston, Ontario: Ronald P. Frye & Co., 1988.

Canada and the Philippines. The Dimensions of a Developing Relationship. Asian Pacific Monograph Series No. 1. North York, Ontario: Captus Press for the Asian Pacific Research and Resource Centre, Carleton University, 1990.

ARTICLES:

"The Organization of the British Military Administration in Malaya," *Journal of Southeast Asian History*, Vol. 9, No. 1 (March, 1968), pp. 96-106.

"The Malaysian General Election of 1969: A Political Analysis," *Modern Asian Studies*, Vol. 4, Pt. 1 (January, 1970), pp. 1-21.

"The State and Peasant Innovation in Rural Development: The Case of Malaysian Rubber," *Asian and African Studies*, Vol. 6 (1970), pp. 75-96; reprinted in David Lim, ed., *Readings on Malaysian Economic Development*, Oxford University Press, 1975, pp. 321-331. "Rubber Strategy for Post-War Malaya," *Journal of Southeast Asian Studies*, Vol. 1, No. 1 (March, 1970), pp. 23-36.

"The Political Structure of the Malayan Union," *Journal of the Malaysian Branch, Royal Asiatic Society*, Vol. 43, Pt. 1 (1970), pp. 116-128.

"Malayan Quandary: Rural Development Policy Under the First and Second Five-Year Plans," *Contributions to Asian Studies*, Vol. 1 (1971), pp. 190-204; reprinted in David Lim, ed., *Readings on Malaysian Economic Development*, Oxford University Press, 1975, pp. 80-88.

"The Draft Development Plan of the Federation of Malaya," *Journal of Southeast Asian Studies*, Vol. 3, No. 1 (March, 1972), pp. 63-96.

"Malayan Labor in Transition: Labor Policy and Trade Unionism, 1956-1963," *Modern Asian Studies*, Vol. 7, Pt. 1 (January, 1973), pp. 21-45.

"A Reply to P.T. Bauer's Comment on Post-War Malayan Rubber Policy," *Journal of Southeast Asian Studies*, Vol. 4, No. 2 (September, 1973), pp. 300-304.

"Traditionalism and Socialism in Burma's Political Development," in S.N. Eisenstadt & Yael Azmon, eds., *Socialism and Tradition*, Atlantic Highlands, N.J.: Humanities Press, 1974, pp. 105-1239; German translation: "Traditionalismus und Sozialismus in der politischen Entwicklung Burmas," in der *Sozialismus und Tradition*, hers. von S.N. Eisenstadt und Yael Azmon, transl. Harry Maòr, Heidelburger Sociologica 15, Tübingen: J.C.B. Mohr (Paul Siebëck), 1977, pp. 117-154.

"The Malayan Post-War Rice Crisis: An Episode in Colonial Agricultural Policy," *Kajian Ekonomi Malaysia* (Malaysian Economic Review), Vol. 12, No. 1 (June, 1975), pp. 1-13.

"Financial Policies in Post-War Malaya: The Fiscal and Monetary Measures of Liberation and Reconstruction," *Journal of Imperial and Commonwealth History*, Vol. 3, No. 3 (May, 1975), pp. 232-248.

"Singapore," *Encyclopaedia Hebraica*, Vol. 25, Jerusalem, 1975 (in Hebrew).

"The Military in Indonesian Development Planning," in Harold Z. Schiffrin, ed., *Military and State in Modern Asia*, Jerusalem Academic Press, 1976, pp. 197-227.

"The Structure of Government in the Colonial Federation of Malaya," *South East Asian Studies* (Kyoto), Vol. 13, No. 4 (March, 1976), pp. 495-512.

"The Indonesian Military and Economic Policy: The Goals and Performance of the First Indonesian Five-Year Development Plan, 1969-1974," *Modern Asian Studies*, Vol. 10, No. 2 (April, 1976), pp. 249-284.

"The Demonetization of the Wartime Japanese Currency Within the British Return to Post-War Malaya," in Denys Lombard, ed., *Indonesie*, Vol. 3, *Actes du XXXIXe Congres des Orientalistes*, Paris: Asiateque, 1976, pp. 177-179.

"Malayan Rubber Policy: Development and Anti-Development During the 1950s, *Journal of Southeast Asian Studies*, Vol. 8, No. 2 (September, 1976), pp. 235-259.

"Education, Development and Change in Malaysia," *South East Asian Studies* (Kyoto), Vol. 15, No. 1 (June, 1977), pp. 23-62.

"The Economic, Social and Political Dimensions of Malaysian Education Policy, in Kenneth Orr, ed., *Appetite for Education in Contemporary Asia*, Development Studies Centre Monograph Series No. 10, Canberra: The Australian National University, 1977, pp. 62-90.

"The Evolution of Development Planning in Indonesia," Proceedings, *Seventh IAHA Conference*, Bangkok: Chulalongkorn University Press, 1979, pp. 813-844.

"Agricultural Policy and Peasant Social Transformation in Late Colonial Malaya," in James C. Jackson and Martin Rudner, eds., *Issues in Malaysian Development*, Southeast Asian Publications Series No. 3, published for the Asian Studies Association of Australia by Heinemann Educational Books (Asia) Ltd., Singapore, 1979, pp. 7-68.

"Trends in Malaysian Development Planning: Goals, Policies and Role Expansion," *Review of Indonesian and Malayan Affairs*, Vol. 14, No. 2 (December, 1980), pp. 48-91.

"Development Policies and Patterns of Agrarian Dominance in the Malaysian Rubber Export Economy," *Modern Asian Studies*, Vol. 15, Pt. 1 (February, 1981), pp. 83-105.

"Labour Policy and the Dilemmas of Trade Unionism in Post-War Malaya," *Review of Indonesian and Malayan Affairs*, Vol. 16, No. 1 (1982), pp. 101-111.

"Ideology and Development Planning in Indonesia,"in Graciela de la Lama, ed., *Southeast Asia, 30th International Congress of Human Sciences in Asia and North Africa 2*, Mexico City: El Colegio de Mexico, 1982, pp. 236-251; Spanish edition: "Ideologia y planaeci para al desarrollo en Indonesia," in Susana-Gonzalez del Solar & Benjamin Preciado Solis, coords., *Asia del Sudests, Actas, Trigesuimo Congreso Internacional de Ciencias Humanas en Asia y Africa y Africa Del Nort 1976*, Mexico: El Colegio de Mexico, 1982, pp. 236-251.

"Changing Planning Perspectives on Agricultural Development in Malaysia," *Modern Asian Studies*, Vol. 17, Pt. 3 (July, 1983) pp. 413-435.

"Higher Education and the Development of Science in Islamic Countries: A Comparative Analysis," *Canadian Journal of Development Studies*, Vol. 4, No. 1 (1983), pp. 62-94.

"Town Carpets from Pahlavi Iran," *Hali*, Vol. 6, No. 4 (1984), pp. 382-2.

"The Evolving Framework of Canadian Development Assistance Policy," in Brian W. Tomlin & Maureen Molot, eds., *Canada Among Nations, 1984: A Time of Transition*, Toronto: James Lorimer and Co., 1985, pp. 125-145.

"The Canada-Indonesia Connection: Foreign Policy, Aid and Trade Relations Over Four Decades," in Bruce Matthews, ed., Southeast Asia: *Problems of the Social and Physical Environment*, published for Acadia University by Lancelot Press, Nova Scotia, 1985, pp. 3-19.

"Agricultural Planning and Development Performance in Malaysia," in Anita Beltran Chen, ed., *Contemporary and Historical Perspectives in Southeast Asia*, Ottawa: Carleton University Printshop for the Canadian Asian Studies Association, 1985, pp. 196-218.

"Colonial Education Policy and Manpower Underdevelopment in British Malaya," in Barbara Ingham & Colin Simmons, eds., *Development Studies and Colonial Policy*, London: Frank Cass & Co., 1987, pp. 193-209.

"Dépenses militaires et croissance économique," *Études Internationales*, Vol. 18, No. 2 (juin, 1987), pp. 389-404 (in French).

"Trade cum Aid in Canada's Official Development Assistance Strategy," in Brian W. Tomlin & Maureen Appel Molot, eds., *Canada Among Nations. 1986/Talking Trade*, Toronto: James Lorimer & Co., 1987, pp. 127-146.

"Japanese Official Development Assistance to Southeast Asia," *Modern Asian Studies*, Vol. 23, Pt. 1 (February, 1989), pp. 73-116.

"Persian Carpets of the Pahlavi Dynasty (1925-1979)", in Ian Bennett, ed., *Twenty Three Persian Carpets from the reign of Mohammed Reza Shah Pahlavi*, London: Quartet Books, 1989, pp. 13-15.

"New Dimensions in Canadian Official Development Assistance Policy," in Brian W. Tomlin & M.A. Molot, *Canada Among Nations: The Tory Record/1988*, Toronto: James Lorimer & Co., 1989, pp. 149-168.

"Canada's Economic Relations with Southeast Asia: Federal- Provincial Dimensions of Policy", *Modern Asian Studies*, Vol. 24, Pt. 1 (February, 1990), pp. 31-73 [with Susan McLellan].

"International Service Delivery. A Strategic Management Plan," *ASHA. American Speech-Language-Hearing Association*, Vol. 32, No. 5 (May, 1990), pp. 48-9 [with D. Elaine Pressman].

"Model for Assessing the Climate for Telematics for Training in the Social Sectors in Developing Countries", in S. Rahman, H. Shrikumar, S.V. Raghavan, eds., *Proceedings of the 10th International Conference of Computer Communication*, New Delhi: Narosa Publishing House for the International Council for Computer Communication, 1990, pp. 71-77 [with D. Elaine Pressman].

"Canada, the Gulf Crisis and Collective Security," in Fen Osler Hampson and Christopher J. Maule, eds., *After the Cold War. Canada Among Nations 1990-91*, Ottawa: Carleton University Press, 1991, pp. 241-280.

"Canada's Official Development Assistance Strategy: Process, Goals and Priorities," *Canadian Journal of Development Studies*, Vol. 12, No. 1 (June, 1991), pp. 9-37.

"Repelita-V and the Indonesian Economy," *Review of Indonesian and Malaysian Affairs*, Vol. 25, No. 2 (Summer, 1991), pp. 35-74.

"European Community Development Assistance to Asia: Policies, Programs and Performance," *Modern Asian Studies*, Vol. 26, Pt. 1 (February, 1992), pp. 1-29.

"ASEAN, Asia Pacific Economic Cooperation and Hemispheric Free Trade for the Americas," *World Competition*, Vol. 16, No. 2 (December, 1992), pp. 131-146.

"Canadian Development Assistance to Asia: Programs, Objectives and Future Policy Directions," *Canadian Foreign Policy*, Vol. 1, No. 3 (Fall, 1993), pp. 67-93.

Economic Development in Bangladesh and Pakistan: A Comparative Analysis of Policies and Performance," *Journal of South Asian and Middle Eastern Studies*, Vol. 17, No. 3 (1994), pp. 32-54.

"Canadian Development Cooperation with Asia: Stategic Objectives and Policy Goals," in Cranford Pratt, ed. *Canadian International Development Assistance Policies: An Appraisal*, McGill-Queens University Press, 1994, pp. 292-312.

"The Dimensions of Asia Pacific Regional Economic Cooperation," *Transnational Law & Contemporary Problems*, Symposium: Regional Trade Agreements, (Vol. 4, No. 4, 1994).

"APEC: The Challenges of Asia Pacific Economic Cooperation," *Modern Asian Studies*, Vol. 28, Pt. 4 (1994), pp. 1-35.

SELECTED OTHER WRITINGS
"Conference Diplomacy, or the Transnational Republic of Scholarship," *Asian Studies Association of Australia, Review*, Vol. 1, No. 3 (April, 1978), pp. 21-2.

"The Role of Money," *Quadrant*, (Sydney, Australia), (March, 1979) pp. 62-6.

"Malaysian Studies in Australian Universities," *Review of Indonesian and Malayan Affairs*, Vol. 15, No. 1 (1981), pp. 126-144.

"By Way of Deception, or Disinformation, or Fabrication?" *Middle East Focus*, Vol. 14, No. 3 (Summer/Fall, 1992), p. 19.